J. Bien, lith.

LIMESTONE BLUFFS, LITTLE TRAVERSE BAY.

GEOLOGICAL SURVEY OF MICHIGAN.

LOWER PENINSULA

1873-1876

ACCOMPANIED BY A

GEOLOGICAL MAP.

VOL. III.

PART I. GEOLOGY.
PART II. PALÆONTOLOGY—CORALS.

BY

C. ROMINGER
STATE GEOLOGIST.

PUBLISHED BY AUTHORITY OF THE LEGISLATURE
OF MICHIGAN

UNDER THE DIRECTION OF THE

BOARD OF GEOLOGICAL SURVEY.

NEW YORK
JULIUS BIEN
1876

PART I.

GEOLOGY

OF

LOWER PENINSULA.

BY

C. ROMINGER.

LIST OF ILLUSTRATIONS.

MAP.

VIEWS.

* In pocket, in back of book.

TABLE OF CONTENTS.

APPENDICES.

To the Honorable the Board of Geological Survey of the State of Michigan.

GENTLEMEN:

I have much pleasure in submitting to your honorable body my final Report, giving the results of the Geological Survey of the Lower Peninsula of Michigan, commenced in the spring of 1873, and prosecuted without interruption during the past four years.

For several reasons, but especially as so many of the results of this survey had to be attained through the combination of fragmentary observations, made at different times and in far separated localities, it was found impossible to call any one to my assistance without danger of incurring endless complications, and of arriving, in many instances, at most unsatisfactory conclusions.

Therefore, with exception of the special report on the salt production of the State (Appendix B), I may claim the work as all my own. That report has been elaborated by my friend, Dr. S. S. Garrigues, the State Salt Inspector, a gentleman who, from his long official connection with that industry, must be better qualified than any other to treat of it in a work of this character.

Very respectfully yours,

C. ROMINGER,
State Geologist.

ANN ARBOR, July 1st, 1876.

CHAPTER I.

GEOGRAPHICAL POSITION AND SURFACE CONFIGURATION OF THE LOWER PENINSULA.

THE Lower Peninsula of Michigan comprises an area of about 35,000 square miles. It is situated between 82° 25′ and 86° 50′ of longitude, west from Greenwich, and 41° 44′ and 45° 47′ of northern latitude.

On the west it is bounded by Lake Michigan, on the north by the Straits of Mackinac, on the east by Lake Huron, Lake St. Clair and Lake Erie, besides the intermediate, river-like arms connecting the three lakes.

The southern limits are formed by the State lines of Ohio and Indiana. In a north and south direction, the greatest length of the peninsula is two hundred and seventy-five miles. In an east and west direction, the greatest width, coincident with a line drawn from Port Huron to Grand Haven, is about 200 miles.

Lake Michigan is 320 miles in length and 100 miles broad at the widest part, its total area being 22,000 square miles. Lake Huron is 260 miles long; 160 miles is the maximum of its breadth, and 20,400 square miles its surface extent. Both lakes have about an equal elevation above the ocean level, which is 578 feet. The elevation of Lake Erie above the ocean is 565 feet. These immense sweet-water basins, carved out in some places to a depth of over 900 feet, are evidently the result of eroding forces, acting on the sedimentary strata which once were spread without interruption across this entire lacustrine area, and these forces undoubtedly were identical with those by which the heavy masses of rock débris, known by the name of drift, were accumulated over a large zone of the northern hemisphere in this and in other continents. The longitudinal axes of Lake Michigan and of Lake Huron approximately have a north and south direction. Coincident with them is the long axis of the Lower Peninsula which they inclose. Its north end is indented by two large bays.

One of them, Little Traverse Bay, extends fourteen miles from west to east, with a width in the centre of about six miles; its geographical position is in latitude 45° 25′, and longitude 85°, at their intersection in the centre of the bay. Only a short distance south of the small bay is the entrance of Big Traverse Bay, which has a north and south direction. Its length from Lighthouse Point to Traverse City, situated at the head of the bay, is thirty-four miles, its width about ten miles. A landspur, parallel with the longitudinal axis of the bay, divides it into two arms; the length of the spur is sixteen miles, with a breadth of one to three miles. On both sides of the bay, and only a short distance from it, are inland lakes of very elongated form, which evidently owe their origin to the same erosive forces which carved out the bay. On the east side of the peninsula, in the same latitude with Big Traverse Bay, Thunder Bay indents the coast in a northwestern direction; its length is about ten miles, equal to the width at the entrance. Fifty miles further south is the entrance of Saginaw Bay. Its direction is southwest, its length forty-five miles, and its width, between Point of Barques and Ottawa Lighthouse Point, twenty-seven miles.

The rise of the peninsula from the level of the lakes is generally gradual, and in a few places only is it abrupt. The surface is of an undulating, hilly character; the hills are rounded and never attain a very great height above the surrounding country. The southern part of the peninsula is lower than the northern. The swell of the land, forming the water-shed of this southern division, coincides with a line drawn in a southwest direction from Port Austin at the entrance of Saginaw Bay, to the southwest corner of Hillsdale County, where it enters the boundaries of the State of Ohio. Within the limits of Tuscola and Sanilac counties, the known surface elevation of this water-shed is about 400 feet above the lake; in Lapeer and Oakland counties it rises to 500 feet; further south, in Washtenaw and Jackson counties, it falls again to about 400 feet; while in Hillsdale, not far from the southern State line, some points with an elevation of 600 feet are recorded, but the water-shed is probably not over 500 feet high. The ascent from the lakes to the height of this water-shed is so gradual that a traveller, in crossing the peninsula from either lake to the other, if he follows the river valleys, can scarcely perceive it. The northern division of the peninsula rises to almost double the height of the southern part; its surface is more broken, and diversified by steeper descents toward the lakes from terrace to terrace. Its highest points in the vicinity of Otsego Lake are, according to the records of the railroad surveys, 1100 feet above the lake level. Otsego Lake has a length of about five miles by a width of not quite one mile; it lies directly west of Thunder Bay, in the median line, and not far from the northern terminus of an extensive high plateau with undulating surface and an average elevation of from 700 to 800 feet.

All the rivers of the northern part of the peninsula have their sources within this plateau, which is dotted with a number of inland lakes, some of which, like Lakes Higgins, Houghton, and St. Helen's, are of large size. The terraces by which the descent from the plateau is made, form a succession of broad belts; their sides are moderately steep and finely timbered; the lowest are wider, gradually slanting toward the shore or overlooking it in bluffs of from 40 to 60 feet. In some places on the west side, the bluffs are from 100 to 200 feet high; and Sleeping Bear Point, a promontory facing Lake Michigan, west of Big Traverse Bay, is said to have an elevation of 500 feet. Opposite this point, twelve miles out in the lake, the Manitou Islands rise abruptly to a height of 200 feet above the water. South of the second correction line, the plateau rapidly declines toward Saginaw Bay. Between the north and south parts of the peninsula, a depressed strip of land extends from Saginaw Bay to the mouth of Grand River on Lake Michigan, having rarely more than 100 feet elevation. Its position is indicated by the river-beds of Bad River, which comes by its watershed in connection with the headwaters of Maple River, the latter emptying into Grand River. An astonishing number of smaller and larger inland lakes are found in every part of the peninsula; all have crystal-clear water, and the principal supply of the head branches of our rivers comes from them. The more important rivers, collecting the waters of the western slope of the peninsula, are the St. Joseph's River, Kalamazoo River, Grand River, Muskegon River, and Manistee River. The three first-named ones have their sources in close proximity to the elevated lands of Hillsdale and Jackson counties. From the same swell of land the river Raisin emanates, flowing eastward into Lake Erie.

Raisin River enters the lake near Monroe; it drains the southern part of Washtenaw County through Saline Creek, Macon Creek, and through its main north arm, which, bending west, enters the southeast corner of Jackson County, and draws its branches from a number of small lakes. The south branches of the river have the drainage of the larger part of Lenawee County, and an arm extends southward into the State of Ohio. The west part of Lenawee and the south part of Hillsdale counties send a portion of their waters southward to the Maumee River in Ohio. The St. Joseph's River, Kalamazoo River, and Grand River almost touch each other within the small area of a few square miles in the county of Hillsdale.

The St. Joseph's River, originating in a number of small lakes and marshes in Hillsdale, flows through the southeast corner of Calhoun County into Branch County and St. Joseph County. It leaves the State at the southwest corner of St. Joseph, and enters it again in the southeast corner of Berrien County with a northerly direction, to enter finally Lake Michigan at the village of St. Joseph.

The streams which form the headwaters of the Kalamazoo River take their rise in Scipio, Moscow, and Somerset townships, in Hillsdale County. The river runs north to Albion, and flows in a due west direction to Kalamazoo, whence it bends northwest, intersecting Allegan County, and falls into Lake Michigan near Saugatuck.

Grand River springs from a few lakes in Liberty township, in the south part of Jackson County, and from a number of other lakes in the northeast quarter of the county. It runs north through Ingham, Eaton, Clinton, Ionia, Kent, and Ottawa counties, when it opens near Grand Haven into Lake Michigan. On the east side of this water-shed a few more rivers deserve notice.

Huron River collects its waters from innumerable lakes and marshes in Livingston and Oakland counties; first it flows southwest; at Dexter it turns southeast and retains this direction, passing through Washtenaw and Wayne counties, until it enters Detroit River in the northern corner of Monroe County.

Clinton River drains the eastern part of Oakland County and all of Macomb County, entering Lake St. Clair near Mount Clemens.

Black River is remarkable for its southern course for nearly fifty miles, parallel with the shore of Huron Lake, at a distance of only five or six miles from it. It begins in the north part of Sanilac County, and enters St. Clair River near Port Huron.

Saginaw River is the receptacle of a whole system of rivers. By the Tittibawassee River, the waters of the north and west, from Gladwin, St. Clair, Isabella, and Midland counties, are led into it; the Shiawassee River collects from the south, in Livingston and Shiawassee counties; Flint River, from the south and southeast, in Genesee and Lapeer counties; and, finally, Cass River brings its waters from the northeast and east, gathering them in the counties of Tuscola, Huron, and Sanilac.

The river system of the northern part of the peninsula consists of the following rivers: Commencing at the southeast side, we find, first, Rifle River and Aux Grees River, which drain the southeastern shore-belt surrounding the before-mentioned high plateau. Sable River is the next largest river north of them. It draws its branches right from the heart of the high plateau, and drains Lake Otsego in the north end of it.

Thunder Bay River, opening into Thunder Bay, spreads its arms north, south and west, reaching the foot of the high plateau. Sheboygan River, on the north end of the peninsula, forms the outlet of three large lakes: Black Lake, with an area of about 16 square miles, Mullett and Burt Lakes, both together with an area of about 45 square miles. These lakes are fed by rivers of good size. Rainy River and Black River empty into Black Lake; Mullett River and Pigeon River into Mullett Lake. On the west side of the peninsula two large rivers deserve to be mentioned yet. Manistee River originates very near the headwaters of Au Sable River on the east side. Its mouth is at Manistee, a little distance to the north of the second correction line. Muskegon River is a still larger river than Manistee; its branches extend to the top of the central high plateau, and are fed by Higgins and Houghton lakes. The mouth of the Muskegon is a short distance south of the first correction line.

Of all the rivers mentioned, none is navigable. In some cases, however, the mouths for a few miles inland from the lake border are wide and deep enough to afford harbor for vessels of medium size. The water-power afforded by these rivers is ample, and those, the branches of which flow through timbered lands, are of vital importance to the lumber business as mediums for the transportation of felled timber, from otherwise almost inaccessible parts of the interior, to ports or railroad stations.

The greatest portion of our world-renowned stores of pine timber would be comparatively worthless to the owners, and to the community at large, without these rivers. Their importance can only be fairly appreciated by one who has seen with his own eyes the lumberman at work. In the fall of the year, hundreds of axemen and teamsters, with horses and yokes of oxen, penetrate for seventy and eighty miles up the rivers into forest desolation, scarcely cutting a rough, narrow road, which seems impassable for man or beast, yet by which, during their stay in the winter, the necessary supplies are conveyed to them from time to time. Arrived at the places with valuable timber, huts are erected, temporary stables built for the animals, and the work begins. Tree after tree sinks to the ground with its mighty crown under the pitiless strokes of their axes. The valuable parts of the trunks are cut into logs of proper length, and drawn on sleighs to the nearest creek, where they are piled up, until, in spring-time, by the melting of the snow, the creeks are swollen into impetuous streams, which are kept back and hemmed in by dams. After the water has risen sufficiently, the braces holding the logs on the banks are removed, when with terrible speed, smashing every thing in their way, they dash down into the muddy pond. This being done, the gates of the dam are opened, and swiftly glide the logs along with the rapid current, accompanied by a crew of men, who remove all obstructions, walking with surprising dexterity to and fro over the floating logs. Finally they reach the mouths of the rivers, which usually expand into lake-like basins, but are sometimes artificially transformed into such. It often occurs that a river-bed for many miles up its course is jammed with logs, representing several square miles of forest, an interesting and curious sight. There are the mills, erected only a few years since, surrounded by acres of ground heaped with mountains of sawdust and other refuse material, witnessing the stupendous amount of work performed. On entering, what a humming, buzzing from all sides—a gigantic beehive; hundreds of persons at work in admirable order, making use of the irresistible steam-power, in the most diversified way, without a minute's loss of time, engine and men working in unison.

A log five feet in diameter floats toward the mill; a minute more, and, fastened to a chain, it moves up the slideway, goes straight under the saw, and in another minute is converted into boards, which, without loss of time, are passed singly through the edging machine, coming out ready for the market. Meanwhile, before a car is loaded to remove them to the lumber pile, all the edging slabs have been transformed into fence pickets and plaster laths, all with the regularity of clock-work. These sights make an impression on the mind of a thoughtful spectator which is more than simple admiration; he feels overpowered by the wonders which man is capable of performing by perseverance and energy, coupled with an intelligent use of the forces of nature.

The rivers have all eroded their valleys into the loose drift masses which almost universally cover the surface of the peninsula in great thickness. Only in rare instances have they carved deep enough to touch the solid rock ledges below the drift; or if such deep cuts did ever exist, they have filled them up again with débris, and the beds of the present streams lie high above those of former times. The peninsula was in its original condition heavily timbered, with the exception of a few marshy flats. Climate and quality of the soil determined the character of the vegetation. In the southern part of the peninsula, deciduous trees, particularly hard-wood timber, prevail. Pine is only sporadically intermingled—the mildness of the climate favoring the growth of oak, hickory, walnut, poplar, etc., which abound here, but become rare further north, where beech, maple, and birch take their place. The sandy soil of the central high plateau is most congenial for the growth of pine forests, which have taken exclusive possession of nearly the entire district. The marshy condition of some other places adapt them for the tamarack, asp, elm, and willow-tree, or for the growth of cedar, while a few parts of the high plateau, proving even too sterile for the pine, afford sustenance to nothing more than a stunted, scrubby growth of *Pinus Banksianus*, and a few creeping herbs which attempt to hide the barrenness of the scene. Such barrenness has, in some instances, been caused by accidental fires, which annihilated forests of large area, totally denuding the surface, which, when of porous sand exposed to the burning rays of the sun and to the exsiccating winds, can not for a long time, if ever, recover its former well-timbered condition. On more fertile soil, with sufficient moisture, the case is different. A few years after a forest is burned down it sprouts again with fresh vigor, but the new growth is generally of a different kind from that which preceded it.

To the first settlers of the country, the heavily timbered forests were a great impediment; with great labor the trees had to be cut down and burned, for no other purpose than to get them out of the way. This system of destruction, first suggested by necessity, has been continued up to recent times, and while it is true that the development of agriculture has been considerably hastened by it, yet it is equally true that, in the lower part of the peninsula, our forests are reduced to such a degree, unnecessarily in some cases, as to render it highly advisable that measures be adopted for the preservation of what we have left, otherwise, I fear, our descendants will sorely feel the consequences of the unwise husbandry of their fathers.

CHAPTER II.

GEOLOGICAL STRUCTURE OF THE LOWER PENINSULA.

(*Surface Material.*)

THE entire surface of the peninsula is covered by heavy drift deposits, with the exception of a few limited localities, in which the drift, subsequent to its deposit, has been washed off by floods, or by rivers carving their courses deep enough to touch the rock beds of older formations. These drift masses are nearly the same in character as those described from the Upper Peninsula in the first volume of the geological reports. The material has been changed somewhat by an admixture of rock débris from the formations encountered by the moving glaciers in their southward course. The glacier drift spread itself in a compact body over the entire surface of the Lower Peninsula, in evidence of which fact the rock beds, wherever they are found denuded, and the nature of the rock has been capable of preserving the marks, bear the traces of its motion on their scratched surface. Not all the drift material found on the lower peninsula has been transported there by glaciers; a large proportion of it must have been carried southward by water, partly in suspension, as mud and sand, partly frozen into floating ice, as the coarser material, the gravel and boulders.

The glaciers deposited moraines, heaps of rubbish composed of all kinds of rock débris in every degree of comminution from the large boulder down to the impalpably fine clay. Much of the drift is not found in this orderless form of moraines, but is disposed in well-stratified layers, assorted according to the weight of its particles by water-currents. It is suggested that floods, acting subsequently on the masses of the moraines, sifted and washed the lighter transportable particles out of them, to deposit them elsewhere as layers of clay, sand, or gravel, but this can not explain all the phenomena we observe in the arrangement of the drift material. We find large boulders, some of them many tons in weight, in the midst or on top of well-stratified drift layers; this could not be if the strata were formed by rearrangement of the moraines; but, by the suggestion that a transportation of the material has occurred through floods with swimming icebergs, no difficulty exists in explaining the position of the hugest blocks within or on top of well-stratified layers; while the mud or sand carried along by the currents settled down into layers, the large blocks carried by the ice over these forming deposits were occasionally dropped and became buried or remained lying on the surface. The glacier period was only the commencement of the drift transportation. A long time of submergence of the land by inundation must have followed the glaciers. The surface of the highest points of the peninsula, 1100 feet above the level of the lakes, is formed of stratified drift sand mixed with pebbles, from which fact we must draw the inference that at one time the water had reached to this height. By looking at the topographical features of the country at present, it is hard to conceive how this could happen, and I make no attempt to suggest the mechanical conditions by which the water level of the lakes could rise so high; but the fact of this occurrence is indisputably proved by the sediments left behind by the water; also the terraces found in the circumference of the peninsula at different heights testify the high elevation of the lake levels in former times. The waters must have receded at different periods for a certain distance, and then kept stationary for a while before a further lowering of their level occurred; and each of these temporary shore lines is marked by a distinct terrace. In many places, such terraces are quite conspicuous, especially so those in proximity to the present shore; the higher terraces, more remote, are sometimes obscured by dense forests covering their slopes, and by the action of atmospheric influences through scores of centuries which has rounded and levelled off their former marked contours; yet any traveller ascending to the central high plateau can not avoid observing that he makes his ascent from terrace to terrace.

The older glacier drift and the later deposits of floods and icebergs are materially of the same composition; both are made up of clay, sand, gravel, and boulders, of the detritus from crystalline and metamorphic rocks, mixed with débris of younger sedimentary strata. The orderless, rubbishy condition of the glacier drift became partially transformed into well-stratified layers by the same floods which deposited the superimposed drift beds, whereby they became blended to such a degree that a distinction of the older and younger drift layers by lithological characters is impossible, and can only locally be made by observation of their direct superposition. The non-stratified condition of the drift is not confined to the lowest beds, but repeats itself in higher positions. The atmospheric influences acting on the loose, non-indurated drift material, instead of sifting and assorting the masses, as sometimes they do, often have the contrary effect; the stratified condition of the superficial masses is obscured by them, and by sliding and other similar causes, they become intermingled. But, leaving this alteration of the surface crust out of consideration, we find extensive accumulations of unstratified boulder drift high above other non-stratified deposits, and separated from them by well-stratified layers of sand and gravel. The coarse boulder drift, covering large surfaces of Washtenaw County and of other counties in the southern part of the State, occupies this higher position, and deeply below it, separated by intervening, well-stratified layers, we find other non-stratified masses again. In the high bluffs on Huron River, a half mile south of Ann Arbor, an instance of this superposition can be directly observed. At the foot of the bluff we can see about 60 feet of a dark blue, indurated, sandy clay, mixed with many smaller pebbles and with a few large boulders, which all bear very distinct marks of glacier striation; the clay has not the least sign of gradual deposit lines; it gives the impression of a solidified mud-stream. Above it we find well-stratified sand layers with discordant bedding and wedge-like intercalations of seams of gravel, amounting in all to about 30 or 40 feet. The top of the hill rises at least 60 or 80 feet higher, and all of it is formed by non-stratified boulder drift, mixed with clay and sand in such proportion as to compose a productive soil on these stony hillsides. The boulders of this horizon are partly large granitic blocks, or green stones, quartz conglomerates, partly blocks of the Trenton, Niagara, Helderberg, or Hamilton group, with characteristic fossils inclosed; also, sand-rock slabs of the Waverly group and from the coal measures are mingled with the others, all bearing distinct glacial striæ on their surface, but otherwise of subangular outlines, indicating little wearing by trituration under water. The coarse boulder drift all through the southern part of the peninsula appears not to occupy the lowest position, in which most frequently a hard, dark blue, sandy clay, with pebbles and some boulders intermingled, is found in layers of considerable thickness. It is known among laborers by the popular name of *hard-pan*. The beds of clay, sand, and gravel in the stratified drift are not deposited in a certain order of sequence which would hold good even for limited precincts; every locality has to be studied for itself, and if denudations of larger horizontal extent are observed—which opportunity sometimes happens in the bluffs of the lake shores—we see constant local changes in the details of structure, although in some principal features a uniformity of the strata may be perceptible. This irregularity in the structure of the stratified drift explains itself, if we consider the conditions under which the deposits were formed and that the already formed deposits were by subsequent causes repeatedly displaced. During the slow emergence of the peninsula from the waters, much of the surface material was shifted about by waves and fluctuations of the retiring lake, and when the river channels began to form, and deep valleys were carved in all directions through the drift masses, immense quantities of material became displaced and deposited anew in a different order, governed entirely by local circumstances; and this process of destruction and building up is to this day in constant operation.

In the report on the Upper Peninsula, I have described, among the drift materials, an impalpably fine red-colored clay deposit of considerable thickness, which rests there frequently in immediate superposition on the older rock beds, and is in some localities—as, for instance, at Au Sable Point, on Lake Superior—overlaid by 300 feet of sand and gravel beds of the drift. In the drift deposits of the Lower Peninsula a similar well-stratified red clay is observed, but there it is not found at the base of the drift. It has a higher position, and is underlaid by stratified sand and gravel beds, while below them follows the non-stratified tough blue clay with pebbles, which, in the southern part of the State, is always the lowest of the drift. The relative position of this red clay to the other drift beds is best seen in the high bluffs lining the shore in the northwest part of the peninsula. The lowest blue gravelly clays, in non-stratified condition, are sometimes visible at the base of the bluffs; above them follow well-stratified sand beds on which the red clay beds rest in almost shale-like, laminated form, amounting to a thickness of from 30 to 50 feet; usually this clay belt is divided by interstratified sand layers into several bands. Certain seams of the clay are soap-like, absolutely free from coarse particles; others contain numerous pebbles, or are mixed with various proportions of sand. The impermeability of this thick clay mass to water causes the issue of copious springs along the bluffs above the horizon of the clay. The upper part of the bluffs, which locally attain a height of 200 feet, is formed of alternating layers of sand and gravel in irregular, discordant stratification. The gravel beds between the sand strata are often five or six feet thick in the centre, and wedge out on both sides into linear seams, which, perhaps, further on, may be seen expanding again, or entirely vanish. Large boulders are mixed into the strata at all heights, but in certain levels of the upper part of the bluffs, boulders are more abundant, and stratification becomes obscure. On top of the bluffs heavy masses of fine sand are deposited, which partly have the character of dunes, partly are stratified, aqueous deposits, but of much more recent origin than the lower portion of the bluffs. Exactly the same exposures of the drift as on the shore of the mainland of the peninsula, are seen on the west side of the Manitou Islands, in connected sections of about 150 feet in height. Sleeping Bear Point, a promontory opposite the Manitou Islands, on the main shore, said to be of 500 feet elevation, is remarkable for its barren, naked surface of a fine, loose sand, without any vegetation. Its base is composed of the same drift layers as the bluffs further south, of which it is a direct continuation. In many other localities of the interior, the same well-stratified red-clay beds are uncovered, always holding a position below the principal coarse boulder drift. The banks of Cass River, near Vassar, in Tuscola County, or the bed of Muskegon River near Big Rapids, give occasion to see the clay beds in their relative position to the other drift strata. In a cut of the railroad between the Big Rapids and Muskegon, close to the first-named village, an interesting section through the drift is laid open. Deepest, at the bottom of the cut, boulder drift mixed with stiff bluish clay is exposed. The large boulders, as well as the smaller pebbles, are plainly marked with drift scratches. Above them are about 30 feet of sand layers with discordant stratification; the layers are bent into tortuous, serpentine flexures. Incumbent on these sand beds is a thick coating of apparently non-stratified boulder drift, differing from the lower boulder drift by less clayey, more sandy constituents, and by having its boulders much less distinctly drift-marked. In the surface of the sand deposits, underlying these upper boulder drift masses, narrow, acute ravines are observed, which are filled with boulder drift. Sections through them are laid open by the railroad cut. It seems as if the surface of the sand deposits had been exposed for a while to the atmosphere, and deep, narrow ravines cut into them by rain-streams, which subsequently were filled out with the boulder drift, without disturbing the sharpness of their angular contours. How this was effected I am not prepared to explain. The flexions of the sand strata, I suppose, are caused by lateral pressure exerted by sliding of the masses. I have frequently observed similarly bent sand deposits in other localities—as, for instance, in the bluffs of Manitou Island.

The incoherent masses of gravel and of sand become in certain localities firmly cemented into conglomerates and sandstones by carbonate of lime, deposited by springs percolating the gravel and sand banks. Such conglomerates, forming large, bulky masses, of concretionary form, are abundantly seen in the above-described bluffs on the shore of Lake Michigan, and more southward, at the mouth of Muskegon and of Kalamazoo rivers; also in the gravel pits along the railroad from South Haven to Kalamazoo, and in a great number of other places. Near the mouth of Kalamazoo River, at Richmond, I have seen such sand rock of the drift in very compact, hard ledges, which would make a durable building stone. Sometimes we find, instead of lime, the sand or pebbles cemented by hydrated sesquioxide of iron, but not in so large masses, and always close under the surface, while the calcareous conglomerates are often found interstratified with other drift beds quite remote from the surface. These ferruginous conglomerates have the same origin as bog-iron ores, from springs holding iron in solution by means of carbonic acid, and depositing it, in some cases, as incrustation over pebbles and sand, and in others, over vegetable stems, which subsequently decay and leave the ore in the porous condition in which usually it is found.

Bog iron occurs very frequently in small patches of marsh land in all parts of the State. Several localities are also known where ore deposits of larger extent have been discovered, but up to the present time no practical use has been made of them, and it is questionable whether any of these deposits is of sufficient magnitude to be an inducement for the erection of furnaces, or for their mining and transportation to other melting works.

Calcareous tufa, a deposit of springs, analogous to bog iron, is sometimes found in large masses spread over springy hillsides. Locally, this tufa is used for lime-burning; sometimes, however, the porous rock mass is sufficiently compact and hard to be used as a building stone, but I have not often seen it so employed in Michigan.

The bottoms of a number of inland lakes are covered with a peculiar modification of calcareous tufa, a white, marly substance, in part composed of the shells of sweet-water molluscs, mixed with white pulverulent carbonate of lime deposited from solution by the lake water. Pine Lake, near Charlevoix, one of the largest lakes in the north part of the peninsula, has its entire bottom covered by this marl, and to a greater or less extent the same is the case with a great many others. I am not aware that any practical use has been made of these shell marls. They would certainly be good fertilizers.

As another surface deposit, peat has been mentioned. Innumerable larger and smaller patches cover the swampy surface depressions throughout the whole State. It is formed by a continued growth of a certain class of plants in wet places, where, submerged, the basal parts of the plants die off, and become decomposed and changed into a coaly substance, which accumulates sometimes to very great thickness. Peat is at present little used in Michigan. Several experiments to prepare it for commerce by compressing it with hydraulic machines have given very good results, as far as its usefulness and heating qualities are concerned, but in the light of a pecuniary transaction the results were less favorable. Fuel is too cheap yet, but the time will come when peat will be appreciated at its true value.

CHAPTER III.

SOILS OF THE LOWER PENINSULA.

By the nature and distribution of the drift material, which has almost exclusive occupancy of the surface of the peninsula, the quality of its soil is determined; the localities where its character is modified by the lower rock formations are of very limited extent, and deserve no particular consideration in this place. The soil possesses two important requisites for vegetation. It gives to the plant a secure hold in its position, and furnishes to the roots the material necessary for life and growth. Soil is composed of pulverulent particles of mineral substances, generally mixed with a proportion of organic matter. The mineral components must contain all the chemical elements which enter into the composition of plants, in a condition available for absorption by the roots. In moist conditions, it has a certain degree of coherence and plasticity; it is porous, readily absorbs water, and retains it with a certain tenacity. These are the general requisites for a soil, to make it adapted for the growth and nutrition of plants.

The chemical elements necessary for the organism of vegetation are oxygen, carbon, hydrogen, nitrogen, sulphur, phosphorus, chlorine, iodine, potassium, sodium, calcium, magnesium, aluminium, silicium, iron, manganese—all of which are to be found distributed in varying proportions almost everywhere on the surface of the earth.

Soil constantly forms by the action of atmospheric influences on the superficial rock beds, slowly effecting their chemical decomposition, or causing mechanical disintegration by frost or mutual trituration. A soil forming on the spot by decay of the underlying rock beds participates in their chemical composition, and may be destitute of certain ingredients necessary for a good soil. Soil formed of drift material, being composed of the greatest variety of mineral species, generally has all the chemical requirements of a good soil.

But we must recollect that the drift material is frequently found assorted according to the fineness of its particles, and that this assorting is sometimes carried to such a degree as to be detrimental to the quality of the material as a soil. A bed of pure clay, or of sand, or of clean gravel will not make a soil of itself, but a mixture of all constitutes the most fertile that we have. The fertility of a soil is, however, not alone conditioned upon its chemical constituents; it depends in a great measure upon its porosity, adhesiveness, and the state of comminution of its molecules. To learn the chemical composition of soils and their molecular structure, analyses of the most complicated kind have been made, which, taking a purely scientific view of the question, are highly interesting, but are, practically, of a value not in proportion to the labor and expenditure of time in making them. The soil of one and the same farm, or of a single acre of ground, often differs so much that a few analyses would not give a correct idea of its quality, at least none more correct than could be reached by a superficial examination, so that, in buying a farm, I would advise one rather to rely on the judgment of an experienced farmer than on the results of a chemist's laboratory.

The good quality of a soil covered by a thrifty vegetation of certain herbs and trees is immediately recognized. The barrenness of a spot, likewise, needs not to be first ascertained by finding out its chemical deficiencies; and, provided we are acquainted somewhat with the elements of vegetable physiology, we will also soon be able to guess at a proper course for its improvement.

A plant draws a great proportion of its nourishment through its roots from the soil. The roots can only take up nutritive parts when in solution. Easily soluble salts must be highly diluted, or they would injure the plants; usually soils contain little of these, and the mineral substances composing them are of themselves so insoluble in water that the roots could draw no benefit from them, if by the admixture of humic acid, which almost every good soil contains, the solubility of these substances were not induced. This acid is a brown substance, originating from the decomposition of vegetable matter in the soil. It has the peculiarity of forming with all earths combinations which are soluble in water; it displaces carbonic acid from the carbonates, and decomposes insoluble silicates, and its salts taken up in solution by the plants can be perfectly assimilated, because humic acid is composed of carbon and water.

Vegetation requires more than liquid nourishment supplied through the roots; plants absorb and exhale large quantities of gases through the roots as well as through the parts above ground. A soil must, therefore, be in a degree porous, or a plant will not live in it. A regular process of respiration exists in plants. The green leaves and other green-colored parts constantly absorb carbonic acid from the atmosphere, and exhale in its place oxygen, provided they are exposed to the light. In the darkness the process is inverted; the plants then take up oxygen and exhale carbonic acid. All the parts of plants which are not green, such as roots, bark, petals, and red or yellow leaves in the fall, constantly absorb oxygen and exhale carbonic acid.

The soil of the Lower Peninsula, being a drift soil, is generally very deep, and contains all the chemical constituents of a good soil. The assortment of the drift material into clay, sand, and gravel beds determines its character as these layers happen to occupy the surface positions, while by intermixtures a great variety of intermediate shadings in the quality of soils is locally produced under atmospheric influences. The distribution of soils over the surface of the State is sometimes very unequal and changeable, so that within limited areas, and often within single farms, a number of variations in the character of the soil are represented. But with the differences seen in the surface configuration of certain districts is also usually found a corresponding contrast in the quality of their soil. The high plateau in the northern part of the peninsula has its peculiar soil, a thick, uniform mass of fine sand, containing few pebbles and a small proportion of argillaceous constituents. In accordance with it is the vegetation; the pine-tree finds a congenial home in these sandy hill lands, and their surface is overgrown with splendid forests of this tree, to the exclusion of almost every other kind. This soil, as long as some humus is mixed with it, may give a fair potato crop, or, by careful attendance, garden vegetables can be raised, but its productiveness is so soon exhausted and its moisture so soon lost, that it can never be used for agriculture on a large scale with any prospect of success.

Other districts, represented by lowlands adjoining the lakes, and to all appearance within comparatively recent times parts of the lake bottoms, are covered by a stiff clay soil overgrown with elm, ash, and kindred trees—as, for instance, the lower part of Saginaw valley and a strip of land bordering Detroit River, from Monroe up to Lake St. Clair. Properly drained, this is the richest soil in the State, giving larger crops and bearing the practiced system of exhaustion better than any other. But the most characteristic soil of Michigan, that which makes it a wheat-producing country in the first rank, is a gravelly clay soil which covers the largest part of the surface in the southern half of the peninsula. It unites all the qualities of a good soil, all the chemical essentials for the plants which it bears in such profusion; its molecules are a mixture of all degrees of comminution, from the finest clay mud up to the boulder, producing a proper degree of porosity, and securing the retention of the necessary moisture by a constant drainage of any accidental surplus of it. A certain variety of this gravelly soil is full of large pebbles and boulders to a degree which makes the inexperienced believe its cultivation hopeless, yet such lands give generally very good returns in wheat and corn crops.

Distributed over the country are patches of light, sandy soil, which contain a sufficient proportion of argillaceous and other mineral ingredients to make them fertile. The easy tillage of these lands and their generally fair returns bring them into high favor with the farmers. The climate of the peninsula, which is the other principal factor in its productiveness, is over the whole extent temperate, extremes of cold or heat being prevented by the surrounding large lakes. From the north to the southern end all the cereals can be planted with little risk of failure. The northern part is somewhat colder, its vegetation coming out two weeks later than in the south, and the winter setting in about that much earlier, which affects somewhat the raising of the more tender fruit crops, as grapes, peaches, etc.

The grape and the peach do well in the southern part of the State, and particularly near the shores of the lakes, where the foggy, humid air prevents late frost, the greatest enemy of these fruits. The west shore up as far as Muskegon has become famous for its peaches and other small fruits. The Traverse Bay region, which has been so strongly recommended as a fruit-growing country, is not fulfilling the expectations entertained of it. They may raise peaches there in seasons when all other places in the south have theirs killed by frosts, but this does not prove the greater mildness of the climate, but simply that the peaches are in bloom there late enough to escape frost. The fruit raised under such conditions may be large and perfect, but in sweetness and flavor it can not compete with fruit grown in a warmer climate.

For the apple, our climate and the deep gravelly soil answer exceedingly well, immense quantities of the most delicious kinds being yearly sent to the markets of all the Eastern and Western States.

CHAPTER IV.

PALÆOZOIC ROCK SERIES.

BENEATH the drift the peninsula is underlaid by regularly stratified rock beds, in undisturbed horizontal position, which represent the upper part of the palæozoic strata.

Of deposits younger than the coal measures, no evidence can be discovered on its surface. It forms the centre-point of an oceanic bay, which seems to have existed, without any important alteration in its limits, from the beginning of the Silurian period to the end of the Carboniferous time. We find within the space supposed to have been the bay an uninterrupted series of marine deposits, following each other in the greatest regularity of superposition, which represent all the known formations deposited on this continent from the Potsdam period on to the Coal formation. The northern shore of this ancient silurian bay coincided in part with the present north and west shore of Lake Superior. Some cliffs of the present lake, formed by upheaved Huronian rock beds, were formerly the cliffs washed by the breakers of the silurian ocean.

We find the rounded, water-washed cliffs, with all their fissures and eroded pot-holes, intimately embraced by the sandstones and conglomerates of the Potsdam period, horizontally abutting against them, with their layers discordantly laminated, as we see the sand masses of a beach formed under our eyes. It needs no great degree of illusion to imagine that you see these sand masses dashed upon the shore by the breakers of the present lake, and quickly hardened into rock. One feels strangely impressed at beholding a landscape with its general features as they must have existed myriads of years before, a space of time during which continents formed and disappeared, during which the place itself has undergone the greatest changes, become covered with sediments, the ocean having receded long ages ago from the spot, and then to imagine glaciers to come, ploughing up the sediments covering the old surface, dredging out a part of the old ocean bed, and finally leaving it filled with the water which now washes the cliffs of the restored shore line, as if it never had left them.

As we recede southward from this ancient shore line, and have passed over a belt of the Potsdam sandstone, we find the Trenton limestones overlapping the sand rock, and still further, belt by belt, successively occur younger rock beds, which follow each other in imbricated superposition. On Mackinac Island we have reached a fragment of the sediments of the Helderberg belt, which resisted destruction when the lakes were carved out. A description of all these rock belts I have given in the geological report of 1873.

On the northern end of the Lower Peninsula, which forms the main subject of consideration in this report, we find the Helderberg group again as the lowest of the exposed rock beds, and only occupying a narrow strip of the northern shore line. The imbricated superposition of younger formations continues southward to the centre of the peninsula, where we find the Helderberg group overlapped by the Hamilton series; following it are the black shales of Ohio, the Waverly group, and a central disk formed by the coal measures.

These concentric arched belts of formations continue across the area now occupied by the lakes, and are met again on the opposite shores of Canada, Wisconsin, and Illinois. The belt of the Helderberg series strikes the Canada shore south of Goderich; the Hamilton group and the black shales are found in Bosanquet township and on Kettle Point, C. W.

On the Wisconsin side, the Helderberg and Hamilton strata barely reach the shore at a place six miles north of Milwaukee. The remainder of the shore of Wisconsin and Illinois, south from there, is composed of the next older rock beds of the Niagara group.

Entering on the special description of the mentioned formations, and of their surface distribution on the Lower Peninsula, I commence with the lowest beds, with the Helderberg group exposed at the northern and southeast ends of it.

CHAPTER V.

HELDERBERG GROUP.

At the foot of McGulpin's Point, a little distance from the former site of old Fort Mackinac, the bed of the lake is formed of ledges of limestone, a series of which continues at the height of 10 or 15 feet above the water level around the base of the promontory. Its higher levels are formed of drift rising in several well-marked terraces, on one of which the lighthouse is erected. The limestone is light-colored, of conchoidal fracture, rather thin and unevenly bedded, abounding in hornstone concretions. It contains a good many fossils characteristic of the upper Helderberg group, but few of them are well preserved. The strata which form the top of Mackinac Island represent the same geological horizon, and if we were to admit a continuity of the strata across the straits, and take those of McGulpin's Point as identical with the highest beds of Mackinac, the calculated dip of the strata toward the south would amount to 30 feet per mile, Mackinac Island being 300 feet above, and its distance from McGulpin's Point 10 miles.

The limestone ledges can be traced in the shoal water westward to the Waugoshance Islands; the projecting part of them is formed by loose limestone pebbles and regular boulder drift, with no outcrops of the underlying limestone ledges. Further west, the formation extends to the Beaver Island group. The larger of the islands, Hog Island, Garden Island, and Beaver Island, are all composed of drift. Loose, angular limestone slabs, inclosing fossils of the Helderberg group, are found abundantly strewn over their beaches, indicating a proximity of the ledges to the surface; the ledges themselves are visible in the bottom of the lake in the circumference of Whiskey and Trout Islands, which likewise belong to the Beaver Island group.

On the east side of McGulpin's Point the limestone ledges

soon disappear under the drift, and from there to Hammond's Bay no more rock exposures are seen along the shore line. On Round Island and on Bois Blanc Island, limestones of a lower position than those of McGulpin's Point come to the surface. The largest portion of the islands is covered by drift and by gravel and sand accumulations, thrown up at a more recent time by the lake. On Round Island the rock escarpments are, on the north side, formed by thick-bedded, light-colored, somewhat porous dolomitic limestones, projecting in a steep bluff of about 50 feet in height. A dense growth of forest trees covers the declivity, hiding the rock ledges from view, when at a distance from the bluff.

On Bois Blanc the exposures are on the southwestern shore, rising in bluffs to about 15 feet above the water level. Under a cover of boulder drift we find highest, thick ledges of a brittle, dolomitic, and partly cherty limestone; the lower beds are thinly laminated slabs of a bluish mottled lime rock with rough, earthy fracture; they are seen extending far out in the bottom of the lake. In the upper thick beds, not unfrequently the often-mentioned acicular crystals are found pervading the mass, which are characteristic of the lower horizons of the Helderberg group. Fossils have not been found. The lime rock of both islands is used to a small extent for the production of lime, but as a building-stone the rock has little value.

From the mouth of Oqueok River in Hammond's Bay, onward to Presque Isle, frequent rock exposures can be observed along the shore, which generally is occupied by sand or gravel beaches; the rocks come out at the ends of projecting land-spurs. The strata seen in these exposures have a higher position than those of McGulpin's Point; they are the transitory beds between the Helderberg and Hamilton groups, which insensibly merge into each other, without having any sharp line of demarkation.

I preferred to describe these latter beds in connection with the Hamilton strata, and have delineated on the geological map accompanying this report the Helderberg group as confined to the narrow spur of McGulpin's Point and to the islands north and west of it.

Rocks of the Helderberg group compose the surface of a restricted area in the southeast corner of the State, comprising

Monroe County, the southeastern part of Wayne County, and the same part of Lenawee County. This triangular segment is the northern terminus of a large body of the formation, which covers the northwestern part of Ohio, and is continued through the State of Indiana. It is on the west side of the Cincinnati axis of elevation; the beds are not disturbed by the uplift in their horizontal position.

In Monroe County the beds of nearly all the creeks present exposures of the ledges; in Lenawee and Wayne counties, the incumbent drift deposits are much heavier and the rock is not so often exposed. The surface of all the rock beds of this region which lie on top is worn smooth and scratched by drift marks.

The lower division of the Helderberg series, identical with the strata forming the base of Mackinac Island, and with the water-lime group of the Ohio reports, has a much greater surface extension in the district under consideration than the upper division corresponding with the limestones of Sandusky. This upper division is well uncovered in the quarries of Trenton village in Wayne County, and likewise in the quarries on Macon Creek, formerly owned by Judge Christiancy. The surface layers of the Trenton quarries are only covered by a thin coating of loamy drift. They are limestones of light color, segregated in thin beds, with uneven rough surface, containing an abundance of fossils, particularly Crinoid stems, Bryozoa, Cyathophyllum cornicula, various Favosites, Atrypa reticularis, Spirifer gregarius, Spirifer acuminatus, etc. The thickness of the beds is about six feet; they are used for lime-burning, and yield a white, quick-slaking lime of very good quality. The beds of the quarry have a very perceptible dip west by southwest, which is evidently caused by a local undulation of the strata. The direction of the dip of the formation at large can not be learned from the measurement and examination of single localities; it is generally hypothetically deduced from the distribution and sequence of the rock beds over areas of large extent. The next lower beds in the quarry are a compact gray, crystalline limestone, in beds from eight inches to two feet in thickness, and in all amounting to about eight feet, which represent the principal quarry rock. They are rich in fossils; the species which I collected there are: Cyathophyllum Hallii, Cyathoph. cornicula, Zaphrentis prolifica, Zaphrentis gigantea, Favosites turbinatus, Fav. hemisphericus, various species of Fenestella and Polypora, Stictopora Gilberti, Stromatopora textilis, Atrypa reticularis, Spirifer acuminatus, Strophodonta concava, Strophod. perplana, Orthis Livia, Lucina elliptica, Conocardium trigonale, Euomphalus Dekewyi, various large forms of Orthoceras, Gomphoceras, Gyroceras, Nautilus, Phacops bufo, Prœtus crassimarginatus, Dalmania selenurus, and bones of fishes.

The base of the part of the quarries at present worked is formed of about 4 feet of very uneven, thin-bedded, concretionary limestones full of hornstone nodules, and coated over by a black, shining crust of bituminous shale; the peculiar segregations called stylolites are also quite frequent in these beds, which (beds) are thrown away as worthless rubbish. Under them, in another part of the quarry, not now worked, are other limestone beds denuded to the depth of 12 feet; several of their thicker seams furnish material quite as good as the best ledges in the upper part of the quarry. The owner of the place bored in the quarry a drill hole through solid limestone for a depth of 60 feet, in search of well-water, but did not succeed in finding any. Selected blocks of the lime rock are cut into door-steps, sills, water-tanks, etc., the rest being used for foundation walls and for the lime-kilns. An analysis of the principal quarry stone gave:

Carbonate of lime..........................	87.5
" " magnesia	10.1
Quartz ore residue, besides small quantities of iron and alumina.........................	2.0
	99.6

The quarries on Macon Creek, on Mr. Christiancy's former property, are opened in the same strata as the Trenton quarries. The rock there is more porous, absorbing water rapidly when dry, and considerably impregnated with rock oil, which exudes from its crevices, and often collects on the water pools of the quarry in a thick scum. In humid state, the rock is dusky drab-colored. The surface layers are rich in fossils identical with those of the Trenton quarries; certain seams are perfectly crowded with Chonetes yandellana, and others with Tentaculites scalaris. Below these fossiliferous beds, the useful ledges of the quarry, about 6 or 7 feet in thickness, follow; they are of the above-mentioned porous character. The better quarry-stone furnishes sills, door-steps, etc., but most of it is used for the production of lime. Its composition is:

Carbonate of lime....	84.0
" " magnesia	13.0
Iron oxide hydr.	0.4
Quartz and bitumen	2.2
	99.6

The deeper strata of the quarry become worthless from a copious admixture of white, cherty concretions. The exudation of rock oil from the crevices induced some persons, a number of years ago, to form a company to bore for rock oil at this locality. A drill hole was sunk to the depth of 700 feet, but without the hoped-for success. The record of the boring I could not obtain. I was informed that not many feet below the rock beds opened in the quarry, a bed of sand rock was struck. This sand-rock deposit seems to be a very constant stratum found at that horizon, not only in Michigan, but all over the Helderberg area of the State of Ohio. Natural outcrops of this sand rock can be observed in the bed of Raisin River, six miles above Monroe; it is there very hard and compact, rich in calcareous cement; several fossils, casts of spirifer, etc., are inclosed in some blocks of the rock, but they are too imperfect for specific determination. The sand-rock stratum, in a soft, friable condition, and occasionally perfectly white, is found in the northeast corner of Raisinville township, on the farm of Mr. Bond, where it forms the surface rock over a good many acres of ground; in places it is overlaid by dolomitic limestones about 8 feet in thickness, which contain the casts of numerous fossils, Zaphrentis, Favosites, several forms of Bryozoa, Atrypa reticularis, Orthis Livia, Conocardium trigonale, Phacops bufo, Dalmania selenurus. Quantities of this sand, which is almost pure quartz without admixture, have been shipped to Pittsburgh for glass manufacture, for which purpose it is said to be of excellent quality. The thickness of the deposit is not seen in this place; only 6 or 7 feet are denuded in the diggings. In Section 16 of Ida township, a sand rock of about 6 feet in thickness forms the top layers of a limestone quarry. The upper strata are friable and soft, their calcareous cement seeming to have leached out while the deeper sited strata are hard and rich in calcareous matter.

The rock contains some casts of bivalve shells and of gasteropods; its fissures and druse cavities are filled with strontianite, cœlestine and calcspar. The sand rock reposes on a hard, compact dolomite rock, mottled with light and dark blue cloudy specks resembling castile soap. The dolomite is composed of

	Per Cent.
Carbonate of lime	54
" " magnesia	42
Quartz sand	4

The lower hard cemented sand-rock beds contain

	Per Cent.
Carbonate of lime	46
White quartz sand	54

Sand-rock ledges of a somewhat different character from those mentioned, but evidently equivalent with them, are exposed on both sides of a road passing the north end of Ottawa Lake. The rock is hard, fine-grained, of dark bluish, or, in weathered condition, of ferruginous brown color, and contains 65 per cent of calcareous matter by 34 per cent of quartz sand. It is quarried for building purposes; intermediate between the harder layers are seams of a coarse-grained, softer sand rock with only a small proportion of calcareous cement. Inclosed in these softer seams, I found dermatic plates of macropetalichthys. South from there, across the State line, near Sylvania, in Ohio, a similar seam of sand rock is found intercalated between the upper and lower Helderberg limestones; and from the geological reports of Ohio we learn that throughout the entire Helderberg area of that State a sand-rock deposit is constantly found in such position. In some localities the sand rock seems to be replaced by an oolith. In the quarries of Plum Creek, near Monroe, and near Little Lake, in Bedford township, the mottled dolomite rock which lies at the base of the sand rock in the Ida quarries, Section 16, is found in the same characteristic form, but instead of sandstone, in the two mentioned localities, oolithic rock beds are superimposed. Their chemical composition is: carbonate of lime, 61 per cent, and carbonate of magnesia, 37 per cent. The thickness of this sand-rock stratum has, within the State of Michigan, never been found to exceed 8 or 10 feet, and in Ohio, also, it forms only a comparatively thin seam. No fossils are known to have been found in it except the few fragmentary specimens which I mentioned, so that a palæontological comparison with other beds is forbidden; but considering its relative position between the upper and lower divisions of the Helderberg group and its lithological character, its equivalency with the Oriskany sandstone of New York becomes very probable, an identification which was first made by the Ohio geologists. A marked change in the nature of the deposits above and below this geological horizon is perceptible. The rock series below the sandstones which has been identified with the water-lime group of New York, is altogether composed of dolomites and contains entirely different fossils from those found in the strata above the sand rocks, which have more of a true limestone character, and rarely contain a high percentage of magnesia. I have previously made the statement that this lower water-lime division has a much greater surface extent within this southeastern corner of Michigan than the higher beds. All the exposures of Raisin River, in Plum Creek, belong to this lower rock series; the quarries in the townships La Salle, Ida, and Bedford are worked in the same beds, and the outcrops on Point-aux-Paux, at Gibraltar, in Swan Creek, and Stony Creek, all represent this water-lime series. The upper strata of this group are frequently but not always found in a brecciated condition, with fragments of various ledges intermingled and re-cemented. The lower, non-brecciated beds have evidently the same lithological characters as the fragments composing the breccia.

By what force the strata were shattered into fragments, it is difficult to suggest, but the cause of the disturbance can not have been a local one, confined to this district only. We find this rock in brecciated condition all over the northwestern part of Ohio and on the islands of Lake Erie. The same occurs again in the equivalent beds of Mackinac, and in the exposures of Goderich in Canada.

A natural section through the whole thickness of the water-lime group is nowhere in the district exposed, and the artificial excavations by quarrying generally comprise vertically only a small series of beds, and they are nearly always of one and the same horizon. Of deep artesian borings, several have been made within the city limits of Monroe to a depth of from 150 to 300 feet, and the boring records of some have been noted down. Such notes are very useful for comparison of strata, if we were only beforehand informed of the geological structure of a locality, in its details; but to learn these details by the results of borings alone is very unsatisfactory.

As an illustration, I give one of the records of a drill hole sunk in the Court-House Square of Monroe to a depth of 140 feet. It reads:

Clay and sand	6	feet.
Gray limestone	3	"
Blue limestone	6	inches.
Dark gray limestone	3	feet.
Blue limestone	1½	"
Gray limestone	14	"
Blue limestone	2	"
Gray limestone	39	"
Blue limestone	5	"
Gray limestone	2	"
Blue limestone	32	"
Blue shale	39	"

We see here a number of limestone beds, varying in color and compactness, amounting to over 100 feet in depth, and below, a deposit of calcareous shales, which could perhaps be taken as representing a part of the Onondaga formation; but the information we receive by this record is insufficient to enable us to form a clear idea of the special qualities of the rock beds, or to distinguish positively certain horizons. From another boring made in the same place, I received, through the kindness of Judge Christiancy, specimens of the rock brought up by the pump, by which I can see that, to a depth of 300 feet below the surface, limestone beds are almost exclusively following each other in continued superposition; but these limestones, of a dolomitic character, sometimes light-colored, sometimes dark, partly laminated, or other specimens of a cellulose structure, full of irregular cavities, clothed with spar crystals, or pieces pervaded with acicular spar crystals, are all without prominent peculiarity by which one can tell whether the boring has passed the water-lime and entered the Onondaga or Niagara group or not. Rocks exactly similar to those brought up from the deepest portion of the drill hole are found in the superficial beds of the quarries near by, and acicular limestones, not distinguishable from those mixed with the upper brecciated limestones, come up from a depth of over 200 feet.

We learn by the borings that no gypsiferous shales are found in the strata underlying Monroe, and that for several hundred feet downward limestones of dolomitic character alternately follow each other; but we have no guiding rule by which to learn exactly where we are.

Among the exposures of the water-lime group, the quarries of Gibraltar, situated about four miles south of the Trenton quarries, are the most northern. There this lower rock series comes to the surface in the bed of the creek where it enters the lake near Gibraltar, and west of the village, at the point crossed by the Michigan Southern Railroad. The surface of the upper ledges is polished by drift action. The rock is a somewhat absorbent, minutely crystalline dolomite of gray color and a laminated structure, sometimes deceivingly resembling an obsolete Stromatopora. The beds are even, from 1 to 2 feet thick, answering a good purpose as a building-stone. They frequently contain large, spherical, concretionary masses, very hard and compact in the centre, but successively becoming more and more porous toward their periphery, which merges into the general rock mass without a defining line separating the concretion from the plasma of the ledge. About 8 feet of the rock beds are denuded in the quarry; no fossils were observed in the place.

West of this locality, near Flat Rock, Huron River runs in rapids over ledges which belong to the water-lime horizon, a drab-colored, crystalline, somewhat porous, but hard dolomite, with flinty concretions. Of fossils, I noticed casts of crinoid joints, vegetable stems, and a small elongated body with email surface, serrated on the edges, which can only be the remains of a fish or crustacean. Similar corpuscles I found in the brecciated limestones of Point-aux-Paux, a locality which will subsequently be described. The rock in the vicinity of Flat Rock is covered by drift of considerable thickness, and does not come near enough to the surface to be opened in quarries. At Newport on Swan Creek, the water-lime strata are found everywhere close under the surface of the level country, polished by drift action. The rock is a light, drab-colored, fine-grained, absorbent dolomite; the surface of the bed is rugose, pitted, as if the strata in soft condition had at one time emerged from the water and been exposed to rain-drops. Seams of black carbonaceous shale separate the ledges and cover their surface with a shining, thin coat. Stylolitic segregations are very common; they are evidently a peculiar sort of shrinkage cracks formed by the contracting of the mud mass during its consolidation into rock; their striated surface is likewise blackened with this shaly coating. In the quarries, only about 8 feet of the strata are uncovered; the upper superficial ones are the best; some of them break in good-sized blocks about a foot in thickness, which are used as a building-stone. However, most of the rock is quarried for lime-burning. The lower beds in the quarries are thin, uneven slabs interstratified with seams of black shale. Fissures and druse cavities in the rock mass are filled with fine crystals of cœlestine and of calcspar. Of fossils, casts of Meristella lævis, and vegetable stems are the most common. The surface of certain seams in the rock is often densely crowded with the shells, which are frequently coated with asphaltum or surrounded by liquid rock oil. The vegetable remains are of various kinds. Some are band-like, compressed stems, which sometimes bifurcate, and are of jointed structure. On certain portions of these stems, annular cicatrices are disposed in remote rows, in shape resembling the pores of the tube of a Favosites. Another kind of stem is narrower, more remotely jointed, and each joint is surrounded by a verticil of long, narrow leaves. I have transmitted specimens of these remains to Prof. Leo Lesquereux, of Columbus, leaving it to him to give his opinion on them at pleasure. He thinks they are of considerable scientific interest, and will probably say something about them in one of his scientific publications.

Three miles southeast of the Newport quarries, we find along the shore of Point-aux-Paux a very good natural exposure of the same rock beds which here are in brecciated condition, while the beds of the Newport quarry are undisturbed. The rock beds project only about 4 feet above the water level, but by undulations of the strata about 15 feet of successive ledges become exposed. The breccia is formed of angular rock fragments; sometimes larger masses, composed of several consecutive layers, retaining their regular stratified position to each other, lie inclosed in it, often also a regular, unbroken seam of limestone alternates with the brecciated layers.

The principal part of the ledges resembles in all particulars the rock of the Newport quarries; the same fossils are found in them, only in greater abundance and variety. Meristella lævis, Leptocœlia concava, Megambonia aviculoidea, casts of several forms of bivalves and gasteropods, and a small spirorbis-like shell, are the usual forms met with, besides a profusion of the above-mentioned vegetable remains pervading the rock beds. Druses of cœlestine and calcspar, and veins of these minerals, filling the fissures of the rock, are very abundant.

Eurypterus remipes and Leperditia alta, the two typical forms of this horizon, I could not find in this locality, but on Put-in-Bay Island both fossils are found in association with the others above mentioned, and in beds which, by their lithological characters, leave no doubt of the identity of the strata in both places. Of the emailled corpuscles with serrate edges, which I found in the dolomite of Flat Rock, and suggested might be the remains of fishes or crustaceans, I found several at Point-aux-Paux. South of Point-aux-Paux, toward Monroe, we find the same rock beds everywhere close under the surface, with only a few feet of drift on them. The quarries alongside of Raisin River, up to Dundee, are all opened in beds of this horizon. In the quarries of Plum Creek, a short distance south of Monroe, by the undulations in which the strata rise and sink, about twenty feet of rock beds come to an exposure. Uppermost are fine-grained, light-colored dolomitic limestones in beds a few inches thick, and in the aggregate reaching six feet. Next below is a compact stratum of oolith from eighteen inches to two feet in thickness, which makes a good building material. Lower are thin, rugose ledges of limestone with intervening narrow seams of a black shale mass; these are succeeded by about two feet of a gray and blue mottled dolomite rock, after which are again thinly laminated limestone slabs with intermediate black shale seams. The surface of these limestone slabs is covered by ramified relief forms, apparently of vegetable origin. The lowest beds in the quarry are bluish gray dolomites in moderately thick ledges, opened to the depth of about eight feet, and representing the principal quarry-stone used for ordinary building purposes. In the whole series of rock beds, fossils are rarely seen, but in nests or in a thin seam, locally, they may be found in abundance. Among the rocks which came out on excavating the cellar of a brewery situated within the quarry, certain blocks are crowded with casts of Meristella lævis, Retzia globosa, Leptocœlia concava, Megambonia aviculoidea and several other bivalves, several Gasteropods, great numbers of a spirorbis-like shell, besides the vegetable stems found elsewhere in the same strata.

In the southwest corner of La Salle town, about six miles west of the lake shore, the brecciated limestones, which in Monroe are in a position on a line with the lake level, are found in the quarries at an elevation of about 100 feet above the lake.

In the quarries near Little Lake, in Bedford township, similar strata to those of the Plum Creek quarries are uncovered. In the upper part of the quarry we find an oolith stratum identical with the one in the other locality. The lower part is formed of brecciated limestones, seams of which are fossiliferous; besides the already-mentioned forms, a Cyrtoceras and some Gasteropod casts are found there, which I have not noticed in the other localities.

Two miles west of Ida village, close to the railroad track, extensive quarries are opened and lime-kilns erected. Close under the surface, light-colored, almost white dolomites, of finely crystalline grain, and of absorbent, porous structure are found; they are much intersected by veins of calcspar, and inclose druse cavities lined with the same material. Certain layers are completely filled with small acicular spar crystals, or the crystals have been dissolved by a partial weathering of the rock, and the places formerly occupied by them are now found as open, narrow slits pervading the rock in all directions. By the same process of weathering, the rock, which originally was a hard mass composed of dolomite spar crystals, cemented together by calcspar, the more soluble calcspar being dissolved by the percolating waters, is left, according to the degree of weathering, either a porous but yet hard mass of minute dolomite spar crystals, or a mealy, crystalline substance friable between the fingers.

An analysis of the dolomite with acicular crystals gave,

Carbonate of lime.............59 per cent.
" " magnesia..........39 "
Insoluble residue not weighed.

The acicular spar crystals are very characteristic of the limestones of this lower horizon of the Helderberg group, everywhere to be found in this district, in Ohio, in Goderich, Canada, and in Mackinac Island where these beds are uncovered. Similar acicular limestones are found in lower geological position in the dolomite beds of the Onondaga group, and in certain beds of the Niagara group. (See report on the Upper Peninsula, page 35.)

Prof. A. Winchell identified the dolomites of the Ida quarries with the Onondaga group, but the position of these beds is not lower than that of the other quarries considered to represent the water-lime group, and no difference in the lithological characters of the strata exists which would justify a distinction. In the deep boring made in the Court-house yard of Monroe for a depth of 300 feet, no particular change in the nature of the rock was observed; nearly all this thickness was made up by dolomites, some of which, by their cellulose character, with cavities once filled with crystals, are similar to beds found in the Onondaga group, but no gypsum beds nor shale deposits, which are significant of this group, were noticed.

The gypsiferous rock beds have been found in the State of Ohio at Sylvania, but in Michigan no positive evidences of the development of this formation have been discovered in the south-eastern end of the State. Remarkable in this region are the numerous sink-holes found over it. Some of them are small, abrupt, funnel-shaped depressions; others are larger and sink more gradually. Many of them are filled with water and form respectable lakes, as Ottawa Lake and Little Lake, while others are dry or filled only for a part of the year. The water in all these lakes is subject to considerable fluctuations during the different seasons. Ottawa Lake, which covers about a square mile of surface, has in the spring of the year a depth of 50 feet; toward the fall it has lowered its level about 25 feet below high-water mark, and its shallowest parts lie perfectly dry. The water usually disappears rapidly when it begins to sink, which is not the effect of evaporation. It escapes by subterranean crevices, which become visible after the water has run off. The steep embankments of the northeast end of the lake are formed by the brecciated limestones of the water-lime group, which are quarried there and burned into lime.

Little Lake, in the town of Bedford, Section 15, is another sink-hole of large dimensions. It sometimes becomes perfectly dry, which never happens with Ottawa Lake. The rock crevices through which the water disappears were quite conspicuous in the emptied lake bottom at the time of my visit. Four miles north of Ottawa Lake, on the land of Mr. Cummins, in the town of Whiteford, between Sections 1 and 2, another large sink-hole is observable, which during the summer and fall-time is perfectly dry and partly overgrown with grass. The centre of this depression is about 18 feet below the level of the surrounding country; a part of its bottom is formed of naked rock ledges fissured by deep, vertical crevices. The owner of the place informs me that during the spring this depression is filled with water which contains large fish, although I saw not a drop of water in it at the time of my visit. When the water begins to sink, it escapes quickly, and at the spot where the crevices are, a whirlpool draws them in with a distinctly audible, rushing noise. The larger fish being unable to get off with the water, are left on the dry bottom to die. From the fact of the appearance in these periodical water-basins of full-grown fish of the kind usually found in Lake Erie, it has become the general belief of the inhabitants that a direct connection exists between these sink-holes and that lake, which suggestion has in it much of probability. All limestone formations are apt to be undermined and eaten out by the water flowing through their crevices, which is more or less charged with carbonic acid, and thus rendered a powerful solvent for the limestone. The old sandy beach-lines encircling this district bear clear testimony to the fact that all this part of the country was at a period not very remote a part of the bottom of Lake Erie, whose waters leached out the softer, more soluble ledges of the lime rock, and left the harder layers as roofs over the eroded cavities. After the receding of the water from this ground, leaving behind a deep, muddy sediment, which forms the present rich soil, the roofs of these subterranean cavities broke down, in some cases forming sink-holes that remain in connection with intricate subterranean channels which doubtless lead into the lake.

The connection of the Helderberg group with the superincumbent younger formations is in this part of the State entirely hidden by drift deposits. At Blissfield, Deerfield, and Petersburg, localities which are only a short distance from the actual outcrops of the Helderberg strata, in ordinary wells, dug to a depth of seventy and eighty feet through drift deposits, no rock ledges have yet been touched, and at Detroit, 130 feet have to be sunk through before the lime rock is reached. In Prof. Winchell's geological map, published in Walling's Atlas of Michigan, the southwest corner of the State is represented as underlaid by the Helderberg group, through a great portion of Cass and Van Buren counties and all over Berrien County. This is an error; the Helderberg strata have nowhere been found as the surface rock underneath the drift in any of the deep borings made at Niles, Cassopolis, Michigan City, or other places.

In a deep boring lately made at the Indiana State Prison, at Michigan City, the drift was found to be 170 feet deep; below it, the black shales of Ohio were struck in a thickness of 76 feet, and, finally, at a depth of 246 feet from the surface, the first limestone beds of the Helderberg group were penetrated. A natural outcrop of the Waverly group is north of New Buffalo, near Brown's Station, not far from the Lake Shore. It is the same case south of the Michigan boundary-line, on Indiana territory, where for many miles no trace of a limestone formation underlying the drift can be found; it is always the subcarboniferous sand rock and its intermediate shale beds which are first encountered.

CHAPTER VI.

HAMILTON GROUP.

ON the map of Prof. A. Winchell, just mentioned, a belt of the Hamilton group is represented as extending from Wyandotte southwestward through Monroe and Lenawee counties, and on the southwest side of the State another belt is laid down as stretching from the southwest corner of St. Joseph County to the north end of Berrien County.

In the southern part of Michigan no strata have ever been discovered which could be claimed as representing the Hamilton formation, and even if such existed, the belt laid down as running through St. Joseph and Berrien counties would be positively misplaced, as its hypothetical course would be not less than 40 or 50 miles further to the southwest. The Hamilton group is, all through Ohio and Indiana, scarcely developed; in the exposures, the beds usually found next incumbent on the Helderberg limestones are the black shales of Ohio, considered as equivalent to the Genesee shale of New York. Only in a few localities of Ohio are some shaly strata of inconsiderable thickness, containing Hamilton fossils, intercalated between the limestone formation and the black shales.

In the northern part of the Michigan peninsula we find the Hamilton group developed as a heavy formation of over 500 feet in thickness. The southern limit of the surface extent of this group, in the region spoken of, is indicated by a line drawn from Partridge Point, in Thunder Bay, northwestward to intersect the principal meridian in the southern part of Town. 34; from there the line goes directly west, through Bear Lake and Pine Lake, and then bends southwest, terminating near Norwood on the shore of Big Traverse Bay. The land-spur across the bay is covered by drift, and presents no outcrops of rock. The continuation of this belt of the Hamilton group, across Lake Michigan and Lake Huron, to the shores of Canada and Wisconsin, has previously been mentioned. North of the indicated line, all of the surface of the peninsula is formed by the Hamilton strata, excepting the small strip of shore at McGulpin's Point, which is described as composed of the upper Helderberg limestones. The Hamilton group in New York is pre-eminently a shale formation, with subordinate beds of limestone; in Michigan it has more the character of a limestone formation with but a subordinate development of shale beds.

Natural sections of large extent, by which the thickness of the formation can be estimated, do not exist; by borings made in Alpena, its thickness is found to be much greater than formerly had been supposed. One of the borings was made more than ten years ago, but no accurate record was kept of it. At that time a bed of rock salt was struck in the bottom of the well, and I myself saw more than a bushel of salt in yellowish crystals which was brought up by the sand pumps; still no further use was made of this discovery, and it is only within the last few years that the strong stream of mineral water discharged from the bore-hole has received attention and been used for its strong medicinal properties. At present it is led by tubings to a bathing institution close to the landing-place at the bay. The mineral water is strongly impregnated with hydrosulphuretted gas. It flows from a higher level than the bottom of the well, but has a considerable proportion of chloride of sodium in solution, which probably rises from the lower part of the bore and mingles with the upper sulphurous water. An analysis made by Dr. Duffield gave 237 grains of solid matter to a gallon of the water, as follows:

Bicarbonate of soda	15.736	grains.
" " lime	55.136	"
" " magnesia	62.920	"
" " iron	1.840	"
Sulphate of lime	30.056	"
Chloride of sodium	68.256	"
Silica and alumina	3.088	"
Organic matter	0.928	"

Sulphuretted hydrogen 3.91 cubic inches per gallon.

Another boring was made four years ago close to the bed of Thunder Bay River. It commenced in rock beds which are at least 100 feet lower than the strata composing Partridge Point. The boring commenced in limestones, which continued, without much interruption by other beds, to a depth of 400 feet below the surface, when blue shales were struck, and a powerful stream of mineral water rose to the top, carrying with it many well-preserved fossils of the shale beds. The fossils were: Cyathophyllum Houghtoni, Cyathoph. Hallii, various species of Favosites, Cladopora, and numerous Bryozoa, Crinoid stems, Atrypa reticularis, Spirigera concentrica, Spirifer mucronatus, Cyrtina Hamiltonensis, etc. The thickness of the shale was found to be 80 feet. Below it, limestones of variable hardness and color were penetrated to the depth of 600 feet from the surface, and from there to 1025 feet, light-colored, partly dolomitic limestones were found. At this depth a bed of solid rock-salt was struck, after which the boring was discontinued. The upper 480 feet of this drill-hole are positively made up by strata of the Hamilton group, which, with addition of the 100 feet of higher strata, would give 580 feet for the thickness of the Hamilton group, and in all probability a part of the limestones below the shales also belong to that group. The lower light-colored limestones represent the Helderberg group, and their dolomitic strata may be equivalent with the lower beds of Mackinac Island, and with the subjacent Onondaga group. The deposit of rock-salt is at all events identical with the rock-salt deposits of Goderich in Canada, and with the Onondaga salt deposits of New York State. The salt brine of Saginaw valley belongs to an entirely different and much higher horizon, to the Waverly formation. After the boring was finished, pumps were set in the tubed hole, and a concentrated brine was lifted to the surface, which, after pumping for a while, became weaker and weaker, until at last a very weak brine only came up. If the pumping was interrupted for some hours and commenced again, a strong brine could be obtained for a while, when the weaker grades would reappear. This discouraged the owners of the well, so that nothing more was done. I told them the reasons for this, explaining to them that the salt being in solid condition, had to dissolve first in the water which runs upon it from above, and required time to become saturated, so that after the strong solution, the quantity of which could only be small, proportionate to the surface of salt rock exposed to the solvent, was pumped out, it was to be expected that only a weak brine could be obtained. But this would have soon remedied itself; by constant pumping a larger cavity would have been formed, and the surface offered to the water for solution would constantly have increased, so that a reservoir would finally be formed capable of furnishing a supply of strong brine which could no longer be exhausted by the pumps. Whether any use was made of these hints, I do not know, but the fact is that this very valuable discovery has lain idle for several years, which is much to be regretted, as I have not the least doubt that, by a little patient application of the pumps, it would soon yield a constant supply of strong brine. The highest beds of the Hamilton series at Thunder Bay are seen at Partridge Point, on the south side of which, in Squaw Bay, the bituminous black shales of Ohio directly overlie them. Sulphur Island, in front of Squaw Bay, is also covered by the black-shale formation.

The top layers on Partridge Point are thin-bedded, hard limestone slabs, seen in the thickness of a few feet; they contain no fossils. Next below them follow calcareo-arenaceous shales of bluish or greenish color, alternating with seams of limestone, which face the lake in a bluff along the north side of the point, projecting about 12 or 15 feet above the water level. The shales and limestone beds are crowded with fossils in a good state of preservation. A great variety of Bryozoa, particularly of the genera Fenestella, Polypora, Hemitrypa, Stictopora, Fistulipora, and Trematopora, belong to the most abundant forms, besides corals, Cystiphyllum Americanum, Cyathophyllum geniculatum, Cyathoph. Hallii, Diphyphyllum Archiaci, and various forms of Favosites, Syringopora, Aulopora, Dendropora. Crinoids are very well represented by the genera Megistocrinus, Dolatocrinus, Nucleocrinus, Pentremites, Lepadocrinus. Of Brachiopods occur: Atrypa reticularis, Spirifer granuliferus, Spirigera concentrica, Cyrtina Hamiltonensis, Terebratula romingeri, etc.; of Trilobites, Phacops bufo and a species of Prœtus. In front of these bluffs, at a distance of about one mile, are two islands, Bear Island and Grass Island, on which I expected to see the next lower beds exposed, but all their surface is composed of boulder drift.

Likewise on the main shore, the rock strata below the shales of the bluffs are hidden from view; between the next point northward, Stony Point, and Partridge Point, a low, swampy space about a mile in width extends, on which no rock ledges can be seen; it is, however, evident, from the strike and dip of the strata, that the beds composing Stony Point are below those of Partridge Point, and that no great mass of rock strata can intervene between them. The ledges of Stony Point are first noticed submerged, while northward, by a gradual rise of the strata, they project about three or four feet above the water level. They are a light-colored limestone, full of large convex masses of various species of Stromatopora, particularly Str. monticulifera and Str. Wortheni. Some deeper ledges of darker color and of a nodular structure, with intermingled shaly seams, are rich in many species of fossils, chiefly Cyathophyllum Houghtoni, Cyathophyllum Hallii, Cystiphyllum Americanum, Diphyphyllum Archiaci, Cyathophyllum profundum, Favosites Hamiltonensis, Favosites nitella, Alveolites subramosus, various forms of Syringopora and of Aulopora, and numerous Bryozoa. Of Brachiopods, I may mention Atrypa reticularis, Spirigera concentrica, Spirifer mucronatus, Spirifer zigzag, Cyrtina Hamiltonensis, Pentamerus aratus, Strophodonta demissa, Strophodonta erratica, Crania Hamiltoniæ, Crania crenistria, with a number of others.

Analogous rock beds form the surface rock over an extended space west and northwest from Stony Point. The hillsides lining the south side of Thunder Bay River, in Sections 28 and 20 of Alpena town, present a number of exposures of the strata in question. The highest beds seen in these localities are light-colored limestones containing few fossils beyond some Crinoid stems and ramulets of Bryozoa. Under them follow nodular limestones abounding in irregular, flexuous seams of black bituminous shale matter. The mass of these limestones is almost entirely composed of different species of Stromatopora, Favosites Hamiltonensis, Cyathophyllum profundum, Cyath. Houghtoni, etc. Somewhat lower strata are of a lighter blue or drab color, with the shaly seams very prevalent throughout the ledges. They are very fossiliferous, containing about the same forms as have been enumerated as belonging to the lower beds of Stony Point, besides a few others not seen there, as Cystiphyllum aggregatum, and large lumps of Chætetes and of a Fistulipora species. At the foot of the hills, below these shaly layers, about 15 feet of light-colored limestones, in beds six or eight inches thick, are the lowest seen in the outcrops; they contain but few fossils, and not any of them characteristic of a certain horizon. The total depth of strata composing these outcrops is from 50 to 60 feet. On the north side of Thunder Bay River another series of rock beds is found, which I suppose to be the next in succession below the section just described. The marshy, level surface on which the north half of Alpena village is situated is underlaid by light-colored limestones inclosing a profusion of Stromatopora plana and many corals, as Favosites, Cyathophyllum, Cystiphyllum, partly in silicified condition. The next deeper strata, exposed on the side of the first lake terrace, contain, besides the aforementioned corals, silicified stems of Favosites radiciformis, Cladopora Alpenensis, Michelinia insignis, Favosites radiatus, Cyathophyllum Hallii, and numerous other fossils. Among the lower ledges of this horizon a bed is almost exclusively filled with disconnected shells of Cyrtina umbonata. In further descending order, beds of a coarsely crystalline, drab-colored, and sandy-looking limestone occur, which contain only a few fossils, but interlaminated with them is a seam of much lighter-colored, smooth fracturing lime rock full of fossils, among which Chonophyllum ponderosum and Strombodes Alpenensis are peculiar to this stratum. Still below them we find compact dark gray or bluish-colored limestones of crystalline fracture, and almost entirely composed of broken shells and Crinoid stems. This rock is quarried in several localities, being the only good building-stone to be had in the vicinity of Alpena. The total thickness of the rock series described on the north side of Thunder Bay River is about 50 feet. The lowest of the beds, all of which were in nearly horizontal position, are visible in the circumference of a small, abrupt hillock on which Mr. Phelps's lime-kilns stand, in an uplifted position, dipping away from the central, bubble-like protrusion at an angle of 25 or 30 degrees. Several such hillocks are noticed within the space of half a square mile. The central mass of the hillocks is a whitish, fine-grained, pure limestone, of brecciated structure, and of smooth, conchoidal fracture, pervaded in all directions by fissures filled with calcspar and mottled by cloudy seams of light green or reddish color. It contains a great abundance of fossils, particularly Stromatopora Wortheni, Favosites Hamiltonensis, Cyathophyllum profundum, Strombodes Alpenensis, Chonophyllum ponderosum, many Bryozoa and various Brachiopods of the usual Hamilton species, etc. The rock makes an excellent white, quick-slaking lime. Similar strata of less brecciated structure, and inter-laminated with soft, soap-like, whitish green clay are uncovered in the race of Mr. Broadwell's saw mill on Thunder Bay River. The clay incloses a profusion of splendidly preserved Bryozoa and corals, also some Crinoids (Dolatocrinus) and Brachiopods. The exact relative position of the strata exposed in this locality I was unable to ascertain. A bubble-like upheaval of the beds has its centre in the river bottom and by the dam thrown across the river—the most instructive portions of the section are thus set under water. Only a short distance up the river, on the side of the road leading to Trowbridge's mills, a small knob is formed by the same light-colored, smooth fracturing, brecciated limestones, which there seem to repose in undisturbed original position on blue calcareous shales, with seams of silico-argillaceous limestone. The river, which passes only about 100 steps from the hillock, has cut its bed through these subjacent shales to a depth of 50 feet, and for a whole mile the ledges are exposed in high bluffs. The shales inclose a great variety of well-preserved fossils: Atrypa reticularis, Spirigera concentrica, Cyrtina Hamiltonensis, Cyrtina umbonata, Spirifer mucronatus, Spirifer divaricatus, Spirifer granuliferous, Spirifer fimbriatus, Terebratula Linklæni, Strophodonta demissa, Pentamerus papilionensis, Crania crenistria, Crania Hamiltoniæ, and numerous Bryozoa, Phacops bufo, etc. A few interstratified seams of a silicious limestone are a conglomerated mass of silicified shells of Cyrtina umbonata and of a few specimens of Spirigera concentrica.

The argillaceous limestones interstratified with the shales were a number of years ago used for the fabrication of hydraulic cement. Expensive kilns stand abandoned at the foot of the river bluffs. Mr. Trowbridge, their former owner, informs me that sometimes an article of very good quality was produced, but the success was so uncertain that the cement never came into reputation in the market, and after a short time he gave up the undertaking. Whether the failure to make a uniform product was in the use of different beds, some of which would not answer, or in the management of the burning process, I can not tell.

From Trowbridge's mills, higher up the river, the strata are hidden from view for several miles ; they appear again under the bridge crossing the north branch of Thunder Bay River. Judging from the rock character and the fossils, the strata belong to about the same horizon as those near Trowbridge's mills.

In Township 32, R. 6, east, Section 34, on the farm of Mr. Marston, close to his dwelling-house, a large funnel-shaped sink-hole without an outlet attracts attention. It occupies the area of a few acres, and has a depth of about 25 feet ; a strong spring issues from the side of the depression and disappears again in its bottom in the crevices of the rock.

The bottom strata, seen in a thickness of about 8 feet, are hard, bituminous limestones, with delicate laminar striation in the direction of the bedding and fissible into thin flags. Near the upper terminus of the rock strata a seam about one foot in thickness of a cellulose, brecciated quartz rock, mottled with various red, brown, or yellowish colors, and containing distinct casts of fossils, is intercalated. Above it follows a coarsely crystalline, tough, brownish-gray dolomite, which contains large Euomphalus-like coiled shells, Cystiphyllum, and indistinct specimens of Stromatopora ; its thickness is from 8 to 10 feet. Next above is a silicious limestone full of silicified specimens of Stromatopora Wortheni, Favosites digitatus, Syringopora nobilis, Spirigera concentrica, and the same large coiled shell as in the dolomites below ; its thickness is 4 or 5 feet, and over the top a few layers of compact, light-colored limestones are spread. About a mile from Marston's the road passes not far from the river, where it intersects the southwest corner of Section 34 in the same town. It flows there in a long series of rapids, over hard, bluish, crystalline limestones containing shell fragments and Crinoid joints. The banks of the river, about 18 or 20 feet high, are all formed of drift, and the relative position of these rock beds can not be made out. On Section 28 of the same township, on Mr. Johnson's farm, in a well 21 feet deep, blue-colored argillaceous limestones and intermediate shale beds were penetrated ; of fossils, I noticed in them Atrypa reticularis, Spirifer fimbriatus, Spirifer granuliferous, and Crinoid stems ; one of the layers was a coarse-grained, gray dolomitic rock identical with the dolomite rock in the sink-hole on Mr. Marston's farm. The horizon of all these rocks seems to be below the strata of Thunder Bay River near Trowbridge's mill. For a circle of many miles around the localities described, rock beds of the same horizon seem to occupy the surface, covered by a more or less considerable coating of drift material. The drift soil of this region is a fertile, gravelly loam, which was densely covered with forest until a number of years ago fires swept through them, totally destroying them for many square miles. By this clearance of the productive soil, numerous settlers were attracted to the spot, whose fields have now a really promising aspect. Wheat, oats, grass, and potatoes give very good crops, which, from the vicinity of the lumbering districts, always find a ready market and good prices. Mr. Johnson told me he raised for three successive years nearly a hundred bushels of oats from an acre of land. I saw some of his oats, which were heavier than any I had seen before, and certainly, even if the hundred bushels to the acre were a slight exaggeration, indicated much fertility of soil. An interesting feature of this district are the numerous sink-holes found in it, hundreds of which may be counted along the headwaters of Thunder Bay River; some are small, funnel-shaped depressions, dry on the bottom, or containing waterpools; others are narrow, vertical clefts, described to me by the woodsmen as sometimes 80 and 100 feet deep; and it is said of one which I passed that a large stream of water rushes across its bottom. A few of these sink-holes, as mentioned before, are of very large size, and form lakes. One of the latter is Sunken Lake in Township 33, R. 6, Section 32. It is about one mile and a half long, and in its widest part 500 yards. During the wet season, it is filled with water, having a depth of 90 feet; its overflow forms a branch of Thunder Bay River, which at that time is used for floating logs from the surrounding pineries to the saw mills of Alpena. During the dry summer season, the water almost totally disappears from the lake, making its escape through the rock crevices in its bottom. Formerly the water flowed off very rapidly, making a strong whirlpool. The lumbermen, in order to keep the water in the lake, threw masses of brush and even whole trees and rocks into the crevices to stop them up, and partially succeeded, but the water soon again cleared its passage through those obstructions;

its efflux was retarded only, not prevented. At the time of my visit in June I found the lake 25 feet below high-water mark. At its west end a vertical rock wall about 15 feet high ascends from the water; the ledges are dolomitic limestone from 18 inches to 2 feet thick, of light gray color, separated by thin, intermediate shale seams; they contain Atrypa reticularis, Spirifer granuliferous, Strophodonta demissa, and Crinoid stems. The position of the beds is visibly inclined toward the lake. The beds next to these, in the ascending line, are exposed at the south shore of the lake; they contain an abundance of Stromatopora Wortheni and Stromatopora monticulifera, Cyathophyllum profundum, various species of Favosites, Alveolites Goldfussii, heads of Dolatocrinus and Megistocrinus, Atrypa reticularis, Strophodonta demissa, Spirifer mucronatus, Spirifer granuliferous, and other fossils. The outlet of the lake when its basin is full is at the south end. When I saw it, the bed of the creek lay perfectly dry, and before reaching its level the water would have had to rise at least 20 feet.

The outlet of Long Lake, in Township 32, R. 8, east, is formed by a similar large sink-hole. During the wet season this basin is full, and a large creek flows in rapids and small cascades toward Lake Huron. In summer-time, the basin, all formed of solid rock, lies perfectly dry, and the water, discharged from the main body of the lake above, runs off through subterranean crevices.

The surface rock of the shore-belt from Long Lake southward to the north point of Thunder Bay, inclusive of Thunder Bay Island and Sugar Island, belongs all to about the same geological horizon. It is composed of an alternation of limestones, partly of gray, partly of black color, with interstratified seams of shales, which are also black or dark gray. Some beds are of nodular, concretionary structure, almost entirely composed of various species of Stromatopora, Cyathophyllum profundum, Favosites Hamiltonensis, Favosites digitatus, and other corals and shells, particularly Brachiopods. The exuberance of fossils in the strata is most beautifully exhibited in the shoals of the lake north of Thunder Bay Island, where any one sailing over them can see for miles the whole bottom paved with corals in convex lumps, from a few inches to some feet in diameter, their white, sparry substance contrasting beautifully with the dark limestone which incloses them.

The fossils found at Stony Point, south of Alpena, are mostly identical with the fossils found in the Thunder Bay Island strata, but I believe the latter to be of a lower position than the first. The fauna of the Hamilton group remains through the whole period essentially the same, and a repetition of fossiliferous rock beds containing the same species in different horizons is a frequently observed fact. The position of the strata of Thunder Bay Island is below that of the shale beds in Thunder Bay River near Trowbridge's mills. The road from Alpena to Long Lake passes the lime-kilns of Phelps, where a whitish brecciated limestone forms the nucleus of several bubble-like hillocks; the same limestone is noticed resting on the shales of Trowbridge's mills. In going north from Phelps's quarries, the surface rock retains the same character for several miles, the various beds which happen to be exposed being sometimes fossiliferous, at other times not, while in places layers are filled with hornstone concretions. Two miles south of Long Lake, we come upon black, shaly limestones containing Atrypa reticularis, Spirigera concentrica, Strophodonta demissa, Strophodonta erratica, Pentamerus papilionensis, Spirifer granuliferous, Cyrtina Hamiltonensis, Cyrtina umbonata, and Terebratula Linklæni, besides corals and Bryozoa. These beds evidently underlie the others. We find the black, shaly limestone continued from there as the highest stratum on the hilltops bordering Long Lake, which have an elevation of about 75 feet above its level. Descending to the lake, underneath the black strata, gray limestones are found, inclosing a few specimens of Stromatopora, Favosites, Atrypa reticularis, Spirifer granuliferous. Lower beds are a coarsely crystalline, crinoidal limestone, and the base of the hillsides, to within about 30 feet of the water level, is formed by an alternation of shales, nodular seams of limestone, and some heavier massive limestone ledges, all of which contain an abundance of specimens of several species of fossils. The fossils are partly in silicified condition. The following is a list of the collected specimens: Stromatopora Wortheni, Stromatopora monticulifera, Cystiphyllum Americanum, Cyathophyllum profundum, Cyathophyllum scyphus, Favosites Hamiltonensis, Favos. digitatus, Cladopora, Syringopora, various Bryozoa, Atrypa reticularis, Spirifer mucronatus, Spirifer granuliferous, Cyrtina Hamiltonensis, Cyrtina umbonata, Orthis Tulliensis, Spirigera concentrica, Terebratula Linklæni, Pentamerus costatus,

Strophodonta erratica, Strophod. demissa, Productella dumosa, a large Myalina Euomphalus, etc.

A few miles east of Long Lake we find the shore of Lake Huron lined with exposures of the black, shaly limestones, agreeing with the strata on top of the hills near the former, everywhere containing an abundance of Stromatopora Favosites, Cyathophyllum profundum, as the prevailing fossil forms, besides other species common only in certain localities; as, for instance, a species of Zaphrentis, which I found in great quantities at Section 34, in Township 32, Range 9, east, but which, in all other localities north and south from there, was rare or missing. I also found Favosites digitatus more common there than elsewhere. On Thunder Bay Island, the variety of fossils in the black limestone strata is greater than I found it in any other place. Besides the above-mentioned leading forms of Stromatopora and of corals, the strata are rich in Bryozoa and in Brachiopods. Among the latter, I may mention Atrypa reticularis, Spirigera concentrica, Spirifer zigzag, Spirifer mucronatus, Terebratula Linklæni, Strophodonta erratica, and Pentamerus aratus. Orthoceras, Gomphoceras, Prœtus crassimarginatus, and Phacops bufo also belong to the more common fossils of the island. Sugar Island represents the same strata, but the rock beds there are mostly covered by drift. Little Thunder Bay is a deep recess in the coast, situated in Township 31, R. 9, Section 75. Its entrance is very shallow, not always deep enough to admit a Mackinaw boat. The head of the recess is formed by a large sink-hole, which in the middle has a depth of 100 feet. A semicircle of rocky bluffs of from 25 to 30 feet elevation surrounds this deep pot-hole. The external portion of the semicircle is formed by the edges of horizontal rock beds projecting in vertical walls; a belt in front of them is composed of loose masses of the same rock, broken off and dipping in rapid inclination or in irregular, uptilted position toward the margin of the water-basin. The strata are the same as on Thunder Bay Island, but of lighter color, and more interlaminated with soft, shaly seams.

One township further north, in T. 32, R. 9, Sect. 6, directly west of Middle Island, on the side of a small creek flowing southeastward into Lake Huron, a chain of vertical rock bluffs, about 16 feet in height, is found commencing about half a mile from the shore, and extending thence about one mile up the stream. The bluffs consist of nodular, unhomogeneous beds of limestones, interstratified with thin seams of shaly substance of black color. Nearly the entire rock mass is made up of specimens of Stromatopora mingled with Favosites, Cyathophyllum profundum, Diphyphyllum archiaci, and other corals, which, by exposure, easily become disintegrated. At the foot of the bluffs, blue shales are exposed which contain many fossils: Atrypa reticularis, Spirigera concentrica, Spirifer mucronatus, Spirifer zigzag, Spirifer granuliferous, Rhynchonella, Strophodonta concava, Strophodonta demissa, Chonetes coronata, Cyathophyllum Houghtoni, Cystiphyllum Americanum, Stromatopora monticulifera, Stromatopora Wortheni, Crinoid stems, and many Bryozoa.

The lumps of coral and Stromatopora composing the upper beds of the bluffs take a good polish. Deceived by some good-looking polished samples, parties in Detroit were induced to buy the land on which the specimens were found, with the intention of opening a marble quarry. The shattered condition of the rock bluffs, which should have warned them at the first glance, was totally ignored, and in the vain hope that, by digging deeper down, a sounder quality of the rock would be found, a shaft was sunk into the shale beds under the bluffs to a depth of 50 feet. It was then that those concerned came to me, asking for advice, which I gave them with sincerity, but a little too late to save their purses.

Another so-called marble quarry was opened a number of years prior to this experiment, by Mr. Crawford, in the vicinity of Adams Point, in Town. 35, Range 5, east, Sect. 24, which gave no better results. The rock has not the compactness and homogeneous qualities requisite for marble. The beds in both mentioned places seem to be identical. A belt of similar limestones, partly covered up by drift deposits, follows the northeastern shore of Grand Lake, connecting the two points. The blue shales below the rock in the one locality are not seen at Crawford's quarry, but there is a probability that the blue shales penetrated in the artesian well at Alpena, 400 feet below the surface, may be the equivalent of them. The next lower beds to this series compose Middle Island, and identical with the Middle Island strata are the outcrops on False Presque Isle, where the ledges project in a low bluff from the east shore of the island, and where, when the lake is quiet, a huge stairway, formed by large rock tables, divided by vertical fissures into rhomboids, can be observed, leading down, step by step, into greater depths, until finally lost to view. Presque Isle Lighthouse Point is composed of the same strata, and intermediate between the lighthouse and False Presque Isle, on several parts of the shore, they come to the surface, the rest of the shoreline being a sand or gravel beach.

Significant of these strata arc two fossils, which I found in every one of the outcrops observed. One is Lucina elliptica, the other a species of Euomphalus, closely related, or perhaps identical with Euomphalus Dekewyi of Billings. Associated with these fossils in the outcrops of Presque Isle are, Stromatopora textilis, Stromatopora Wortheni, Diphyphyllum rectiseptatum, Favosites (rare), Spirigera concentrica (small, globose form), Spirifer gregarius, Atrypa reticularis, and Pentamerus. On Middle Island, I found, in addition to the first, Cystiphyllum, Atrypa reticularis with very fine ribs, a new species of Pentamerus (P. nucleolus), a Strophodonta, two species of Bellerophon, a Pleurotomaria, and several other Gasteropods, a large Myalina (M. carinata), Avicula flabella, and casts of other bivalves, Orthoceras, and a Nautilus with quadrangular oblong diagram of volutions. The scarcity of Favosites and Cyathophyllum in the strata of all the localities under consideration is peculiar; in all the rock beds, above and below, these two genera are the predominating types. The rock ledges composing Middle Island are best exposed on the north side of the island; the ledges are uneven-bedded, not thick, a dark gray-colored, somewhat brittle limestone; some beds are mottled with porous, lighter-colored dots, and sparingly intermingled with flint concretions. The whole thickness of the exposed beds successively coming to the surface is not over 20 feet. The exposures at Presque Isle Lighthouse Point exhibit at the water's edge limestones entirely similar to those of Middle Island; higher beds denuded during the excavation of the foundation for the lighthouse are an easy weather ing limestone with an abundance of cherty concretions.

At Crawford's quarry the shore-belt rises in two terraces, partly covered by drift, partly presenting rock exposures. At the water's edge, rock bluffs projecting to a height of from 10 to 15 feet are composed of drab-colored limestones mottled with darker, more compact spots, while the surrounding lighter-colored rock mass has a certain degree of porosity. Lucina elliptica was the only fossil noticed. About 12 feet above the vertical bluffs is the level of the first terrace, the intervening space being apparently made up of limestone ledges of similar character to the lower beds. On this first terrace rises a second, its elevation above the first being about 25 feet. This likewise is formed of a continued series of lime-rock ledges, and these represent the quarry rock of the so-called Crawford's marble quarry.

The rock of this second bluff is deposited in uneven beds of quite unhomogeneous structure, not suitable for large blocks, and not susceptible of an equal polish; some portions are porous, with dull, earthy fracture. Nearly the entire bulk of these rock beds is composed of several species of Stromatopora, Str. monticulifera, Str. Wortheni, and Str. textilis. Other fossils observable are Cyathophyllum profundum, Eridophyllum simcoense (similar to), Favosites (various forms), Atrypa reticularis, Strophodonta erratica, Lucina elliptica, Lucina sp. nov. and Orthoceras. The top of the second terrace is covered by drift deposits. From this level, undulating highlands extend southward, meeting the highlands surrounding the head branches of Thunder Bay River. Rock beds similar to those of Crawford's quarry, or somewhat higher beds, are, all over these high plains, not very deeply covered by drift, and are frequently denuded. The principal denudations of the rock are confined to certain belts striking in a southeast and northwest direction. One of these belts may be indicated by a line drawn from the north end of Long Lake to the mouth of Oqueock River in Hammond's Bay; another limestone belt can be followed from the head branches of Thunder Bay River (north branch) to Rainy River and Sheboygan Lake.

The surface rock most frequently seen on these high plains is light-colored, of crystalline grain, and principally contains the already-mentioned species of Stromatopora; a species of Diphyphyllum is also quite common (Diphyph. rectiseptatum). In some localities, shaly beds, intermediate between the limestones, are very fossiliferous. On McArthur's farm, 8 miles southwest of Crawford's quarry, I collected from the material thrown out in digging a well, Favosites Hamiltonensis, Favosites digitatus, Cyathophyllum profundum, Chonophyllum ponderosum, Aulopora conferta, Stromatopora

Wortheni, Fistulipora, Atrypa reticularis, Pentamerus costatus, Streptorhynchus, Strophodonta concava, Strophodonta nacrea, Productella navicella, Cyrtina Hamiltonensis, Spirifer granuliferous, Spirifer mucronatus, Lucina elliptica, several casts of Gasteropods, and dermatic plates of fishes. A continuation of the same range of rock exposures of the lower division of the Hamilton group is seen on Rainy R ver, 4 miles from its entrance into Black Lake (Sheboygan Lake), and in the rock bluffs facing Black Lake in Town. 35, R. 2, east, Sect. 7. In both localities, from 30 to 40 feet of strata are exposed. Highest are light-colored limestones, with Stromatopora and Cyathophyllum profundum, 20 feet in thickness, and somewhat variable in the structure of the single beds. Below these are about 12 feet of calcareous shales full of well-preserved fossils, viz.: Cyathophyllum profundum, Cyathophyllum Houghtoni, Cyathophyllum resembling C. cornicula, Cystiphyllum Americanum, Favosites digitatus, Favosites Hamiltonensis, Zaphrentis, Syringopora nobilis, Fistulipora, Chætetes and other Bryozoa, Atrypa reticularis, Spirigera concentrica, Strophodonta demissa, Strophodonta concava, Spirifer zigzag, Spirifer granuliferous, and fragments of Prœtus. Lowest are hard, smooth-bedded limestone strata containing few fossils.

Westward from Black Lake, the environs of Mullett Lake and Burt Lake, and all the district north of them, up to the Straits of Mackinac, are deeply covered with drift deposits, with the exception of the foot of the promontory at McGulpin's Point, which, as we have seen before, presents the upper strata of the Helderberg group. Much the larger portion of this district is covered by hard-wood timber and has a rich soil, which has attracted a good many settlers, and amply rewarded the labor bestowed on it. North of Burt Lake and in the vicinity of Turtle Lake, the land is sandy and poor, covered by pine forests, but toward Little Traverse Bay it becomes much better again. The soil in the vicinity of Sheboygan is a heavy but fertile clay. The clay of the drift formation furnishes an excellent material for brick manufacture. The north shore of Little Traverse Bay has no rock exposures. High drift bluffs ascend from the lake, and terrace by terrace the land rises into a plateau of about 250 feet elevation, which extends from the bay up to Cross village.

The south shore of the bay ascends likewise in terrace form, and the hilltops are composed of drift, but the lower levels along the shore are formed by an almost uninterrupted string of rock exposures, from the head of the bay clear round to Big Traverse Bay, where the last beds of the Hamilton group dip under the black shale at the village of Norwood, in the south corner of Town. 32, Range 9, west. The Hamilton group, as developed on the west shore, is chiefly a limestone formation, but its rock character differs in many respects from the Thunder Bay series. The first outcrops at the head of the bay are found about a mile and a half east from the mouth of Bear Creek, which enters the bay at the foot of the newly built village of Petosky, the present terminus of the Lansing and Saginaw Railroad. Below the railroad depot, vertical rock bluffs of 45 feet elevation face the bay; eastward the bluffs become lower, and finally disappear altogether, giving place to a sand and gravel beach which lines the east end of the bay.

The lowest strata of these bluffs are seen on its eastern end, a blue, argillaceous, hard lime rock cropping out at a level with the water-line. The higher beds have almost the same lithological character, being light drab-colored, porous dolomites, with a dull, earthy fracture. The lower strata are very even-bedded, of finely laminated structure; they contain numerous band-like, compressed, carbonaceous, vegetable stems, similar to Psilophyton, and bones of fishes; the casts of small bivalve shells, or branching forms of Favosites also cover the surface of some ledges, but generally fossils are rare in these lower beds. The upper strata forming the vertical part of the bluffs are not always so regularly stratified; by weathering, the seams of the bedding become obliterated on the surface of the exposed walls, which sometimes appear to be one solid mass. By digging into them, however, the stratification becomes clearly observable. Some parts of the rock are mottled with darker, more compact blotches than the rest of the substance, which in a dry state rapidly absorb water. These blotches seem to be portions of the rock unaltered from their original condition, while the lighter-colored surrounding mass has been leached out by percolating waters, which dissolved the sparry calcareous cement, whereby the fine crystals of the less soluble dolomite spar were held together, leaving the latter a soft, porous skeleton.

Fossils are very abundant in these upper layers, but are not equally distributed in the horizontal extension of a bed. We may, in one part, for a distance of many yards, scarcely see a fossil imbedded, when suddenly the same stratum becomes so completely crowded with them that the whole rock mass is a compact agglomeration of fossils, leaving no room for any inorganic limestone particles between. It is Stromatopora pustulifera in particular which is so abundant; it grows in strumose, globular masses, often several feet in diameter, tightly crowded together, and sparingly intermingled with other fossils. About 8 or 10 feet above this seam of Stromatopora pustulifera, another band follows, which is equally rich in a different species of Stromatopora, Stromatopòra cespitosa, a form of similar structure to the first, but growing in clusters of ramified stems, or in more massive, globose form, and with much larger pustules, and always with well-preserved tissue fibres, which in Stromatopora pustulifera are nearly always obscure. The massive forms of Str. cespitosa resemble Stromatopora monticulifera, but I do not believe them to be identical. Associated with the Stromatoporas, a number of other fossils are found in this locality, viz.: Favosites Hamiltonenis, Favosites digitatus, Cyathophyllum juvenis, Cystiphyllum Americanum, Diphyphyllum rectiseptatum, Atrypa reticularis, Spirigera concentrica, Terebratula Linklæni, Pentamerus papilionensis, Spirifer fimbriatus, Strophodonta erratica, Conocardium (a small form), Pleurotomaria cavumbilicata, Phacops, Gomphoceras, Orthoceras, etc. A few years since, on the shore in front of the rock bluffs of Petosky, lime-kilns were built, which at the time of my visit were not so far finished as to be in working order; but the experiments made with the rock on a small scale proved it to be well adapted for the purpose. As a building-stone it has not much value; it does not sufficiently resist atmospheric influences.

Prof. A. Winchell considers the position of these beds as lowest in the rock series of Little Traverse Bay, but from my own observation I am inclined to consider them as representing the upper part of the series, and as equivalent with other strata which by Winchell have been designated as buff magnesian limestone. The rock bluffs just described are interrupted at the location of Petosky village, and replaced by a drift terrace. A quarter of a mile southwestward, close to the railroad bridge across Bear Creek, a few ledges of the same rock seen in the bluffs are uncovered in the ditches of the road bed, and descending at this point to Ingall's mill, situated about 40 feet lower, we find, next under these ledges, hard, bluish-colored limestones containing Stromatopora monticulifera, Stromatopora Wortheni, and Cyathophyllum profundum. At Porter's old mill site, below the limestones, 6 or 8 feet of blue shales come out in the bed of the creek, filled with specimens of Cyathophyllum profundum, Favosites Hamiltonensis, Atrypa reticularis, Strophodonta erratica, etc. Then follow limestones again, which form the bed of the creek downward to the foot of the race at Ingall's mill, amounting to about 20 feet in the outcrop. They contain nearly the same fossils as the shale beds above. Following the bed of the creek down to its mouth, rock ledges are again several times uncovered, but their exact position with regard to the ledges of the upper part of the section is not seen. The total descent which the creek makes from the top of the railroad bridge to the lake shore is 90 feet, all of which is made up by limestone beds, with the exception of the mentioned seam of shales. About one mile west of the mouth of Bear Creek, an ascending section through the strata can be observed by following the lake shore westward, commencing about at the bottom of the section given above. The lowest ledges seen, partly submerged under water, are hard blue limestones of rugose surface, and interlaminated with seams of black bituminous shale. They contain Cyathophyllum profundum, Stromatopora Wortheni, Stromatopora monticulifera, and Atrypa reticularis. A few hundred steps farther, in a low bluff, about 12 feet of the next higher ledges are seen resting on the former; they consist of light-colored, brittle limestones, of fine-grained, conchoidal fracture, interstratified with calcareous shales. In places, the rock beds contain only few fossils, while the same strata may be crowded with them some steps farther on. The most common forms inclosed are Cyathophyllum profundum, Cystiphyllum Americanum, Favosites Hamiltonensis, some Bryozoa, Spirifer pennatus, Spirifer mucronatus, Cyrtina Hamiltonensis, Strophodonta erratica, Strophodonta nacrea, Pentamerus papilionensis, and Atrypa reticularis. The outcrops are then interrupted by a high drift bluff which comes up to the shore; at its foot sometimes one of the ledges of the beds referred to sticks out. On the other side of the drift bluff, which is only a few hundred yards wide, another outcrop of rocks faces the bay, which are the next higher beds succeeding those last mentioned. The lowest portion of them is a drab-colored, porous dolomite, full of Stromatopora monticulifera and Stromatopora Wortheni, Cyathophyllum profundum, Favosites Hamiltonensis, etc. The upper portion is laminated with seams of a black, calcareous, combustible shale, which contain an abundance of Strophodonta erratica, ramulets of Favosites digitatus, and other fossils. The thickness of this dolomitic series is about 8 or 10 feet. Above it is a stratum of soft blue shale of variable thickness, from 1 to 4 or 5 feet, which contains many finely preserved fossils, such as: Cyathophyllum profundum (Acervularia profunda), Cyathophyllum Houghtoni, Cyathophyllum Hallii, Cystiphyllum Americanum, Favosites Hamiltonensis, Favosites nitella, Aulopora conferta, Syringopora, Stromatopora plana, Stromatopora monticulifera, Stromatopora Wortheni, a great variety of Bryozoa, Atrypa reticularis, Spirigera concentrica, Spirifer mucronatus, Spirifer granuliferous, Cyrtina Hamiltonensis, Strophodonta erratic, Terebratula Linklæni, Crania Hamiltoniæ, Crania crenistria, Crania(?) radicans Winchell, Pholidops, Phacops bufo, etc. Above these shales follow drab-colored, porous dolomites similar to the beds at the base of the section, and containing about the same fossils; from 10 to 15 feet of them terminate the outcrops in that locality.

Several outcrops comprising about the same series of strata are found by following the shore westward for two or three miles. About three miles east of Khagashewung Point, the section through the heretofore considered beds is continued into higher strata (the so-called buff magnesian limestone of Winchell), which I believe to be equivalent with the Stromatopora beds composing the bluffs of Petosky. The section is as follows: Lowest, partly submerged under the water, are blue, hard limestones full of Stromatopora, Cyathophyllum profundum, and Favosites Hamiltonensis; above them are alternating seams of nodular limestones and of black, combustible shale, crowded with fossils similar to those in the former stratum. Next follow several feet of gray limestones; some beds of them are of very fine grain, like lithographic stone, but brittle; they contain but few fossils; a fossiliferous seam, with Cyathophyllum profundum, Favosites, and other fossils, overlies them; then come again from 6 to 8 feet of the brittle, smooth-fracturing limestones, interlaminated with shaly seams, and fossiliferous in nests. The limestone with smooth fracture like lithographic stone contains 98 per cent of carbonate of lime, 1 per cent carbonate of magnesia, and 1 per cent of insoluble silicious matter. Superimposed on these beds are drab-colored, porous dolomites, with Stromatopora monticulifera, Stromatop. Wortheni, Cyathophyllum profundum, Favosites Hamiltonensis. The outcrop is at this horizon interrupted; it is the place where the fossiliferous blue shales of the other sections should be found, with the incumbent fossiliferous dolomites. A short distance behind the top of the bluffs which exhibit this section, a second terrace rises, which is composed of dark, drab-colored, crystalline dolomites, identical with those composing the rock bluffs of Khagashewung Point, or with the buff magnesian beds of Prof. Winchell.

Khagashewung Point, for more than a mile's length, is lined with vertical rock bluffs about 15 feet high. The lowest strata exposed along this point are light-colored, smooth-fracturing limestones, interlaminated with thin seams of shale, and with a bed of a crystalline limestone almost entirely composed of Crinoid joints. Fossils are not numerous in them, and are of the usual kinds found in the other outcrops. Above them are some beds of a blue, argillaceo-arenaceous lime rock, containing many specimens of Cyathophyllum profundum, Favosites Hamiltonensis, Cystiphyllum Americanum, and Atrypa reticularis. Then follow light-colored limestones with earthy fracture and of thinly laminated structure, linear carbonaceous seams pervading them in the bedding plains. Their thickness is only a few feet, and they resemble the laminated, dolomitic beds at the foot of the Petosky bluffs, inclosing the same fish-bones and a few stems of Favosites. The higher part of the Khagashewung cliffs is formed by layers of a porous, crystalline dolomite, of a brownish yellow color, in thick, homogeneous beds, of variable finer or coarser grain. Fossils are generally rare, but in certain seams casts of Brachiopods, or dispersed specimens of Favosites, Cyathophyllum profundum, etc., are noticed. Other beds are a coarsely crystalline, crinoidal limestone, with many other fractured shells besides the Crinoid joints. Atrypa, Spirifer, Cyrtina, Strophodonta, Rhynchonella, are the recognizable forms; Prœtus and Phacops are likewise to be found.

The highest beds observed on Khagashewung Point are thin-bedded, light-colored, brittle limestone ledges, lying in a few places on top of the brownish dolomite rock. From the saccharoidal, compact beds of the dolomite can be obtained good-sized blocks, which would answer for building purposes, being of sufficient durability and easily dressed. The position of the outcrops near the lake shore is very favorable for the opening of quarries, and for the transportation of the rock by vessels.

An analysis of this dolomite gives:

Carbonate of lime..............	58	per cent.
" magnesia.........	38	"
Alumina and iron oxide hydr...	1.5	"
Insoluble residue..............	0.5	"

West of Khagashewung, to the mouth of Pine River, the shore presents numerous other outcrops of the beds below those forming the point, which, however, rarely emerge more than a few feet above the water level. Proceeding from the point westward, we first find the beds containing an abundance of Stromatopora, of which, in the dolomites of the cliffs, not a single specimen could be found. Further on, below the Stromatopora beds, light-colored, brittle limestones with conchoidal fracture are brought to the surface by the undulations of the strata; in places, these beds are rich in fossils, in others not. Strophodonta nacrea, Strophodonta demissa, Strophodonta erratica, Chonetes Emmetensis, Spirifer pennatus, Spirifer mucronatus, Cyrtina Hamiltonensis, Terebratula Linklæni, Atrypa reticularis, Spirigera concentrica, Pentamerus papilionensis, several forms of Bryozoa and corals, and some rare forms of Trilobites have been collected from them. In a few spots the still lower beds of hard blue limestone with Cyathophyllum profundum and Favosites Hamiltonensis, in alternation with black shale seams, are noticed. The blue fossiliferous shale beds (acervularia beds of Winchell) just reach the surface in the lake bottom half a mile west from the dock of Charlevoix. On the point, 3 miles west from the dock, some larger outcrops border the lake shore in low cliffs, elevated 5 or 6 feet above water-mark. Lowest is the blue, hard lime rock with Cyathophyllum profundum, Favosites Hamiltonensis, Atrypa reticularis, etc., and above are light-colored, smooth-fracturing, brittle limestones with seams of shale, which are in this locality very fossiliferous. There are: Spirifer pennatus, Chonetes Emmetensis, Strophodonta nacrea, and all the other fossils enumerated previously as existing in equivalent beds exposed west of Khagashewung Point and east of Charlevoix. From the frequent occurrence of a species of Stictopora in these beds, Prof. Winchell termed them Bryozoa beds. The shore line has here a north and south direction. Three miles south of the locality just treated of, some other exposures are found, and at about five miles from it we see the Hamilton group for the last time, exposed near Norwood.

The beds at Norwood are higher than any of those in the sections yet described. In the bluffs which have about 12 feet elevation above the water level, we can observe about 25 feet of strata brought to the surface by an undulation. Lowest are dark, bluish gray, rough-fracturing limestones, with intermediate seams of shale, inclosing many specimens of Favosites. Above are thinly bedded, hard limestones, alternating with ledges or nodular seams of flint limestone, and flint beds of a laminated, banded structure; their thickness is about 8 feet. Some thicker ledges of limestone follow, having a smooth, conchoidal fracture. Next higher are gray, compact limestones with many fossils: Stromatopora similar to Str. Wortheni, Caunopora (thin stems with a ventral canal, of thickness from a straw to a goose-quill), Favosites Hamiltonensis, Favosites digitatus, Cyathophyllum Houghtoni, Cyathophyllum geniculatum, Aulopora, Strophodonta erratica, Pentamerus (a large, globose form), and several others. The highest strata are coarse-grained, crystalline dolomites, of light gray color, some 4 or 5 feet in thickness, which contain Stromatopora and other fossils in very imperfect preservation, while numerous druse cavities, once the beds of fossils, are lined with spar crystals and partially filled with rock oil.

A chemical analysis of the dolomite gave:

Carbonate of lime	56	per cent.
" magnesia	39	"
Alumina and iron	2.8	"
Insoluble residue	0.4	"

In immediate superposition on the dolomite beds, the black shale formation, the equivalent of the Genesee shales of New York, is deposited.

In the drift composing the lake terraces on the south shore of Little Traverse Bay, large numbers of slabs of a tough black shale are intermingled. The shale is easily ignited, burning with a bright flame, and is by many persons taken for coal, or as an indication of the existence of coal in that district. The shale contains a great abundance of well-preserved fossils of the Hamilton group, in calcified condition ; fan-like expansions of Fenestella, Polypora, each genus represented by various species, Stictopora, Fistulipora, and other Bryozoa are in great perfection ; several forms of Stromatopora, incrusting other fossils, or in laminar expansions, Cyathophyllum Houghtoni, Cyathophyllum profundum, Cystiphyllum Americanum, Favosites Hamiltonensis, Favosites digitatus, Aulopora, Syringopora, Tentaculites, Conocardium, Atrypa reticularis, Spirigera concentrica, Pentamerus papilionensis, Terebratula Linklæni, Strophodonta erratica, Strophodonta nacrea, Phacops bufo, and Prœtus crassimarginatus have been noticed.

During the description of the Hamilton series of Little Traverse Bay, several seams of similar black shales interlaminated with the other strata have been pointed out, but in none of the outcrops were more than a few inches of such shale beds noticed, while the slabs found in the drift seem to have been parts of thick ledges. It is most likely the lower seam of the two, exposed below the horizon of the blue fossiliferous shales (acervularia shales), from which the drift specimens originate.

The thickness of the rock series of the Hamilton group exposed along the shore of Little Traverse Bay is not accurately determinable. No continued sections through more than 50 feet of strata are seen in one place, and the rock character of beds in their horizontal extension is subject to so many variations, that no sure conclusion on the identity of rock ledges in distant outcrops can be based on it. The palæontological features of the strata are also not strongly marked. Although certain forms of fossils are generally associated in certain layers, the majority of fossils characteristic of the Hamilton group are so equally distributed throughout its whole thickness, that all of them can be found in almost any position at the base or in the upper horizons. There are layers filled with the same species of Stromatopora found in repeated superposition, which can not be distinguished if found in different localites, unless the sections exhibit the strata fully denuded so that their relative positions to other strata and to one another may be observed. The strata have retained their original position, but their horizontality is not perfect; they rise and sink in undulations, adapting themselves to the surface on which they were deposited. By means of these undulations, lower or higher strata come repeatedly to an exposure, or disappear again, if we follow the horizontal level of the shore line of the bay, which approximately runs parallel with the strike of the formation, and would consequently always present the same rock beds if the strata remained perfectly horizontal. I estimate the thickness of the exposed rock beds at from 125 to 130 feet. In the bluffs near Bear Creek, where we see the upper part of the series, 45 feet of rock beds are exposed in direct, vertical superposition, and by the slight rise of the strata toward the east, about 10 feet more of lower beds come to the surface. A continuation of this section downward is offered on Bear Creek, where we see, near the railroad bridge, some beds representing the rock of the bluffs, without being able to ascertain exactly which part of them. At all events, in the interval from the bridge to Porter's mill, about 15 feet of strata, lower than any in the bluffs, can be seen; then follow 6 or 8 feet of blue shale, and below are again limestones amounting to about 20 feet in thickness, reaching the base of Ingall's mill-race. Lower down the section can not be followed, but we find the same strata seen at Ingall's mill on the shore exposures west from the mouth of the river, which beds, all added, make a series of something over 100 feet in thickness. If we add to them the 25 feet of strata seen in the exposures of Norwood, which are higher than any of the others, we have an estimated total thickness of 125 feet, which estimate may be perhaps as little lower than the actual measurement would give. The direct superposition of the rock series of the Norwood exposures on the dolomites of Bear Creek bluffs or of Khagashewung Point is not seen; an interval of several miles separates the outcrops, which may hide some intervening ledges under its drift cover.

The Hamilton exposures on the east and west side of the peninsula exhibit not enough of lithological similarity to allow an identification of certain beds or groups of beds on the two sides; also the palæontological features of certain horizons in the group are not well enough marked to enable us to make such identification. The fauna of the Hamilton area remained uniformly the same from the beginning to its end, as I have intimated once before in a previous page. We find differences in the association of fossils in various beds, but these are rather induced by local conditions favoring the development of certain forms and uncongenial to others, than by a change in the character of the fauna, whose standard representatives always make their appearance again, if they have been missing for a while in some of the layers.

My estimate of the thickness of the Hamilton series in Thunder Bay region, about 600 feet, is based on the results of the artesian borings heretofore given, which I will briefly recapitulate. I stated that the strata of Partridge Point and the next lower Stromatopora beds of Stony Point, with the intercalated fossiliferous shale beds, amount in the aggregate to at least one hundred feet, and that their superposition on the beds in which the artesian boring begins is directly observable. The drilling went first through 400 feet of limestone strata of not accurately specialized character in the records kept of the boring, and below them, through a shale bed of 80 feet in thickness, containing a great variety of characteristic Hamilton fossils, proving positively a thickness of 580 feet for the Hamilton series at this spot. This shale deposit I suppose to be identical with the blue shales penetrated to a depth of 50 feet under the limestone bluffs in Town. 32, R. 9, Sect. 6, by the exploring shaft of the attempted marble quarry. The rock series composing Middle Island, Presque Isle, and other localities, underlies the blue shales, and is in this report considered a part of the Hamilton group, and is not overestimated by allowing for it a thickness of 60 or 70 feet, which would give to the Hamilton series of Thunder Bay region a total thickness of 650 feet. According to the boring record, nearly 500 feet of lower strata in the drill-hole, down to the salt-rock deposits of the Onondaga group, should be claimed as representatives of the Helderberg group.

CHAPTER VII.

BLACK SHALES OF OHIO—GENESEE SHALES OF NEW-YORK.

By this name a series of black bituminous shales are designated, which in the States of Ohio and Indiana are found in immediate superposition on the limestones of the Helderberg series, and which in the north part of the Michigan peninsula rest on the beds of the Hamilton group, as do the Genesee shales of New York, which are generally considered the equivalent of the black shale.

By their lithological character, the black shales approach the shale and sand-rock beds of the Waverly group next succeeding them.

A change of the ocean bed, causing a total change in the material of the deposits, had already begun while the black shales were forming; but the fossils inclosed within the shales, and in a series of shale and sandstone beds above them, in the so-called Portage and Chemung group, exhibit a yet greater affinity to the fauna of the subjacent limestone formation than to the fauna of the incumbent, lithologically nearer related beds of the subcarboniferous shale and sandstone formation. This is the regular order, in the succession of strata, within the State of New York, and as in the States of Ohio and Michigan a similar order in the character of the rock beds resting on the black shales was observed, they were naturally supposed to be the equivalents of the Portage and Chemung group.

By the study of the fauna found in the upper part of this arenaceous shale formation above the black shales in Michigan, Prof. A. Winchell came to the conclusion that those of the Chemung and Portage groups had a different character from the complex of fossils found in the supposed equivalent Michigan strata, which latter he declared emphatically to be of carboniferous type. He selected for this upper arenaceous rock series the name of

Marshall group, and, subsequently, from studying the Waverly group of Ohio, he recognized the identity of his Marshall group with the Waverly group.

Between these fossiliferous Marshall sandstones and the black shales, in Michigan, nearly one thousand feet of rock beds of prevalently shaly, partially sandy, and sometimes calcareous character, are intercalated, which are claimed, by Professor Winchell as representatives of the Devonian fauna, with the same emphasis as he asserts the carboniferous character of the other. He combines them with the black shales into a separate group, which he names *Huron Shales.* We will subsequently have occasion to learn that the shales, above the black shale and below the Marshall sandstones of Michigan, inclose absolutely the same fossils as are found in the Cuyahoga shales of the Ohio geologists, and which by Winchell himself are considered as of a marked carboniferous faunal type, and as intimately connected with the fossiliferous sandstones of Marshall. The differences in the faunas are certainly not existing in this special case, and viewing the question from a general standpoint, the contrast between the fauna of the Chemung group and the fauna of the Waverly group is by no means so striking, that for the one a positively Devonian type can be claimed, and for the other a carboniferous.

The group of the *Huron Shales*, according to this view, shrinks back to the small basal portion of them, the black shales, which have been long known under this name, and are likely to continue to bear it for some time to come.

Another objection to the adoption of this name is its similarity to the name *Huron group*, in well-established use for the lower metamorphic rock series of the Lake Superior district, which would unavoidably cause much confusion.

A belt of the black shale formation intersects the north part of the peninsula. Its northern limits have already been delineated in describing the southern limits of the Hamilton group, extending in an arch from Partridge Point, in Thunder Bay, to Norwood, in Big Traverse Bay. The southern extension of this belt is all hidden under drift deposits. Approximately, the slate belt is supposed to extend on the west side to the neighborhood of Frankfort, in the central part of the peninsula to Otsego Lake, and on the east side to touch the shore line some miles south of Harrisville.

In unweathered condition the black shale is hard and slate-like, of very even bedding, of finely laminated structure, fissible in thin leaves, which have some degree of elastic flexibility. Its color is usually a perfect black. In weathered condition, it becomes grayish, and splits open into paper-thin, laminar fragments; exposed to the fire, it burns with a flame, but it is rarely rich enough in bitumen to sustain the heat for its own combustion. Seams of iron pyrites, or nodular concretions of it, and fine granular crystals are invariably found pervading the beds; also subordinate seams of lime rock, which frequently have cone-in-cone structure, are found interstratified; but, most remarkable, are large, spherical, calcareous concretions, which not unfrequently are of almost mathematically true globe form, and sometimes of a diameter of from 5 to 6 feet—usually, however, of from 1 to 2 feet. The concretions must have formed while the shale mass was soft and bulky; by subsequent pressure of the incumbent sediments, the shale diminished its bulk, and was bent around the hard globes which did not yield to the pressure.

The concretions are sometimes formed of a granular lime-rock mass, and often inclose organic remains, as bones of fishes or pieces of wood; in other cases they have a sparry structure, with elongated fibrous crystals radiating in all directions from the centre to the periphery. The spar crystals are usually carbonate of lime darkened by bitumen, but in some localities it is a sparry carbonate of iron which composes the concretions. The analysis of concretions of granular limestone structure, from the shales of Norwood, gave:

Carbonate of lime	89	per cent.
" " magnesia	2	"
Insoluble residue, bituminous and silicious,	7.5	"

On the surface of some slabs of cone-in-cone structure interlaminated with the black shales, I found at Norwood large dermatic plates of Aspidichthys and specimens of a Lingula: fragments of wood (Dadoxylon) are likewise of common occurrence in that and other localities.

North of Norwood, the black shales form bluffs 10 or 15 feet in height, which, rising a short distance back from the shore line, repose on the ledges of the dolomite beds of the Hamilton group described in previous pages. South of Norwood village, the shales come close up to the shore in vertical bluffs of similar height; the total thickness of strata seen in the bluffs, and in the hillsides rising behind them, is not over 35 or 40 feet. South of Norwood, the black shales are overlaid by light greenish, arenaceous shales which have frequent outcrops along the shore line for 9 or 10 miles southward, but this is all that can be seen of them; back from the shore, every thing is covered by drift. Fossils were not discovered in the light shales.

The black shales are exposed northeast of Norwood on Pine Lake, and near Bear Creek the railroad to Petosky has laid open several sections through them, showing sparry, globular concretions inclosed; pieces of Dadoxylon are likewise found there.

In the ravines of the creeks leading into Mullett Lake and Black Lake, the black shales are frequently exposed. In Thunder Bay district, outcrops are along the south branches of Thunder Bay River. In Town. 31, R. 7, Sect. 19, the large globular concretions of the shale formation are composed of carbonate of iron, and weathered specimens transform on the surface into a bright-colored, reddish ochre. A number of years ago some parties opened exploring ditches in search of that mineral paint, but abandoned the project when they found nothing but unaltered concretions of carbonate of iron below the outer superficial crust which contained the decomposed ochraceous masses. On Squaw Point, and on Sulphur Island near Thunder Bay, the black shales are well exposed; further south toward Harrisville, they are mostly covered by drift, and only here and there in a ravine can an outcrop be seen. On the opposite side of Lake Huron, at Kettle Point, in Canada, the black shales are splendidly exposed, where their superposition on fossiliferous limestones similar to those of Norwood can be seen. In this locality, the spherical concretions in the shale are larger and more abundant than I have seen them elsewhere.

In the south part of the State, the black shales are not well exposed; the drift, however, contains large quantities of the shale intermingled in the belt which is supposed to be underlaid by the shales, and in all the deep artesian borings the black shales have been found.

At Ann Arbor the drill hole sunk in the Court-House Square struck the black shales at a depth of 525 feet below the surface, their thickness there being 85 feet. In the south part of Washtenaw County, and in the northwestern corner of Monroe County, in well borings, the black shales are found usually not more than about 100 feet below the surface. Frequently a stream of hydrocarburetted gas escapes from the drill holes after the black shales have been reached.

On the farm of Mr. Kinear, on Saline River, near Milan Village, a well was bored with an auger through 106 feet of drift deposits, partly clay, partly gravel. When the auger came upon the black shales, suddenly, with a sort of explosion, hydrocarburetted gas escaped from the opening, carrying with it mud and water to a height of 30 feet above the surface. I visited the spot three weeks after, and found the gas still escaping in a continuous stream, which, at the opening of an inch iron pipe, burned with a bright, illuminating flame 8 inches high. On several other farms in the vicinity, similar gas wells were accidentally found while boring for water.

CHAPTER VIII.

WAVERLY GROUP.

THE light-colored, greenish, arenaceous shales, on top of the black shale exposed along the shore of Big Traverse Bay, may possibly be an equivalent of the Erie shales of the Ohio geologists, but no fossils have been found by which this question can be determined, and no outcrops of equivalent beds are seen in any other part of the State. The shales in the southern part of the peninsula, which were considered by Winchell as a part of his Huron shales, occupy a higher position, and must be identified with the Waverly group.

The Waverly group is the most important rock series on the lower peninsula—not only because it forms the surface rock over the greatest part of it, but for its economical value. It is the repository of the Michigan salt brine, and furnishes almost the only good building-stone we have on the peninsula. The Huron grindstones, famous for their excellence, are likewise taken from this group. The Michigan salt group of Prof. Winchell is a series of rock beds above the Waverly group, which I shall consider in connection with the subcarboniferous limestones; they contain large quantities of gypsum, but no salt brines of practical value.

The Waverly group forms, underneath the drift, the surface rock over half the extent of the peninsula, but its natural outcrops are very limited, either horizontally or vertically. The upper division of the group is much better exposed than the lower, which in part is only known through the results of deep borings, information of a very unsatisfactory kind. The vicinity of Port Austin and the shore belt east and west from it offer a very good field for the study of the upper part.

From the west end of the village, to Flat Rock Point, the shore is nearly all the way lined by low cliffs of a coarse-grained, soft, whitish sand rock, in thick, massive beds. The cliffs have an elevation of from 8 to 10 feet above the water-level, and on the rising ground back from the shore, additional ledges of a similar sand rock are superimposed, bringing the total thickness of this sand-rock deposit to 30 or 35 feet. West of Flat Rock Point, the cliffs are interrupted, and at the base of the massive ledges, thin-bedded, more finely grained, sandy flagstones, partly of red, partly of greenish color, come to the surface. Some distance further on, at the mouth of a small creek, lower beds of a micaceous greenish sand rock, rich in calcareous cement, and partly conglomeratic, barely emerge from the water, and in seams are very fossiliferous. The fossils are Nucula Hubbardi, Solen quadrangularis, Goniatites Marshallensis, Orthoceras, Rhynchonella, Productus, and other forms identical with those found in the sandstones of Marshall. Toward the mouth of Pinegog River, west of the creek, the rocks disappear, but Hat Point, 3 miles from that spot, is again formed of rock cliffs, 15 or 18 feet high, composed of the same coarse-grained sand rock as the cliffs of Flat Rock Point. One of the rock masses forms a small island in the shape of an inverted cone, resting on a slender base, and expanded above into a discoid platform overgrown with trees. This, bearing a general resemblance to a hat, gave the point its name. At the foot of the cliffs, the greenish, micaceous sand-rock ledges come out, but show no fossils. The cliffs of Hat Point recede some distance from the shore in a southeast direction, forming the margin of a terrace; westward, bluffs of drift sand take their place; only at intervals does the sand rock show itself on the surface, in small, circumscribed spots—as, for instance, on the roadside near Mr. Smalley's farm-house. On Mr. Klump's farm, southeast of Oak Point, the sand rock is covered by fossiliferous limestone ledges, which represent the basal part of the next higher group of rocks. South of Port Crescent, on the branches of Pinegog River, the water frequently flows over denuded ledges of a sand rock, and through this whole district only a thin coating of drift, rarely more than 20 feet in thickness, is spread over the rock, which resembles the finer-grained beds below the cliffs of Flat Rock, but contains no fossils in the localities examined by me. Further south, toward Badaxe and Verona, the drift is much deeper, and the rock beds are not within reach by well-excavations of ordinary depth. Very large metamorphic boulders are strewn over the surface of some fields, but the soil of this vicinity is generally good.

On the east side of Port Austin, we find the cliffs of Point of

Barques composed of the same coarse-grained sand rock as Flat Rock Point; they rise vertically from the lake to a height of about 20 feet; the rock is harder and more greenish than at Flat Rock, more like the cliffs of Hat Point. An impression of a Goniatite and casts of a Rhynchonella are the only fossils I observed in it. The strata at the base of the cliffs are of a darker greenish tint and of finer grain, and are so undermined by the water that large masses have tumbled over into the lake, or stand like inverted conical masses, as at Hat Point, resembling at a distance barks at anchor. It is from this that the name of the point is derived.

In the drift masses covering the cliffs, slabs of a calcareo-ferruginous sandstone are quite abundant, which are almost totally composed of casts and shells of Rhynchonella camerifera and Centronella Julia, together with a few other shells and stems of bryozoa. These fossiliferous, loose rock fragments were long since discovered, but their exact position in the series was not known. By following the sand beach east of Point of Barques, toward Burnt Cabin Point, quantities of similar fossiliferous slabs, but evidently freshly broken from the ledges, are thrown out by the lake; the stratum, consequently, must be denuded under the water-level, and have a position only a few feet below the base of the cliffs. The reddish, thin-bedded flagstones next below the cliffs of Flat Rock are probably representatives of the same horizon. I found in them, sparingly however, specimens of Rhynchonella camerifera. The cliffs of Point of Barques, at the old mill erected there, recede from the immediate vicinity of the shore, and continue southeastwardly, as a terrace-like bluff of about 30 feet elevation, at some distance from the lake, passing the grindstone quarries and extending to Willow Creek. The low shore belt in front of the bluffs is underlaid by the grindstones which have frequent exposures between Burnt Cabin Point and the grindstone quarries, and beyond them to Willow Creek, with some interruption by sand beaches.

The grindstone quarries are opened in a part of this shore belt where the rock faces the lake in vertical bluffs of from 5 to 15 feet elevation. A thin coating of boulder drift covers the surface of the level ground extending to the foot of the terrace formed by the cliff rock of Point of Barques, half a mile back from the shore. The layers found next under the drift are thin-bedded, brittle slabs of chocolate-brown color; below them is usually found a band of conglomerate not over a foot in thickness, composed of pebbles of sizes ranging from that of a pea to that of a hazle-nut. Then comes a fine-grained, micaceous, greenish-colored sand rock, and a few feet below the upper conglomerate another seam of it often follows; but these conglomerate bands are not regular; they wedge out on both sides, while, in places, no such seam is developed. The conglomerates contain a large proportion of calcareous cement, and are usually very hard. The sand-rock beds between the conglomerates often contain single pebbles scattered through them, and globular concretions from the size of an egg to that of a man's fist, of extremely hard, calcareous sand-rock mass, which, split open, are nearly always found to inclose some kind of a fossil, bones of fish, or Goniatites, etc.; the same fossils are found in the conglomerate seams. The sand-rock ledges inferior to the conglomerates represent the useful quarry rock, having a total thickness of about 16 feet. It is a middling, fine-grained sandstone, micaceous, of bluish or greenish color, in places very regularly stratified, and all through homogeneous, splitting in even beds, with sometimes ripple-marked surface. In some parts of the quarries, however, the bedding is discordant, as it is found in every sandstone formation, involving a greater proportion of waste. Sometimes also layers are damaged by single quartz pebbles scattered through them, which unfit them for use as grindstones. The rock is split into plates of any desirable thickness, dressed roughly with the hammer, and is then finished by a steam-turning machine; portions also are sawed into strips for use as whetstones. Grindstones of 6 and 7 feet in diameter can be easily obtained. The blocks not well suited for grindstones are either dressed on the spot as building material, or are shipped in the rough, to be used for the same purpose.

I have already mentioned the occurrence of Goniatites and Fish remains in the conglomerate beds and in the calcareous concretions; the same fossils, although more rarely, are also found in the other parts of the rock series. Teeth and spines of various fishes of the shark family are found in great perfection; among these I may mention a tooth of an Orodus 4½ inches long. This specimen, besides a number of others, I gave into the hands of Prof. Newberry for description, the study of fossil fishes being a specialty of his. Of Goniatites, I collected three different species. Some seams contain also numerous casts of bivalve shells, most of them identical with forms found in the sandstones of Marshall and Battle Creek. Carbonaceous vegetable fragments, among them Calamites and Lepidodendron, are of common occurrence. The lower beds of the sand rock are largely intermingled with shale fragments, and the underlying shales being eroded on the surface, the sand rock resting on them fills out their furrows.

In the bluffs on the lake shore, below the solid body of sand rock which is designated as the *grindstone*, a series of blue shales, interlaminated with seams of sandstone, is exposed, emerging about 5 or 6 feet above the water-level. Similar shaly beds are noticed in the bed of Willow Creek, under the mill at Huron City. At that locality the sand-rock ledges much prevail over the shaly material, certain seams of this sand rock being completely filled with the casts of a Rhynchonella, intermingled with a species of Productus and a few other shells. The surface of some layers is often covered with relief forms resembling Fucoides caudagalli. On the south side of Willow Creek, the hill over which the road to Port Hope leads is again capped by the grindstones. The hill forms toward the lake a steep escarpment about 50 feet high, which continues southward about a mile beyond Point of Barques Lighthouse. Twenty feet of the top part are solid sandstone ledges, containing irregular seams of conglomeratic structure; the lower portion of the escarpment, down to the level on which the lighthouse stands, is made up by arenaceous shales, alternating with seams of sand rock. The shales contain casts of bivalves and other fossils, similar or identical with those found in a bed of calcareous sand rock below them, the same on which the lighthouse is built.

This sand-rock ledge, having a thickness of from 2 to 3 feet, is even with the water-level a few hundred yards north of the lighthouse; at the lighthouse it has risen about 5 feet, and further south it may be seen in the bluffs 8 or 10 feet higher than the level of the lake. The shale bluffs above the sand-rock ledge are at a distance from shore at the lighthouse and north of it; a quarter of a mile south of the lighthouse, however, they come up close to the shore line, and cover the ledge from above, while below it, as basal part of the same bluffs, shale beds similar to the upper ones make an outcrop. These bluffs continue for about half a mile, when they again recede from the shore, which further south is a low sand beach.

The sand rock of Point of Barques Lighthouse is coarse-grained, partly conglomeratic, full of nodules and granular crystals of iron pyrites. In undecomposed condition, it is rich in calcareous cement, and very hard; its color is partly dark bluish, or, in weathered condition, ferruginous brown; much weathered portions which have lost nearly all their cement are softer and often whitish. The bed is quite fossiliferous. The surface of the ledge is rugose by fucoid-like ramifications spread over it, and seams of it are often densely crowded with casts of a Rhynchonella; of other Brachiopods, a species of Orthis, a Productus, a Syringothyris, a Spirifer of a large kind, Streptorhynchus, Rhynchospira, Spiriferina, Terebratula, are generally plainly recognizable, but are too imperfect for specific determination or identification with forms of other remote localities.

In addition to the Brachiopods, several Lamellibranches of the genera Cypricardella, Schizodus, Aviculopecten, and of Gasteropods a large Pleurotomaria (Huronensis Winchelli), were found, as well as a species of Goniatites, and a large form of an annulated Orthoceras. A Prœtus, the head of a Cyathocrinus, and stems of other Crinoids, together with traces of Bryozoa, complete the list of fossils found there by me.

The order of sequence of the strata composing the section from Port Austin to Point of Barques Lighthouse, is differently represented in Prof. Winchell's report of 1861, in which the same locality is described. It will be remembered that I consider the rocks of Flat Rock Point, Hat Point, and Point of Barques as identical, and occupying the highest position in the series; next below them are thin-bedded ledges of sandstone with a fossiliferous seam containing Centronella Julia and Rhynchonella camerifera. A band of conglomerate rock follows, and then we come upon the grindstones, which in their fossils are identical with the sandstones of Marshall; to the latter, shales, with seams of sandstone, are subjacent, and last and lowest in the section is the sand-rock ledge of Point of Barques Lighthouse.

Prof. Winchell commences his section with the calcareous sandrock ledges west of Flat Rock Point, which he correctly identifies with the sandstones of Marshall, but places as the highest of the exposed strata, and, under a preconceived theoretical opinion on the general dip of the strata, he believes that he descends to lower beds, when, moving eastward, he really ascends to the cliffs of Flat Rock; proceeding on to Point of Barques, he still is under the impression that he descends to lower horizons. From Point of Barques toward the Lighthouse, the section is actually changed into a descending one, which is considered by him as a direct downward continuation of the former. Unfortunately, this section is laid across a synclinal undulation of the formation, and begins at one end with the same rock beds (Marshall sandstone) which on the other end are found very near the base (grindstone ledges). Under the impression that he has all the while descended, he stands again on the horizon from which he started. An almost uninterrupted section through all the above-described rock beds can be seen in Willow Creek, 5 miles above its mouth; the layers between the coarse-grained upper sandstone and the grindstone series are particularly well denuded there in the bed and banks of the creek.

The sand-rock ledge of Point of Barques Lighthouse, whose fossils I have enumerated, is designated by Prof. Winchell as the dividing stratum between his Huron shales and his Marshall group; the sand-rock bed is pretended to represent the Devonian fauna, the shales above it, the fauna of carboniferous character. He enumerates 19 species of fossils found in the sand rock to prove its Devonian character. Six of them are identified with Hamilton species, identifications which must be questioned, and 13 species are newly described by the Professor, which, as new forms, can have no great value in the instituting of comparisons, their generic types being as much at home in the Devonian as in the carboniferous rocks. The shales above this sand rock contain a majority of all the species in common with it. The conformity of rock material and stratification in this part of the formation, above and below the imaginary division line between the Devonian and carboniferous deposits, is so perfect that no one could accept this stratum as the terminal deposit of the Devonian ocean, even if the fact were ignored that at least 500 feet of rock beds below this horizon present the faunal characters of the Cuyahoga shales of Ohio, which form the upper division of the Waverly group.

From Lighthouse Point southward, as far as Forestville, in the north part of Sanilac County, rock beds approximately of the same horizon with the grindstones of Huron City are near the surface along the shore line. The outcrops are insignificant compared with the stretch of sand and gravel beach interrupting them, but it rarely requires the removal of very deep drift masses in order to uncover the rock beds.

At Port Hope, the grindstones crop out in the lake bed close to the docks. More extensive denudations are to be seen one mile and a half north of the village, at the shore; the land behind it rises in several terraces formed of coarse boulder drift with metamorphic and crystalline blocks and of Niagara and Helderberg or Hamilton limestones, besides a large proportion of fragments from the underlying sand rock, some of which are rich in the shells usually found in the Marshall and Battle Creek sandstones. The boring of a salt well at Port Hope, to a depth of 787 feet, is recorded as follows:

Drift	16	ft.
Greenish micaceous sandstone	6	"
Blue arenaceous shale, with occasional seams of sand rock	510	"
Very hard rock (not more particularly specified)	1	"
Dark blue shales	154	"
Arenaceous shales	29	"
Coarse, whitish sandstone, saturated with strong salt brine	71	"

Further south, in the creek near Sand Beach, greenish and bluish micaceous sand-rock ledges interstratified with shales are exposed in seams filled with a species of Chonetes. The same beds, with Chonetes and impressions of Goniatites, are well exposed at Rock Falls, the ripple-marked surface of the ledges in the latter place being covered with Caudagalli fucoids in relief, as well as other singularly-shaped prominences of organic origin.

At White Rock, south of the village, the arenaceous shale beds below the horizon of the grindstones ascend in steep bluffs of 25 feet elevation from the lake bed, for the distance of about a mile. Indistinct casts of fossils, amongst which Goniatites is recognizable, are found on the surface of the arenaceous flags; this is the last rock exposure on the shore of Lake Huron, which washes upon a drift beach for the remainder of the distance down to

Port Huron. Mr. Thompson sunk two artesian wells at White Rock—one to the depth of 555 feet, the other to 700. In both, blue shales, alternating with arenaceous layers containing much iron pyrites, extended to the depth of about 450 feet below the surface, when a porous gray sand rock was struck, saturated with a strong and very pure salt brine. The thickness of the sand rock was about 100 feet, and below it blue shales were found again, which were penetrated to a depth of 50 feet. Mr. Thompson had saved specimens of his deeper drill hole, representing almost every interval of 5 feet, which he kindly presented to me, and by which I could form a more correct idea of the character of the rock beds than could be obtained from any descriptive record.

Of other deep borings made within the district under consideration, I may mention the salt well at New River, only two miles south of the grindstone quarries, bored to a depth of 1029 feet.

It begins in the grindstone, which is there 15 feet in thickness, underlaid by soft blue shales 30 feet thick; to them follow alternately shale and sand-rock ledges to the depth of 800 feet. There, as the record says, a rotten, bad-smelling, soft rock was penetrated, and then 100 feet of a porous, coarse-grained, whitish sand rock was found, saturated with brine, below which the boring was continued for a few feet into blue shales. Salt brine was already found at a depth of 90 feet below the surface, but it continued to increase in strength as a greater depth was reached. In the sand rock at the bottom of the well, it has a strength of 85 salinometer degrees.

At Port Austin, one of the oldest salt wells was bored to a depth of 1200 feet, but the boring record has been lost. Lately, Mr. Skene made a new boring to the depth of 1225 feet in a locality one mile west of the village and about 200 yards from the shore line of the bay. The boring, after the penetration of a few feet of drift, begins in the conglomerate band of the grindstone series, following which are greenish-blue micaceous, fine-grained sand-rock ledges. Another conglomerate bed is found 125 feet below the surface, and from that a strong current of sweet water rises to the surface. From there to 163 feet are arenaceous shales; at 204 feet is a gray sandstone, and the first signs of brine were observed at from 204 to 315 feet, shales with arenaceous seams occur at 317 feet, and a conglomeratic sand rock 20 feet thick. There was a strong discharge of sweet water from the bore hole, from 336 to 1100 feet (764 feet), all of which was through bluish shale, with only a few intermediate strata of sandstone. At 1120 feet are bright-red and chocolate-colored shales 40 feet thick, while from there to 1225 feet is white sand rock saturated with brine; underneath lie shales again.

Inland from the shore line, whose geological structure has been described in previous pages, we find the greatest part of the surface of Huron County covered by deep drift deposits. The upper coarse-grained sand rock comes to the surface in Bingham township, near the head-waters of Cass River. Similar outcrops are found in the northwestern towns of Sanilac County, in Greenleaf and Argyle, and in Tuskola County, in the towns of Elkland and Novesta, where the bed of Cass River is formed by the upper coarse-grained sand rock inclosing vegetable remains, Lepidodendron. Further up the river, at Indian Rapids, in Town. 13, R. 12, Sect. 7, some lower beds of finer-grained sand rock interlaminated with shale form vertical bluffs about 20 feet high on both sides of the river. One of the interlaminated seams is soft, almost entirely composed of mica scales and carbonaceous vegetable substance. The sand rock is mostly thin-bedded, and without fossils as far as observed.

On the north side of Saginaw Bay an outcrop of the upper sandstones of the Waverly group forms the bed of Rifle River for the distance of a mile. The locality is in Town. 21, R. 3, Sect. 16. The rock is coarse-grained, whitish or greenish, with ferruginous spots, moderately soft and irregularly stratified in discordant bedding. Its thickness can not well be estimated, but 30 or 40 feet of the strata are distinctly seen successively rising to the surface. No fossils were observed in it. The hills on both sides of the river are all composed of drift. The strata dip southward, and a few miles lower down calcareous beds of the next higher formation, having the same southern dip, form rapids in the river, but the immediate contact between the Waverly rock and these limestones is not seen.

In this upper portion of the peninsula, no other natural outcrops of the Waverly group are known to me, but the formation has been found in several deep borings made for salt; two made in Tawas City and one lately at Sable City. Of the latter boring I have no details, being only informed of their success in finding a good supply of brine. Of one of the borings at Tawas, in the establishment of Grant and Sons, I copied an accurate record from the books of the firm, which reads as follows:

Sand	30 ft.	drift.
Clay, yellow	20 "	
Sandstone, whitish	60 "	
Sandstone, red	15 "	
Sandstone, gray	5 "	
Sandstone, red	40 "	
Shale, light-colored	10 "	
Shale, arenaceous red	30 "	
Shale, light-colored	5 "	
Shale, arenaceous red	88 "	
Shale, blue	35 "	
Sandstone, red	40 "	
Shale, hard, light-colored	60 "	
Sandstone, red	5 "	
Shale, white	15 "	
Sandstone, red	5 "	
Shale, hard, light-colored	40 "	
Sandstone, red	5 "	
Shale, white	3 "	
Shale, arenaceous, light-colored	3 "	
First indications of brine.		
Shale, white, hard	164 "	
Sandstone, gray	195 "	
Abundant supply of strong brine.		
Shale, blue	10 "	
Total	905 ft.	

A few years later, another company bored a well at Tawas with the same success, but I did not find out the particulars of the boring.

In the south part of the State, natural exposures of the Waverly group are found in the counties of Jackson, Hillsdale, Branch, and Calhoun. In the west part an outcrop is known at Brown's Station, in Lake township, Berrien County, and other exposures are near Holland, in the south part of Ottawa County. At Napoleon village, in Jackson County, sandstones of the Waverly group have been quarried as a building-stone since the first settlement of the

State. The quarries are about half a mile south of the village, with the rock beds close under the surface, on the summit level of a slight undulation.

The sandstone is of middling coarse grain, greenish-yellow, intermingled intimately with kaolin-like granules, by which the firmness of the rock is impaired. For ordinary uses, however, it is durable enough, and selected blocks are used for ornamentally-cut door and window sills, etc. The beds are not very thick, often irregular through discordant stratification, and alternation with shaly seams. The thickness of all the rock beds uncovered in the quarries may be 50 feet. Fossils have never been found.

Southwest of Napoleon, at Stony Point, a station on the Jackson and Hillsdale Railroad, sandstones entirely similar to the Napoleon rock are quarried. The quarries were first opened in an uptilted mass of sand-rock ledges in vertical position, in all probability an effect caused by forces of the drift period, by an underwashing of the strata, and consequent disruption from the main body of the deposits, which were found behind the loose portion in regular horizontal position. The bottom of the valley on the side of which the quarries and rock escarpments are, presents no rock ledges; it is deeply eroded, and the erosion is filled up with drift material. In the quarries, about 35 or 40 feet of strata are exposed; the highest beds are thin-bedded, soft flagstones of discordant stratification, the lower strata being in beds of from 1 to 4 feet in thickness. The vertical clefts dividing the beds are rather irregular, oblique, or curved, which causes considerable waste in shaping the blocks. The rock is moderately coarse-grained, light, drab-colored, and sufficiently compact to make a valuable building-stone. Fossils are generally rare, but abound locally in certain seams; the species are all identical with the forms found in the sandstones of Marshall and Battle Creek. I collected in the quarry: Nucula Hubbardi, Nucula stella, Solen quadrangularis, Solen scalpriformis, Sanguinolaria similis, Myalina Michiganensis, Allorisma, Bellerophon galericulatus, Chonetes Illinoisensis, Orthoceras, Goniatites, and others. The same rock beds are laid open in many localities in the vicinity of Jonesville, of Hillsdale, Osseo, and Moscow, but the quality of the rock is not always so well adapted for use as a building-stone, its general character and the fossils inclosed proving, however, the identity of all the outcrops. Every locality has certain species of fossils for itself or more abundant than in others, nearly all as casts, but sometimes with the shell, with all its delicate surface decorations, most perfectly preserved. Other exposures of the Waverly sandstone are near Homer, and near Condit Station, south of Albion. At the latter place a quarry is opened in a sand rock exactly similar to the Napoleon sandstone, and like it perfectly destitute of fossils. The beds of the quarry amount to about 20 feet; below them are a bluish-colored micaceous sandstone alternating with shale beds, and from this seam issue copious springs. Besides that afforded by the superficial outcrops of the district, something is added to our knowledge of its geological structure by deep artesian borings. In the Court-house square of Hillsdale two artesian wells have been drilled, one to the depth of 1350 feet, and another to that of 1550. No register of the borings was kept; however, from some attentive citizens, who watched the progress of the boring, I have received the following general statements, drawn from memory: Under a cover of several feet of drift, a soft, thinly laminated, micaceous, bluish sand rock, 20 feet in thickness, was first penetrated; under it, to a depth of 1120 feet, the principal rock found was shale of bluish color, interlaminated with arenaceous seams, and sometimes with harder ledges, believed to be of calcareous nature; the color of the shales became dark bituminous in the lower portion of the section. Next to the shale a hard, red-colored rock containing much iron pyrites was found, and the water was strongly saline. In the deeper of the two borings, below the hard red rock, a white limestone 50 feet in thickness was penetrated, and below it a softer, likewise calcareous rock continued downward as far as the drilling went. The lime rock in the bottom part of the drill hole very probably represents the Helderberg limestone, which, according to the record, is in that locality about 1400 feet below the surface. The dark bituminous shales above, equivalent to the black shales, can not be distinguished from the incumbent shales of the Waverly group, but we can see the considerable aggregate thickness of these formations.

In the city of Albion, several borings were made to a depth of 300 or 400 feet. Near the flour mill at Albion, a flowing well of slightly mineral, palatable drinking-water was opened by boring to a depth of 281 feet, all through solid sand rock, with the exception of 10 feet of drift on the surface. Below the sand rock the boring was continued for 100 feet through blue shales, without reaching their limit. At Marengo, 6 miles west of Albion, a boring went through 60 feet of drift before striking the sand rock, which was found 200 feet thick. Below it shales were penetrated through a thickness of 200 feet.

From Albion westward the valley of Kalamazoo River offers frequent exposures of the upper sandstones of the Waverly group, as far as Battle Creek, and for some distance further. The sandstones of Marshall and Battle Creek have become famous through the abundance of their fossils. Prof. Winchell has described a large number of species from these localities, some of which are in good preservation and easily recognized; but a great proportion of those described, the originals of which are deposited in the University Museum of Michigan, are mere fragments offering so few species characteristic, that it would have been better to omit all description until additions to the collected material should justify it. The most common forms of fossils in this rock are casts of bivalves, their shells being rarely preserved. I enumerate Nucula Hubbardi, Nucula stella, Nucula Iowensis, Nucula bellastria, Myalina Michiganensis, Solen quadrangularis, Solen scalpriformis, Sanguinolaria similis, Edmondia equimaryinalis; likewise various forms of Orthonota, Cyrtodonta, Allorisma, Avicula, and Aviculopecten. Several forms of Productus, Spirifer, Spiriferina, Rhynchonella, Bellerophon galericulatus, Bellerophon rugosiusculus, Goniatites Allei, Goniatites Marshallensis, Nautilus of various kinds (Trematodiscus), also different forms of Orthoceras, fish remains of the shark tribe, and vegetable remains (Lepidodendron), as well as traces of corals and Bryozoa, are observed. Formerly a number of quarries were worked at Marshall along the bed of Kalamazoo River, which are now abandoned. The superficial rock ledges are a micaceous soft sand rock of yellowish-brown color, splintered into thin, uneven slabs by exposure; the deeper, more protected rock beds are harder, of bluish color, and rich in calcareous cement. Interlaminated with them are seams of a blue arenaceous shale. The harder rock answers a good purpose as a building material. The fossils are confined to certain seams, or at least rarely are found in other parts of the rock. Within the city of Marshall, a great number of artesian wells have been opened by boring through the sand rock to a depth of from 60 to 100 feet, a copious stream of sweet water, rising several feet above the surface, being found in all the borings without exception.

The west part of the city of Battle Creek is built on rock ledges of the Waverly group. The upper strata, opened by digging out cellars, and seen on the slope of the banks of the river, are a middling, coarse-grained, yellowish sand rock, resembling the sand rock of Napoleon or Condit Station. Some beds are of moderate thickness, and are used for foundation walls; others are thinly laminated, of discordant stratification, and worthless. Some vegetable stems and concretions of iron pyrites are inclosed within them. Their total thickness is about 30 or 40 feet.

Below these strata, in the bed of Kalamazoo River, and emerging a few feet above it, are micaceous sand-rock ledges, thinly laminated, alternating with harder calcareous sand-rock ledges crowded with fossils of the same kinds as enumerated from the sandstones of Marshall, with additional forms peculiar to the locality. The higher elevations surrounding Battle Creek are all composed of heavy drift accumulations, partly well stratified sand and gravel beds, partly coarse, non-stratified boulder drift in a position above the stratified deposits. In the northeast part of the city the rock beds are covered by 70 feet of drift. An artesian well bored in that part of the city went below the drift stratum through 43 feet of sand rock, when the drill struck a cavity, sinking at once 3 feet, and a copious stream of water rose in the bore-hole to within 16 feet of the surface. The boring was continued through 326 feet of blue shales, until at 440 feet it was given up.

Twelve miles north of New Buffalo at Brown's Station, on the Lake Michigan shore road, and about 1½ mile east from the shore line, a brownish or violet-colored sand rock is found under a drift cover only a few feet in thickness. By exploring ditches, about 4 or 5 feet of the rock ledges have been laid open, which contain some of the most characteristic forms of the sand rock at Marshall: Nucula Hubbardi, Allorisma, etc.; but this is all that I could observe—the flat, level shore belt presenting no larger denudation or deeper sections into the rock. Hard, thin-bedded flagstones resembling the rock at Brown's Station are frequently thrown out by the lake, all along the beach from Michigan City northward; similar flagstones are also largely intermingled with the lower unstratified clayey boulder drift of this vicinity, which induces me to believe that this rock series underlies the whole southwestern corner of the State; but the drift is generally too deep to allow of denudation of the rock beds by natural erosions, or by the ordinary excavations in well-digging, etc.

The next known outcrop of the Waverly group on the west shore is on Black River, near Holland, in Ottawa County, and some miles further north, near Grand River, it is seen for the last time. The outcrops at Holland are about 4 miles north of the village, in the flats bordering Black River. They comprise only a limited vertical series of beds, some of which are thinly laminated, while others are in thick, regular ledges, which are quarried for building uses. Their lithological character is nearly the same as that of the grindstones in the quarries on the Lake Huron shore, a greenish, middling, fine-grained, micaceous sand rock. In seams, a great number of the usual fossils of the Marshal sandstone are found; other parts of the rock are almost destitute of them. I found in the quarry, Nucula Hubbardi, Nucula stella, Nucula Iowensis, Solen quadrangularis, Solen scalpriformis, and other bivalves; also Bellerophon, Nautilus, Orthoceras, Goniatites, etc. North of Ottawa County, nearly all the land west of the Grand Rapids and Indiana Railroad line is supposed to be underlaid by the Waverly group as far as the head of Big Traverse Bay, but no sign of a rock ledge comes to the surface on this whole space until we come upon the green shales south of Antrim Village.

At Muskegon, several deep borings have been made—one a number of years ago by Mr. Whitney, to the depth of 1230 feet; another, the deepest ever made in Michigan, reaches a depth of 2627 feet. Of the first boring a register was kept to a depth of 657 feet. The boring commenced in drift deposits, which were penetrated 223 feet before the first ledges of solid rock were struck. The following shows the descending order of the beds:

Sand rock	50 ft.
Iron pyrites	3 in.
Sand rock	16 ft.
Shale	3 "
Sand rock	22 "
Shale	17 "
Shales and sand rock alternating	326 "

At a depth of 330 feet below the surface, and also at 643 feet, copious water streams were found, which rise to the surface, making an overflow of mineral water of quite an agreeable, refreshing taste. In the lower part of the boring salt brine was found, which, however, does not rise and mingle with the upper streams.

Of the deep boring, an accurate record of which would have been of great scientific interest, I could only get the general results, given from memory, by one of the superintendents of the work.

Drift deposits	235 ft.
Shales of lighter and darker color, alternating with seams of sand rock	450 "
Strong flow of mineral water.	
Blue shales, with some harder seams	775 "
Hydro-carburetted gas, drops of rock oil, and saline water.	
Soft blue shale	150 "
Red shale	150 "
Lime rock, with seams of shale	300 "
Salt-bearing rock, with seams of sandstone	50 "
Dark-colored lime rock	250 "
Gypsum beds, alternating with limestone	195 "

Dark, loose, porous lime rock, 82 feet thick, forms the bottom part of the bore-hole. It is to be regretted that no special pains were taken to preserve a regular set of specimens from each pumping. Few of them were kept in the office, mostly of shaly or arenaceous character, but of the horizons of the lime rock and gypsum beds, which I was very desirous to see, I could find nothing preserved. It is probable that the lower 800 or 900 feet of the boring penetrates the Hamilton and Helderberg groups, and that the salt brine found in the lower end of the well belongs to the Onondaga series, like the salt wells of Alpena, and of Goderich in Canada.

In previous pages, I have led the reader over the different outcrops of the upper division of the Waverly group, as developed in Michigan, and, occasionally, I gave an account of deep borings made in places vicinal to the outcrops. This upper division, principally composed of sand rock with intermediate subordinate seams of shale, has, as far as known by means of the deep borings in different parts of the State, a thickness of from 250 to 350 feet. The higher portion of the deposits is a porous, middling, coarse-grained sand rock, with little calcareous cement, and rarely fossiliferous. Prof. Winchell named these strata Napoleon group, to distinguish them from the lower, often very fossiliferous beds, composed of more fine-grained micaceous sand rock, with seams of harder ledges rich in calcareous cement, which lower division he names Marshall group. He asserts the two divisions to be always separated by a seam of shale several feet in thickness, but such a regularity in the disposition of the rock beds of this horizon does not exist; shale beds are found everywhere in alternation with the sand-rock ledges, and in the different exposures of limited vertical extent, it is almost impossible to tell which of the special sand-rock ledges or shale beds we have under observation. Neither is the presence or absence of fossils in the rock beds a feature to be relied upon. A large portion of the lower beds, considered to represent the Marshall group, contains no fossils, yet the absence of fossils at Napoleon is no proof that those particular strata do not contain any. The rock of the quarries at Stony Point is so absolutely similar to the Napoleon sandstone, and is generally so barren of fossils, that nobody would doubt its identity with the other. It is only lately, by the more extensive opening of the quarry, that fossiliferous seams were discovered, which were before not known to exist.

It has been stated that Prof. Winchell considers the sandstones of Marshall as the lower terminus of the carboniferous rock series, typically distinct by its fossils from the next subjacent shaly beds which he connects with the Devonian rocks by the character of their fauna. Such a difference in the fauna is not perceptible; the fossils of the Marshall sandstones and the subjacent shales are not only generically in full harmony, but a great number of species are common to both. This lower shale formation is the surface rock in the south part of Hillsdale County and Branch County; the transition from the upper sandy division to the lower is not defined, as should be expected in rock beds with two distinct faunas; the beds are in fullest conformity of deposition, and the material composing them does not change. In the upper we have a sand rock with subordinate beds of shale; in the lower we have the same sort of shales alternating with subordinate beds of the sand rock. The outcrops of the shale formation in the counties mentioned are never of great vertical extent, and their horizontal extension is much interrupted by incumbent drift deposits. An artificial section through this shale formation is recorded by Dr. Bennett, of Coldwater, and specimens from all the pumpings during the progress of the boring were carefully saved by him and kindly handed over to me. The locality of the boring is a few miles west of Coldwater, near Branch Station. The following details of the boring can be given:

Drift	26 ft.	
Soft blue shales	177 "	
Hard blue shales, containing Crinoid stems and Chonetes	13 "	
Soft blue shale	4 "	
Hard blue lime rock, with quartz	1 "	
Soft shale		10 in.
Hard calcareous sand rock		10 "
Soft sand rock		4 "
Water rising to the surface.		
Hard calcareo-argillaceous sand rock, with many shell fragments	2 "	6 "
Soft shale	2 "	
Pyritous shale		7 "
Soft blue shale, with many shells	4 "	5 "
Hard blue rock (lime rock)	1 "	9 "
Soft blue shales	3 "	3 "
Argillaceous hard lime rock, of blue color, with many shells	1 "	8 "
Blue shale	2 "	
Hard sand rock	2 "	8 "
Soft shale with fossils	2 "	10 "
Hard calcareous sand rock, with shells, Crinoid stems, etc	1 "	
Shale and sand rock alternating, containing fossils and iron pyrites	33 "	
Hard blue limestone, with calcspar and pyrites, shells	1 "	
Salt brine.		
Shale and sand rock, with shells	11 "	6 "
Hard blue lime rock, with shells	1 "	6 "
Soft blue shale, with seams of sand rock, pyrites, and dark bituminous particles.	22 "	

Similar shales, alternating occasionally with a seam of sandstone or limestone, continue to a total depth of 447 feet below the surface.

Only half a mile east from this drill-hole, on a higher level, in a brick-yard, shale beds of a seemingly higher position than those penetrated in the drill-hole are well denuded. The exposure comprises about 25 feet of strata, principally a soft blue shale with interstratified seams of arenaceous, thin-bedded flagstones, and full of lenticular iron-ore geodes of concentric structure, containing sometimes a loose, shaking nucleus. The superficial crust of the geodes is generally transformed into hydrated sesquioxide of iron; the internal portions are gray, compact, amorphous protocarbonate of iron. The shale beds, otherwise horizontal, are considerably flexured in serpentine lines, which disturbance in all probability was caused during the drift period by pressure of the advancing glacier masses on those beds which they encountered. The base of the hill capped with this shale is all enveloped by a mantle of drift deposits. No fossils were found in this locality.

Similar shales are uncovered in another brick-yard on the north side of the city of Coldwater; they are likewise crowded with iron geodes, some of which are fossiliferous, inclosing Chonetes Illinoisensis, etc. Below the shales, argillaceo-micaceous sandstones come to the surface, which contain iron geodes similar to those of the shales. All the hillsides north of Coldwater River valley, for several miles eastward from Coldwater, are composed of this shale formation covered by a more or less thick coating of drift material, but in other parts of the State, brick-yards generally use the drift clay. In the vicinity of Coldwater, all the clay used for brick-making is derived from the shale beds of the Waverly group, which are ploughed up and left to the influence of the weather for about a year, by which time the shale has decomposed into a soft, plastic clay. In the brick-yard of Mr. Merritt, 2 miles south of Union City, Town. 5, R. 7, west, Sect. 16, the surface beds are sandy shales with seams of calcareo-ferruginous rock, containing many small cylindraceous nodules composed of compact carbonate of iron, besides a number of partially very finely preserved fossils. Below these beds are yellowish gray soft shales, used for brick-making, which also contain numerous kidney-ore concretions of lenticular form.

The ore nodules were formerly collected and melted in a blast furnace at Union City, which is now given up. Half a mile north from the brick-yard on Mr. Randall's farm, the shale beds are seen in outcrops along the banks and in the bed of Coldwater Creek, amounting in the exposures to about 30 or 40 feet. The lowest strata seen in the bed of the river are dark blue hard shales, with gray carbonate of iron geodes and concretions of iron pyrites; above them some arenaceous seams pervade the shale beds, following which are the beds seen in the brick-yard. The fossiliferous, calcareo-ferruginous bed, and to some extent also the kidney-ore geodes, contain the following species of fossils: Chonetes Illinoisensis, Strophomena rhomboidalis, Terebratula eudora(?) several Spirifers not accurately determined, Spirigera lamellosa, Lingula, various species of Nucula, Myalina, Platyceras, Loxonema, Pleurotomaria, Bellerophon cyrtolites, Bellerophon galericulatus, Goniatites Oweni, Nautilus, Prœtus, some Bryozoa, and others, not yet properly determined.

South of Coldwater, in the town of Algansee, on Pencil Creek, in the ravines of drift-covered hills, the shale formation, with its intermediate seams of sandstone and of kidney-ore geodes, can he seen nicely exposed. Some of the iron geodes are fossiliferous. In the town of Reading, the shale formation is everywhere found under a thin coating of drift when digging wells, etc.; natural outcrops in the ravines and beds of creeks are also often encountered. The shale is sometimes considerably arenaceous and pervaded by regular sandstone ledges. These latter often contain fossils, but the best preserved are always found in the calcareous or ferruginous seams or in the geodes. Besides the other forms mentioned previously as found near Union City, I found in an outcrop in Reading a large Nautilus digonus.

The drift deposits of this region contain in places large quantities of fragments of the Marshall sandstone, inclosing an abundance of fine fossils; one of these localities is near Round Lake, in Sect. 32, of Allen township, where, by the excavation of a road bed, masses of this sand rock were thrown out. To the west and southwest of Coldwater, the shale formation is very soon lost under the drift cover spread over the entire southwest part of the State. The drift of all the western counties, as St. Joseph, Kalamazoo, Van Buren, and Allegan counties, is mixed with large quantities of kidney-ore nodules from the shale formation, which are crowded with finely preserved fossils, identical with those found in the exposures of Branch County. To enable a comparison with the fossils of other strata, I will enumerate the forms collected from these nodules in the drift. The larger portion of them are not specifically determined, because a great many of them are undescribed forms, while in some cases I have used specific names with the intention of indicating a similarity rather than a full identity.

Of corals a species of Zaphrentis and a Pyrgia are noticed. Of Crinoids, heads of Platycrinus and numerous stems of other forms occur. Bryozoa, as Fenestella, Polypora, Stictopora, and Trematopora entirely compose certain ferruginous rock fragments. Brachiopods are represented richly by Lingula, Discina, Productus semireticulatus, Productus punctatus and two other small species of Productus, Streptorhynchus crenistria, Spiriferina spinosa, Spirifer setigerus, Spirifer Carteri, Syringothyris, Spirigera lamellosa, Terebratula Eudora, Meristella, Chonetes Illinoisensis, entirely composing large boulders; Rhynchonella, two species, Strophomena rhomboidalis, and Orthis; of Lamellibranches, five species of Nuculoid shells, Myalina, Modiola, Cyrtodonta, Orthonota, Cypricardinia, Conocardium, Lucina, Allorisma, Schizodus, and several forms of Aviculopecten. Of Gasteropods, I distinguish four species of Platyceras, a Pleurotomaria, Loxonema, Murchisonia, Bellerophon galericulatus, Bellerophon cyrtolites, and a Tentaculites; of Cephalopods, Trematodiscus digonus, various forms of Orthoceras and Nautilus, Goniatites Oweni, Goniatites Allei, fragments of Prœtus or Phillipsia, numerous specimens of Cypridina, and Fish remains.

A large proportion of these species I can recognize among the collections I made from similar iron geodes from localities in Ohio, at Sciotoville, and in the strata of Bagdad, and other exposures of the Cuyahoga shales, which latter, in lithological characters, also bear considerable resemblance to our Michigan shale formation. Prof. Winchell, who made a special study of these Ohio fossils, correctly recognizes the Cuyahoga shales as equivalent or analogous with the Marshall sandstones. I can not conceive, therefore, how he could overlook the similarity of the fauna of the shale beds of Michigan to those, except on the assumption that he never paid any attention to the collection of fossils from the shales; but if so, he had no grounds upon which to attempt a demonstration of their Devonian age. The surface configuration of Ohio is very favorable for the study of the Waverly group; it forms a chain of hills extending from the north end to the south end of the State, which are deeply intersected by valleys of erosion, presenting on their slopes sections through the whole series in direct, uninterrupted superposition, and laid open sometimes for miles in extent. Such advantages we do not enjoy in Michigan. The Waverly series was evidently at an earlier period likewise intersected by deep erosions, but during the drift period these valleys became completely filled up again with the rubbish of the drift. Subsequent erosions denuded some rock beds superficially, in limited spots, but no deep cuts through them are laid open; our deepest natural sections do not comprise in any one place more than 50 feet of strata, and of a portion of the lower beds of the Waverly series, which is nearly a thousand feet in thickness, we have little more information than what we get from artesian borings by means of the material pumped up in pulverized condition, a very imperfect mode of studying a formation, the value of which is even lessened by the negligence with which the records of such borings are generally kept. The lower division of the Waverly group is not a shale formation throughout; it incloses in several horizons thick masses of porous sandstones, which are of the highest economical value for us, as the repositories of a concentrated salt brine. The brine, however, does not seem to be confined to this lower horizon, but pervades the whole rock series, in which the sand rock acts as a sponge, absorbing into its pores the saline liquid and retaining it, if the conditions for its retention are otherwise favorable.

In search of this brine, boring experiments have been made in all parts of the State, while in other deep borings, made for a different purpose, brine has been found accidentally. It has been ascertained by these borings that salt brine is not confined to certain localities or to a certain limited geological horizon, but can be found in all parts of the peninsula which are underlaid by the Waverly group, and at the same spot in higher and lower horizons.

Incidentally, I have recorded several deep borings, while giving a description of the general structure of the Waverly group. A number of others, particularly those made in districts where no superficial outcrops of rock ledges are known, are of interest, and may be mentioned here.

A drill-hole to the depth of 770 feet was made in the Court-house square of Ann Arbor, whose progress I carefully watched, so that I can vouch for the correctness of the record:

Drift above coarse boulder drift, below stiff clay beds mixed with pebbles and a few large boulders	155 ft.
Blue arenaceous shales interstratified with seams of fine-grained sandstone	150 "
Black bituminous shales, evolution of hydro-carburetted gas and rock oil in drops	28 "
Gray sandstone, coarse, containing brine of 1142 spec. weight, leaving 19 per cent residue by evaporation, which is almost pure chloride of sodium	92 "
Blue shales, with subordinate sandstone layers and seams of iron pyrites	100 "
Black shales, very bituminous, with iron pyrites,	85 "
Dark blue arenaceous shales, with iron pyrites and traces of fossils	22 "
Black bituminous shales, with iron pyrites	68 "
Limestone, bluish-colored, with flint	70 "
Total	770 ft

Commenting upon this section, a parallel could be drawn between the upper 178 feet of shale and the Cuyahoga shales of Ohio; the lower black portion, 28 feet in thickness, would correspond very well with the black shales on top of the Berca grit. The sand rock with salt brine, 92 feet, I compare to the Berca grit stones.

The next 275 feet of shales and arenaceous layers have to be taken as the equivalents of the Bedford-Cleveland-Erie shales, and black shales of Ohio, and the lowest 70 feet of lime rock as representing the Helderberg series. In the heretofore described boring at Hillsdale, the brine was found at a depth of 1100 feet below the surface, and no large sand-rock deposit was met with in the whole interval.

In the boring at Coldwater, brine was struck at 282 feet below the surface. At Constantine, in St. Joseph County, a drill-hole was sunk to a depth of 680 feet below the surface, the boring record of which reads:

Drift....................................	93 ft.
Blue calcareous sand rock..................	30 "
Blue shales, with red seams................	160 "
Gray sandstone...........................	100 "
Strong brine.	
Hard silicious rock........................	5 "
Evolution of inflammable gas.	
Blue shales..............................	85 "
Hard silicious rock........................	10 "
Softer rock..............................	10 "
Black shales, readily combustible...........	160 "
Total...............................	680 ft.

From the upper series of the strata a stream of mineral water rises to the surface, which is used for medicinal purposes, a bathing institution having been established at the spot.

At Niles, a boring was made to the depth of 600 feet, but no accurate record was kept. Mr. Finley, a gentleman who was connected with the enterprise, gave me from memory the following data:

Drift....................................	70 ft.
Sandstones thinly laminated and of variable hardness, about......................	300 "
Issue of strong salt brine.	
Dark shales about........................	250 "
Evolution of much hydro-carburetted gas.	

Of several other deep borings made in the southwest part of the peninsula, I could not learn the particulars. The boring made in the State Prison at Michigan City has already been mentioned.

Borings in the western central portion of the peninsula, at Grand Rapids and vicinity, described in Prof. Winchell's report of 1861, need no repetition here. In all of them the Waverly group is found to be the repository of the brine. The borings never were carried deep enough, under the preconceived false impression that the salt brine had its site in the higher gypsiferous rock series, in the Michigan salt group of Winchell.

In the borings at Muskegon, salt brine was found at a depth of 1250 feet from surface, which would appear to come from the Waverly group; the salt brine found at the depth of 2400 feet in all probability is within the rock series of the Onondaga group.

There remain yet to be given some accounts of borings executed in the salt-producing districts of Saginaw valley. The salt wells of Caseville have a very great depth; one of them is 1735 feet below the surface, but, unfortunately, no record of the boring was kept. I am informed, however, by persons who were present when the boring was made, and who gave attention to the matter, that the upper 900 feet went principally through a blue shale, sometimes through red shales, with no important seam o harder rock in the whole interval. At 900 feet, a large body of a whitish sand rock was struck which contained strong brine; another supply of brine was found near the bottom of the well, likewise in a sand rock. No limestone formation, or any other rock series indicating a lower horizon than the Waverly group, was met with in the boring, which commenced in the top part of the above-named series, immediately below the incumbent gypsum formation.

One of the first borings made in Saginaw valley, and at the same time the most accurately recorded, is the well of the East Saginaw Salt Mining Company. Dr. Lathrop, who kept the records, communicates to me the following details of it:

Drift	92	ft.
Sandstone	78½	"
Dark shale	26	"
Light shale	14	"
Sandstone with seams of coal	23	"
Brine, 10 degrees salinometer.		
Shales	12½	"
Sandstone with seams of coal	10	"
Blue shales	36½	"
Brine, 14 degrees salinometer.		
White sandstone	106	"
Limestone, fœtid	4½	"
Sandstone	5½	"

Limestone	4 ft.
Sandstone	6 in.
Limestone	6 ft.
Sandstone	1½ "
Limestone	8 "
Sandstone	6 in.
Limestone	5 ft.
Sandstone	6 in.
Limestone and sandstone, mixed	12 ft.
Sandstone	2 "
Limestone, sandstone, and shale mixed	14 "
Shales	3 "
Sandstone, light color	11 "
Salinometer, 26 degrees.	
Shales	38 "
Sandstone, fine-grained, blue	2 "
Salinometer, 40 degrees.	
Shales	13½ "
Sandstone, hard	2 "
Salinometer, 44 degrees.	
Shale	3 "
Sandstone, hard	6 in.
Shale	4 ft.
Shale, arenaceous, darker and lighter	18 "
Sandstone, hard, blue	8 "
Salinometer, 60 degrees.	
Sandstone, softer, blue	2 "
Salinometer, 64 degrees.	
Shales, dark	15 "
Sandstone	5½ "
Shales, dark	3½ "
Sandstone, hard, blue	1 "
Sandstone, gray, coarse	3 "
Shales, dark	7 "
Sandstone, micaceous, softer and harder	5 "
Sandstone and light-colored shale	5 "
Salinometer, 90 degrees.	
White soft sand rock	5 "
Very hard rock	2 in.
Shales, dark	6½ ft.

Hard, calcareous sand rock	10 in.
Shales, dark	2 ft.
White sand rock mixed with shale	8 "
Sand rock	99 "
Salinometer, 94 degrees.	
Shales generally of bright red color	64 "

These latter extended as far as the drilling was carried, which was to a depth of over 800 feet.

Since the time of this first boring, many more than a hundred other salt wells have been sunk in Saginaw valley, in all of which about the same general order of superposition of rock beds is observed. The coal measures and the subcarboniferous limestone formation are in all of them superimposed on the salt-bearing sand-rock beds of the Waverly group. A weak brine is found even within the coal measures, but the valuable brines are always found lower, within the Waverly group, at a distance of from 600 to 1000 feet below the surface. Beneath the sand rock saturated with the strongest brine there are found in nearly all the wells red-colored shales, which are for the practical salt man a sure guide in his boring that he has reached or nearly passed the salt-producing level. North of Saginaw River, the same results are obtained by deep borings. At Kawkalin, two salt wells have been sunk, one to a depth of 810 feet, the other to 1133 feet. The drift is there about 100 feet thick, then follow about 300 feet of shale and sand rock, with seams of coal, then 100 feet of limestones and gypsiferous shales. About 700 feet below the surface, a sand rock from 90 to 100 feet in thickness is found, which is saturated with a strong brine. In the deeper well, below the sand rock, is a series of red shales.

Southeast of Saginaw, 6 miles from Bridgeport, a very deep boring has been made lately by Mr. Blackmar. The boring penetrated

Drift	90 ft.
Shale	270 "
Coarse sand rock	90 "
Brine, 63 degrees.	
Blue shales	45 "
Red shales	200 "
Gray arenaceous shale	850 "

Sandstone	110 ft.
Strong brine.	
Gray shale	20 "
Limestone	2 "
Total	1764 ft.

Further south, at Flint, a boring of 1200 feet was made a number of years ago, concerning which Dr. Clark gives me the following general information:

Drift	68 ft.
Sandstone	67 "
Shales and sandstone, with seams of coal	35 "
Sandstone	108 "

From the depth of 260 feet a strong stream of sweet water rose to the surface. From there to a depth of 1200 feet, alternations of shale and sandstone occurred, and in the lower portion of the drill-hole a strong salt brine was found.

At Flint, several other deep borings were made through the coal measures into the Waverly group, but in none of them could the existence in that locality of the subcarboniferous limestone series be ascertained. A boring made in Section 5 of the town of Owosso, in Shiawassee County, is reported to me by Mr. Courier, of that place, as follows:

Drift	121 ft.
Shale	20 "
Coal	4 "
Shale	54 "
Hard rock	15 "
Shale	33 "
Sand rock	220 "
Limestone	3 "
Shale	64 "
Limestone	3 "
Soft shale	20 "
Sandstone with brine	77 "

after which were blue and red shales to the depth of 1000 feet below the surface.

I have now given a description of the observations which I was enabled to make on the surface distribution and structure of the Waverly group, from an examination of the different natural outcrops, and from the results communicated to me of different deep borings made in all parts of the State, and will proceed to briefly recapitulate the principal facts derived from such investigation.

The Waverly group seems to be spread in a basin-like sheet over all the peninsula, with exception of the country north of the river systems of Au Sable River, on the east side, and of Manistee River, on the west side, besides a triangular area in the southeast corner of the State, which is occupied by the Helderberg group and by the black shales, as may be seen by a glance at the geological map connected with this report. This basin-shaped rock series is, in the centre of the peninsula, overlaid by the coal measures and by the subcarboniferous limestone, but is everywhere there within the reach of deep borings.

The essential constituents of the formation are sand rock and shales, with subordinate admixture of calcareous or ferruginous layers or nodular concretions. It is a shore deposit. All shore deposits are composed of coarse materials, carried there from the neighboring continental surfaces; their nature depends upon the nature of the surface material of those continents, and the deposition of the sediments under the changeable wave action on an ocean shore is necessarily more irregular than that which takes place in the deep water remote from the shore.

The stratification often becomes discordant, and frequent changes in the material are induced by local influences; while in one place a shale bed forms, in another near by a sand-rock ledge may be accumulated. This fact is noticed in every shore deposit, recent or old. A comparison of the strata in different outcrops of the Waverly group will for these reasons rarely allow of an identification of certain beds, and often not even of their exact horizon in the series. Still greater must be the discrepancy in the results of boring experiments, where direct observation of the rock beds is excluded, and we have to depend on the examination of comminuted fragments; and what makes the case worse yet, is that these fragments can rarely be examined by the scientific observer himself—he has to depend on the statements made to him by well-borers, who have rarely much knowledge of lithology, while each calls the rocks by his own names, which are not always easily understood.

By the fossils contained in the rock beds we can sometimes ascertain their horizon, but the fossils are so unequally distributed that we may, in a seam which in one place contains tens of thousands, fail to find a single one in another not far removed; and where outcrops are generally of so very limited extent, we often have the bad luck to hit upon just such a barren portion, leaving us without a key by which to ascertain the exact position of one bed in relation to others.

The thickness of the Waverly group in Michigan is considerable, probably never less than 1000 feet, and in some places more than that. Its thickness seems to be greater in the northern and central parts of the peninsula than in its southern part. The upper division, prevalently a sand rock, with only subordinate layers of shale, and seams of harder sand rock cemented by much calcareous matter, has an approximate thickness of from 300 to 350 feet. Fossils are more abundant in the lower beds than in the upper, and are locally distributed. The great preponderance of Lamellibranches is remarkable, but I do not take this to be a peculiarity of the fauna during that period, being inclined to consider the nature of the deposits in connection with the animal forms inclosed by them. Lamellibranches are inhabitants of the sands of shore lines, and consequently must preponderate over dwellers in the deep sea, which by chance only are thrown out amongst them, just as is the case on the shell beaches of the ocean of the present day.

The lower division, chiefly a shale formation, is much greater than the upper; it is interstratified with arenaceous beds and with seams of calcareous and ferruginous concretions; frequently, also, several heavy sand-rock masses, sometimes 100 feet in thickness, are found interstratified between the shales, as is proved by deep borings. Whether these heavy sand-rock deposits occupy a certain equivalent position in different localities, or are local deposits, can not be positively asserted. All we know of the matter is derived from the results of a few borings. If we compare the boring records of the salt wells in different parts of the country, we find that, after penetration of the upper sand-rock division, usually not less than 400 feet of a shale formation are found before the deeper massive sand rock beds are struck, which latter, in the technical language of the salt manufacturer, are called the salt rock, because they supply him with strong, valuable brine. The brine is not confined to a certain horizon in the Waverly group ; it seems to pervade all of it, but has accumulated only in beds sufficiently porous to absorb it from the surrounding rock mass, and sufficiently protected from the percolation of surface waters to retain the solution of the salt in concentrated form. These conditions are much better fulfilled by the deeper beds than by the more superficial. In the majority of salt wells, high above the productive level, there is found a weak brine which increases in strength the nearer we come to the principal, more deeply situated repository. Experience has taught the salt manufacturer that, after exhaustion of the first salt rock, by boring deeper, sometimes, but not always, another sand rock saturated with strong brine can be found, termed by him the second salt rock ; but this designation is not applicable to a rock having a certain geological position, as it relates only to the conditions of a locality, and as the equivalent of the second salt rock in one well may be in another the upper or first salt rock.

In the salt wells of Tawas, Caseville, Port Austin, Port Hope, White Rock, etc., the salt rock is inclosed by the deeper shaly division of the Waverly group. The upper strata of the formation, as the sandstone of Point of Barques, and the grindstones, contain no salt in these localities ; they have been leached out owing to their superficial position. The salt wells of Saginaw, on the other hand, seem to furnish their supply of brine from the upper sand rocks corresponding to the Point of Barques sandstone or the grindstones. They are deeply buried under the coal measures and the carboniferous limestone, which prevent the atmospheric waters from percolating through them. The brine contained in these beds even rises into the superincumbent layers of the coal series, with the waters circulating below it, which all are under a certain hydrostatic pressure driving them upward to the surface.

From all the facts known, we must suppose that the salt exists in the strata as a solution, retained in the porous sand rock as in a sponge. Indications of solid rock salt have never been noticed in any of the salt wells of Saginaw district. I have stated that brine is found in almost every part of the State where the Waverly group can be reached by deep borings; in many localities a brine of equal strength with the best brines of Saginaw district has been found, without an attempt made to utilize it.

The manufacture of an article as cheap as salt depends not only upon the supply of good brine, but upon the expense of converting the brine into the merchantable article. In this respect, only large saw-mill establishments, with their immense mass of waste fuel, can enter into successful competition with the Eastern and Canadian salt works, with a fair chance of profit. In all other cases, its manufacture would hardly more than pay the expense of the fuel used for evaporation of the brine.

An exposition of the salt-manufacturing process, of chemical analyses of the salt brines of different localities, statistical records of the salt production in Michigan, etc., are given in an appendix elaborated by the State salt inspector, Dr. Garrigues, who kindly offered his help, and, being in the possession of all the facts relating to the matter, was far better qualified to make this part of the report than I could be, however well disposed.

CHAPTER IX.

CARBONIFEROUS LIMESTONE.

THE rock beds succeeding the Waverly group indicate important changes in the condition of things caused by the altered nature of the ocean sediments. The sandy material so much prevailing toward the end of the Waverly period begins to vanish; in place of arenaceous ledges interlaminated with the still continued shaly sediments, we find beds of limestone, and gradually the shales become narrower subordinate seams, until the upper part of the series is exclusively a limestone formation. The upper limestones resemble, in rock character and by their fossils, the upper division of the subcarboniferous limestones of the Mississippi valley; the lower part of the formation, which, locally, incloses heavy gypsum beds and attains a considerable thickness, is indubitably the equivalent of the inferior division of the western subcarboniferous limestones, but can not be exactly parallelized with a certain horizon of that series.

The lower gypsiferous part of the group has been described by Prof. A. Winchell under the name of *Michigan salt group.* I have previously stated that the salt brines of Michigan are derived from the subjacent Waverly group. Gypsum and salt are frequently found associated in other parts of the world, which circumstance probably induced Mr. Winchell to locate the salt in this higher rock series; but the fact of the occurrence of the salt brine in a lower position can not be denied on the ground of mere theoretical speculation. The carboniferous limestone series is very unequally developed on the peninsula; in some parts we find it scarcely represented, while in others the upper calcareous division is well developed, but not the lower gypsiferous beds, which seem to be of restricted local extent. The lowest beds of the group can be ob-

J. Bien, lith.

QUARRY OF THE GRANDVILLE PLASTER CO.

served in the vicinity of Caseville, on the farm of Mr. Klump, in Town. 18, Range 11, Sect. 18, where bluish drab-colored limestone beds of dolomitic, or partly of arenaceous character, repose on the upper coarse-grained sand-rock ledges of the Waverly group, similar to those exposed some miles east of the place, at Hat Point.

The limestones contain a species of Productus with very convex ventral valve, shallow, sinuated in the median line, and covered by from 40 to 50 fine sub-equal ribs, a Retzia similar to Retzia vera Hall, Terebratula (similar to Eudora), Spirifer Marionensis, and Spiriferina spinosa. At Oak Point, a short distance north of the locality just mentioned, fragments of similar fossiliferous, arenaceous lime rock are thrown out by the lake, and in its bottom, a short distance off shore, larger angular blocks of the same are found. Some of the slabs thrown ashore are almost totally composed of fragments of Brachiopod shells, besides other bivalves, Crinoid joints, stems of Bryozoa, etc. In dredging out the harbor at Caseville, rounded, strongly drift-worn limestone boulders of the same lithological character, and inclosing similar fossils, are brought up with the mud masses; among them are dark, bluish-colored, fine-grained limestones, crowded with shells of Lamellibranches, Myalina, Modiolopsis, Schizodus, with some Brachiopods, Rhynchonella, Retzia, Terebratula, etc., intermingled. Other calcareous rock boulders are of a slaty, laminated structure, of a dark, nearly black color, and filled with band-like, compressed stems, divided by regular constrictions into suborbicular segments. The bands seem originally to have been hollow utricules, with veinous, longitudinal carinæ; their substance is brownish, horn-like, and semi-translucid; most probably they are vegetable organisms. Other palæontologists to whom I showed the specimens suggest that they are related to Graptolites. A short time after I found these slaty boulders, whose position was not known to me, I discovered in the bed of Rifle River, at Island Rapids, Town. 21, R. 3, Sect. 28, the same rock in place; besides the stems mentioned, it contains a Productus and some shells resembling Modiolopsis. It forms the lowest beds in the rapids, visible to a thickness of 3 or 4 feet; above them are from 6 to 8 feet of limestones, of crystalline structure and dark gray color, full of Crinoid joints and shells or their fragments. Among them I recognized a large Aviculopecten, a Rhynchonella, Spiriferina spinosa, Productus, and quite numerous specimens of an annulated Orthoceras, resembling Orthoceras annulato-costatum of Meek and Worthen. The specimens are thickly incrusted with laminated strata of an amorphous limestone mass, which resemble the incrustation by a Stromatopora, but have no trace of organic structure. The siphon of the Orthoceras is central. An outcrop of the underlying Waverly sandstone, two miles above Island Rapids, has been previously described. The immediate contact of the superimposed limestones with the sand rock is not seen; the river bed in the interval is formed by drift, and the slopes of the hillsides bordering the river are all drift. Another locality where these lower beds of the carboniferous limestone series can be observed is on Cass River, 30 miles south of Caseville, in Town. 13, R. 11, Sect. 16. At the farm-house of Mr. W. H. Brown, situated close by the river bed, the water flows in rapids over the oblique edges of rock beds dipping at a moderate angle down stream. Here we find a coarse-grained whitish sand rock with small punctiform, ferruginous dots, and sometimes containing stems of Lepidodendron and other vegetable remains. Interstratified with them are greenish, micaceous sand-rock ledges and arenaceous, shaly seams. This sand rock is the equivalent of the Point of Barques sandstone, and forms, with few exceptions, the bed of Cass River for 6 or 8 miles up its course to Indian Rapids, which were mentioned when I gave a description of the outcrops of the Waverly group. Only a few steps below Mr. Brown's house, the sand-rock ledges are overlapped by a bluish argillaceous limestone of a dull, earthy fracture and moderately soft. It was from this rock that the Indians used to carve their smoking-pipes. It contains numerous nodular concretions of Zincblende, or Druse cavities filled with this mineral, or with Brownspar and Dolomitspar. The Zincblende is mistaken by the inhabitants for Galena, and the same mistake occurs on the old maps of surveyors, lead ore being indicated as occurring in the vicinity of Cass River. Stories are afloat according to which Indians used to gather large quantities of lead on Cass River and transform it at once into bullets, but I have little belief in such accounts, especially since I have failed to find any thing to substantiate them; the only mineral observed by me was Zincblende. This lime rock contains a moderate number of fossils, Productus, Spirifer Marionensis, Spiriferina spinosa, Syringopora ramulosa, and Orthoceras (annulato costatum?), the same as those found in the bed of Rifle River. Some vegetable remains can also be observed. The thickness of this limestone may reach 8 or 10 feet; above it is a seam of coarse-grained, drab-colored, rusty dolomite rock, which is crowded with casts of Spirifer Marionensis and various kinds of Lamellibranches, Terebratula Eudora? Retzia, and others. Purer calcareous beds, nearly all composed of shell fragments like those at Oak Point, are interstratified here, and higher we find blue argillaceo-arenaceous limestones, of an absorbent, porous character, which contain somewhat abundantly the Productus species mentioned several times before, but few of other fossils. A hard, calcareous bed with flint concretions overlies them, and then follow arenaceous shales and harder sand-rock ledges of a bright red, or yellowish green and red variegated color; some of the layers are in brecciated condition. The total thickness of the red layers may be 15 or 20 feet, of the entire section exposed in the river bed, 50 feet. Further down stream, the strata disappear under the drift, and no rock is exposed in the bed of Cass River until Tuscola village is reached, where small outcrops of the coal measures are observed. Up stream, between Brown's farm and Indian Rapids, by undulations of the rock beds the Waverly sandstone becomes sometimes bent downward into a synclinal trough, and the intermediate depression is filled out with the higher fossiliferous limestones, containing Zincblende concretions.

Next above the described rock series the horizon of the gypsum deposits begins, but a direct superposition of the strata is nowhere observed, and the gypsum, as I have intimated before, is only found in local deposits, many places on the same geological level with these bearing no signs of it whatever. The largest exposures of the gypsum formation are found on the shore of Lake Huron, at Alabaster Point, where beds of pure gypsum, covered by only a few feet of drift, lie quite near the surface. The gypsum beds are deeply eroded by the solvent action of atmospheric waters; during the glacier time, also, much of the soft rock became destroyed, or intersected by large, deep grooves which are now filled up with drift material. The practical quarryman in search of gypsum is guided in his explorations by certain surface indications.

The surface in those places where the gypsum is close under it is full of small pot-holes and intermediate hillocks, and he knows by experience that the depressions indicate places where the superficial gypsum beds have been dissolved, or carried away by some cause, while in the hillocks he is always sure to find a well-preserved mass. In the quarries of Messrs. Smith, Bullard & Co., the superficial gypsum bed is 15 feet thick; large masses of white or rose-colored granular gypsum and smaller fragments of the same pure substance are cemented together by seams and veins of gray argillaceous gypsum into one solid, compact bed, variegated and mottled in some spots like castile soap, or of much coarser brecciated structure where the larger masses of pure gypsum are cemented. Below the gypsum bed follow calcareo-arenaceous, thinly laminated flagstones, and shale beds of dark greenish drab-color, seen uncovered in a thickness of about 6 feet. The flagstones are very fossiliferous; particularly abundant is a Myalina, next so are Allorisma, Aviculopecten, Edmondia, Retzia globosa, and Spiriferina spinosa. The owners of the quarry have bored to the depth of 20 feet below its bottom, and have found only a few feet down another very thick gypsum bed, which for the present is not opened. About 4 miles south of Alabaster Point, the gypsum formations rise in bluffs along the shore to the height of about 25 feet. The strata in question seem to be next above the gypsum of the Alabaster Point quarries. Lowest, at the water level, heavy, somewhat concretionary masses of gypsum project; above them follow about 10 feet of soft green shales full of small nodular concretions of gypsum. The shales are covered by an arenaceo-calcareous rock, in beds of from 4 to 6 inches in thickness, which in one place where gypsum has been quarried is directly covered by drift masses, the surface of the ledges being plainly drift-marked in a direction from northeast to southwest. Only a few steps further south from this locality, these upper drift-marked ledges are overlaid by from 6 to 8 feet of arenaceous shales, or by soft greenish sandstones of discordant stratification, and frequently ripple-marked; and on them a seam of brittle limestone 15 inches or 2 feet thick, with many flint concretions, forms the top of the bluffs. This calcareous rock with flint nodules forms the surface rock under the drift, extending from here down to White Rock Point, where a number of additional light-colored limestone beds are found connected with it, and laid open in a few limited escarpments along the lake shore. Next above these limestones of White Rock Point follow the limestones of Aux Grees Point; but a direct contact between the beds is not seen, the interval from White Rock Point to Point Aux Grees being filled by a sand beach, and the country back from the shore being all deeply drift-covered.

Gypsum beds are frequently penetrated in boring for salt in Saginaw valley, but from these not much is to be learned of the detailed structure of the gypsum formation, and the limits of this horizon, either upward or downward, are not clearly recognizable. In some of the bore-holes of Saginaw valley, no gypsum beds were found at all, but the presence of gypsum within the rock beds is perceived in these wells notwithstanding, by the large quantity of gypsum which the water holds in solution. The manufacturers have to carefully close off from their pipes the water streams coming from the gypsiferous horizon, as it will incrust their cavities in a very short time and cause obstructions. In the salt wells of Kawkalin, the gypsum is struck at a depth of 400 feet from the surface. In some wells of Bay City the gypsum horizon is about 700 feet below the surface. Further south, in Blackmar's salt well, near Bridgeport, and in the borings at Flint, Lansing, etc., no gypsum beds were found.

West of Alabaster Point, for a distance of 30 miles the gypsum formation can be found near the surface on all the head branches of Aux Grees River. In Town. 21, R. 5, Sect. 20, the shales inclosing gypsum beds are seen in the bed of Aux Grees River and on its banks. Shales of blue or greenish color, interstratified with calcareo-arenaceous seams, inclose large concretionary masses of pure white, rose, or salmon-colored granular gypsum, in quantities which would invite to mining enterprises, but for the fact that gypsum has a limited demand, and that the necessary supply can be much more cheaply quarried in the gypsum beds near the shore, which, from present appearances, are not likely to be exhausted for a great many years to come. Some miles northeast from this latter spot, in Town. 21, R. 5, Sect. 12, is another similar exposure of rich gypsum deposits, and numerous smaller exposures are noticed in the beds of creeks between that locality and the lake. In the central part of the peninsula, along the supposed northern division between the coal field and the Waverly group, no rock exposures whatever are known; likewise along the same geological belt arching across the south part of the peninsula, no gypsum deposits have ever been discovered, but on the western edge of the belt we meet again with large gypsum deposits in the vicinity of Grand River. The gypsum formation is found close under the drift extending from the southern limits of the city line of Grand Rapids to within a mile or more south of the village of Grandville, covering in all about 6 or 8 square miles, and found everywhere over that space within a distance of not more than 50 feet from the surface. Some spots there may be found where the gypsum beds have been destroyed during the drift period, but, as a rule, it may be with safety looked for everywhere in the district. Seven gypsum quarries are now in operation in the vicinity of Grand Rapids, situated on both sides of Grand River, and if the demand for gypsum were to increase tenfold, there would still be no lack of material.

In most of the quarries, a bed of pure gypsum much cut up by erosions is found close under the drift; below that bed are dark gray shales with seams of argillaceous limestones and arenaceous beds, amounting to various thicknesses, in different localities; then follows a gypsum bed from 8 to 12 feet in thickness, and under it are again shales and limestone beds with thin seams of gypsum.

In the plaster quarries of the Grand Rapids Plaster Co., on the west side of Grand River, the upper layers in the bluff are soft arenaceous shales, interlaminated with seams of limestone and arenaceous flagstones, having an abundance of globular or lenticular nodules of rose-colored granular gypsum, as well as seams of a brown gypsum, in large, columnar crystals, together with thin seams of a perfectly colorless, translucid selenite. At the base of the bluffs, two thick beds of gypsum project, partly composed of pure white or reddish granular gypsum with gray, veinous, mottled seams; partly of a more impure brecciated mass of gypsum and gray limestone cemented together, which latter, if the limestone is mingled in undue proportion, has to be thrown aside as waste rock. In this locality, the gypsum is mined by driving subterranean galleries into the bluff. A view of the mine is represented in the plate accompanying this report. A large plaster mill is erected close to the mine, where the impurer gypsum is ground for agricultural purposes, the purer rock being selected and ground separately for conversion into plaster-of-paris, while the finer granular masses are occasionally used for ornamental purposes, such as the

J. Bien, lith.

QUARRY OF THE GRAND RAPIDS PLASTER CO.

cutting of it into vases, etc., and polishing it. The rest of the quarries are worked in the ordinary style of stone quarries. In the Grandville quarries, of the Grand Rapids Plaster Co., we find highest a series of argillaceous, drab-colored, easy weathering limestones with seams of shale, which, locally, are found to be quite fossiliferous, containing several forms of Lamellibranch shells, Schizodus, thick-shelled, large Nuculas, and other forms; Brachiopods, such as Chonetes, and an Orthoceratite, Crinoid stems, Bryozoa, etc., are also found; but in particular, Fish remains in somewhat worn condition are abundant. Scales, teeth, dorsal spines, and numerous coprolites, mixed with water-worn pieces of shale, sandstone, and quartz pebbles, and cemented by carbonate of lime, compose the fossiliferous seams. The non-fossiliferous portions of this rock, which, on chemical analysis, gave,

Carbonate of lime	48
" magnesia	27
Hydrate of iron oxide and alumina	4
Argillaceous residue	18
	97

might perhaps be converted into hydraulic cement. Below these upper strata a white gypsum bed, a few feet in thickness, follows, which in some places lies directly under the drift, and is very much eroded and cut up into isolated blocks, quite surrounded by drift material. The next lower strata, amounting to about 4 feet, are argillaceous limestones and soft, dark gray shales, which rest on a heavy bed of gypsum from 8 to 12 feet in thickness. The lowest strata seen in the quarry are again limestones and dark shales with thin seams of white gypsum. In the lately opened Wyoming Plaster quarries, about half a mile northwest of the Grandville Plaster quarry, 25 feet of rock beds are uncovered. First come about 8 feet of drift, then 3 feet of a calcareous laminated sand rock with purer limestone seams of a greenish-gray color; next lower is a 5-foot bed of white gypsum, then calcareous sand rock and dark bluish shales, amounting to 7 or 8 feet; lowest is a plaster bed, already penetrated to a depth of 17 feet without having reached its limit. The lime and sand-rock beds are very plainly ripple-marked, and on some of the slabs are the relief casts of large, irregularly reticulated sun cracks; their surface is covered by thin laminæ of colorless, translucid selenite.

Fossils I could not find in this quarry, except some small fragments of the before-mentioned water-worn fish-bones. The thickness of the gypsiferous rock series can not be estimated from the exposures in the quarries; by borings it has been ascertained to be about 160 feet. In an artesian well sunk at the principal business place of the city, in Mr. Powell's block, a lime rock 36 feet in thickness was first penetrated under the drift; then followed an alternation of shales, gypsum beds, and lime-rock ledges, to a depth of 204 feet from the surface. The bottom of the well is in sand rock, and a fine stream of pleasant potable mineral water discharges from the tubing to refresh the thirsty. A more detailed account of a boring made in Beyrich's brewery to a depth of 236 feet may give an idea of the sequence of rock beds in the vicinity of Grand Rapids:

Drift	35 ft.	
Limestone	1 "	6 in.
Blue shales	7 "	
Gypsum	1 "	6 "
Blue shales	6 "	6 "
Flinty rock (?)	3 "	6 "
Shale, soft	7 "	
Blue shale, harder	1 "	
Shale, soft	7 "	6 "
Flint	2 "	6 "
Shale	6 "	6 "
Pyritous rock	1 "	6 "
Shale	7 "	6 "
Pyritous rock	1 "	6 "
Shale	11 "	
Pyritous rock	1 "	
Shale	2 "	6 "
Pyritous rock	2 "	
Shale	8 "	
Pyritous rock	2 "	6 "
Sand rock	3 "	4 "
Shale	4 "	

Sand rock	5 ft.	2 in.
Gypsum	5 "	
Sand rock		6 "
Shale	2 "	6 "
Gypsum	5 "	
Blue shale	4 "	6 "
Hard, flinty rock		6 "
Gypsum	6 "	
Shale, blue	4 "	6 "
Pyritous rock	8 "	
White sand rock	55 "	
Blue shale	6 "	
Total	236 "	

There is an ample flow of mineral water from this spring, quite as pleasant to drink as that from Mr. Powell's well, but it is not a water fit for brewing purposes, to supply which the boring was originally intended.

The upper calcareous division of the carboniferous limestone series is, at Grand Rapids, directly superimposed on the gypsiferous shale formation; the beds of transition from one to the other could formerly be seen in the river at the foot of the rapids, but at present all that part is filled up and covered over with large buildings.

The approximate thickness of the limestones at Grand Rapids is 50 or 60 feet; the lowest beds are in streaks mingled with sand granules or alternating with thin seams of sand rock; the higher are free of arenaceous admixture, and are stratified in moderately thick beds, which contain some fossils and many druse cavities filled with brown-colored spar crystals. Most observable among the fossils are large fish-teeth, various forms of Fenestella, Polypora, Trematopora, Lithostrotion mamillare, and a few Brachiopods. In a few quarries, close to the west side of the river, these strata can be seen. Formerly they were more extensively exposed in the river bed and in the banks on the east side, but by the erection of dams across the river and of buildings along its sides, nearly all are now hidden from observation. Next above these massive beds, which serve a good purpose as a building material for rough walls, follow thinner-bedded limestones interlaminated with calcareous shales. These are uncovered in some old quarries not far from the Detroit and Milwaukee Railroad depot, and are used for lime-burning; the fossils inclosed are Allorisma clavata, Productus Flemmingii, Lithostrotion proliferum, Lithostrotion mamillare, numerous Bryozoa, Phillipsia, and a few others. In the river bed west of the Milwaukee depot, other limestone ledges of a reddish color and of silicious character overlie the former, but the river is at present rarely low enough to allow of their being seen. North of Grand Rapids the limestone formation is soon lost under the heavy drift masses; also eastward, through the towns of Ada and Cascade, all is covered by drift, but the numerous limestone fragments intermingled with the drift make it probable that the formation underlies these towns. Westward from Grand Rapids the sand-rock ledges of the Waverly group form the surface rock under the drift, and are denuded in a few limited spots. The supposed extension of the carboniferous limestone belt passes northward over Newaygos, curves diagonally through Osceola County, and, taking an eastern direction near the second correction line, strikes with a curve southeastward toward the north shore of Saginaw Bay. The first outcrops of the limestone along this described course are found at the headwaters of Rifle and Aux Grees rivers, whence they continue to the lake shore. The rest of the interval exhibits no rock ledges of any kind, and the drift is so deep that erosions by rivers, or ordinary wells or other artificial excavations never reach the underlying older strata.

Southward from Grand Rapids the opportunities for following the carboniferous limestone belt are not more favorable than to the northward; we find it first denuded at Bellevue, 60 miles southeast of Grand Rapids. Borings at Middleville, Hastings, and other places, lying in the supposed direction of the limestone belt, did not reach to the rock beds at a depth of over 100 feet. At Bellevue, over a space of about 6 square miles, the carboniferous limestone is at the surface, or covered only by drift deposits of moderate thickness. In the bed of Battle Creek, and in a railroad cut south of Bellevue village, we find as the lowest strata of the exposures a greenish-white sand rock of middling fine grain, partly soft and friable by pressure with the fingers, partly hard, and firmly cemented by an abundance of sparry calcareous material. Such calcareous sand rock reflects the light from its fractured surfaces in the same manner as if they were the fissure plains of a crystal or of innumerable parallel crystals; its chemical composition is 69 per cent of quartz with 30 per cent carbonate of lime. Upward in the series the arenaceous beds are gradually replaced by pure limestones, but thin seams of quartz sand are yet occasionally wedged in between the calcareous layers. Not unfrequently the strata of this horizon are in brecciated condition; locally they are found to be very fossiliferous—numerous Fish-teeth (Helodus, Cladodus, etc.), Productus Flemmingii, Bellerophon sublævis, Zaphrentis spinulosa, Fenestella, Polypora, and Trematopora being the forms noticed. The next higher strata are pure, light-colored limestones with smooth, conchoidal fracture, in beds of variable thickness, interlaminated with concretionary seams of Hornstone; fossils are generally not very abundant, but certain seams are crowded with them over widely extended surfaces. The stems of Lithostrotion proliferum, also Syringopora ramulosa, Allorisma clavata, and various Bryozoa, are not uncommon. The numerous quarries of Bellevue are opened in these beds, which reach 8 or 10 feet in thickness. Their chemical composition is:

Carbonate of lime	96
" magnesia	1.0
Hydrate of iron oxide	0.5
Insoluble residue	1.5

In the quarries, we observe above these limestones a stratum of a brown ferruginous dolomite with dull, earthy fracture, and about 2 feet in thickness, and following next to it about 3 or 4 feet of light-colored limestones identical in appearance with the beds below. Higher still is another belt of brown, ferruginous dolomite rock, about one foot in thickness, and either in continuous layers wedging out at both ends, or in seams of irregularly-shaped septaria surrounded by calcareous shale. A few feet of light-colored, thin-bedded lime rock deposited on top of the brown concretionary seam are the highest strata noticed.

The brown dolomite rock is composed of

Carbonate of lime	56
" magnesia	23
Iron oxide hydrate, with some alumina	5.5
Silicious residue	9.0

8

The total thickness of the strata exposed at Bellevue I estimate to be about 50 or 60 feet. The rock is generally quarried for lime-burning; as a building-stone it is used in the vicinity, and large quantities of it have been used in the construction of the foundation for the State House at Lansing. The rock was broken into fragments, and filled into the bottom of the ditches for the foundation, over which a liquid hydraulic cement was poured. South of Bellevue, along the valley of Battle Creek, the rock soon disappears from sight; at the junction of the creek with Kalamazoo River, the beds of the Waverly group are near the surface, and between Bellevue and Battle Creek outcrops of the gypsum formation should appear in the bed of Battle Creek, but no indications of this mineral have ever been found there.

The trend of the formation is to the southeast; travelling in this direction, the first indications of the carboniferous limestone are found again some miles north of Albion, and from there across the centre of Jackson County many isolated patches of the limestone are met with. It is often impossible to determine the exact stratigraphical relations of these outcrops to the surrounding sand rock and shale strata of the coal measures; the beds have been evidently considerably disturbed during the drift period, segments of hills having been carried away by the advancing stream of drift masses from their original resting-place, and deposited, as they are now found, in more or less uptilted, irregular position inclosed within the drift, but with the relative stratigraphical order of the beds to one another fully preserved. Several such large masses of carboniferous limestone within the drift are intersected by the Michigan Central Railroad in the interval between Albion and Jackson. A short distance northeast of Parma village the carboniferous limestone underlies quite an extensive area, and several quarries were once worked in it. The rock is of dark-bluish color, full of sparry and silicious veins; it contains Allorisma clavata, Crinoid joints, etc. As a building-stone it has little value, nor is it good for lime-burning, having too great an admixture of silicious matter. Above the blue lime rock is a brown, cellulose dolomite rock equivalent with the brown dolomitic seams of the Bellevue quarries; its composition is,

Carbonate of lime	63.7
" magnesia	11.4
Hydrated iron oxide and alumina	18.4
Silicious residue	2.9

South of Parma, in the township of Spring Arbor, the carboniferous limestone has many outcrops; one is on Mr. Roberts's farm, Sect. 17, where a quarry was opened forty years ago by the present owner for the purpose of burning lime, which in those early days of settlement was a great desideratum and found a ready sale. The quarries are on the slope of a hill facing south. Lowest is a sand rock of light greenish color and moderately fine-grained; part of it is soft and porous, while other beds are rendered very compact through an abundance of calcareous cement. In alternation with the sand rock are soft, plastic, light-colored shales or arenaceous shales. Above the sand rock, which in the upper ledges changes into a sandy limestone, beds of a pure lime rock follow with a thickness of from 8 to 10 feet; some of the beds are of crystalline structure; others have a smooth, conchoidal fracture, and are often in brecciated condition, re-cemented by veins of calcspar. On top, the brown dolomite, so often mentioned before, is found again. Fossils are quite rare in this locality. Along the wagon-road from the quarries to Jackson, several other outcrops of the carboniferous limestone are passed by within the limits of Spring Arbor township. On Mr. Shoemaker's land, in Summit township, 3 miles south of Jackson, another exposure of the carboniferous limestone can be observed. At the foot of a hill sloping toward a marshy flat land, there is a rather coarse-grained, whitish-green sand rock containing flint concretions, and cemented hard by calcareous matter. Above it are beds, still arenaceous, which should be classed as limestones; they are partially in brecciated condition, inclosing within an arenaceous, re-cemented lime-rock mass, pure limestone fragments with smooth, conchoidal fracture. Still higher beds are a purer lime rock, not brecciated, with some flint nodules, and crowning the section we find again 4 or 5 feet of the brown, ferruginous dolomite rock, partly of cellulose structure, easily decaying into angular fragments of a rough, earthy surface. The purer beds of the limestone contain,

Carbonate of lime	94	per cent.
" magnesia	1	"
Iron	1	"
Quartz sand	4	"

The entire section comprises about 18 feet of strata. North of Jackson, on Portage River, about a mile east of its entry into Grand River, the carboniferous limestone is found on top of a hill, the southern slope of which is formed by steeply inclined sand rock and shale beds, with seams of coal. Their dip is southward.

The lowest beds of limestone exposed are of a nodular, brecciated character, composed of rounded lumps of a light-colored, smooth fracturing limestone, with seams of green-colored harder and softer shaly substance filling the interstices; the higher beds are a smooth, compact, brittle lime rock of light color, also in shattered condition, and full of stylolithic segregations. Fossils are rare; sometimes a Productus, Allorisma clavata, Bellerophon sublævis, or a species of Rhynchonella, is inclosed. The strata seen in the quarries reach a thickness of 15 feet. Mr. Wright, the owner of one of the quarries, drilled a hole within its limits to a depth of 53 feet. First, 9 feet of the upper lime rock in the quarries were penetrated, then 5 or 6 feet of the greenish, brecciated lime rock, followed by 2 or 3 feet of a reddish-colored limestone. Below came 8 or 10 feet of hard, calcareous sand rock, and, lowest, a coarse, soft sandstone. Only about 30 steps from this bore-hole, across the road, a shaft of 25 feet in depth was dug, which first went through highly inclined black shales, and then through sand rock belonging to the coal measures.

On the opposite, south side of Portage River, the sloping hillside over which the road to Jackson leads is formed by coarse-grained, soft sandstone similar to the sandstone of the Jackson coal mines. Near the top, greenish calcareous sand rock, with seams of greenish shale, is seen in the road ditches, and right above it are 5 feet of well-stratified limestones with delicate laminar striation resembling a Stromatopora, but apparently not of organic origin. The same limestone beds are pervaded by numerous vertical flexuose channels, laterally anastomosing, and much resembling moulds formed around the clustered stems of a Syringopora. Some of the cavities were filled with spar, but I could not discover organic structure. The limestone of Portage River makes an excellent white lime; its composition is,

Carbonate of lime	96.9
" magnesia	1.0
Alumina and iron	0.7
Insoluble residue	1.4
	99.0

North of Portage River, along the eastern margins of the central coal field, no outcrops of the carboniferous limestone are known. South of Saginaw district, through borings made along this line, or more toward the centre of the peninsula, the carboniferous limestone series is found very poorly represented, and frequently seems to be altogether missing.

At Lansing, many deep borings have been sunk, one to a depth of 1400 feet, and one in the yard of the Lansing Hotel to a depth of 740 feet, of neither of which was I able to get a record. Another well in the State Reform School, having a depth of 506 feet, was carefully recorded; but the identification of rocks by comminuted, sand-like particles, as they are brought up by the sand pumps, is so difficult that one can rarely get from the well-borers, who generally keep such records, names appropriate to the various formations encountered. Contemplating such a record, with the intent to form an idea of the exact nature of the superimposed rock series, one is often disposed to give up in despair, if he is over-scrupulous to give rein to his imagination, or to arrange things to suit his own notions. The register of the boring at the Reform School reads as follows:

Drift (alternations of clay, sand, gravel and boulders)	101 ft.
Soft sand rock	3 "
Hard fire-clay	4 "
Soft, white sand rock	13 "
Soft, sandy fire-clay	15 "
Hard sand rock	119 "
Hard fire-clay, alternating with beds of sand rock variable in color from whitish to blue.	64 "
Cherty lime	1 "

Gray lime....................................	4 ft.
Sandy fire-clay mixed with seams of harder rock	51 "
Soft sand rock..............................	37 "
Hard gray limestone.......................	2 "
Soft white sand rock.......................	15 "
Blue limestone..............................	1 "
White fire-clay..............................	1 "
Sand rock....................................	4 "
Fire-clay with iron pyrites.................	50 "
Soft sand rock..............................	5 "
Blue limestone..............................	16 " 6 in.

In deep borings made at Flint, no rocks similar to the carboniferous limestones have been found, neither does the record of Blackmar's salt well, south of Bridgeport, say any thing of limestone beds perforated; but in nearly all the boring records of Saginaw and Bay City, the horizon of the carboniferous limestones is plainly discernible. In the Saginaw Bay district, we find fine, natural exposures of the carboniferous limestones, northward on the branches of Rifle and Aux Grees rivers.

If we follow Aux Grees River from the point where I have described the gypsum beds (in Town. 21, R. 5, Sect. 20), upward to Sect. 30 of the same township, we find the creek running over arenaceous limestone ledges, and in its banks about 12 feet of limestone strata are seen above the water-line. The lower arenaceous limestones are interstratified with dark, blackish shales. One of the lower beds is also pervaded by the Syringopora-like ramifications of cherty substance which I have described in the limestones found north of Jackson, on Portage River; here also no organic structure can be discovered. The upper portions of the ledges in the outcrop are light-colored, smooth-fracturing limestones, containing many hornstone concretions, and of fossils, an abundance of Allorisma clavata, with other species, such as Productus Flemmingii, Syringopora ramulosa, Zaphrentis spinulosa, and various forms of Fenestella. A chain of outcrops of these limestones extends between the parallel streams, Rifle and Aux Grees, to Point Aux Grees. This point is a low land-tongue of not over 10 feet elevation above the lake level. On both sides for the distance of a mile it is lined with low cliffs of calcareous sand-rock ledges, with flint nodules, the upper, more limestone-like arenaceous beds of which contain Zaphrentis spinulosa, Lithostrotion proliferum, Syringopora ramulosa, and Productus Flemmingii. Above the arenaceous beds are 6 or 8 feet of light-colored brittle limestones with an abundance of flint nodules, interlaminated with thin seams of greenish shales. The limestones contain, besides the fossils mentioned, Fenestellas and other Bryozoa. In former years the limestone was quarried there, but at present the place is abandoned. The Charity Islands are composed of the same rock beds as Point Aux Grees. On the largest of them, on which a lighthouse is built, the northeast shore presents the best exposures. The bluffs are nowhere over 8 feet high, being generally lower. One place exhibits a very interesting example of discordant stratification. The lowest beds, a light-colored, ripple-marked, calcareous sand rock, project in a gentle arch about one foot above the water level, and from both sides higher strata dip away from the convexity at a sharp angle, resembling the anticlinal position of an uplift, with about 50 feet of rock beds on each side of the arch, in an imbricated order, and having at their projecting ends about the same level. The higher ledges of this anticlinal series are still arenaceous, but the lime prevails, and for them the name of lime rock is more appropriate than that of sand rock. They contain flint concretions, Zaphrentis spinulosa and Lithostrotion proliferum, and the surface of nearly all of them is ripple-marked. Over the surface of this anticlinal series, horizontal limestone ledges are deposited in obvious discordance with the subjacent ones. These upper ledges are a pure lime rock, free of sand, but inclosing numerous flint nodules, and interlaminated with thin seams of calcareous shale. Lithostrotion proliferum, Syringopora ramulosa, Fenestella, Polypora, Productus Flemmingii, Allorisma clavata, and Fish-teeth are the usual fossils, but are not found in great abundance. The thickness of these upper horizontal beds is about 8 feet. Higher strata are not observed on the island ; its west side is low, marshy, and covered with loose rock débris and sand. The subjoined sketch illustrates the irregularity of stratification which I have just descrbed :

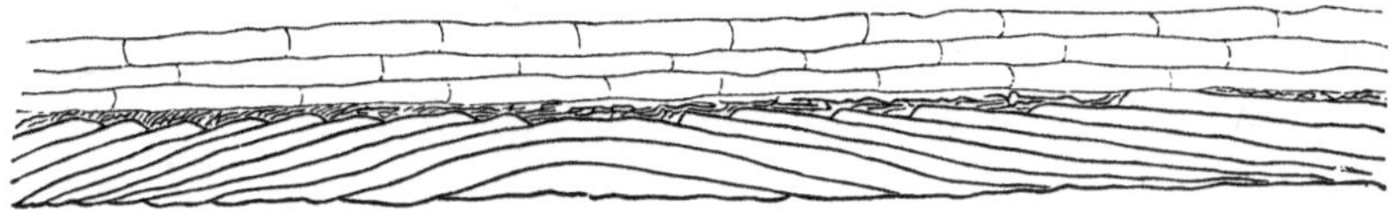

The most complete exposure of the carboniferous limestones is seen on Wild Fowl Bay, 6 or 8 miles southwest of Caseville. We find on the shore there, below the water level and emerging above it, a greenish-white calcareous sand rock, visible in a thickness of 4 or 5 feet. Next above is a layer of gray limestone with cherty nodules, about 1 foot in thickness, overlaid by a thin seam of shale; then a 6-inch bed of delicately laminated limestone, and a seam of sand rock of a few inches; on it lie several somewhat differing ledges of an arenaceous limestone of laminated structure, amounting to 2 feet, upon which follow in the order given, an 8-inch layer of dark gray bituminous limestone with smooth fracture, a blackish, thinly laminated calcareous shale, 2 feet thick, full of scales, teeth, and bones of small fishes, besides a species of Cypris, or Cythere, and a dark gray limestone of smooth, conchoidal fracture, in three 1-foot beds, of which the upper one is pervaded by Syringopora-like, flexuose, anastomosing channels, similar to those already described as existing in several outcrops in other localities. The section is terminated by about 10 feet of light-colored arenaceous limestones, with an alternation of purer calcareous and prevalently sandy seams. These upper beds contain many fossils, Zaphrentis spinulosa, Lithostrotion proliferum, Syringopora ramulosa, various forms of Fenestella, Polypora, etc., Productus, Allorisma clavata, and Fish-teeth (Cladodus, Helodus). The higher levels of the slope are covered by drift. A mile east from the shore, on the farm of Mr. Crawford, and on the adjoining lands forming the plateau of a lake terrace, a series of lime-rock ledges is uncovered, which appear to be the next higher strata to the section just described. The beds are light-colored, pure limestones, occasionally interstratified with a thin seam of sand rock; certain seams are full of hornstone concretions, while others are quite free of them. Fossils are also very unequally distributed, being rare in some of the layers, while others are crowded with silicified corals, Lithostrotion proliferum, and Lithostrotion mamillare, which are also found loose, strewn about the fields in immense numbers and beautifully preserved.

The highest layers found on this plateau are brown, ferruginous, cellulose dolomites of a rough, earthy fracture, irregularly traversed by veins of quartz or calcspar. Further east, the rock ledges disappear under heavy drift masses. The purer ledges of the limestone on Crawford's farm have been used for lime-burning, but at present the kilns lie idle. The islands of Saginaw Bay, lying in front of Wild Fowl Bay, are all underlaid by this limestone formation. On several of them, particularly on Mr. Heinzelman's Island, quarries are opened which provide the cities along Saginaw River with the necessary stone for foundation walls and like purposes. To supply a local demand, a portion is converted into lime.

CHAPTER X.

COAL MEASURES.

In regular order of succession, the carboniferous limestone formation is followed by a complex of sandstone and shale deposits with intermediate seams of coal, termed *coal measures*.

This series occupies the central portion of the Lower Peninsula, and is supposed to cover about one fifth part of its entire surface; but over its greater extent the formation is hidden by drift deposits, and its limits on the north and west sides of the basin are rather taken for granted than known. The thickness of the formation could be ascertained in a few localities only; it seems in Michigan not to exceed 300 feet, and is often less—a thickness which, compared with the development of the coal measures in our neighboring States, Ohio and Illinois, is very insignificant. In proportion to the thickness of the formation is also that of the inclosed seams of coal, of which we generally find only one of sufficient thickness for mining enterprises, while our neighbors can boast of six or seven productive beds, besides a number of smaller intermediate seams not taken into account.

The approximate limits of the coal measures on the peninsula are within a line drawn from Sebawing, on Saginaw Bay, toward Holly, in the south part of Genesee County, and from there prolongated in a southwesterly curve to Jackson. From Jackson the line goes west, passing a few miles north of Albion; it then strikes northwest, passing some distance east of Bellevue, to Hastings, whence, northward, the extent of the formation is only guessed at. The western edge of the coal measures is supposed to intersect the Detroit and Milwaukee Railroad line near Lowell, thence to go north, touching Big Rapids, and from there to run in a northeastern curve, diagonally through Osceola County and the northwest corner of St. Clair County. The line does not seem to transgress the second correction line; it goes parallel with it along the northern end of Gladwin County, from which point the formation is again known through actual outcrops; it enters the northwest corner of Bay County, and extends in a southeast direction toward the mouth of Rifle River, striking the shore of Saginaw Bay. The rim of the formation is a few miles north of the Rifle River valley.

The first discovery of coal in Michigan was made in the vicinity of Jackson, situated near the southern rim of the coal field. The formation is there, in various places, naturally exposed, and is found, in digging cellars or wells within the city limits, under the cover of only a few feet of drift.

A coarse-grained, whitish sandstone is the highest of the rock series. The east side of Grand River presents various bluffs of this sand rock, in the northern part of the city. Walker's coal mine is located in one of these, and its lately erected buildings are closely attached to the vertical rock walls from which the material for their erection was quarried. A short distance south of the coal mines is the Michigan State Prison, which stands on the sand-rock ledges of the coal measures. Its walls are built of the same material, dug out from the spot, or from others in close proximity to it.

This upper sand rock has an approximate thickness of 30 feet. By an undulation of the strata, some shale beds below the sandstone come to the surface in the interval between the State Prison and Walker's coal mine, but this is the greatest depth to which natural sections go; the deeper beds are only known by artificial borings, of which I will enumerate some, communicated to me by Mr. Walker, and by other parties. The shaft of Walker's coal mine is 54 feet deep, commencing in sand rock 26 feet, followed by shale beds with kidney-ore nodules, 17 feet; bituminous coal, 4 feet; fire-clay, 7 feet. Below the shaft an excavation to a further depth of 30 feet went through nothing but shales and arenaceous rock seams. Total depth of excavation, 84 feet.

Half a mile east of Walker's mine is Porter and Hubert's mine, the shaft of which, 64 feet deep, commences in drift 11 feet in thickness, followed by,

Sandstone, coarse, whitish	30 ft.
Shale, dark	17 "
Coal	4 "

Fire-clay opened for several feet.

Mr. Walker records of a boring made a short distance north of his coal mine, near the pottery works, the following series of rock beds in descending order:

Sandstone	20 ft.
Sandy fire-clay	2 "
Hard shale	2 "
Hard sandstone	2 "
Soft greenish shale	2 "
Sand rock, hard	6 in.
Green shale	2 "
Sandstone, hard	8 "
Sandstone and shale	2 "
Black shale	3 "
Gray fire-clay	5 "
Bluish fire-clay	7 "
Cherty sandstone	3 "
Black shale	7 "
Coal, hard	8 in.
Coal, soft	3 " 6 "
Fire-clay, black and white	8 " 6 "
Gray chert rock	2 " 6 "
Fire-clay	9 " 1 "
Black shale and chert	10 " 6 "
Brown shales with kidney ore	11 " 6 "
Hard white sandstone	41 "

Other test-borings made on the land of the Coal Mining Company of Jackson, as recorded by Mr. Walker, are:

No. 1 begins below the sand rock:

Black shale with kidney ore	12 ft.
Fire-clay	6 "
Black shale	13 "
Coal, bituminous	4 "

No. 2:

Black shale	8 ft.
Fire-clay	5 "
Black shale	9 "
Coal	4 " 6 in.

Carbonaceous shales, sand rock, and iron pyrites below.

No. 3:

Sandstone	2 ft. 6 in.
Fire-clay	5 " 6 "
Black shale	16 "
Coal	4 " 6 "

Carbonaceous shales and sandstone as in No. 2.

No. 4, situated close to the State Prison ground:

Sand rock	27 ft.
Dark shale	2 " 10 in.
Coal	2 " 6 "
Slaty coal	8 "

Sand rock below.

No. 5, behind the chemical works:

Drift	11 ft.
Sandstone	30 "
Black shale	13 "
Coal	4 " 6 in.
Coal, poor	9 "

Hard sand rock at bottom of boring.

No. 6:

Drift	2 ft.
Sandstone	16 "
Coal	2 "

No. 7:

Drift	4 ft.
Sandstone	27 "
Black arenaceous shale	16 "
Black shale	2 " 10 in.
Coal	4 "

No. 8:

Sandstone	23 ft.
Black shale	8 "
Hard rock with pyrites	6 "
Black shale	10 "
Coal	4 "

No. 9 is a boring made on the west side of Grand River, in the hillside opposite the coal-mine locality.

Drift	6 ft.	
Sandstone	27 "	
Conglomeratic sandstone	2 "	
Bituminous shale		8 in.
Small coal seam.		
Soft black shale	2 "	
Black shale with kidney ore	19 "	
Bituminous coal	1 "	
Fire-clay		8 "
Fine-grained sandstone	3 "	
Black shale	1 "	6 "
Fire-clay	7 "	
Sandstone and shale alternating	40 "	

The shaft of the Woodville mine, 3 miles west of Jackson, intersects,

Drift	12 ft.
Sandstone	30 "
Dark shale	43 "
Coal	4 "
Shales	3 "

This mine is now abandoned.

We see, by a comparison of these sections, many minor differences in the sequence and thicknesses of the strata, but a general conformity conspicuous throughout. The highest position is always taken by a light-colored, coarse-grained sand rock of from 25 to 30 feet in thickness; below it, invariably, shales or alternations of sandy fire-clays with shales are found, in a maximum thickness of 40 feet, but usually in much thinner beds. Next a bed of coal between 3 and 4 feet in thickness follows in almost every one of the localities, and under it are arenaceous shales or sand rock. In the exposures at Jackson, the upper sandstone is frequently found in thick, tolerably compact beds, which are useful in supplying building-stones; other beds are thinly laminated, of irregular, discordant stratification, often soft and friable between the fingers. Between the harder solid ledges conglomeratic seams are frequently wedged in, or kidney ore and pyritous masses are disseminated; locally the ledges are colored a dark chocolate brown by a ferruginous cement uniting the quartz granules. Occasionally, also, a narrow coal seam can be observed, and vegetable remains, such as Calamites, are not uncommon. In an outcrop east of the Jackson Pottery the sand rock is locally bent into serpentine curves, as if the ledges had been corrugated by some force pushing sideways on them before they were fully indurated. The outcrop is capped by heavy masses of boulder drift and clay, and at the foot of the sand rock the clay pits of the pottery are opened.

The shale beds below the sand rock are usually of a dark, blackish, silky, shining color, partly hard and slate-like, partly soft and very fissile. They contain a species of Lingula, and often also compressed shells of Lamellibranches, besides trunks of Stigmaria, Sigillaria, and Lepidodendron transformed into iron pyrites. Nodules of kidney ore are abundantly intermingled with the shales. Interstratified with the latter there is frequently found a fine-grained, argillaceous sand rock, called fire-clay by the miners, in which trunks and leaves of Stigmaria are almost always plentifully inclosed. Some of the stems are found covered with leaves radiating in all directions, as if the apex of a branch had been immersed in the liquid clay paste without any disturbance or compression of the expanded leaves. The leaves are long and band-like, flat at the outer part, subcylindrical, clavate, and connected at the basal ends with the stems.

The coal of the Jackson mines is bituminous, of a strong, resinous lustre, with delicate laminar striation parallel with the bedding. Split open in this direction, it presents a mottled structure; a part of the mass is a shining, amorphous bitumen; another part is porous, with the vegetable structure of charcoal. It breaks vertically with a smooth, shining cleavage, with nearly square angles. Compressed stems of Lepidodendron and Sigillaria can often be recognized in the mass, either transformed into bitumen or preserved by a mould of iron pyrites. A seam of iron pyrites is found almost invariably interstratified with the coal, but can be readily separated; the remainder of the coal is not contaminated with an unusual proportion of the pyrites, still the quantity is large enough to render it unfit for blacksmith's purposes. The iron pyrites of the mines can be sold to advantage for a price equal to that of the coal, to the sulphuric-acid manufactory at Jackson. The heat-producing qualities of the coal, for boiler use, etc., are excellent; it burns with a bright flame, leaving a small residuum of ashes. Its tendency to bake in the furnace, renders a breaking up of the half-melted mass necessary to the securing of a sufficient draught. This is remedied by setting the bars of the grates wider apart than in those intended for the use of hard coal. By distillation at red heat, the coal gives off 44 per cent of volatile matter.

The strata beneath the coal in some of the borings just recorded are found to be arenaceous shales and fire-clay, while in others the coal was directly underlaid by a sand rock. Prof. Winchell terms this sand rock, Parma sandstone, asserting that, in this position, a large body of sand rock is invariably deposited throughout the coal area of Michigan. Such regularity in the sequence of strata does not exist in the coal formation. The beds in it are usually of local extent, so that a position which in one place is occupied by a shale bed may in a neighboring locality be filled by a ledge of sand rock. The whole series is a constant alternation of shale and sandstone beds, and every natural or artificial section teaches us that an immense variety exists in this alternation. The deeper part of the formation incloses several heavy sand-rock beds, which in lithological characters are almost alike, so that in the limited exposures presented to our view, the determination of the exact relative positions of such beds becomes practically impossible. In case we adopt this Parma sandstone, we will rarely have an opportunity to identify it with any degree of certainty.

Two miles west of the Woodville coal mine, we find on Sandstone Creek, close to the Michigan Central Railroad, another abandoned mine. The surface rock is a soft dark shale with concretions of kidney ore and iron pyrites, which latter often represent trunks of Stigmaria. The coal seam, a little over 3 feet in thickness, had only this soft shale for a roof. The mining therefore required too costly timbering, and was consequently abandoned. On the sloping hillside, north of the mine, at the foot of which the shales are well exposed in the creek bed, and at a higher level, a patch of subcarboniferous limestone is found, apparently in undisturbed position; the top of the hill is formed by drift. This position of the strata is decidedly abnormal, and one or the other of the rocks must be dislocated; but every thing is so covered up by drift and sod, that it can not be told, from the visible surface exposures, which of the two is in its place and which dislocated. Numerous similar abnormal positions of the strata can be noticed along the southern margin of the coal field. One of the localities has already been mentioned incidentally while describing the carboniferous limestone of Portage River. At that place the coal measures lean in steeply inclined position against the slope of a hill, capped with the carboniferous limestone. East from the limestone quarries the shales of the coal measures inclose thick beds of plastic fire-clay, full of the stems of Stigmaria, and abounding in kidney-ore concretions. The Jackson Pottery draws large quantities of its clay from these diggings. The owner of the clay pits informs me that he bored with an auger through 50 or 60 feet of soft shale and clay, and found no hard rock bed to resist its progress.

In Spring Arbor township is another coal mine on Sandstone Creek, which, like the before-mentioned one, two miles further north, in the bed of the same creek, has only shales for a roof; it was worked, however, at the time of my visit. Its coal seam is 3 feet thick, and resembles the coal of the Jackson mines. The shales incumbent on the coal are about 30 feet thick. They contain numerous geodes of kidney ore and stems of Stigmaria transformed into iron pyrites. Below the coal, for a number of feet, shales continue, and then a heavy sand rock follows. Not many steps from the mine a well was drilled to the depth of 65 feet; its lower part went through sand rock altogether, and at the depth mentioned a copious stream of good, drinkable water was struck, which rose to the surface, and has since continued to flow freely.

North of Albion, the quarry of Mr. Fisk is indicated in Winchell's geological report for 1861 as a typical exposure of his Parma sandstone. The sandstone is a whitish, coarse-grained, partly conglomeratic, soft rock, similar to some layers of the sandstones of Jackson. Mr. Geiger, a well-borer, living in the immediate vicinity of the place, informs me that he bored through 19 feet of the sand rock, and struck a bed of good coal, 3 feet in thickness, underlying which were other sandstones. This coal seam would be unusual if the incumbent rock has really the position Mr. Winchell gives it; but from my own observations in the surrounding country, I am inclined to take the sand rock as the equivalent of Mr. Winchell's Woodville sandstone.

North of Jackson County, in Eaton and Ingham counties, the presence of seams of coal has been ascertained through artesian borings; but none appeared to be valuable enough to induce mining enterprises. At Mason, a mile south of the village, the upper coal sandstone is naturally exposed in the bed of the creek, and a thin coal seam has been lately discovered beneath it. In a drill hole sunk in the court-house yard of the village, thin seams of coal were likewise penetrated.

Four miles north of Mason, a large mass of coal connected with shale and sandstone beds in stratified order, was found standing in almost vertical position in the surrounding drift; the discoverers entertained great hopes of making their fortunes, and, indeed, succeeded in selling the place at a high price to a speculative genius, who, after I told him what he had bought, vanished from the place, leaving behind a good deal of money and some unpaid debts. In the mineral well of Mr. Frost, at Eaton Rapids, a seam of coal was struck at a depth of 120 feet from the surface; the incumbent rock beds were alternating strata of shale and sand rock, amounting to 100 feet; the upper 20 feet were drift.

In the banks of Grand River, two miles above Eaton Rapids, the upper sand rock of the coal measures projects in bluffs about 12 or 15 feet in height; the rock is of a darker bluish or ferruginous color than usual, and is interstratified with blue shales. It contains Calamites and other vegetable remains, and pyritous concretions.

In the artesian borings at Lansing, no coal of appreciable thickness was found. At the rapids of Grand River, one mile and a half above Lansing, the upper coal sandstone makes an outcrop, and has been quarried on a small scale. Six miles south of Lansing, near the railroad from Eaton Rapids to Lansing, a bed of coal 8 feet in thickness was said, some years ago, to have been discovered on the farm of Mr. Minie, but the report did not turn out to be correct.

At Charlotte, in Eaton County, a boring was made to a depth of 730 feet. In this the sand rock of the coal measures was struck below a drift cover of 50 feet; some small seams of coal were found beneath the sandstone, but I was not able to find out the details of the boring record. The facts which I mention were communicated from memory by accidental observers of the boring.

In the vicinity of Chester, Eaton County, the coal comes close to the surface and often crops out in the ravines of little Thornapple Creek. In one of these outcrops, a coal seam of 3 feet comes out under black shale beds, and is underlaid by light-colored shales, and fire-clay containing Stigmaria. Lately a number of experimental borings have been made in the vicinity of Chester. The coal formation is found considerably eroded and partially swept off during the drift period. The shales and inclosed coal seams are generally deprived of the protecting roof of sand rock and lie close under the drift, which is a very unfavorable condition for mining. The coal seams appear also to be often replaced by hard black bituminous shales. Of one of the borings at Chester, I received the following record: Drift, 8 feet; hard black shales, slate-like, and inclosing thin seams of coal, from 6 to 8 feet; whitish, fine-grained sand rock, containing Stigmaria, Lepidodendron and Calamites, 7 feet; whitish plastic fire-clay, 30 feet; black shales with pyrites, 30 feet; white fire-clay with hard, ferruginous bands, found at the bottom of the bore-hole.

The most instructive natural section through the coal formations which we have in the State, is seen at Grand Ledge, in the valley of Grand River, 10 miles below Lansing. The river has carved its bed there to a depth of about 60 feet below the general surface level of the country. The upper part of the hills bordering the valley is formed of drift; the lower presents a section through the rock beds of the coal measures. The village of Grand Ledge is located nearly in the centre of the outcrops, which continue up and down the river for about a mile. The strata rise and sink in undulations, which bring the higher and lower beds to repeated outcrops on the same level. The order of stratification, often visible in sections of large horizontal extent, gives a fair opportunity for observing the changes to which a stratum in its horizontal extension is often subject with regard to thickness and quality of material. The observed variability explains why, in the numerous sections seen within the limited space of a few miles, no one exactly corresponds with the other, although many of them represent about the same horizon.

The upper part of the formation is a coarse-grained sand rock from 25 to 30 feet in thickness. In the locality where I saw it best exposed, the rock occupies one of the depressed curves of an undulation such as has been alluded to, and at both ends of the exposure lower rock strata come up alongside the upper beds on the same level. The sand-rock ledges form a compact body, with only insignificant intermediate seams of shale, or with an occasional coal seam of a few inches thickness wedged in. Calamites and other vegetable imprints, besides concretions of kidney ore and of iron pyrites and conglomerate seams, are usually found inclosed within the rock mass. In grain and hardness, it fully resembles the upper sandstones of Jackson; its color, however, is a somewhat darker yellowish shade. Locally the rock becomes very hard and has a dark, chocolate-brown color from containing an abundance of ferruginous cement; a part of this brown rock is coarsely conglomeratic. Next below this sand rock, which borders the river in vertical cliffs for nearly the length of a mile, we find blue shales of arenaceous character, interlaminated with thin layers of sand rock, all amounting to a thickness of about 15 or 20 feet. Under these is a coal seam 2½ feet in thickness, and of very good bituminous quality. It wedges out in places or changes into a black, carbonaceous shale. This seam is worked at times by single workmen, as a temporary occupation when they have little else to do. The coal seam rests on a gray, argillaceous, laminated sand rock with softer shaly seams, which both inclose a large quantity of coaly vegetable remains, Lepidodendron, similar to Lepid. Wortheni, Stigmaria ficoides, trunks and leaves. The thickness of the beds is about 5 feet. Lower comes a fine-grained, whitish sand rock in even, compact beds, 8 feet in thickness. Directly under this sand rock is a 15-inch bed of good bituminous coal. Lowest in the outcrop are about 25 feet of additional strata, principally sand-rock ledges, with some intermediate shale seams. In the bed of the river at this spot, large, hard sand-rock slabs, of very even bedding, and from 2 to 3 inches in thickness, are laid open, which would make excellent flagstones for paving sidewalks. The aggregate thickness of the given section is about 90 feet; it begins with the centre of the synclinal depression and is followed downward with the stream. Up stream a rise of the strata is seen, but the next lower strata to the upper sand-rock deposit are not uncovered as plainly as at the lower end of the depression. After passing a covered interval of about 60 steps, in going up stream, the following descending section is observed:

Drift, up to the plateau of the hillsides........30 ft.
Blue soft shales with kidney ore..............15 "
Sand rock with Stigmaria.................... 2 "
Thinly laminated shaly sand rock............. 4 "
Black carbonaceous shale, or coal in its stead... 1 "
Sand rock with Stigmaria, from............1 to 2 "
Blue shales, partly arenaceous, containing kidney ore............................ 7 "
Black shale or coal..................several inches.
Sand rock with Stigmaria.................... 2 ft.
Blue shale.............................. 2 "
White ripple-marked sand rock thinly laminated 4 "
Nodular white sand rock, with ferruginous dots and interlaminated with seams of shale, visible.............................. 3 "
The lower beds are submerged.

This section is directly continued by an artesian boring, made at the Mineral Spring Hotel, to a depth of 105 feet. The boring begins in the last-mentioned sand rock, which is found to be 20 feet thick; beneath follow 5 feet of fire-clay, then 40 feet of white sand rock, a seam of coal 16 inches thick, carbonaceous shales from 3 to 4 feet, and lighter-colored shales 12 feet. At 80 feet below the surface a conglomeratic sand rock is struck, from which a copious stream of water rises to the surface. The sand rock continues to the depth of 105 feet, where another water-stream is struck. The water has an agreeable mineral taste. On the opposite side of the river, subsequent to this boring, another well was opened, which seems to be in subterranean connection with the well of the Mineral Spring Hotel, whose tube had to be shortened 2 feet in order to secure an overflow after the other well began to discharge its stream.

A good section through the formation can be observed in the ravines of a creek entering Grand River from the south, a short distance west of the village, and another, in the bluffs just below it, and opposite the section last described. Highest in this latter, under a few feet of drift, are 15 feet of arenaceous shales with nodular seams of sand rock and kidney-ore concretions, and a band of carbonaceous shale with seams of coal; beneath follow 8 feet of a fine-grained, greenish-white sandstone in thick, even beds, identical with the sand rock found in the first section intermediate between the two coal seams. This rock is quarried and worked into cut-stone, window and door sills; it is of fine quality, better than any of the coal-measure sand rocks I had seen before. The beds at one end of the quarry are much thicker than at the other, and seem to wedge out. Under the quarry-stone a foot or two of arenaceous shales, laminated by black, coaly seams, follow, and then a coal bed 15 inches thick. The coal is of very good quality, even for blacksmiths' use, and is occasionally obtained by working the quarry for its sand rock. The coal seam rests on bluish arenaceous shales, and, lower, beds of sand rock form the base of the bluff and the bed of the river. The banks of the river, at intervals for the distance of 8 miles, present more limited outcrops than those near Grand Ledge, but after that no more rock is denuded in the river-bed until Ionia township is reached, where, in Section 23, the upper sand rock of the coal measures comes to the surface, or is only covered by a thin coating of drift. The quality of this sand rock is superior to the equivalent beds at Grand Ledge or at Jackson; it can be quarried in blocks of large dimension, and is of proper durability for building purposes. It has a reddish tint or is a variegated red and white. In the quarries I observed an interesting example of discordant stratification. The surface of a sand-rock ledge is seen deeply eroded by furrows and excavations as if it had been a long time exposed to the action of the atmosphere, and this eroded surface is coated with a smooth, argillaceo-ferruginous cuticle. On this ledge another deposit of sand rock follows, which fills out all the inequalities of the lower bed. We must, therefore, suggest a temporary emergence of the lower stratum before the next ledge could be deposited over it. From Mr. Blanchard, of Ionia, I received the record of a boring in the vicinity of the quarries, made to a depth of 450 feet. It penetrated in

Sand rock................	80 to 110 ft. in thickness.
Shales and fire-clay..........................	4 ft.
Coal from..........................	20 in. to 4 "
Fire-clay............................	2 "
Sand rock, fine-grained......................	40 "
Coal seam, thickness unknown.	

The deeper strata were alternations of sand rock and shales. At 300 feet below the surface, a copious stream of sweet water was struck, which rises in constant flow to the surface, proving very refreshing to the laborers of the quarry.

West and north of Ionia, the coal formation disappears under the drift, and no other borings have been made in these directions by which we could ascertain the extent of its distribution as the surface rock. To encounter the coal formation again, we have to return eastward. In Ingham County, shale beds inclosing a coal seam come to the surface on Cedar River, near Williamston; not far off from this exposure, a shaft has been sunk, and for several years past a mine has been in operation which produces a good quality of bituminous coal. The shaft commences in a drift-mass 15 feet thick; right under the drift a coal seam of 20 inches is found; next to this is fire-clay with seams of sand rock, 12 feet; black shale, 3 feet; white, soft fire-clay, 3 feet; kidney ore, 6 inches; black, slate-like shales containing Lingula, Discina, Productus, and compressed Lamellibranches, 2 feet; coal from 3 to 3½ feet; fire-clay, 4 feet; the shaft extends about 12 feet below the coal seam, through gray shales. A seam of pyrites is generally connected with the coal, but can be easily separated; otherwise the coal is tolerably clear of pyrites. Specimens of Sigillaria and Lepidodedron are common in the pyritous seam. Besides the vertical shaft, a sloping gallery is driven to the bottom of the mine, in which the sequence of the rock strata can be studied most commodiously. Mr. Rush, the agent of the coal mine, has explored the vicinity of Williamston for coal, and kindly gave me the results of his experiments, which I set down here. In a boring 4 miles west of Williamston, close to the river, were found,

Drift	18	ft.
Black slate	4	"
Coal	2½	"
Fire-clay	6	"
Black shale	12	"
Shaly sandstone	10	"

Half a mile south from the latter place a boring went 60 feet through drift, without reaching the older rock beds.

A boring at the railroad depot of Williamston gave

Drift	16 ft.	
Sandstone, soft, white	12 "	
Coal		6 in.
Light shale	6 "	
Dark shale	8 "	
Coal	3 "	
Fire-clay	3 "	
Black shale	2 "	
Fire-clay	4 "	
Black shale	4 "	
Fire-clay	4 "	
Black shale	13 "	
Light shale	7 "	
Black shale	5 "	
Fire-clay	3 "	
Shale	14 "	

Half a mile southwest of the depot another boring went through

Drift	28 ft.
Sandstone	6 "
Light gray shale	10 "
Dark shale	6 "
Black shale	7 "
Coal	1 "
Fire-clay	4 "
Shale	3 "
White sand rock to end of the boring	20 "

In a boring 200 yards north of the coal shaft, across the river, there were encountered,

Drift	4 ft.
Sandstone	13 "
Dark gray shale	1 "
Coal	3 "

Below, fire-clay and shales.

North of the locality just mentioned were found :

Drift	18 ft.
Coal	7 "
Fire-clay	6 "

and black slate and lighter shales to the depth of 60 feet in all below the surface.

The above experiments show a uniform distribution of a coal seam about 3 feet in thickness over this whole district. Its position is often too superficial, without a proper roof, for advantageous mining. In nearly all the borings two seams of coal are found, of which the upper one is generally too narrow to be of practical value. The two seams are separated by from 15 to 20 feet of intermediate beds.

The next disclosures of the coal measures we find on Shiawassee River, near Owosso, and Corunna, in both of which places coal mines are opened. The shaft of the Owosso mine is close to the river, within the village limits. It begins in a blue shale with coaly, vegetable remains, under which a coal bed of 15 inches is found resting on fire-clay 6 feet in thickness; then another coal seam, likewise of 15 inches, succeeds. The bottom part of the shaft, which is 40 feet deep, is formed by shales and fire-clay; the fire-clay is partly of a hard, sandy nature, and contains numerous stems and leaves of Stigmaria ficoides. The coal is of a rich bituminous quality and tolerably free of sulphur, but the seams are too thin to be profitably mined. Several companies tried to work it, but gave it up after a short time, as not returning enough to cover the expense.

At the Detroit and Milwaukee Railroad depot, a boring to the depth of 307 feet has been executed. Its record runs:

Drift	40 ft.
Fire-clay	5 "
Blue shale	20 "
White arenaceous shale	8 "
Blue shales, partly arenaceous	107 "
Coal	6 in.
White sandstone	16 ft.
Shales	22 "
Blue sand rock, alternating with shale	46 "
White sand rock	11 "
Dark shale	5 "
Sand rock	27 "

Shales to the bottom of the boring.

The bottom of the Shiawassee valley, near Corunna, is all formed of rock beds of the coal measures, where the erosions of the drift period have not destroyed them and filled their place with débris.

The upper sand rock of the formation is in many places entirely swept away, and the shale beds below lie denuded at the surface. The two mines opened at Corunna, a mile or two east of the village, have begun their shafts in the shale beds; one of them, the more northerly situated, was abandoned at the time of my visit; the other, located within a short semicircular bend of the river, was worked. In the oblique drift leading to the bottom of the mine, the following section is offered:

Drift	9 ft.
Shale, dark, partly black	30 "
Sandstone	4 "
Black slaty shales, containing Lingula and Discina, besides compressed Lamellibranches	6 "
Coal	1 "
Fire-clay	4 "
Black slaty shales, as above	8 "
Coal from	3 to 4 "
Fire-clay	4 "
Black shales	4 "

Arenaceous shales continue to the bottom, which is 80 feet below surface. The beds are found in the mine rising and sinking in undulations. The fire-clay seams are usually arenaceous and contain stems of Stigmaria. The shale beds contain lenticular concretions of kidney ore, in the non-decomposed condition of gray, amorphous carbonate of protoxide of iron; seams and nodules of iron pyrites are also found dispersed throughout the whole formation. In the coal seam the pyrites are concentrated into a band of a few inches in thickness. The coal is of bituminous quality, of the same character as the Jackson coal. Not far off, west from the mine, the shale formation is found covered by the upper coarse-grained sand rock inclosing stems of Calamites. The visible thickness of the rock is about 15 feet, but it is probably thicker if it could be seen better exposed. Other outcrops of the sandstone are to be found in the river bed 4 miles above Corunna. The coal measures are frequently noticed in the bed of the Shiawassee below Owosso, as far down as St. Charles. A locality of particular interest is near the mouth of Six-Mile Creek, 6 miles north of Owosso. In the bluffs of the Shiawassee River we observe the lower part formed of blue shales, with seams of sand rock and abundant concretions of kidney ore; the top is drift with a considerable intermixture of angular débris from the underlying strata. Under the shale, emerging a few feet above the water and partly submerged, are layers of a black, shaly lime rock, visible in a thickness of 4 or 5 feet, containing numerous fossils, partly in calcified, partly in pyritous condition; particularly observable is a large nodose Nautilus, described by Meek and Worthen under two different names, N. latus and N. Winslowi. A large Orthoceras is quite common, and other forms are Spirifer cumeratus, Productus nanus, a Spirigera, Chonetes, Myalina, Platyceras, Bellerophon, Crinoid stems, and compressed specimens of a Zaphrentis.

The same limestone is seen a quarter of a mile off in the bed of Six-Mile Creek; its ledges are there more even-bedded flagstones, less shaly than those seen in the Shiawassee River. Close under the lime rock is a 15-inch bed of coal, quantities of which have been taken from the river bed when the water is very low. The coal reposes on a soft, plastic clay of greenish-white color, which incloses stems of Stigmaria and large, calcareous, nodular masses of cone-in-cone structure. Stems of Stigmaria are also found in the upper shales of the bluffs and in the geodes, when split open fronds of ferns are sometimes found, but their occurrence is rare. A few steps from the mouth of Six-Mile Creek, some parties made an experimental shaft about 30 feet deep, and from that point drilled to 100 feet below the surface. From the material thrown out of the shaft, I see that shales of various color, with seams of sand rock and conglomerate, besides an abundance of kidney ore, compose the surface layers as far as the shaft went. Mr. Ott, the owner of the land, informed me that four beds of coal, amounting in all to 11 feet, were found in the boring. He gave the same account to Prof. Winchell, who has described in his report for 1861 the details communicated to him, to which record I refer the reader. The record in itself is somewhat doubtful, and the hesitation to take it as a true representation of facts is increased by the subsequent acts of the discoverers of so rich coal deposits (11 feet within a vertical thickness of 20 feet of strata). Mr. Ott ends his story by saying that the men, after they had reached the depth of 100 feet, left the place at once, not to return again.

The valley of Flint River cuts through the carboniferous series near Flushing, northwest of Flint. Two miles above Flushing the bed of the river is formed by a hard, fine-grained sand rock full of Stigmaria, stems, and leaves; several feet of it emerge above the water-line. Above follow about 4 feet of blue arenaceous shales, likewise with Stigmaria stems; next higher are 5 feet of dark shales containing kidney-ore concretions; above them is black shale with thin seams of coal, amounting to about 3 feet in all. Greenish, micaceous sandstones 25 feet in thickness follow, above which 15 feet of dark gray shales constitute the highest ledges of the section. The sand rock is in part thinly laminated with discordant stratification. Another part is in regular beds, varying from 18 inches to 2 feet in thickness. The rock incloses fine specimens of Calamites and thin, coaly veins, besides numerous concretions of iron pyrites. It can be quarried in tolerably large blocks, and is used for cut-stone of a fair appearance. At the time the building contracts for the State House at Lansing were let out, this sand rock was offered to the building committee as a first-class material, by parties from Flushing. In consequence of this offer I was ordered by Governor Baldwin to examine the quarries and the rock, which I did, reporting conscientiously, to the best of my knowledge, that I considered the rock of the Flushing quarries as of middling good quality, suitable for buildings of less weight than the State House was likely to have, but that, for an edifice of such dimensions, I did not think the rock had sufficient firmness. I expressed also my doubts in regard to its durability when exposed to the severe winter frosts. These views were not mere surmises, but were based upon the appearance of several buildings in Flint, in the construction of which the Flushing stone had been used. These buildings had then been standing about ten years, and I found their sills and water tablings so much damaged by exfoliation within that short time that I could not think of recommending the stone. I make this statement in justification of my report to the committee, which roused against me the indignation of the Flushing quarrymen. I have no doubt their anger has passed off ere this, as, upon reflection, they must see that I could not honestly have acted otherwise than I did in the matter.

In Saginaw Bay district, thin coal seams were frequently found in boring for salt, and several experimental borings in search of coal were made in the district a good many years ago, but no sufficient inducements for coal-mining could be discovered. During the last few years the report of the discovery of rich beds of cannel coal in the valley of Rifle River has caused great excitement, not only in Saginaw district, which is specially interested in such a discovery, but throughout the whole State. In order to ascertain the actual state of the case, I examined the Rifle River district with particular care, and give here a brief statement of the observations made.

The first explorations for coal on Rifle River were induced by some pieces of cannel coal found in the bed of the river by a settler living close by it. Some gentlemen of Bay City, hearing of the fact, began to examine the surroundings of the locality indicated to them, and after experimenting awhile, succeeded in finding, at a depth of only 18 feet below the surface, a deposit of black shales and cannel coal, the latter, according to their reports, having a thickness of 7 feet. They sunk a shaft to the depth of 27 feet; the upper 14 feet of the excavation were loose drift masses; under them, seemingly, a three-foot ledge of a hard, calcareous sand rock was found; then came a hard black slate a few feet in thickness, the lower 7 feet in the shaft being thought to be all cannel coal. When I visited the spot, the shaft was full of water, and I could not ascertain the facts as accurately as would have been desirable; but from the examination of the material taken out of the shaft, which was all there yet with the exception of a few barrels of coal taken away, I came to the following conclusions: That the sand rock next under the drift and above the black slate was not a ledge in its natural position, but a large boulder of the arenaceous beds of the lower horizon of the subcarboniferous limestones, the same rock which forms the cliffs on Point aux Grees; that the remainder of the excavation went through a deposit of a black, highly bituminous slate, 10 feet in thickness. Three feet of these slates were considered as such, and the rest were taken for cannel coal; but I rather think the proportion is inverted. The true cannel coal in the promiscuous mass thrown out from the shaft was the smaller part of the whole, and even admitting that the best pieces of the coal had been picked out from the heap before I saw it, the quantity taken away could be but very small in comparison with the slate masses left there. The transitions of the slate rock into cannel coal of good quality are represented in all gradations; much of the slate is so rich in carbon, that it burns freely, but leaves so large a proportion of ashes as to make it unfit for fuel.

The seams of true cannel coal interstratified with the slates burn with a residue of a small quantity of pulverulent ashes. The slates contain numerous specimens of a small Lingula, and on several slabs I found clusters of fish-scales scattered over a space having the outlines of a small fish in decomposed, compressed condition. After my first visit to the coal shaft, it was pumped out, was somewhat deepened, and a gallery was driven from its bottom 30 feet sideways. Some weeks later, when I visited the shaft again, I found it abandoned and filled with water, but from the additional rubbish thrown out, it can be seen that the black slate is underlaid by an arenaceous fire-clay inclosing stems and leaves of Stigmaria.

The position of the shaft is in Town. 19, R. 4, Sect. 3. In the same section two other experimental borings were made on the opposite side of the river. In one, sand rock was struck under a cover of 25 feet of drift; the boring went 20 feet into the sand rock, and was then interrupted, no signs of coal being found. The other boring, executed by Mr. Ortmann, of East Saginaw, was continued to a depth of 190 feet. First came drift 21 feet, and then alternations of blue shales and sand rock; near the bottom a seam of iron pyrites was found, and under it black shales, but no coal.

Another drill-hole, three quarters of a mile southeast of the above borings, sunk to a depth of 100 feet, struck sand rock and shale beds under a drift cover 60 feet in thickness, but found no signs of coal. Another boring to the depth of 100 feet, in Sect. 17 of the same town, went altogether through drift, without reaching the rock. Further east, on the lower part of Rifle River, Mr. Ramsdall made some experiments, in Town. 19, R. 5 east. He found drift, 36 feet; sandstone, 35 feet; blue shale, 34 feet; pyritous rock, 2 feet; blue shales, 14 feet, until, at 120 feet below the surface, the boring was given up. South from there, in Town. 19, R. 4, Sect. 10, he found,

Drift sand	75 ft.
Clay	25 "
Sand rock	7 "

Shales of various color, partly black, and a 4-foot bed of fire-clay were the rock beds next penetrated to the depth of 200 feet; at the bottom a dark gray hard rock was found—no coal.

Another boring in the same town had, at the time the record was given to me, reached a depth of 122 feet, and was still within the drift. Several other borings were made in the vicinity of Rifle River with no better success.

A natural outcrop of the coal-bearing rock series is seen in the river bed, Town. 19, R. 4, east, Sect. 4, below a dam built across it. Highest is a yellowish, rather soft sand rock, from 10 to 12 feet in thickness, interstratified with some seams of dark bluish shale, and containing ferruginous concretions and vegetable remains (Calamites). Lower are from 2 to 3 feet of a shaly, micaceous sand rock, of irregular, discordant stratification, thinly laminated by intervening linear coaly seams, and with the strata frequently distorted into serpentine flexions. Next below are 15 inches of a dark blue arenaceous shale with kidney ore, its strata also flexured, or broken into a brecciated mass. The lowest visible beds are a white sand rock inclosing numerous water-worn, ferruginous pebbles and pieces of shale, besides thin, linear seams of coal. About 5 feet of it emerge from the water. Other outcrops are found further down the river. On Mr. Kinney's farm, Town. 19, R. 5, east, Sect. 10, blue arenaceous shales, with some thick ledges of sand rock forming the top part, are all that can be seen. Still further down the river, within the village of Omer, the bed and its banks are formed of a white, soft sand rock of discordant stratification, interstratified with some thin shale beds, and containing narrow veins of coal not over an inch in thickness. Toward the mouth of the river the formation disappears under drift deposits. While the explorations on Rifle River were going on, some boring experiments had also been made along the line of the Lansing and Saginaw Railroad, near Deep River, and near Standish, which were attended by a somewhat better success than most of the experiments on Rifle River. At Deep River station, Mr. Stephens sunk a drill-hole to a depth of 120 feet, and found,

Drift	28 ft.
Light-colored sand rock	57 "
Blue shale	7 "
Coal (cannel)	5½ "
Black shale	5 "
Coal	2½ "
Soft shales, with seams of sand rock and iron pyrites	12 "
Solid limestone, entered	2 "

Below the drift deposits a stream of sweet water was struck, which rises in a constant flow to the surface. From the material brought up by the sand pump, it is impossible to determine with accuracy the thickness and quality of a coal seam, which is found in connection with a coal-like slate rock, as in this boring. Mr. Stephens, the owner of the place, after obtaining so favorable indications, determined to investigate the matter thoroughly by sinking a shaft down to the coal beds, and I am informed that the work is already in fair progress, which, if accomplished, will finally solve the question as to whether valuable coal beds can be expected within this district or not. It is to be hoped that of the 13 feet of black deposits found in the boring, 7 feet may turn out to be good cannel coal, as the supposition is; but even a somewhat thinner seam would be a discovery of great importance for Saginaw district.

At Standish, another boring for coal was in progress. When I was there, it had reached the depth of 129 feet; it went through

Drift	52 ft.
Sand rock	27 "
Blue arenaceous shales with seams of iron pyrites and narrow bands of coal	27 "
Coal	13 in.
Blue shales and fire-clay	14 ft.
Sand rock	2 "
Shale	6 "

Subsequently, as I am informed, a thicker coal seam was met with by a continuance of the boring. On Tittibawassee River, at Mr. Shattuck's farm, 6 miles west of Saginaw City, explorations have been in progress for several years back, by which the presence of a coal seam has been ascertained. Last fall they commenced to sink a shaft to the coal bed, but since then I have not heard how far the work has advanced.

The coal fields of Michigan, supposed to cover a space of 8000 square miles, are up to the present day of very inferior importance in the economy of the State. Only four mines are in actual operation, and these are worked with but a small force of men.

Searching for the causes of this neglect of apparently so great stores of wealth buried beneath our feet, we find one of them in the imperfect exposure of the rock beds, which, with the exception of those in a few limited districts, are all deeply covered by drift deposits. This would be no serious impediment, if the coal seams were spread in a continuous sheet over the surface of a certain horizon; we could then without much risk go down and uncover them; but all coal deposits are confined originally to certain limited basins, and if we consider that the coal series, as the youngest of the stratified rock beds found on the peninsula, has been without protection by later deposits, exposed to the vicissitudes of untold ages, we must expect to find a large proportion of the deposits destroyed and swept off; in particular, during the drift epoch, the coal formation must have suffered immense destruction from the moving glacier masses. The direct proof of this is furnished by the large quantity of débris of the coal measures mixed with the drift material; but the drift action has not only destroyed a large proportion of the coal formation, but has at the same time filled up the eroded gaps with loose drift material, hiding the extent of destruction from observation, and thus rendering our mining operations always hazardous in a deeply drift-covered region, because we have no means whereby to know how much of the supposed underlying rock strata has escaped destruction.

The same erosive forces have acted on the coal formation of Ohio, but there the valleys of erosion intersecting it have not been filled again with drift masses. The erosion has rather facilitated access to the coal beds, and laid the strata open for observation in natural sections miles in length. There success to miners' enterprises is assured by the same revolutionary forces which have proved so detrimental in the case of ours. Another reason for the small development of the coal-mining industry in Michigan is undeniably the fact that we have no large stores of coal to invite the capitalist to invest his means in the trade.

The best coal seam we have is not over 4 feet thick, while often the average thickness of a vein does not exceed 3 feet. We have discovered only one practically useful coal seam as far as the series is explored. This, however, does not explain why our already opened mines, in profitably workable beds, do not produce more coal through the employment of a greater force of men, when our demand for coal is so great that millions of dollars are yearly sent abroad for the article. It is not the lack of coal; our now known beds would supply for a long time to come all we want for consumption. One of the reasons for so large an import of foreign coal is in the quality of the home production; its highly bituminous quality and rather large percentage of pyritous admixture unfit it for certain purposes, for iron smelting and for blacksmiths' use, for instance, while for family use a highly bituminous coal is rendered objectionable by the large quantity of fœtid smoke evolved through imperfect combustion. For gas production, the coal, otherwise very suitable, is little used on account of the inconvenience of purifying the gas from sulphur.

As fuel for steam production, the Michigan coal can compete with any coal imported for that purpose, and is superior to many of them. The production of our mines is far behind the consumption of coal for steam generation. Let us hope, however, that the coal-mining industry of the State, as long as it offers an article equally useful and fully as cheap or cheaper than the article imported, will receive the patronage of our manufacturers to a greater extent than it has heretofore done.

I have attempted, in the foregoing part of the report, to describe the geological structure of the Lower Peninsula of Michigan as accurately as the conditions allow.

From the statements made, we learn that the formations composing it are exclusively of sedimentary origin, and the deposits all superimposed on each other in undisturbed horizontal or nearly horizontal position. In some parts of the continent where the strata are disposed with similar regularity, they are found deeply eroded, and the valleys and ravines carved through them present opportunities for observing the rock beds, exposed in sections of large vertical and horizontal extent, in which not only every stratum can be studied accurately in all its qualities and local peculiarities, but can also be clearly seen the relative positions which the superimposed strata hold to each other. The strata of Michigan are doubtless similarly eroded. The power and destructive action of these erosive forces are illustrated impressively by the ocean-like basins of the lakes surrounding us, which are their handiwork. Yet not only were all these wounds in the rocky skin of the earth healed in time through being filled up with débris carried from the destruction of other places, but a thick coating of the filling material was also spread over the levelled surface so as to hide from view even the scars. We are learning to comprehend what a great advantage this healing process was for man, who subsequently took possession of this portion of the globe, prepared for him and his welfare long, long years before the human race existed.

This loose, porous mass of débris, in proper comminution to make a soil, and being composed of every variety of mineral substance necessary for the sustenance of vegetable life, formed the destiny of this strip of land ; it makes it an agricultural country. No great mineral wealth is hidden here under our feet which we could have reached through the gaps, so it were better they were closed and levelled, to enable us to harvest golden ears of wheat and corn from their surface, than that we should enter shadowy subterranean passages in search of gold, endangering our lives and without any certainty of success in the end. Still we are not entirely deprived of mineral wealth, which by many is thought an indispensable requisite for the household of a rich State. We have our modest share of coal, left as yet nearly untouched, but which, when exhumed, will be fully adequate for the supply of our demand for home consumption. We have tapped stores of salt brine, reserved for our benefit in the sponge-like sand-rock beneath us in inexhaustible quantities, drawing enough for all domestic wants, for curing thousands of barrels of delicious fish, caught in the cool, crystal waters of our lakes, and sent far abroad as an article of commerce, besides an immense surplus from which to provide our Western neighbors, in exchange for their coin. Then we have gypsum of snowy whiteness, laid open on the surface in quantities to last for generations to come for all the uses to which it is devoted. We have stone, lime, and sand enough to build our edifices; our grindstones have acquired fame over all the country adjoining us. Can we claim more for our peninsula, whose principal pride it is to produce the best wheat and the finest apples grown anywhere? If we had more, I fear it would demoralize us. But this is not all; we have our mining country set apart from this lower Arcadian land by a broad, intervening lake, where, to compensate for the scarcity of metal in the other part, nature has deposited its metallic treasures in an exuberance that challenges the competition of any other spot on the globe. Mountains of iron ore of the better kind are passed by unnoticed, because we find there plenty of it of a yet richer quality. Copper in malleable metallic condition lies there in blocks heavy enough to load down a three-master to a sinking condition, while, in finer granular condition, it is disseminated, in incredible quantities, through mighty sedimentary sand-rock masses and conglomerates forming a mountain range of over one hundred miles in length. Silver in pure metallic state is also found in no small quantity, and daily there are fresh discoveries of it.

Nature has well equalized the division of its gifts. The broken, hilly character of the mineral district, and its northern climate, although rendering it healthy and pleasant as a place of habitation, do not recompense the farmer as well for his labor as they do the miner, and, therefore, all industrial efforts in this region are directed to mining. The population of a district congenial for agriculture throws all its energy into the tillage of the land; another finds itself predestined for a manufacturing district by some natural advantages offered, such, for instance, as our lumbering districts. Each one of these will dispose of the surplus of its products to the other in exchange for its surplus; and only by such a division of occupation and interests, in accordance with external climatic and geological conditions, can the necessary life and circulation come into the social organism, and secure its healthy and durable existence. It would not add to our prosperity if all the natural advantages possessed by a single part of the State were to be equally distributed over the whole. The two peninsulas, united into a twin State, form the happiest union that could be made; both have their great advantages—one upholds the other; but if I were asked to say, which is the best, my choice would fall upon the lower. As an agricultural district, it is absolutely self-sustaining, if we moderate our claims to the necessities of life. A mining district without agriculture, if yet full of gold, would let its inhabitants starve to death, if the agriculturist did not come to their relief.

When it became my duty to investigate the Lower Peninsula, I was already informed of the general facts concerning its structure, and I felt somewhat uneasy when I thought that I had no prospect of discovering any great mineral wealth within it, because I knew that there is a general feeling that the geologist should make numerous new discoveries, and report at length about the details of the rock formations, etc. I believe that I have done conscientiously all that could be done under given circumstances, but I have had to be more brief in the description of many things than was my wish, for the simple reason that I had not the opportunities to make more extended observations, on account of the very unfavorable and restricted exposures of the rock beds, which, as already explained, are in the greatest part of their extension covered by an unbroken mantle of drift masses. Perhaps I could have entertained the reader a little better by giving hypothetical speculations on things which could not be seen; but this would have been in opposition to my principle, which is to give facts only, as a guidance for the enterprises of explorers, and for the student of the earth's history.

The benefit to the commonwealth of a geological investigation consists not only in adding discoveries of new stores of minerals to those already known, but to a much greater extent, I think, in causing to be fairly understood the uselessness of explorations for certain minerals in places where they do not exist. Thousands and thousands of dollars have been spent in this way, which could have been saved to their owners, if they had had a clear comprehension of the structure of the earth's crust which they explored, or had asked advice of some one better informed than themselves, before they commenced their work; and in such sense, I know that the contributions to knowledge which I have made in this report will return to the State an ample equivalent for the expense of the investigation.

As an appendix to the foregoing report, exclusively devoted to the description of the Lower Peninsula, is added the report of Dr. Garrigues on salt production in Michigan. Two other special reports, on the roofing slates of Huron Bay, and on the silver-bearing rocks of the Ontonagon district, give the results of a short journey to the Upper Peninsula which I made by special order of the Geological Board.

APPENDIX A.

OBSERVATIONS ON THE ONTONAGON SILVER MINING DISTRICT AND THE SLATE QUARRIES OF HURON BAY.

BY

C. ROMINGER.

APPENDIX A.

OBSERVATIONS MADE ON A CURSORY TOUR THROUGH THE ONTONAGON SILVER MINING DISTRICT.

THE discovery of silver in the sedimentary rock beds of Iron River, in Ontonagon County, has recently attracted considerable attention on the part of miners and capitalists.

On my return from the examination of the Huron slate quarries, of which the report is given elsewhere, some gentlemen of Marquette, interested in the new mining district, asked me to go along with them and examine into the conditions under which the silver is found, which invitation I gladly accepted. In the first report on the Upper Peninsula, little has been said about the region in question, and at the time of its issue the discovery of silver had not yet been made, for which reason I think that the small contribution which I can add to our knowledge of this mining country will be welcome to those interested in its geology and in the development of its mineral resources. Ontonagon district has the same geological structure as the northeasterly part of Kewenaw peninsula, of which it is a direct continuation.

A ridge of copper trap, with a strike from northeast to southwest, and with a northern dip, divides it into an east and west part. The east part is a mountainous plateau with marshy flats, from which Ontonagon River collects its waters through branches, one of which is fed by a large inland lake, the Gogebic Lake.

After winding its way for a while along the foot of the ridge, and having united with its affluents from the south and north, the Ontonagon breaks transversely through the trap range and hastens in a direct northwestern course down the western slope to the lake.

The surface rock of this east side of the central trap range is the red Lake Superior sandstone inconformably abutting against or overlapping the trap rock, with horizontally disposed layers.

On the western slope of the ridge we find the trap rock overlaid by a heavy series of sand rock, conglomerate, and slate deposits, resting conformably on the trap, and participating in its upheavals. The age of these beds is intermediate between the trap and the horizontal sandstone deposits; but between all three of the indicated groups so great lithological affinities exist, that it is most natural to consider them as the consecutive products of one and the same epoch, in the commencement of which the just-formed strata were displaced by volcanic action, which subsided toward the end and left the last deposits undisturbed.

The trappean series is not clearly definable from the conformably incumbent higher beds which form the western slope of the range. The crystalline or amygdaloid trap seams are underlaid by conglomerates and by ripple-marked brown sandstones which are absolutely undistinguishable by lithological characters from similar rock beds found deposited above the trap, and the only way in which the two horizons can be distinguished is by observation of their relative positions to the underlying or incumbent strata of a certain well-marked lithological character.

The absence of all trappean rocks distinguishes the upper division from the lower, in which a constant alternation of trap with the sedimentary beds is observed.

The lately discovered silver-bearing rocks are sedimentary strata inclosed within the more recent non-trappiferous division, which conformably leans with its uplifted beds against the higher trappean hill range, forming a sloping belt of lower hills between the higher range and the lake.

In the north part of Kewenaw peninsula, this shore belt is formed by sandstones very little affected by the upheavals, and lithologically very similar to the horizontal sand-rock beds on the east side; they seem to be somewhat younger than those forming the belt at the foot of the Ontonagon range, and are, as far as known, not metalliferous.

In the interval between the mouth of Ontonagon River and the Porcupine Mountain spur, this rock series under consideration is of somewhat different lithological character; its beds are considerably dislocated by upheavals, and certain seams of the formation are rich in metallic silver, while others are so in metallic copper.

The thickness of this rock series in Ontonagon district is very great, amounting to at least 3000 or 4000 feet. The higher beds are prevalently of a dark grayish or greenish color, of argillaceous and arenaceous composition, and of rather fine-grained slaty or flaggy structure; the lower are prevalently brown-colored sand rocks and conglomerate. The metalliferous seams are above the brown sandrock and below the gray slaty upper division, and have a much wider distribution than at first was supposed. The metal-bearing beds have actually been found by explorers, from Ontonagon River for 30 miles westward, in every locality where denudations of the rock beds could be seen; and beyond all doubt the existence of the metalliferous beds is not confined to this narrow district. On the other hand, it is not to be expected that the beds are everywhere charged with the metal in quantities which would pay for mining it: some spots may be found unusually rich, others where the same strata are barren of metal.

The silver and the copper are generally found in two separate seams which are only a few feet apart. The lowest seam is charged with scales and granules of metallic silver. In the upper seam the copper is found in similar fine scaly particles and granules, but in much greater quantities than the silver. The silver was first discovered in the rock beds exposed on Little Iron River, at the location of the Scranton mine; and, subsequently, in the valley of Big Iron River, the same strata were discovered either in natural outcrops or through test-pits, so that now a half dozen mining companies are located along Iron River valley, within the distance of a few miles.

The general direction in the dip and strike of the strata is conformable with the strike and dip of the copper range, from northeast to southwest, with northwestern dip; but this direction is only ideal, deducible from the geographical extension of the rock belts, while in actual field observation we find the strata dipping and striking in so many directions, that every locality is governed by its own rules. We find the rock bent in short curves, in synclinal or anticlinal position, or that abrupt breaks in the continuity of the strata cause considerable complications in the reciprocal position of the layers. In examining the bed of Iron River for two miles upward from its mouth, the strike and dip of the strata were found changing continually, so that for a while, in ascending the river bed, we actually descended into lower and lower strata, and then, in the further progress upward, began to rise from the lower beds to the higher, and this several times repeated.

At the mouth of Iron River, brownish, thin-bedded, sand-rock layers with intermediate shaly seams are seen in the banks, with an approximate strike northwest and a northwest dip. A short distance up the river runs in rapids over rocky bars, obliquely crossing its bed, which are lower strata than those at the entrance; their strike is about 15° north of west, with a dip east of north at an angle of about 20°. Ascending in the river channel, we pass over the edges of constantly lower and lower strata; these lower beds are dark bluish or blackish gray slaty layers of a fine-grained, sandy and argillaceous rock with fine micaceous scales; the surfaces of the thin slabs are ripple-marked. With the ascent the dip and strike of the strata constantly change. At a no greater distance than 150 steps above the former place where strike and dip were measured, the strike had changed to be south of west with a dip south of east. The strata here are still lower, thinly laminated flagstones containing some calcareous cement, but of the same dark, arenaceous, slate-like rock mass as the higher beds. The dark rock contains globules of calcareous concretions, and seams of softer shaly structure alternate with the ripple-marked harder slabs. Weathering slaty pieces are covered with a green efflorescence of carbonate of copper oxide. We have arrived now at the foot of low, stair-like falls, where, by a bend of the river, across the strike and with the dip of the strata, which latter is here south of east, instead of descending further in the series as we were doing, we ascend, step by step, into higher beds, similar in character to those seen before.

By another flexion of the river bed, it comes parallel with the strike of the strata, and without ascending or descending in the series, we move up its course, remaining on the same horizon; but soon, by another bend, a descent into lower beds, while still ascending the river, begins. The stamp works of the Ontonagon Mining Company are now in sight; the strike of the strata approaches gradually an almost due east and west direction, with a dip northward at a steep angle, and still, while ascending the river, we steadily descend upon lower beds. The rock below the stamp mill is in thicker, much more massive beds than seen before. Some seams approach also to the structure of ordinary sand rock, but the general character of the rock material has not changed much.

The sum of the thickness of the rock series passed over between the mouth of the river and the stamp mill, which is two miles up, can not be much less than 1500 or 2000 feet.

Under the more thick-bedded, argillaceo-arenaceous rocks mentioned, follow thinly laminated, blue, shaly layers, and then a bed, or several beds, of a rather coarse-grained, grayish sand rock, hardened by an abundant admixture of calcareous cement, and interlaminated by thin flexuose seams of a shining black shaly substance. This latter is the *silver-bearing rock*, varying from about 1 foot to 4 and 5 feet in thickness. Further up the river the strata retain the same direction, and in descending order, below the silver-bearing sand rock, we find at once a change in both the color and composition of the rock; we go through a series of brown sandstones and coarse conglomerate beds, of very great thickseness, which seem to be directly followed by the trappean rock series. The miner has in this brown sand rock an infallible indication that he is below the silver-bearing beds; thus, when he sees in an outcrop the dark bluish slate-like beds and the brown sand rock coming in close contact, he knows that the silver-bearing rock band must be found between. The silver is contained in the sand rock in thin leaflets and granules, in pure metallic condition; the black shaly seams covering the surface of the ledges are generally richest in metal. Narrow fissures in the sandstone are also sometimes filled out with paper-thin sheets of silver, and the small druse cavities are lined with a film of it. Remarkable is the occurrence of rock oil in some of these druse cavities. In the sand rock containing the silver, thin seams and granular specks of vitreous copper ore are usually found interspersed; the miners consider them as sulphuret of silver, but I examined the ore and found it composed of copper alone with no silver.

By repeated synclinal or anticlinal curves in which the strata are bent, in various localities higher up the river, either higher or lower beds are brought to the surface. The silver-bearing bed is found again a mile south of the stamp mill, on the properties of the Cleveland and Collins Mining Companies, which join each other; also in Little Iron River. At the Scranton mine the ore is found under the same conditions, always resting on a foot wall of brown sand rock or conglomerate, and with a hanging wall of blue slaty rock.

A very interesting fault in the strata is observable in the river bed, about fifty steps up stream from the Collins mine.

At the mine the silver-bearing bed strikes diagonally across the river, 25° east of north, with a dip south of east. An abrupt break interrupts the strata then, and a belt of almost vertical ledges of brown conglomeratic sandstones crosses the river bed in a direction 25° south of west, with a dip northwestward, and on the other side of this belt similar conglomeratic sand-rock ledges come in contiguity to it, which strike in the direction of northwest and dip northeast with moderate inclination. In the bed of Mineral River, east of Iron River, entirely similar exposures are observed. A seam of sandy rock beds, which contain sometimes immense quantities of fine scaly or granular metallic copper, is found quite as uniformly distributed as the silver-bearing seam. It is found only 6 or 8 feet above the argentiferous beds.

The Nonesuch mine is opened in these cupriferous beds; its situation is in Town. 50, R. 43, Secs. 1 and 12. The strike of the formation is there 50° east of north, dip south of east, at an angle of 30°. The hanging wall of the mine is formed by blue arenaceous slates seen in a thickness of several hundred feet, exposed in the bed of the creek. The ore bed is an argillaceous and partly conglomeratic, greenish-gray sand rock, densely crowded with fine copper scales or coarser granules of that metal. Its thickness is about 8 feet. Some few feet below the ore bed, which is naturally exposed in the creek, another sand-rock seam is noticed which can be identified with the argentiferous sand-rock seams of the mines in Iron River.

The same superposition of the two ore beds I have noticed in the bed of Mineral River. At the base of the ore beds of the Nonesuch location, the brown sand rock and conglomerate beds are well denuded in the bed of the creek, in descending toward the stamp works of the mine.

The proportion of metallic copper mixed with this sand rock is very great, fully as great as in the best picked specimens of the Calumet and Heckla conglomerate, but the finely comminuted condition of the copper causes a great loss in the stamping and washing of the rock.

In Union River, a short distance west of Little Iron River, at the foot of the Porcupine Mountains, brown sand rock and conglomerate ledges of great thickness are uncovered in the bed of the creek, dipping at an angle of from 20° to 30° in a northeast direction.

The beds can be directly followed in descending series by going up stream toward Union mine, where they are seen in conformable superposition on the amygdaloid trap belt in which Union mine is opened. Under the amygdaloid belt other conglomerates and sand-rock strata are found, which can not be distinguished in lithological characters from the upper beds. A natural exposure of the two sand-rock belts with the amygdaloid rock between is seen in a ravine close to the side of the road leading from Union mine to the Nonesuch mine. The foot-wall sand rock of the Nonesuch mine seems to be the analogue to the hanging wall of the Union mine. On the west side of the Porcupine Mountains, the shore belt has the same geological structure as the Iron River district, and in all probability the silver-bearing rock seams can be found there also.

The silver is extracted from the rock by stamping all the rock as it comes from the ledge, without selection, and subjecting the stamped rock to the amalgamation process. The results of the experiments were quite variable, yielding, per ton of rock, from fifteen to fifty dollars' worth of metallic silver. The process of amalgamation was very imperfectly carried out, leaving in the sediments which settled from the wash-water a considerable proportion of amalgam globules. I am fully convinced, therefore, that, by proper management of the process, the average quantity of silver per ton would not be less than thirty dollars. The silver seems not to be confined to certain localities, but to have a wide horizontal distribution in this rock seam; still it would be unreasonable to expect that in every locality where these rock beds are found, they should contain silver in quantities to make mining remunerative.

REPORT ON THE SLATE QUARRIES OF HURON BAY.

BY special order of the Board of Geological Survey, I left on August 23d, 1875, for Lake Superior district to examine the slate quarries on Huron Bay, with a view to reporting on the conditions under which the slate rock is found, and upon the quality of the rock as a roofing material. I spent in all two weeks on the excursion; therefore it can not be expected that I will give an exhaustive report on the complicated geological structure of this country, full as it is of upheavals. Yet I will endeavor to make a general statement covering all important facts connected with the distribution and qualities of this valuable rock species.

Let me here acknowledge the kind assistance received on this occasion from Mr. S. C. Smith, a gentleman favorably known for a great many years back as one of the most successful explorers of the Lake Superior country. He accompanied me on the excursion, and, aided by his minute acquaintance with the district, in which he had spent the whole previous season in explorations, I was enabled to see, during the short time at my disposal, nearly all the more important outcrops dispersed throughout its dense forests.

Glancing over the geological map of the Lake Superior district, issued with the report of 1873 on the Northern Peninsula, we see the area of the Huron mountains, which attain an elevation of about 1200 feet above the lake, represented as composed of the Laurentian rock series, mainly crystalline, granitic and dioritic, massive, or with obscurely stratified structure.

On its northern margin, at the foot of the mountains, which reach close up to the shore, this granitic rock series is surrounded by a narrow belt of horizontal strata of the Lake Superior sandstone, inconformably abutting against it. Southward, nearly reaching up to the highest crest of the mountain range, the Huronian rock series leans inconformably against it, with its uplifted beds, alternating between Slate rock, Quartzites, Diorites, and Jaspery strata, interstratified with heavy seams of iron ore in the form of magnetite, or as a red or brown iron oxide. These latter two are designated by the miners as red and brown hematite.

The western and northwestern slope of the granitic knot is surrounded by slates which belong likewise to the Huronian series, but differ from the slates of the Marquette district. It is not as yet clearly ascertained what position this slate occupies relative to the iron-bearing series.

The slate rock extends, at the head of the Bay of L'Anse, close to the shore, the outer edge of the shore line being formed by horizontal ledges of the Lake Superior sandstone, in plainly visible inconformable superposition on the uplifted edges of the slate rock. Mr. Hurley, of Marquette, during last summer, opened a quarry in this sand rock, and, as I am informed, found a very good marketable stone equal to the Marquette brown stones. In the slate exposures along the shore, we can see the strata frequently flexured in a series of synclinal and anticlinal axes. The slate is in shattered condition, with cleavage planes intersecting the lines of stratification at various angles; its color is a light green or bright red, or variegated. Hard and soft seams frequently alternate; it is not durable, nor does it split regularly, and can not therefore be used as a roofing slate. At intervals, belts of a metamorphic rock, intermediate in structure between a very compact glassy sandstone and a Diorite, are intercalated between the slate layers. Some of these belts are massive, like an intrusive volcanic rock, while others are distinctly bedded and alternate with thinner seams of slate rock. In places the tough, hard rock is rotten on the surface, and, when such is the case, lumps can be taken and crushed into sand by a mere pressure of the hand.

The thickness of the shale rock in the exposure can not well be estimated, as the strata repeat themselves several times on account of their synclinal and anticlinal position; but the rock is so much alike in its totality, that an identification of the corresponding strata on opposite sides of the axes of elevation can rarely be made. In one of the synclinal crevices, I noticed an interesting case of the filling up of the gap by horizontal layers of sandstone.

The bed of a creek which descends in a series of rapids, from the northern slope of the Huron mountains to the head of L'Anse Bay, presents a splendid section through at least 1000 feet of slate rock, with an approximate strike from northwest to southeast, and a southern dip. This slate is of darker color and more compact than the slate in the shore exposure, but is not at all suited for roofing purposes. Contact of the slates with the granitic rocks cropping out at the summit of this slope is not seen. Deep drift masses, mixed with slate and granitic blocks, occupy a large space between them.

The slate rock suitable for roofing is found on the northwest side of the Huron mountain range, in the vicinity of Huron Bay. A fine road 15 miles in length has been made from L'Anse to the slate quarries, which are about 3 miles south of Huron Bay, in Town. 51, R. 31, Sect. 28. From the Methodist Mission on the shore of L'Anse Bay, the road goes directly east, and for several miles along the surface rock is the horizontally stratified red sandstone which covers the entire land-spur between Huron and L'Anse Bays, with the exception of a knoll of so-called trap rock protruding on the west side of the head of the bay like an island.

Near the big bend of Silver Creek, where it changes its course from west to northeast, the road makes a steep descent and crosses the stream. The slate formation is here well uncovered; the strata are steeply inclined, dipping south, with a strike from northwest to southeast, showing, however, greater or less local variations in direction through tortuous plications on a large scale, or through minor zigzag corrugations, which frequently occur.

The slates exposed at this locality are of a blackish color, hard, silicious, and with irregular, uneven cleavage, unfitting them for roofing purposes; frequent seams of a compact, hard quartzose, hornblendic and feldspathic rock, in grain resembling a metamorphosed sandstone, alternate with the slates. Its color is either a greenish black or a light grayish shade. The road intersects the strike of the strata almost rectangularly, presenting, in its further progress, belts of slates several hundreds of feet in thickness, alternating with the hard quartzose rock generally designated by the name of trap, all retaining the same general strike and dipping direction.

We pitched our camp in the northeast corner of Sect. 25, of Town. 51, R. 32. The exposures of the slate rock at the bridge across Silver Creek are in Sect. 27, of the same town. Northeast from our camping-ground, in Sect. 19, of Town. 51, R. 31, after crossing over continued slate beds, with southern dip and the general northwest and southeast strike, we came to a high hill composed of a belt of hard, blackish-colored trap rock, about 500 feet in width, of obsoletely stratified structure, with rhomboidal cleavage cracks, and much resembling a basaltic igneous rock mass. On the other side of the crest of this hill the slate rock is met again with the same dip and strike as before. The slate is here more evenly laminated, but not of a quality that can be used for roofing.

The direct distance from our camping-place to the location of the slate quarries was three miles. In going there we had to intersect obliquely the strike of the strata, which is over all this space in the general northwest and southeast direction, with a southern dip, without a change of the direction which would cause a repetition. The thickness of the slate deposits must, consequently, be enormously great. In Section 30, after crossing two creeks running parallel with the strike of the strata, we came upon a belt of trap rock protruding as an abrupt hill range above the surrounding slate. This possibly may be the direct continuation of the trap range we found the day before, in Sect. 19, or, perhaps, a distinct belt, of which there seem to be many intercalated with the slate formation.

In Section 28 we enter the valley of another creek, along which the slate quarries are located. No change in the strike and dip of the strata is observed. The useful slate rock is a seam of the immense series already transgressed, differing from the rest only in possessing a more regularly laminated character. It is susceptible of being split into large, even slabs of any desired thickness, with a fine, silky, homogeneous grain, and combines durability and toughness with smoothness. Its color is an agreeable black, and very uniform. Several companies have located their quarries along the creek which runs parallel with the strike of the strata, and a tram-road about 3½ miles in length has been built down to the bay, where a dock is erected for the unloading of vessels and for convenient shipment of the slate.

I followed the exposures of the slate rock, which, however, are not all of the better quality, along the section lines of 28, 27, 26, and 25. Not far from there, in the next township, Range 30, Mr. Hurley has commenced to work a quarry, which so far furnishes a product fully equal in quality to that of the other quarries. On the town line between Secs. 24 and 25, I found another belt of trap protruding as an abrupt hill above the surrounding country. Its strike is nearly east and west, its dip south, and on both sides are slates of conformable strike and dip. The trap belt is about 60 feet wide, a dark hornblende rock, with quartz and chlorite veins, and divided into rhomboidal blocks by cleavage cracks, altogether resembling rather an intrusive mass than a sedimentary layer.

Along the tram-road, toward the bay, after intersecting a series of roofing slates, a dark belt of trap rock of about 100 feet thickness is crossed. Following this is a belt of white quartzite about

200 feet wide, succeeding to which are other slates of the inferior unmarketable quality. All these strata are conformable in strike and dip. Near the bay the horizontal sand-rock ledges are again encountered.

In the quarry of the Huron Bay Slate Company, the slate dips south, at an angle of from 45° to 60°. Three cleavage plains intersect the slate and divide it into rhombical blocks. The principal cleavage, with which alone it can be split into roofing slabs, is identical with the plane of stratification.

By another cleavage, intersecting the slates in horizontal direction, the walls of the quarry appear as if composed of a sequence of thick horizontal beds.

The rock mass here is frequently cleft by narrow, vertical fissures, which are filled out with different mineral substances essentially distinct in genetic character.

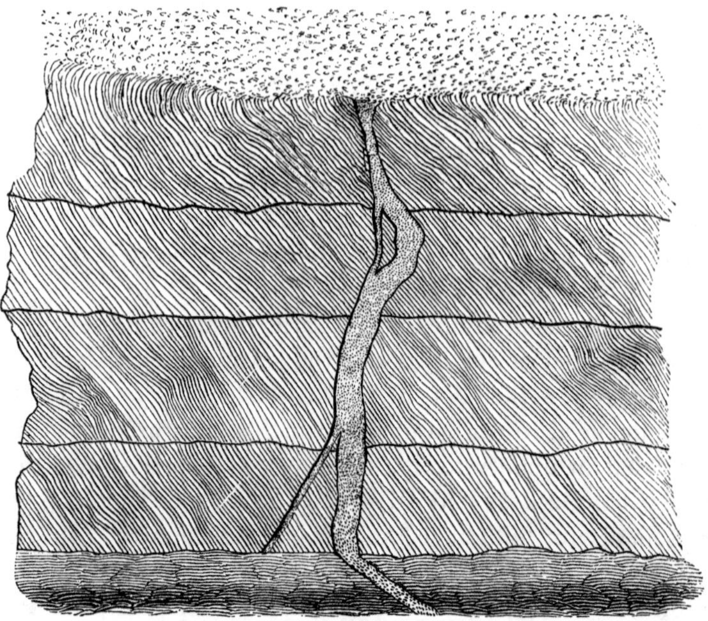

One of these fissures seen in the walls of the quarry, of irregular, somewhat tortuous form, in some places wide, in others narrow, and more than once divided into two branches, which subsequently unite, is filled with a compact, dark, greenish-colored rock mass, of amorphous or finely crystalline fracture, and interspersed with acicular sparry crystals, together with granular crystals of pyrites and some leaflets of a shining brown mica. This mass is most intimately united with the slate wall on both sides, and has all the appearance of an injected igneous body. Near the surface the fissure is wider, and the inclosed rock substance spreads laterally over the immediately surrounding surface. The greatest width of the vein is perhaps a foot, but it shrinks in places to not more than half an inch.

Another class of fissures, which are of more frequent occurrence, are filled with milk-white quartz, mixed with calcspar and iron pyrites crystals. These are rarely over an inch wide, and the matter filling them is evidently deposited there from aqueous solutions percolating through the fissures. In some of them, the walls are straight and smooth; in others the slate has broken through in zigzag lines, with strongly indented, saw-like edges, often slightly dislocated so as to bring the teeth and indentations in opposition.

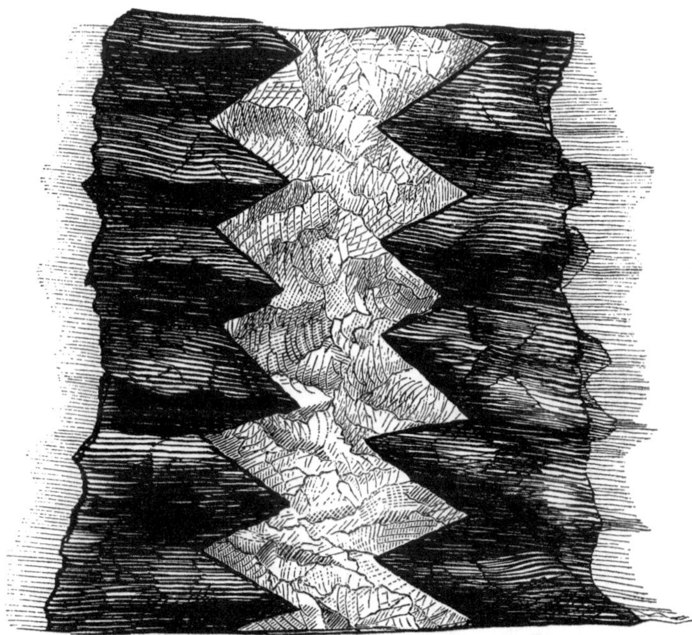

The process of quarrying the slate is attended with great waste, which is to some extent unavoidable. The slate is often unfavorably cleft, and the uplifted layers are sometimes curved or warped to such a degree as to make them unfit for roofing; but, besides this, a great waste occurs in getting out the rock, which is altogether done by blasting with powder. Necessarily, therefore, a great proportion of the loosened rock is shattered into worthless fragments.

I trust the managers and workmen of our quarries, most of whom have been at work in the slate quarries of the Eastern States, know how best to do the business; but I would take the liberty of suggesting that, by cutting narrow gangways into the walls, at intervals, the intermediate blocks or pillars could be taken out by a crowbar without the use of much powder. This would save a great part of the slate now destroyed, and in the end would be found to be a quicker process than the present.

At the time of my visit nearly 40 men were engaged in the quarry, turning out daily about 17 squares of roofing slate, which brings in the Chicago market from $7 to $8 per square.

The slate is of an excellent quality, and bears favorable comparison with the best slates of the Eastern States. In durability and in color, which is a uniform black with a grayish hue, it excels them all.

The opening of the quarries in this remote place, in the midst of a wilderness, was attended with great preliminary expense. The building of roads, the transportation of machinery, and the hire of men and constant transportation of supplies, had to be paid for at extra rates; then a long time was required in which to bring the quarry to a productive condition. I think, however, from all I can observe, that the worst difficulties have been encountered and overcome, and that nothing now stands in the way of the future prosperity of this highly commendable enterprise, undertaken at so great an expense and risk.

Several other quarries have been recently opened, in close proximity to that described above, some of which have produced already small quantities of slate for shipment, equal in quality to that of the first. The masses of good slate already discovered in the district promise an inexhaustible supply.

APPENDIX B.

REPORT ON THE SALT MANUFACTURE OF MICHIGAN.

BY

S. S. GARRIGUES, PH.D.,

STATE SALT INSPECTOR.

TABLE OF CONTENTS.

APPENDIX B.

SALT IN MICHIGAN.—HISTORICAL.

It was known from the earliest settlement of the country, that the Indians formerly supplied themselves with salt from springs existing in the peninsula, and numerous reservations of land supposed to contain the springs were made by the general government, and it is a matter of record that many years before Michigan was organized into a State government, attempts were made to manufacture the article.

By the act of admission of this State into the Union, in 1837, it will be recollected, the State authorities were permitted to select seventy-two sections of salt-spring lands.

A State geologist—the lamented Dr. Douglas Houghton—was appointed at the first meeting of the Legislature thereafter, who, in his report to the Legislature in January, 1838, says he regarded it important that the spring lands be selected for State purposes, at as early a day as possible, and most of his examinations the season previous were devoted to that end. Dr. Houghton's explorations resulted in finding many indications of saline springs, particularly on the Grand and Tittibawassee rivers, in Kent and Saginaw Counties, and also in St. Clair, Macomb, Wayne, and Jackson Counties. The Legislature passed an act for the improvement of the State springs in 1838, and by virtue of his appointment, Dr. Houghton was authorized to make examinations and to institute experiments, which he did on the Grand and Tittibawassee rivers with partial success.

Although public attention was at that time directed to our salt springs, and practical investigations relating to their development were for a time vigorously prosecuted, these experiments failed of complete success, and the subsequent death of Dr. Houghton, by depriving the State of one on whom it had relied to give intelligent direction to these enterprises, discouraged in a measure their further prosecution.

Guided, however, by the information thus furnished, other investigators took up the matter, and on a thorough examination of the subject became so fully satisfied of the existence of rich saline waters in our State, that they at once determined to extend their experimental researches still further, and soon demonstrated in the most satisfactory manner the entire correctness of the theory advanced.

Saginaw valley has the honor of having practically proved the wisdom of our first State geologist, in regard to the saline resources of the State, and demonstrated in a few short years, to an extent hardly to be credited, their unlimited supply, as well as their profitable and beneficial nature. Encouraged by the information furnished by the geological surveys, borings in several localities have been extended to other groups of rocks, much older and lower than the preceding, viz., Onondaga salt group—the representation in this State of the group so called in the State of New-York—and though their productiveness is not yet perhaps satisfactorily established, sufficient encouragement has been received to afford reasonable hopes that these rocks may yet yield a supply of salt sufficient to render them a source of profit, thus adding immensely to the saline wealth of the State.

WELL-BORING MACHINERY.

The proper location having been selected for the salt well, a drill house, 16 by 30 feet, with a tower, is erected. This is large enough for a boiler, small portable engine, and a forge for repairing tools and keeping the drill sharp.

The tower or derrick has a height of 50 feet, or is high enough to draw out the drilling poles. The tool with which the boring or drilling is done is a drill, 3 feet long, shaped at one end like a chisel, and made of the best quality of steel.

The drill is screwed into the sinker, which is a round iron bar 40 feet long and 3 inches in diameter, and weighing about 2000 pounds.

Attached to the sinkers by strong screws are the "jars;" these are about 7 feet long and made of good iron. The "jars" are two slotted links, moving up and down within each other, and are intended to increase the force of the blow of the drill upon the rock by allowing it to fall with a sudden jerk.

The jars are attached by a screw to the drill pole, which is, in turn, connected by a swivel to a chain. The chain is fastened to an ordinary "walking-beam" of wood, driven by an engine of small horse-power.

The beam rises and falls continually over the mouth of the well, the chain which suspends the tool passing over the end of the beam, being so arranged that it can be let out as the hole deepens, at the same time lifting the tool or drill and allowing it to drop with measured stroke on the rock, which is thus gradually drilled out. A workman sits at the mouth of the well, having the pole grasped by his hands, and after every stroke the poles are slightly turned so as to turn the drill which is working on the bottom, thus keeping the well true and circular in shape.

While the well is in process of boring, the tools are frequently removed and the sand pump introduced to remove the loose matter from the bottom of the well, which is done by means of a suction valve. The sand pump removes all the ground rock sand, and takes up at times stones an inch or more in size. In commencing the well, a strong wooden box 8 inches square, made from 2-inch plank, is driven down into the ground, say from 14 to 16 feet. Inside of this, an 8-inch iron tube or casing is put down as fast as the alluvial or drift material overlying the rock formation is broken up by the drill and taken out by the sand pump; this continues until the solid rock is reached.

At this point, considerable care should be taken that the opening into the rock is perfectly round and well finished by the drill; for the casing should be set so firmly in the rock as to prevent any sand or gravel from running in under the tube, and thus getting in on top of the drill and endangering its becoming fastened in the well.

The rock-drilling now commences and continues to the depth to which it is proposed to sink the well. After the drilling is done, the sides of the well are smoothed off with a tool called a reamer.

In most of the salt wells on the Saginaw River an offset is placed in the well at a short distance above the lower sand rock. Below the offset the size of the well is lessened half an inch in diameter.

On this offset is made the so-called rock-packing, the hole being drilled bevelling so as to receive a tightly-fitting iron collar or funnel-shaped piece of metal. A tube corresponding to the size of the upper part of the well is made to rest on this rock-packing as the offset, and runs to the top of the well; in this way, all the weak brine from the upper rock and any fresh water that may come into the well above the offset are shut off. Below the offset, the tube continues in reduced size to the locality of the lower sand rock, at which point the pumping chamber containing the pumping valves is placed.

In the early history of salt-well boring in Michigan, the pressure of the brine in the well tube forced it within 100 feet of the surface. More recently, owing no doubt to the great demand for brine, it does not rise so high. It only requires a small amount of power, after the pumping rods are properly balanced, to lift the brine out of the well into the settling tanks.

PUMPING BRINE.

Often, in starting up a new salt well, the brine is weak—that is, shows a small percentage of salt by the salinometer. This arises from the fact that a large quantity of fresh water or weak brine from the upper formations has passed down into the well during the time the well was opened or being tubed. To test this point, and to bring the brine up to the usual strength of salt brines, the pump is put in operation and run for some time. If the brine continues to show an increase of strength on being tested by the salinometer, the pumping is continued until the strength of brine remains permanent at such a percentage as wells of equal depth in the same locality have shown.

If, however, the brine does not increase in strength, there are strong probabilities that there is a leakage of fresh water or weak brine into the well at the offset. This should be remedied at once—the more so if the well is a deep one, such as most of those in the Saginaw Valley are; for in this case the offset in the well is below the so-called gypsum formation, and you are drawing in and mixing with your strong brine a weak brine from these formations which has a higher percentage of gypsum.

This mixing of the two brines in the well and tubing causes a precipitation or separation of the gypsum upon the pumping rods and in the pumping chamber. If this is not stopped, it will eventually close up the valves, and prevent them from being drawn out of the chamber. More than one instance has been known where parties have suffered much extra expense in not attending to this kind of leakage.

A manufacturer, in starting up his well pump, may also find that he has a short supply of brine, and the brine in the well tube runs down as soon as the pump is stopped. In this case he may have strong suspicions that his well tube is defective, or that the joints are not put together tightly, causing a leakage. To ascertain where this is, the tubing should be lifted out, the lower valve being allowed to remain in. As the tubing is being drawn, the pressure of the column of brine in the tube on the joints or imperfections will show where the leakage is. If the tubing is imperfect, it should be taken out and replaced by perfect tubing. When the leakage is at the joint, a new thread should be cut upon it, or the joint should be screwed together more tightly.

It is very important that the salt manufacturer should ever be on the lookout for these leakages, as they may and do often arise from a jarring of the tubing in running the pump faster than the supply of brine comes to the pumping chamber, causing a vacuum and producing the so-called pounding of a well. The capacity of a well has been very materially affected by such a leakage, increasing the expense of pumping from 50 to 100 per cent.

The supply capacity of a well is also very materially increased by the position of the pumping chamber in the well. In the early history of salt wells in Michigan, the pumping chamber was generally placed a short distance below the offset. More recent tests go to prove that the best location for the pumping chamber is at or very near the point where the largest supply of brine comes into the well, and that point is the lower portion of the sand rock, or within a short distance of the bottom of the well.

In pumping a well, it is also important that the weight of the pumping rods should be evenly counterbalanced by a weight on the other end of the walking-beam; this relieves the engine, the only weight to be lifted being the brine.

The stroke of the piston in the pumping chamber should be made as long as possible, and the motion of the engine should not be over 32 revolutions to the minute. In this way, about the entire supply of brine in the well is obtained, without forming a vacuum, thus preventing the pounding of the well and the danger of parting the pumping rods or jarring the tubing loose at the joints, causing leakage.

The capacity of salt wells varies in different localities, from 12 to 20 gallons per minute—the size of the well and the quantity and porosity of the sand rock having much to do in increasing the amount. A good well will fill a cistern 20 x 30 x 6 feet in about 20 hours. A salt well in Saginaw City owned by Pierson, Wright & Co. produced enough brine during a manufacturing season of eight months to make over 26,000 barrels of salt. At East Tawas, the wells, 3½ inches in diameter, fill a cistern of the above size in about twelve hours. At Port Austin, the well fills a cistern in seventeen hours.

TESTING THE STRENGTH OF BRINES BY SALINOMETER, WITH COMPARATIVE TABLES.

The following table is extracted from Alexander Winchell's Report on the Geology of Michigan, published in 1861; it has been thought advisable to reprint it at length as a guide to our salt manufacturers.

"Pure water dissolves, at ordinary temperature, a little over one third its weight of salt, or from thirty-five to thirty-six hundredths. The amount varies somewhat with the temperature, and the results of different experiments are, moreover, not perfectly accordant; but from the most accurate observations, it appears that 100 parts by weight of pure saturated brine, at temperatures from 32° to 70° Fahr., contain from 26.3 to 26.7 parts of salt. Some earlier determination, however, gave but 25.7 parts, and upon this figure the table was calculated.

"The specific gravity of a saturated brine at 60° Fahr. is 1.205 pure water, being 1.000. The salinometer employed in many salt works for fixing the value of brine is an areometer with an arbitrary scale divided into 100 parts. The density of water on this scale is represented by 0° and that of saturated brine by 100°. Each degree of the salinometer, therefore, corresponds very nearly to one quarter of one per cent of salt. In the following table, the true specific gravity, with the corresponding degree of the salinometer, and of the hydrometer of Baumé, is given in the first three columns. The succeeding columns give the percentage of salt in a pure brine for each degree of the salinometer, the number of grains of salt to the wine pint of 36,625 cubic inches, and the number of gallons of such brine required to yield a bushel of salt weighing 56 pounds.

"From this table the properties and capabilities of any brine may be ascertained by knowing its strength as shown by the salinometer. Suppose, for instance, the salinometer shows 53°. The table shows at a glance that this corresponds to 13.78° of Baumé's hydrometer, a specific gravity of 1.100, and a percentage of 13.62; while a wine pint of the brine would furnish 1092 grains of a solid residue, and 44.7 gallons would produce a bushel.

"If the strength of a brine is expressed by giving its specific gravity, and we wish to compare the strength as thus stated with that of another brine given in degrees of the salinometer, or the number of grains in a pint, and we look in the column of 'specific gravity' in the foregoing table, and find the number which agrees nearest with the given one, then on the same horizontal we have all the synonymous expressions for the same strength, and it is seen at once whether the brine with which we wish to make the comparison is stronger or weaker.

"Or suppose, thirdly, that a land-owner desires to know the comparative strength of a brine spring on his premises, while he possesses no instrument for taking specific gravity. Let him evaporate a wine pint and weigh the residue, or take it to the apothecary to weigh; then the number of grains found in the fifth column of the table will show him all the equivalent expressions.

TABLE GIVING A COMPARISON OF DIFFERENT EXPRESSIONS FOR THE STRENGTH OF BRINE, FROM ZERO TO SATURATION.

Degrees Salinometer	Degrees Baumé.	Specific Gravity.	Per cent of Salt.	Grains of Salt in one Pint.	Gallons for a Bushel of Salt.
0	0	1.000	0	0	Infinite.
1	.26	1.002	0.26	19	2599
2	.52	1.003	0.51	38	1297
3	.78	1.005	0.77	56	863
4	1.04	1.007	1.03	75	647
5	1.30	1.009	1.28	94	516
6	1.56	1.010	1.54	114	430
7	1.82	1.012	1.80	133	368

Degrees Salinometer.	Degrees Baumé.	Specific Gravity.	Per cent of Salt.	Grains of Salt in one Pint.	Gallons for a Bushel of Salt.
8	2.08	1.014	2.06	152	321
9	2.34	1.016	2.31	171	285
10	2.60	1.017	2.57	191	256
11	2.86	1.019	2.83	210	232
12	3.12	1.021	3.08	229	213
13	3.38	1.023	3.34	249	196
14	3.64	1.025	3.60	269	182
15	3.90	1.026	3.85	288	169
16	4.16	1.028	4.11	308	158
17	4.42	1.030	4.37	328	149
18	4.68	1.032	4.63	348	140
19	4.94	1.034	4.88	368	133
20	5.20	1.035	5.14	388	126
21	5.46	1.037	5.40	408	120
22	5.72	1.039	5.65	428	114
23	5.98	1.041	5.91	448	109
24	6.24	1.043	6.17	469	104
25	6.50	1.045	6.42	489	99.7
26	6.76	1.046	6.68	510	95.7
27	7.02	1.048	6.94	530	92.0
28	7.28	1.050	7.20	551	89.5
29	7.54	1.052	7.45	572	85.3
30	7.80	1.054	7.71	592	82.3
31	8.06	1.056	7.97	613	79.5
32	8.32	1.058	8.22	634	76.9
33	8.58	1.059	8.48	655	74.5
34	8.84	1.061	8.74	676	72.1
35	9.10	1.063	8.99	697	69.9
36	9.36	1.065	9.25	719	67.9
37	9.62	1.067	9.51	740	65.9
38	9.88	1.069	9.77	761	64.1
39	10.14	1.071	10.02	783	62.3
40	10.40	1.073	10.28	804	60.6
41	10.66	1.075	10.54	826	59.1
42	10.92	1.077	10.79	848	57.6
43	11.18	1.079	11.05	869	56.1
44	11.44	1.081	11.31	891	54.7
45	11.70	1.083	11.56	913	53.4
46	11.96	1.085	11.82	935	52.2
47	12.22	1.087	11.08	957	50.9
48	12.48	1.089	12.34	979	49.8
49	12.74	1.091	12.59	1002	48.7
50	13.00	1.093	12.85	1024	47.6
51	13.26	1.095	13.11	1047	46.6
52	13.52	1.097	13.36	1070	45.6
53	13.78	1.100	13.62	1092	44.7
54	14.04	1.102	13.88	1115	43.8
55	14.30	1.104	14.13	1137	42.9

Degrees Salinometer.	Degrees Baumé.	Specific Gravity.	Per cent of Salt.	Grains of Salt in one Pint.	Gallons for a Bushel of Salt.
56	14.56	1.106	14.39	1160	42.0
57	14.82	1.108	14.65	1183	41.2
58	15.08	1.110	14.91	1206	40.4
59	15.34	1.112	15.16	1229	39.7
60	15.60	1.114	15.43	1252	38.9
61	15.86	1.116	15.68	1276	38.2
62	16.12	1.118	15.93	1299	37.5
63	16.38	1.121	16.19	1322	36.9
64	16.64	1.123	16.45	1346	36.2
65	16.90	1.125	16.70	1370	35.6
66	17.16	1.127	16.96	1393	35.0
67	17.42	1.129	17.22	1417	34.4
68	17.68	1.131	17.48	1441	33.9
69	17.94	1.133	17.73	1465	33.3
70	18.20	1.136	17.99	1489	32.7
71	18.46	1.138	18.25	1513	32.2
72	18.72	1.140	18.50	1538	31.7
73	18.98	1.142	18.76	1562	31.2
74	19.24	1.144	19.02	1587	30.7
75	19.50	1.147	19.27	1611	30.3
76	19.76	1.149	19.53	1636	29.8
77	20.02	1.151	19.79	1661	29.4
78	20.28	1.154	20.05	1686	28.9
79	20.54	1.156	20.30	1710	28.5
80	20.80	1.158	20.56	1736	28.1
81	21.06	1.160	20.82	1761	27.7
82	21.32	1.163	21.07	1786	27.3
83	21.58	1.165	21.33	1811	26.9
84	21.84	1.167	21.59	1837	26.5
85	22.10	1.170	21.84	1862	26.2
86	22.36	1.172	22.10	1888	25.8
87	22.62	1.175	22.36	1914	25.5
88	22.88	1.177	22.62	1940	25.1
89	23.14	1.179	22.87	1966	24.8
90	23.40	1.182	23.13	1992	24.5
91	23.66	1.184	23.39	2018	24.2
92	23.92	1.186	23.64	2045	23.8
93	24.18	1.189	23.90	2072	23.5
94	24.44	1.191	24.16	2098	23.2
95	24.70	1.194	24.41	2124	23.0
96	24.96	1.196	24.67	2151	22.7
97	25.22	1.198	24.93	2178	22.4
98	25.48	1.201	25.19	2205	22.1
99	25.74	1.203	25.44	2232	21.8
100	26.00	1.205	25.70	2259	21.6

"In making use of the table, it must be remembered that it will prove accurate only for *pure solutions of salt.* In this state, the chloride of calcium and magnesium which existed to some extent in our brines will cause the table to make a showing too favorable. As the percentage of impurities is a variable quantity, it was impossible to make allowance for them in the table. Though we can not therefore construct a table practically accurate, it is not thought best to discard all attempts at a table. As long as it is thought desirable to use the salinometer, it seems to be a matter of convenience to have at hand the ready means for converting its reading into the equivalent expressions.

"It must also be borne in mind that brines of the same strength possess different densities, depending upon the temperature, the density rapidly diminishing as the temperature rises. It is consequently necessary to experiment on brines at a uniform or standard temperature. The ordinary standard for hydrometrical operation is 60° Fahrenheit's thermometer, but the standard temperature at the Onondaga salines is 52°, that being the natural temperature of the brine as it issues from the well.

BRINE ANALYSES.

The first practical attempt at salt-well boring in Grand Rapids was commenced August 12th, 1859, and finished October 14th, being 257 feet deep. A sample of brine taken at this time was analyzed by Prof. Fish, with the following results:

Specific gravity	1.01752
Fixed constituents	2.33385 per ct.
Carbonate of iron	0.00145
" lime	0.00473
" magnesia	0.00084
Free carbonic acid	0.00603
Silicic acid	0.00025
Sulphate of lime	0.13120
Chloride of calcium	0.27641
Chloride of magnesium	0.07196
Chloride of potassium	0.01561
Chloride of sodium (salt)	1.73696
Loss	0.08841
	2.33385

"Salt operations in Saginaw valley were first commenced in 1859. Through the influence of Dr. George A. Lathrop, the East Saginaw Salt Manufacturing Company was organized in April of that year, and commenced operations in May following. First well completed in March, 1860; first salt made in July, 1860."

Soon after passing into the first rock, indications of salt brine were found, and the following table shows the strength of brine obtained therefrom at various depths:

At 90 feet	1 degree.
" 102 "	2 degrees.
" 211 "	10 "
" 212 "	14 "
" 487 "	26 "
" 516 "	40 "
" 531 "	44 "
" 559 "	60 "
" 569 "	64 "
" 606 "	86 "
" 636 "	90 "

An analysis of brine from this well made by Prof. Douglass, on April 11th, 1860, is as follows:

Specific gravity	1.179
Saline matter	22.017 per ct.
Chloride of sodium (salt)	17.912
" calcium	2.142
" magnesium	1.522
Sulphate of lime	.116
Carbonate of iron	.105
Chloride of potassium	.220
Water	77.983
	100.000

Composition of brines taken from various salt wells on Saginaw River, in October, 1862, and analyzed by Dr. C. A. Goesmann—this investigation being directed to ascertain their commercial value:

Portsmouth, Bay County, Michigan. Depth of well, 664 feet. Brine, 54° by salinometer.

Sulphate of lime (gypsum)	0.4884
Chloride of calcium..................	0.3472
" magnesium................	0.4333
" sodium (salt)..............	12.5315
Saline matter.....................	13.8004
Water	86.1996
	100.0000

Gillmore Well, Bay City, Michigan. Depth of well, 505 feet. Brine, 65° by salinometer.

Sulphate of lime (gypsum)	0.3961
Chloride of calcium..................	0.5302
" magnesium	0.4115
" sodium (salt)..............	15.2674
Saline matter.....................	16.6052
Water	83.3948
	100.0000

The two brines, as the depth of the wells will show, are from the upper salt-bearing sand rock, and are quite characteristic of this formation, as shown by the large percentage of gypsum and low percentage of chlorides.

Swift & Lockwood's Well, Saginaw City. Depth of well, 860 feet. Brine, 86° salinometer.

Sulphate of lime (gypsum)	0.0983
Chloride of calcium..................	2.6430
" magnesium	1.0685
" sodium (salt)..............	17.5103
Saline matter.....................	21.3201
Water	78.6799
	100.0000

East Saginaw Salt Manufacturing Company, East Saginaw. Depth of well, 806 feet. Salinometer, 80°.

Sulphate of lime (gypsum)	0.1516
Chloride of calcium	2.2665
" magnesium	0.9629
" sodium (salt)	16.8636
Saline matter	20.2446
Water	79.7554
	100.0000

Bangor Salt Manufacturing Company, Banks, Bay Co., Michigan. Depth of well, 774 feet. Brine, 95° salinometer.

Sulphate of lime (gypsum)	0.0722
Chloride of calcium	2.9611
" magnesium	1.2612
" sodium (salt)	19.8595
Saline matter	24.1540
Water	75.8460
	100.0000

These three specimens of brine, as the depth of the wells will show, are from the lower salt-bearing sand rock, called the Napoleon sandstone by Winchell. The analysis shows a decrease in the percentage of gypsum, an increased percentage of the earth chlorides, and increased quantity of salt.

These are the representative brines of the Saginaw River, and are those which are mostly worked for their salt.

Composition of brines taken from wells outside of the Saginaw valley:

Ayres & Co.'s Salt Well, Port Austin, Huron Co., Michigan. Depth of well, 1198 feet. Brine, 88° salinometer.

Sulphate of lime	0.0129
Chloride of calcium	3.1274
" magnesium	1.5675
" sodium (salt)	17.6161
Saline matter	22.3239
Water	77.6761
	100.0000

Grant & Co.'s Salt Well, East Tawas, Iosco Co., Michigan. Depth of well, 905 feet. Salinometer, 85°.

Sulphate of lime (gypsum)	0.0350
Chloride of calcium	3.4843
" magnesium	1.2433
" sodium (salt)	15.6141
Saline matter	20.3767
Water	79.6233
	100.0000

The analyses of these brines show a marked increase in the earthy chlorides, and are without doubt from a lower saliferous horizon, located in the Devonian strata, and consequently intermediate between the Onondaga formation and the Michigan salt group—this same formation having been struck at Caseville, Huron County, at the depth of 1750 feet, and at Blackmar's Mills, 13 miles east of East Saginaw, at the depth of 1675 feet. The new wells going down at Oscoda, Mich., are without doubt in this formation also.

Composition of brines taken from wells on the Lake Shore of Huron County, and representing an excellent quality of brine for salt manufacturing—nearly approaching the Goderich brines in freedom from the earthy chlorides:

Sand Beach Well, Huron County. Depth of well, 702 feet. Brine, 84° salinometer. Analysis by Dr. S. P. Duffield.

Sulphate of lime (gypsum)	0.2539
Chloride of calcium	0.3000
" magnesium	0.1591
" sodium (salt)	22.5673
Saline matter	23.2803
Water	76.7197
	100.0000

White Rock Well, Huron County. Depth of well, 566 feet. Brine, 78.5° salinometer.

Sulphate of lime (gypsum)	0.2623
Chloride of calcium	0.5373

Chloride of magnesium	0.4106
" sodium (salt)	18.9134
Saline matter	20.1236
Water	79.8764
	100.0000

The following analyses of Michigan brines, made by H. C. Hahn, Ph.D., will show the chemical composition of other brines not included in the above list:

Oneida Salt Company, Crow Island, Zilwaukie. Specific gravity of brine, 1.1864.

Sodic chloride (salt)	19.304
Calcic chloride	2.623
Magnesic chloride	1.343
Calcic sulphate (gypsum)	0.080
" carbonate	trace
Magnesic carbonate	"
Ferrous carbonate	0.0054
" chloride	0.0032
Magnesic bromide	traces
Carbonic acid	"
Water	76.269
	99.6276

New-York Solar Salt Company, Zilwaukie. Specific gravity of brine, 1.1930.

Sodic chloride (salt)	19.914
Calcic chloride	3.040
Magnesic chloride	1.419
Calcic sulphate	0.073
" carbonate	0.0010
Magnesic carbonate	0.0006
Ferrous carbonate	0.0058
" chloride	0.0038
Water	75.042
	99.498

Michigan Solar Salt Company, Zilwaukie. Specific gravity of brine, 1.1900.

Sodic chloride	19.671
Calcic chloride	2.916
Magnesic chloride	1.381
Calcic sulphate	0.082
" carbonate	0.0010
Ferrous carbonate	0.0123
Magnesic carbonate	0.0015
Carbonic acid	trace
Water	75.715
	99.7800

Smith, Kelly & Dwight Well, at Oscoda, Iosco Co., Michigan. Specific gravity, 1.182. Depth of well, 1070 feet.

Sodic chloride (salt)	17.93
Calcic chloride	4.21
Magnesic chloride	1.93
Calcic sulphate	trace
" carbonate	"
Saline matter	24.19
Water	75.81
	100.000

RECEPTION AND SETTLING OF BRINE.

The salt manufacturer having satisfied himself in regard to the quantity and quality of the brine supply, must now be prepared with cisterns to store his brine during the process of settling.

These cisterns or outside settlers were formerly built in size 20 by 30 feet and 6 feet deep, having a capacity of 25,000 gallons. More recently the size of these has been increased to suit the wants of the manufacturer. They are built of sound 2 to 3 inch plank, well and properly keyed together by strong gripes, and are also calked to prevent leakage. These cisterns are elevated on piling or framed timbers, high enough to allow the settled brine to flow through pipes to the blocks.

The connections from the cisterns into the pipes are 6 inches above the bottom, the flow of the brine being controlled by gates. The supply pipes from the cisterns are usually made of wooden pump logs having a 3-inch bore.

The brine, as shown by the analyses, contains a small percentage of carbonate of protoxide of iron, held in solution by an excess of carbonic acid.

If the brine was boiled down or evaporated with this iron in, it would give the salt a red color and very materially affect its commercial value.

As soon as the cistern is filled with brine, preparation should be made to settle it. A tight box large enough to hold a barrel or more of water is placed on the top of the cistern. In this a proper quantity of fresh burnt lime is slacked with fresh water, enough being afterward added to fill the box, so as to make a whitewash or milk of lime. This mixture being a caustic lime, is freely sprinkled over the brine. The brine is then thoroughly "plunged"—that is, it is stirred up until the lime is well mixed with the brine. The caustic mixture of lime having a strong affinity for the carbonic acid extracts the same from the brine, thus releasing the iron which is precipitated with the lime to the bottom of the cistern as an insoluble peroxide of iron. The brine is then allowed to rest for 48 hours, when it is quite clear and ready for the boiling house or block. This process is called "settling," and on the care with which it is conducted depends much of the success in making good salt.

EVAPORATION OF BRINE.

Having made a stock of settled brine, the next process in the manufacture of salt is the evaporation of the brine; and this is effected by three different methods:

1st. By the direct application of fire-heat to kettles and pans.

2d. By the use of steam, either exhaust steam from saw-mills, or steam generated by flue boilers built expressly for the purpose.

3d. By solar evaporation.

EVAPORATION OF BRINE IN KETTLE BLOCKS.

A kettle block for evaporation of brine consists of a wooden building, 140 feet long by 45 to 50 feet wide, with an elevation of 18 feet, so framed as to admit of the steam passing out at the ventilators. In this building are set from fifty to sixty kettles, having each a capacity of from 100 to 120 gallons. The kettles are set in two rows over arches running from the mouth or furnace to the chimney. These are called "arches." These arches run close together, with a dividing wall between them; the kettles are set close together in a row, resting on the dividing wall on the one side and on the inside wall on the other.

The fire arch or furnace at the front is 3 feet from the bottom of the kettles; from here the bottom of the arch gradually rises so that under the back kettles the space is only 10 or 12 inches. Here the flue passes into the chimney, which is about 40 to 50 feet high.

Between the arches and the salt bins, which are under the same building, is the sidewalk. On this sidewalk the salt boiler operates in drawing the salt from the kettles into the draining baskets, which, when it is sufficiently drained, are wheeled off to the salt bins on this sidewalk or platform. The bins, which run the entire length of the block, are divided off in sections, and are made with open floors for the proper drainage of the salt.

Through the centre of the block, just on top of the middle wall, two sets of pump logs or pipes are laid—one for fresh water, and one for the settled brine, each of them being supplied with faucets for each kettle.

The kettles, after being well cleansed, are filled with brine, and boiling soon commences after the fire is under good headway. A scum rises to the surface, which is taken off with a skimmer.

Of late years, owing to the dry and light material used for fuel (being the refuse slabs from saw-mills), the first ten or fifteen kettles in the arch are protected from the excessive heat by patent arches, which are built over the fire flue, and directly under the bottom of the kettle. By this arrangement and a narrowing of the flue, the heat is distributed more evenly through the entire arch, and the kettles boil more regularly.

Soon after the brine commences to boil, the crystals of salt commence to form on the top, and then fall to the bottom. When the brine is boiled down to about one third, the salt is dipped out with a ladle and thrown into a basket, which is placed over one side of the kettle. The salt is allowed to remain in the basket for two or three hours, the bitter water containing the earthy chlorides being thus drained off. Thorough drainage is considered an important point in this mode of manufacture. The balance of the brine or bitter water remaining in the kettle is now bailed out and thrown into the drainage trough. The kettle is then rinsed out with fresh water, and again filled up with brine.

The difference of the time in which the front and the back kettles boil down varies from four hours in the front to twelve hours in the back. The kettle blocks are generally run day and night by four men, two boilers and two firemen, taking tours of twelve hours each. The average product of a good kettle block is seventy-five barrels of salt per day of twenty-four hours.

EVAPORATION OF BRINE IN PAN BLOCKS.

Pan blocks are buildings of various dimensions, built to accommodate the size of the pan, settlers, and salt bins.

The pans are made of quarter-inch boiler-plate iron. They vary from 90 to 120 feet in length, being divided into sections of 30 or 40 feet, are 12 to15 feet wide, and from 10 to 12 inches deep. With some the sides are straight, the salt being raked to the side, lifted out with a shovel, and thrown on the draining boards. In others, the sides are flanged, and the salt is raked directly on to the draining boards.

Pans of the above size rest on three walls as in kettle blocks, the arches running directly under the pan to the chimney at the end. As the firing of these blocks is done mostly with slabs and light fuel, the first 30 or 40 feet are also protected by patent arches thrown across the flues, thus dividing the heat more generally throughout the block.

The brine boils very rapidly in these blocks, and as the salt makes fast, it requires much care and attention on the part of the workmen to keep the salt from baking on the bottom of the pan; this is prevented by raking out the salt almost as fast as it makes.

Improvements in heating pan blocks have been made of late years in those localities where the price of fuel is a consideration. A pan block of an improved plan for boiling the brine has been erected by Messrs. Ayres & Co., of Port Austin, Huron County.

The block is 120 feet long, 43 feet wide, outside post 10 feet high, and centre post 18 feet high—almost too high to carry off the steam in winter. The length was also calculated for four pans. Three pans only were put on, being each 30 feet long and 16 feet wide on bottom, sides flanging and bolted to the draining boards.

The pans rest on seven walls, which are so arranged that they make two fire flues in the centre and two return flues on the sides.

The centre and outside walls run the entire length and width of the pan. All the walls are a foot wide at the top. The two fire flues which are under the middle of the pan on both sides of the centre wall are 2½ feet wide. Height of grate to pan, 3½ feet. The return flues are next to the outside walls, under the sides of the pan, and are 2 feet wide. This gives a heating surface of 180 feet in length on both sides of the middle wall. The outside flues run into the chimney, which is placed at one side of the front of the block—the space under the pan being reduced to one foot.

The advantage of this arrangement of the flues is that, as the brine boils freely over the fire flues, the salt, as it makes, is thrown to the cool side of the pan, and therefore it is not so liable to bake to the bottom of the pan before it is raked out. Another advantage is in the economy of the heating surface, the entire amount being well used up before it gets to the chimney. This is shown in the amount of salt made—Ayres & Co. reporting the making of 140 barrels of salt with 13 cords of hemlock wood in a day of 24 hours.

The brine for pan blocks is settled cold in the outside cisterns, and in most instances is brought to saturation by the inside steam settlers. The salt, as it makes in the pan, is drawn out by rakes upon the draining boards, where it remains for a time, when it is shovelled into barrows and taken to the store bins for further drainage.

It is very desirable that the draining boards should be so arranged in pan blocks that the workmen should not be compelled to walk over them in the operation of drawing or wheeling off the salt.

EVAPORATION OF BRINE BY STEAM.

The evaporation of salt brine by the steam process is now producing the largest portion of salt made in Michigan.

In describing the arrangements of a steam salt block and the accompanying process, we have selected the steam salt block, drill

J. Bien lith.

WORKS OF THE BUFFALO SALT CO.

house, cisterns, and saw mills of the Buffalo Salt Company, managed by Sears & Holland, of East Saginaw, and represented in the accompanying view.

This steam salt block is 140 feet long, 122 feet wide, and has an elevation of 52 feet to the top of the ventilator. Height of ventilator, 16 feet. Included therefore in the above space are the inside settlers, grainers, salt bins, and packing room.

The inside steam settlers are 136 feet long, 9 feet wide, and 6 feet deep, made of 4-inch plank, well keyed together and tightly calked.

This block is supplied with seven grainers, 136 feet long, 7½ feet wide, and 16 inches deep.

Over each grainer are the draining boards running the entire length. Passing through each settler and grainer, and near the bottom, are 4-inch galvanized tubing, four to five in number, depending on the size of the grainer, through which exhaust or live steam is forced.

In the steam as in the kettle process, the brine is first pumped into the outside settlers, where it is partially settled. It is then drawn into the inside steam settlers, where it is heated up by the steam pipes and brought to saturation—that is, a point just preceding the formation of salt crystals. It is allowed to remain until all sediment of iron has fallen to the bottom, by which time it becomes clear as crystal.

The brine is now ready to be drawn into the grainers, which are filled to about two thirds their capacity, or nearly full. As the settled brine comes into the grainers quite warm and fully saturated, it soon commences to make salt, which forms on the surface of the brine, and then falls to the bottom of the grainers, when a new lot of crystals are formed, to fall in the same way. The brine is also occasionally stirred so as to make the crystals fine. Thus the evaporation continues for twenty-four hours, the temperature being kept at from 170° to 175° of Fahrenheit. The brine being sufficiently evaporated by this time, the workmen commence the "lifting." This is done by first washing the salt in the brine that is left in the grainers, and then taking it out with shovels and throwing it on the draining boards, where it remains a number of hours for drainage.

A large "lift" or "draw" fills the boards with salt, and it is a beautiful sight to see the salt as it comes white and sparkling from the brine. The salt should remain on the draining boards to drain thoroughly, twenty-four hours if possible, before going to the bins. It lies in the bins two weeks to complete the drainage, when it is ready for inspection and barrelling for shipment.

SOLAR EVAPORATION OF BRINE.

The first preparation for solar evaporation is to have a series of covers or wooden vats. The covers are rectangular in shape, being 16 by 18 feet and from 6 to 8 inches deep. They are raised on wooden supports 2 to 3 feet from the ground, and are arranged in sets or strings. Each cover has a movable roof, which can be run on or off to protect or expose the brine, according to the weather. At the end of the string of graining covers, somewhat higher and deeper, are the "strings" of settling covers into which the brine is led from the store reservoirs or cisterns. No lime is used in settling the brine in this process; for in these deep rooms, the brine absorbs a portion of oxygen from the air, by which means the carbonate of iron, which is dissolved in the recent brine, is converted into an insoluble peroxide of iron. In Syracuse, a second series of covers are used to get rid of the gypsum, which separates or is deposited in the form of a crystal. As the quantity of gypsum is very small in the Saginaw brines these rooms are now dispensed with.

As soon as there is a show of salt crystals, the first stage of the process is accomplished, and the saturated brine known as salt pickle is ready for the last stage. It is then drawn into the salt room or graining vats, in which the salt soon commences to crystallize on the bottom of the covers.

"One of the conditions required for the production of a good, large-grained solar salt, which is most esteemed in the market, is that the bottom of the covers in the salt room should be as smooth as possible, rough surfaces favoring the deposition of numerous small crystals. It is also necessary to have the salt covers supplied with a sufficient supply of good pickle, so that the salt already deposited may always be covered. An exposure of the salt uncovered to the air favors the formation of new small crystals, and the addition of an unfinished or not sufficiently concentrated pickle produces the same effect. It is also important that the waste or exhausted pickle from which the greater part of the salt has crystallized should be discharged from time to time, as its presence not only impairs the quality, but diminishes the quantity of the salt deposited."

The time required for the evaporation of sufficient pickle to make a crop of salt depends largely upon the weather, dry and clear weather being, of course, most favorable; six weeks to two months is the usual time. Three crops of salt a season are gathered—the first about the middle of July, the second in the early part of September, and the third at the end of October. The second crop is generally the best, as it is coarser than the others.

The crop of solar salt is gathered by first loosening it from the bottom of the "covers" with a rake or spud. It is then washed in the pickle that is still left in the cover, and "gathered" to the street gunwale. Here it is shovelled into draining tubs, to remain a short time before being emptied into the salt carts for removal to the salt bins for further drainage.

TREATMENT OF CRUDE PRODUCT.

The legal time, fourteen days, required for drainage having passed, the bins are opened and the salt is packed in barrels holding five bushels, or 280 lbs.—each barrel being branded with the name of the firm or person manufacturing the same.

GRADES AND QUALITY OF MICHIGAN SALT.

The salt product has been divided by the State Inspector into the following grades:

Fine.—In barrels, 280 lbs., suitable for general use for all family purposes.

Packers.—In barrels, 280 lbs., suitable for packing and bulking meat and fish. One of the best and purest grades of salt, and branded when coarse, C Packers C.

Solar.—In barrels, 280 lbs.; when screened, branded C Solar C for coarse and F Solar F for finer grades. Solar salt suitable for bulking meats.

Second Quality.—All salt intended for No. 1 of any of the above grades, when for any cause it is condemned by the inspector, is branded Second Quality and sold as such. This salt is good for salting stock, hay, hides, etc.

ANALYSIS OF SALT.

Experience proves that the best quality of salt can be made from Michigan brines, and that a great preponderance of the salt sold in the market has been found as pure and as efficient an antiseptic as any mined or manufactured elsewhere, either in our own or foreign countries.

The following are the analyses of the various grades of Michigan salt:

Kettle Salt made by the East Saginaw Salt Company, East Saginaw, Michigan. Analyzed by Dr. C. A. Goesmann:

Sulphate of lime	0.3165
" calcium	0.3564
Chloride of magnesium	0.1408
Moisture	3.3441
Chloride of sodium (salt)	95.8422
	100.0000

Carrollton Salt Company, Carrollton, Michigan. Kettle Salt, analyzed by Dr. H. C. Hahn:

Sulphate of lime	0.405
Chloride of calcium	1.127
" magnesium	0.517
Moisture	3.292
Chloride of sodium (salt)	94.669
	100.000

Pan Salt made by Bay City Salt Company, Bay City, Michigan. Analyzed by S. S. Garrigues, Ph.D.:

Sulphate of lime,	0.697
Chloride of calcium	0.329
" magnesium	0.340
Moisture	1.346
Chloride of sodium (salt)	97.288
	100.000

Pan Salt made by Taylor & Co., Zilwaukie. Analyzed by Dr. H. C. Hahn:

Sulphate of lime	0.088
Chloride of calcium	0.737
" magnesium	0.445
" sodium (salt)	98.730
	100.000

Steam Salt made by Buffalo Salt Company, East Saginaw, Michigan. Analyzed by Dr. H. C. Hahn:

Sulphate of lime	0.478
Chloride of calcium	1.365
" magnesium	0.694
Moisture	3.478
Chloride of sodium (salt)	94.366
	100.000

Steam Salt made by New York and Michigan Salt Company, at Zilwaukie. Analyzed by Dr. H. C. Hahn:

Sulphate of lime	0.363
Chloride of calcium	0.699
" magnesium	0.313
Moisture	3.308
Chloride of sodium (salt)	95.327
	100.000

SOLAR SALT.

Solar Salt made by East Saginaw Salt Company, East Saginaw. Analyzed by Dr. C. A. Goesmann:

Sulphate of lime	0.3165
Chloride of calcium	0.3564
" magnesium	0.1408
Moisture	3.3560
Chloride of sodium (salt)	95.8333
	100.0000

Solar Salt made by New York and Michigan Salt Company, at Zilwaukie. Analyzed by Dr. H. C. Hahn:

Sulphate of lime	0.173
Chloride of calcium	0.743
" magnesium	0.417
Moisture	2.197
Chloride of sodium (salt)	96.470
	100.000

Average analysis of common salt, made by Dr. C. A. Goesmann, of Syracuse salt:

Sulphate of lime	1.2550
Chloride of calcium	0.1550
" magnesium	0.1369
Moisture	3.0000
Chloride of sodium (salt)	95.4531
	100.0000

Amount of salt made in Michigan by the different processes for the last seven years:

	1869.	1870.
Kettle salt	335,663 bbls.	301,900 bbls.
Pan "	42,000 "	56,430 "
Steam "	176,761 "	255,142 "
Solar "	15,264 "	15,507 "
Total	569,688 bbls.	628,979 bbls.

	1871.	1872.
Kettle salt	290,550 bbls.	202,300 bbls.
Pan "	68.080 "	65,800 "
Steam "	336,162 "	435,920 "
Solar "	37,645 "	20,461 "
Total	732,437 bbls.	724,481 bbls.

	1873.	1874.	1875.
Kettle salt	192,250 bbls.	181,200 bbls.	117,000 bbls.
Pan "	127,700 "	130,500 "	199,100 "
Steam "	471,129 "	685,888 "	741,429 "
Solar "	32,267 "	29,391 "	24,336 "
Total	823,346 bbls.	1,026,979 bbls.	1,081,865 bbls.

	Kettle Salt.	Pan Salt.	Steam Salt.	Solar Salt.
1869....	335,663 bbls.	42,000 bbls.	176,761 bbls.	15,264 bbls.
1870....	301,900 "	56,430 "	255,142 "	15,507 "
1871....	290,550 "	68,080 "	336,162 "	37,645 "
1872....	202,300 "	65,800 "	435,920 "	20,461 "
1873....	192,250 "	127,700 "	471,128 "	32,267 "
1874....	181,200 "	130,500 "	685,888 "	29,391 "
1875....	117,000 "	199,100 "	741,429 "	24,336 "

FUEL.

The fuel used in kettle blocks is cord wood, mixed soft and hard, refuse slabs, and sawdust from saw-mills. Mixed wood now costs $1.25 per cord, delivered at block. Slabs cost 45 to 50 cents per cord at the mills.

A kettle block will consume 10 cords of mixed wood in 24 hours, or 16 cords of slabs in the same time.

Pan blocks on the Saginaw River are run almost entirely with slabs and sawdust from the saw-mills. On the lake shore, mixed cord wood is the fuel used. A pan block 90 feet long, and 16 feet wide, as above described, will use 13 cords of mixed wood in 24 hours, making 140 barrels of fine salt.

Steam blocks are mostly heated during the day with the exhaust from the saw-mills. This is the steam that has been made in the mill boilers. Having performed the work of running the mill engines, it is then exhausted into the pipes connected with the salt block, which carry it through the settlers and graining vats, and causes the evaporation of the brine. If the mill does not run at night, the boilers are connected directly with the steam pipes in the salt block, and live steam is used, the fuel being the sawdust left from running the mill in the day-time.

BARRELS, MATERIAL, AND COST.

The salt barrels of Michigan are now mostly made of pine staves and heading. In some localities, elm staves and ash heading are used. Most of the pine staves are made of the refuse lumber from the saw-mills. The elm stave is mostly made from stave bolts cut for that purpose.

There were manufactured into salt barrels, on the Saginaw River, last year, staves, heading, and hoops as follows:

Staves	16,195,480
Heading	6,138,000
Hoops	9,872,000

The barrels are mostly made by hand in cooper-shops connected with the salt blocks. The average cost of salt barrels is from 28 to 30 cents each. The Rules and Regulations on Cooperage are as follows:

COOPERAGE.

(REGULATIONS IN REGARD TO BARRELS.)

All staves must be of such length that when the barrel is finished it shall not be less than 30½ inches, or more than 31½ inches long. Soft-wood staves, whether rove or cut, to be ½ an inch thick. Hard-wood staves $\frac{7}{16}$ of an inch thick after seasoning. Staves not more than 4 inches wide, of sound timber, and properly jointed.

Heading must be ⅝ of an inch thick, of good, sound lumber, free from holes or unsound knots, smooth for branding. No basswood will be allowed for either staves or heading.

Hoops to be 1 inch wide and ¼ of an inch thick, 10 to each barrel, shaved and well set.

Barrels for fine salt must have heads 17½ inches in diameter. Chime to be 1 inch from point of croze. Bilge from 21 to 21½ inches in diameter outside.

Solar salt may be packed in barrels not less than 30 inches in length with a head 16½ inches. Barrels charred on the inside must be rejected.

LABOR.

The work connected with a kettle block can be accomplished by 7 men and 1 two-horse team, divided as follows: 2 boilers, 2 firemen, 1 engineer, 1 salt-packer and 1 teamster.

The capacity of pan blocks being greater than that of kettle blocks, more labor is required, and is divided as follows: 4 boilers, 3 firemen, 2 engineers, 2 salt-packers, and 2 or 3 teamsters.

Steam blocks being run with exhaust steam, the same firemen who run the mill during the day are employed. At night an extra man is put on. The number of boilers varies with the capacity of the block, being from 4 to 6 men, engineers 2. In many of the steam salt blocks the boilers also pack the salt, after they have finished lifting the same.

In the early history of the salt manufacture, the supply of good labor hands was not equal to the demand. Of late years, the supply has been largely in excess.

The average price of labor in 1864 was $2 a day. In the present year, the average pay per day for salt laborers is $1.25.

FIXED OUTLAY IN DETAIL.

The following figures give the fixed outlay of E. F. Gould's steam salt block at Carrollton, Saginaw County, Mich.:

Size of block, 177 feet long, 84 feet wide, with an elevation of 26 feet. It has 2 inside settlers and 5 graining vats.

Size of settlers, 126 feet long, 7½ feet wide, and 6 feet deep.

Size of grainers, 126 feet long, 7 feet 9 inches wide, and 15 inches deep.

Outside settlers, 20 x 30 feet, 6 feet deep, 4 in number.

Bin room for storing 3000 barrels of salt unpacked. Shed room for 3500 barrels of packed salt.

Capacity of block, 125 barrels a day, and has 2 salt wells.

Engine and boilers for two wells	$2,800.00
Drilling salt wells	2,200.00
Poles for wells	250.00
Tubing "	1,400.00
Pump chamber and valves	250.00
Salt block, cisterns, settlers and grainers	9,600.00
Tubing and connection to salt block	3,500.00
Total	$20,000.00

The cost of the Buffalo Salt Company's block, as described in this article, was $4000 for tubing and $6000 for block, cisterns, settlers and grainers.

COMPANIES, CAPITAL, AMOUNT OF SALT MADE, NUMBER OF KETTLES, GRAINERS, PANS AND COVERS, DEPTH OF WELLS, ETC.

Salt Works and Location.	Salt made in 1875.	Capital Invested.	No. of Blocks.	No. of Grainers.	No. of Kettles.	No. of Pans.	No. of Covers.	No. of Wells.	Depth of Wells.	Mode of Manufacture.
Bay County.	bbls.								feet.	
John McGraw & Co., Portsmouth...	43,837	$25,000	1	10				3	1000	Steam.
M. Watrous & Son, “ ...	8,471	20,000	1	4				1	1000	“
A. Miller, “ ...	48,812	60,000	2	9				4	1050	“
S. McLean & Son, Bay City.......	25,135	50,000	3	8				3	1050	“
S. H. Webster, “	15,981	20,000	1	5				1	1040	“
A. Rust & Co., “	27,134	20,000	1			3		2	1000	Steam and Pan.
Hay, Butman & Co., “	New	20,000	1	5				1	1036	Steam.
N. B. Bradley & Co., “	29,264	30,000	2	7				2	1000	“
William Peter, “	17,081	20,000	1	6				1	1047	“
Eddy, Avery & Co., Bay City.......	35,292	35,000	2	3		3		3	1050	Steam and Pan.
H. M. Bradley & Co., “	21,243	20,000	1	5				1	1000	Steam.
Pitts & Cranage, “	23,292	25,000	1	5				2	960	“
N. W. Gas and Water Pipe Co., Bay City............................	11,660	20,000	1			2		1	740	Steam and Pan.
Folsom & Arnold, Bay City.........	10,135	25,000	1	5				2	954	Steam.
Chapin & Barber, “	31,096	20,000	2	5	60			2	938	Steam & Kettles.
Dolson, Chapin & Co.,“	26,796	25,000	2	6	60			2	950	“ “
John McEwan, “	14,529	20,000	1	4				1	935	Steam.
Atlantic Salt Co., “	2,563	58,000	1		60		404	2	800	Kettles and Solar.
J. P. Hall, “	New	20,000	1	4				1	823	Steam.
Carrier & Co., “	15,329	20,000	1	4				2	735	“
Moore & Smith, Banks............	3,791	20,000	1	3				2	830	“
Leng & Bradfield, “	5,351	23,000	1			3		1	800	Pan.
Taylor & Moulthop, “	4,781	25,000	1			2		2	840	Steam and Pan.
Keystone L. & Salt Co., Banks......	6,196	20,000	1	3				1	980	Steam.
H. W. Sage & Co., Winona.........	51,989	40,000	1	10				4	1020	“
W. H. Malone, Salzburg............	New	20,000	1	4				1	1023	“
Ladrach Bros., “	5,060	10,000	1		50			1	1000	Kettles.
L. L. Hotchkiss & Co., Salzburg....	8,728	20,000	1	5				1	1013	Steam.
Saginaw Co.										
East Sag. Salt Mf. Co., E. Saginaw...	30,208	110,000	3		120		493	3	806	Kettles and Solar.
A. P. Brewer, “ ...	18,960	25,000	1	5				2		Steam.
C. & E. Ten Eyck, “ ...	5,705	15,000	1	3				1		“
Warner & Eastman, “ ...	New	20,000	1	6				1		“
Sears & Holland, “ ...	22,956	75,000	2	7		3		2	750	Steam and Pan.
Thompson & Camp, “ ...	15,240	20,000	1	4				1	750	Steam.
Burnham & Still, “ ...	3,329	15,000	1	3				1	762	“
Gebhart & Estabrook, “ ...	New	20,000	1	5				1	820	“
George Rust & Co., “ ...	21,941	20,000	1	6				2	820	“
Eaton, Potter & Co. “ ...	4,515	10,000	1		60			1	825	Kettles.
Bundy & Youmans, “ ...	12.575	15,000	1		60			1	820	“
H. Beschke, “ ...	New	10,000	1			2		1	828	Pans.
Sturtevant & Green, Saginaw City..	21,907	30,000	2	5	60			2	830	Steam & Kettles,
Swift & Lockwood, “ ...	15,848	20,000	2	4	60			2		“ “
Barnard & Binder, “ ...	26,367	50,000	2	4		2		3	830	Steam and Pan.
Conrad Kull, “ ...	14,931	10,000	1		60			1	802	Kettles.
Geo. F. Williams & Bro., “ ...	16,168	20,000	1			3		1	800	Pans.
C. T. Brenner, “ ...	5,319	10,000	1	3				1	770	Steam.
Pierson, Wright & Co., “ ...	24,752	25,000	1	5				2	741	“
Chicago Salt Co., Florence........	3,300	50,000	2		120			2	800	Kettles.
Shaw & Williams, “	25,609	25,000	1			3		1		Pans.
H. B. Allen, Carrollton..........	5,621	10,000	1			1		1	800	“
E. F. Gould, “	11,350	20,000	1	5				2	800	Steam.
T. Jerome & Co., “	19,350	25,000	1			2		1	746	Pans.
E. Litchfield, “	Not run	75,000	3		180			1	743	Kettles.
H. Ballentine & Co., Carrollton.....	“	30,000	1		60			1	763	“
Saginaw Valley Salt Co., “	5,000	20,000	2		120			1	780	“
H. P. Lyon & Co., “	11,941	20,000	2		60		500	1		Kettles and Solar.
A. J. Bliss & Bro., Zilwaukie.......	17,431	20,000	2	5		2		2	835	Steam and Pans.
John F. Driggs & Co., “	5,153	25,000	2		60	2		1	840	Kettles and Pans.

Salt Works and Location.	Salt made in 1875.	Capital Invested.	No. of Blocks.	No. of Grainers.	No. of Kettles.	No. of Pans.	No. of Covers.	No. of Wells.	Depth of Wells.	Mode of Manufacture.
Rust, Eaton & Co.,, Zilwaukee.... .	23,432	25,000	2	4	60			1	800	Steam.
New York and Mich. Solar Salt Co., Zilwaukie..........................	13,877	270,000	1	4			2695	3	860	Steam and Solar.
W. R. Burt & Co., Melbourne.......	49,117	75,000	2	8				4	950	Steam and Pan.
Lake Shore.										
Frank Crawford, Caseville, Huron Co.	29,065	30,000	2	3		3		3	1760	" "
Pigeon River Furnace Co., Caseville.	5,206	30,000	1	6				1	1760	Steam.
Ayres & Co., Port Austin...........	13,994	20,000	1			3		1	1198	Pans.
New River Salt Co., New River...	6,964	15,000	1			3		1		"
Port Hope Salt Co., Port Hope.....	14,883	20,000	1			3		1	785	"
Jenks & Co., Sand Beach...........	New	20,000	1			3		1	702	"
Thomson & Bro., White Rock......	32,414	20,000	1			6		3	565	"
Grant & Son, East Tawas, Iosco Co.	Not run.	20,000	1	4				1	905	Steam.
Weekes Bros., " "	8,895	25,000	1	4		1		1	835	"
Loud, Gay & Co., Oscoda..........	New	50,000	1	8				3	1103	"
Smith, Kelly & Dwight, Oscoda ...	New	25,000	1	4				1	1070	"
Totals.............	1,081;	2,216,000	95	240	1310	55	4092	119		

SYSTEM OF INSPECTION.

The irregularities that crept into the manufacture of salt, deteriorating its quality and value, soon made it evident that some system of inspection should have to be adopted to protect the careful manufacturer against the ignorance and carelessness of others.

As early as the year 1865, a system of local inspection was adopted by a number of the salt manufacturers, which had a tendency to improve a portion of the salt product. The inspection, however, not being a general one, and there being no State law by which offenders could be punished, the effectiveness of the inspection was greatly diminished, and it soon became evident that some more stringent system, backed by a State law, would be the only way to secure uniformity of manufacture.

To meet this point, a committee of the then existing Saginaw and Bay Salt Association was appointed in 1868 to draft a law meeting the wants of the salt manufacturers. The law as perfected by the Association was presented at the next session of the State Legislature and passed by them—approved March 6th, 1869, and amended by an Act approved April 16th, 1875.

AN ACT TO REGULATE THE MANUFACTURE AND PROVIDE FOR THE INSPECTION OF SALT.

Section 1. *The People of the State of Michigan enact*, That no salt manufactured in this State after this act takes effect shall be sold within the State, nor exported therefrom, until the same shall first be duly inspected, as provided in this act. Any person who shall violate the provisions of this section shall pay, for the use of the people of this State, as a fine, the sum of twenty cents for each bushel of salt sold or exported, contrary to the provisions of this act. In case any manufacturer of salt shall knowingly sell, or export, or permit to be sold or exported, salt, contrary to the provisions of this act, he shall, on conviction thereof, be liable to a fine not exceeding one thousand dollars, or imprisonment in the county jail not exceeding ninety days; *Provided*, That nothing in this act shall apply to any salt packed and in the hands of dealers when this act takes effect.

SEC. 2. Immediately after the passage of this act, and every six years thereafter, there shall be appointed by the Governor of this State, by and with the advice and consent of the Senate, an Inspector of Salt, who shall be a person of competent skill and ability, and who shall hold his office for six years and until his successor shall be appointed and qualified, unless sooner removed for cause. He shall at all times be subject to removal by the Governor, for cause; and in addition to other causes which may arise, incompetency, or inefficiency in the performance of the duties devolved on him by this act, shall be deemed good cause for removal. In case of vacancy in the office, it shall be the duty of the Governor to fill the same, by appointment, immediately upon receiving notice thereof, and such appointment shall hold until the close of the next session of the Senate, and in the mean time the Governor shall, with the consent of the Senate, appoint to fill the vacancy, for the unexpired portion of the term.

SEC. 3. Immediately after his appointment and qualification, the inspector shall divide the salt-making territory of this State into so many inspection districts as he may judge necessary, and shall appoint for each district one or more competent and efficient deputy inspectors, who shall hold office at the pleasure of the inspector, and for whose acts he shall be responsible. Such districts may be changed from time to time, as may be necessary. The inspector shall give his entire time, skill, and attention to the duties of his office, and shall not be engaged in any other business or occupation.

SEC. 4. The inspector shall be entitled to receive an annual salary of twenty hundred dollars. He shall also be allowed the further sum of five hundred dollars annually for the expenses of providing and furnishing his office, and for clerk hire, stationery, books, printing, and travelling expenses. His deputies shall be entitled to such sums, in each case, as he may approve, not exceeding in any case the sum of one hundred dollars per month for the time actually employed. All salaries and expenses provided for by this act shall be retained by the inspector out of the money received under Section 5 of this act, and accounted for, and paid out by him as provided in this act: salaries to be paid monthly.

SEC. 5. Each person, firm, company, and corporation, engaged in the manufacture of salt, or for whom any salt shall be inspected, shall from time to time, as salt is inspected or offered for inspection, pay, on demand, to the inspector, or the deputy of the district where the salt is inspected, three mills for each bushel of salt inspected or offered for inspection; *Provided*, That the same may be required to be paid in advance; *And provided further*, That but one inspection fee shall be paid upon the same salt. In case any person, firm, company, or corporation shall neglect or refuse to pay such inspection fees, on demand, at his, their, or its office or manufactory, the party so refusing shall be liable to an action therefor, in the name of the inspector, and the certificate of inspection, with proof of the signature of the inspector, or deputy giving the same, shall be *prima facie* proof of the liability and the extent of the liability of the party so in default; and it shall be lawful for the inspector and his deputies to refuse to inspect salt manufactured at the works so in default until the amount due is paid. All money received by or paid to any deputy inspector under this section shall be forthwith paid to the inspector. The inspector shall keep just and true accounts of all money received under this section, and an account of the amounts received from or paid by each person, firm, company, and corporation engaged in the manufacture of salt, and all other things appertaining to the duties of the office, and the said books and accounts shall always, during office hours, be subject to the inspection and examination of any person who may wish to examine them, shall be deemed the books of the office, and shall be handed over to his successor in office, together with all the money and effects appertaining to the office.

SEC. 6. The inspector shall, before entering upon the duties of his office, take the oath prescribed by the constitution of this State, which oath shall be filed in the office of the Secretary of State. He shall also execute a bond to the people of this State, in the penal sum of ten thousand dollars, conditioned for the faithful performance of the duties of his office, which bond shall have at least two sureties, and shall be subject to the approval of the State Treasurer, and when approved shall be by such Treasurer filed and deposited in his office; and the inspector shall renew his bond every year. Any person or corporation injured by the neglect or default of such inspector, or by his misfeasance in office, or by the neglect, default, or misfeasance of any of his deputies, may maintain an action on such bond, in the name of the people, for the use of the party prosecuting, and shall be entitled to recover the full amount of damages sustained.

SEC. 7. Each of the deputies appointed by the inspector shall take the oath of office prescribed by the constitution, and shall give bond to the inspector in such sum, and with such sureties as he may approve, conditioned for the faithful performance of his duties as such deputy; and in case said inspector shall be obliged to pay any sum for the neglect or default or misfeasance of any deputy, he may recover of such deputy and his sureties on such bond the amount he was obliged to pay, with accruing costs.

SEC. 8. The inspector shall keep his principal office in either Saginaw or Bay County, and the deputy for the district in which such office is located may occupy the same office. This office shall be kept open at all times during business hours. All the books, records, and accounts shall be kept at this office, and each deputy shall, at least once in each week, make written report, by mail or otherwise, to the inspector, of the salt inspected by him during the week, stating for whom, and the quality and quantity thereof. Abstracts of these reports shall be entered in books provided for that purpose. Said inspector shall, in proper books, keep a full record and account of all his transactions; and such books shall also be open for the examination of all persons wishing to examine the same during office hours.

SEC. 9. The inspector shall not be in any way concerned in the manufacturing or selling of salt, or have any interest whatever, directly or indirectly, in any salt manufactory or erection for manufacturing salt in the State of Michigan, or in the profits of any such manufactory.

SEC. 10. It shall be the duty of the deputy, in each district, to visit, once in each day, Sundays excepted, each salt manufactory in his district, when in operation, and to ascertain if there be therein any salt of bad quality, and such as ought not to pass inspection.

SEC. 11. It shall be the duty of the inspector in person to visit the manufactories in which salt is made, that may be in operation, in the different districts, as often as practicable.

SEC. 12. The inspector or deputy, at each visit, as provided in this act, shall carefully examine the salt in the bins, and the brine in kettles, or pans, or vats, in which the salt is manufactured. If the salt in the bins or any part thereof is of bad quality and such as ought not to pass inspection, or if the brine in the kettles, or pans, or graining vats has not been cleansed, he will direct and see that the owner, or occupant, or boiler, or other person having charge of the manufactory, remove the bad salt from the bin and place it with second-quality salt, or throw it among the bitterns, as the inspector or deputy may direct, and that the impure brine in the kettles, or pans, or graining vats be thrown out, and new brine substituted.

SEC. 13. No lime nor lime-water shall be used by any person in the manufacture of salt, in the kettles or pans, or graining vats, used for manufacturing, under a penalty of twenty-five dollars and costs for each offence, to be sued for in the name of the people of this State; *Provided*, That iron vessels used in the manufacture of salt may be whitewashed, when cool, to prevent the accumulation of rust.

SEC. 14. Every person desiring to have salt inspected shall apply to the inspector or deputy inspector of the district where the same shall be, which inspector or deputy inspector shall thereupon actually examine the salt so offered for inspection, in the package in which the same may then be.

SEC. 15. To facilitate such examination, it shall be the duty of the person or company offering the salt for inspection, to unhead or bore the barrel, or to open the bag or other package in which the salt is contained, as may be directed by the inspector or deputy inspector, so as to expose the salt to his touch, view, and examination.

SEC. 16. The inspector or deputy inspector shall not pass any salt as good unless he shall find it to be well made, free from dirt, filth and stones, and from admixture of lime, or ashes of wood, and of any other substance which is injurious to salt, fully drained from pickle, the bitterns properly extracted therefrom, and manufactured as directed by this act and by the rules and regulations of the inspector.

SEC. 17. The person or company offering the same for inspection shall in all cases provide the necessary force to lift the salt while the inspector or deputy weighs or measures it, and shall also furnish the necessary help and material to brand the salt for and under the direction of the inspector or deputy inspector.

SEC. 18. Each manufacturer shall provide a scale or balance at his works, to be examined from time to time, and approved by the inspector, in which all the salt offered for inspection at his works may be weighed.

SEC. 19. Each inspector or deputy shall deliver to the party for whom he shall inspect salt, a certificate of the quantity and quality inspected, and shall thereupon direct the employés of the manufacturer to brand or mark, under his personal supervision, with durable paint the package containing the salt so inspected, with the surname of the inspector at length and the initials of his Christian name, with addition of the word inspector, in letters at least one inch in length, and shall also cause to be marked or branded by the employés of the manufacturer, upon the head of the barrel, cask, or package, the weight prescribed for such barrel, cask, or package by the inspector, when such weights are in conformity to the rules and regulations prescribed by the inspector in that regard ; and if such weights do not correspond to the rules and regulations, he shall cause the same to be repacked so as to conform thereto.

SEC. 20. If the said salt shall be put up in barrels, it shall not be marked unless the barrels are thoroughly seasoned, stout, and well made, with such number of hoops as shall be prescribed by the inspector, to be well nailed and secured.

SEC. 21. Every person who shall falsely or fraudulently make or counterfeit, or cause to be made or counterfeited, or knowingly aid and assist the false or fraudulent making or counterfeiting the mark or brand of any inspector or deputy inspector, on any package containing salt, shall be deemed guilty of felony, and on conviction thereof shall be subject to a fine of not less than one hundred nor more than one thousand dollars, or be imprisoned in the State prison for a term not less than one nor more than six years, or both, in the discretion of the court.

SEC. 22. No manufacturer or other person shall pack, or cause to be packed, in barrels, casks, boxes, or sacks, any salt, until an inspector shall have determined, upon actual examination, that the same is sufficiently drained of pickle, and otherwise fit to pack.

SEC. 23. The inspector and his deputies, in their daily examination of the several salt manufactories, shall examine all bins of salt, for the purpose of ascertaining whether any salt is packed contrary to the provisions of the last foregoing section.

SEC. 24. If any manufacturer or other person shall pack any salt before the inspector or one of his deputies shall have determined that it is fit for packing, he shall forfeit the sum of twenty-five cents for every bushel of salt so packed.

SEC. 25. Barrels, casks, or sacks in which salt shall have been packed and inspected, shall not again be used for the packing of salt therein, until the marks or brands made by the inspector shall be first cut out or removed; and if any person shall pack, or cause to be packed, or shall aid or assist in packing any uninspected salt in any such barrels, casks, or sacks, without first cutting out or removing such marks or brands, he shall forfeit, for every bushel of salt so packed, the sum of one dollar.

SEC. 26. It shall be the duty of every manufacturer to brand or mark with durable paint every cask or barrel of salt manufactured by him, with the surname at full length of the proprietor or owner of the manufactory at which the same shall have been made, and the initial letters of his Christian name, and if the same shall have been manufactured for a company or association of individuals, he shall mark or brand, in like manner, upon every such cask or barrel, the name by which the company is usually called; *Provided*, That no second-quality salt shall be so marked.

SEC. 27. No inspector or deputy inspector shall inspect or pass any barrel, cask, box, or sack of salt which shall not be marked or branded in the manner prescribed in the last section, and the inspector or deputy shall not affix his brand to any barrel of salt which shall not have been so branded by the manufacturer offering the same for inspection; *Provided*, That none of the provisions of this section shall apply to second-quality salt; *And provided further*, That the inspector may, by regulations prescribed by him, provide that both the brand of the manufacturer and that of the inspector shall be put upon each package at the same time.

SEC. 28. Salt of an inferior quality—dirty, damaged, or condemned—may be sold loose, or in bulk, by the manufacturer thereof, at the works, the inspector making bills of the same, designating the quantity by weight, as in ordinary cases, and distinguishing the same as "second quality;" or such inferior salt may be packed in barrels, boxes, casks, or sacks, and branded by the inspector with the words "second-quality salt," in plain letters not less than one inch in length, and such inspector shall add the initials of his name, and no other or different brand shall be placed thereon; and said second-quality salt, subject to the provisions of this section, may be sold or exported by the owner as such.

SEC. 29. Every person who shall forge or counterfeit the name so required to be put on by the manufacturer, or shall cause or procure to be put on any barrel or cask in which salt shall be packed the name of any person other than that which properly should be placed thereon, according to the provisions of this act, shall, for every such barrel, cask, or sack, forfeit the sum of one hundred dollars, and shall also be liable for all damages to the party aggrieved.

SEC. 30. The inspector shall, by regulation, from time to time, specify the quantity of salt that shall be contained in bags or other packages which shall be offered for inspection; and it shall not be lawful for him to authorize the inspector's brand to be placed upon any package that does not correspond with said regulation.

SEC. 31. The inspector shall, by regulation, require that all ground salt manufactured and put up for the market shall be legibly marked on each keg, box, sack, bag, or other package containing the same, with the words "ground solar," or "ground boiled," or "ground steam," or "ground Chapin," as the fact may be; such marking to be done in letters of not less than an inch in length.

SEC. 32. If the inspector shall consent to, connive at, aid or abet the smuggling of salt, or the transportation of the same away, so as to evade the inspection thereof, or shall accept of any bribe, or sum of money, or any gift or reward whatsoever, upon any express or secret or implied trust, or confidence that he shall connive at, or consent to any evasion of the laws for the inspection of salt, such inspector shall forfeit his office, and pay to the use of the people of this State the sum of one thousand dollars.

SEC. 33. If any deputy inspector shall be guilty of the offences specified in the last section, or any of them, the inspector appointing such deputy shall forfeit to the use of the people of this State the sum of two hundred and fifty dollars, for the recovery of which his bond shall be put in suit.

SEC. 34. The inspector and each of his deputies shall be exempt from serving on juries, and from all military service, except in case of actual invasion or insurrection; and the commission or appointment in writing of any such officer or deputy shall be evidence of the facts stated therein.

SEC. 35. The inspector shall have power, from time to time, to make and ordain such necessary rules and regulations as he may deem expedient, concerning—

First. The manufacturing and inspection of salt not inconsistent with the provisions of this act.

Second. The daily examination, and the reporting by his deputies, of the operation and extent of the several salt manufactories, so as to determine whether the quantity of salt inspected at each manufactory is equal to the quantity actually manufactured thereat.

Third. The districting of the salt-making territory in this State, and the duties of his deputies under this act, and he may alter and revoke such rules and regulations at his pleasure.

SEC. 36. The inspector shall have power to annex penalties, not exceeding ten dollars in any case, to the violation of such rules and regulations. Such rules and regulations shall be printed and posted up in the office of the inspector, and in each manufactory, and published at least once in some newspaper in each county where salt is manufactured, and shall, after they have been posted and published as aforesaid for one week, be binding upon all persons concerned.

SEC. 37. It shall be the duty of the inspector and of his deputies, upon being applied to by any manufacturer to inspect salt in his district, to inspect the same forthwith; and in no case shall the inspector or any deputy delay the inspection of salt beyond twelve hours of daylight, excluding Sundays, after such application, unless such manufacturer shall consent to the delay. For a violation of this section by the inspector, or any one of his deputies, the in-

14

spector and his sureties shall be liable to the party aggrieved in the sum of fifty dollars over and beyond all actual damages sustained.

SEC. 38. Nothing contained in this act shall be construed so as to prevent the sale or exportation of the bitterns from any manufactory of salt, such bitterns to be sold or exported in bulk, or if in casks or barrels, to be branded as bitterns, and sold or exported as such.

SEC. 39. In case of any vacancy, from any cause, in the office of the inspector, the deputy who has been longest continuously in office shall possess the powers and perform the duties of inspector until such vacancy shall be filled; and the bond of the inspector and his sureties shall continue to be liable for the acts of all the deputies, until such vacancy shall be filled.

SEC. 40. The inspector shall annually, in the month of December, and on or before the fifteenth day thereof, make a report to the Governor of this State, which shall contain—

First. The number of districts into which the salt-producing territory of this State may then be divided, with the name and locality of each, and the number and capacity of the works of each district.

Second. The quantity and quality of salt inspected in each district during the preceding year.

Third. The amount received and expenses incurred under this act for the preceding year, in detail.

Fourth. Such suggestions and recommendations as he may think proper to make concerning the manufacture of salt, and the operation of the inspection laws upon the same, and as to what further legislation on the subject, if any, would be advisable. A copy of such report shall be published immediately after its date, in some newspaper in the Saginaw valley.

SEC. 41. The inspector shall establish a grade of "fine" salt, the grain of which shall be at least as fine as the average grain of salt made in kettles. He shall cause the word "fine" to be marked on the packages containing such salt, in large letters, and the word "fine," with or without qualification, shall not, under any circumstances, be placed on salt of coarse grain; but all other grades shall be designated on the packages by some truly descriptive mark or brand, and the inspector may mark salt "second quality" for imperfect grain, as well as for any other defect.

SEC. 42. Nothing in this act contained shall be construed to prevent the sale or shipment of salt in bulk, after the same shall have been duly inspected and a certificate thereof given by said inspector or any deputy; and nothing in this act shall be construed to prevent manufacturers from putting such private trade-mark or brand on their salt as they may see fit; *Provided*, It contains no untruth or statement calculated or intended to deceive the purchaser.

SEC. 43. In case the inspector shall, at the time of making any annual report, have a surplus of money arising from the inspection fees, in this act provided for, in his hands, he shall apportion back and pay such surplus to the persons, firms, or corporations for whom salt has been inspected during the last preceding year, in proportion to the amounts paid by them respectively for inspection fees.

RULES AND REGULATIONS ORDAINED BY STATE INSPECTOR OF SALT.

1. It is hereby *Ordained*, that, in the manufacture of salt by fire heat, the brine when received into the cistern shall remain at least forty-eight hours after the first plunging before it shall be drawn thence into the kettles or pans. The use of lime or any other substance in the manufacture of salt, by being mixed with or added to the water in any stage of the process, without permission of the inspector, is hereby expressly forbidden.

2. The cisterns of each block shall be thoroughly cleansed at the opening of the manufacturing season, and as often and whenever it may be required afterward by the inspector, and it is required that each block shall have at least four cisterns of the ordinary capacity.

3. The connections by which water shall be drawn from the cisterns into the blocks shall be inserted so as to receive the water at least six inches above the bottom of the cisterns.

4. Each manufacturer shall provide a good basket, of sufficient capacity to hold one entire drawing for each kettle in operation, into which the salt shall be drawn and there remain over the kettle for thorough drainage before being discharged into the bin, and the basket shall be well cleansed before being replaced over the kettle, and such salt shall remain in full view until the inspector, in his daily examination, shall have an opportunity to see it before it is broken to pieces.

5. The bins shall be kept clean and no salt put therein except such as is of first quality. After a bin has been emptied, it shall be washed out and so cleansed that the opening in it shall admit of the proper drainage of the salt. The floor of all salt houses shall be raised at least six inches from the ground to allow drainage, and there shall be a sufficient number of bins attached to each block, of convenient size, for storage of all the salt which may be made at such block while it is undergoing the process of drainage.

6. All salt shall stand in the bins at least fourteen days before packing, and the term will be taken to commence from the last discharge of wet salt into the bin. Salt in the bins shall be levelled off evenly at the top and so kept; nor will the packing of any such salt be allowed until the same has been declared fit for that purpose, upon actual examination by the inspector; and the packing of any salt without express permission, although fourteen days may have expired, will not be allowed.

7. Whenever it shall be found that salt has been pickled, or otherwise packed in a wet condition, so that the barrels will drain, it will have to be emptied again, and the persons packing such salt will be held liable to a penalty of ten dollars for each and every offence.

8. It is hereby declared unlawful for any manufacturer, boiler, or packer of salt, or any other person by their permission or procurement, to throw water upon or otherwise wet any salt in the bin or in the barrel before, whilst, or after packing the same; and the same is expressly forbidden. Any person so offending shall forfeit and pay a fine of ten dollars for each and every offence. Nor shall any such person discharge any wet salt into the bins or upon salt previously deposited therein, under a penalty of ten dollars.

9. Salt of an inferior quality that has been condemned by the inspector may be sold in bulk as "second quality," and if packed must be branded in large letters "second quality," payment of dues being made in the usual manner.

Every manufacturer of salt shall be provided with a suitable place of deposit for "second quality" and "refuse" salt, where the same shall be discharged and shall remain subject to the observation of the inspector; and such inferior salt shall not be mixed with nor sold as best salt. Whenever required by the inspector, the person in charge of a manufactory shall cause any wet or inferior salt to be removed to the place of deposit for such salt, or, at his option, and in his presence, may return the same to the cisterns to be dissolved.

10. The quantity that may be packed in each barrel shall be 280 lbs. of salt. Solar, ground, dairy, and table salt may be packed in quantities of 280 or 320 lbs., at the option of the manufacturer, and the latter qualities, if intended for market, in sacks, may be packed in barrels, in sacks, or put in barrels with the empty sacks. The tare of barrels is fixed at 22 lbs. for staves of soft and 25 lbs. for staves of hard wood.

11. Each packer shall make a hole $\frac{7}{8}$ inch in diameter in one head of each barrel packed, for the convenience of the inspector, and shall aid the inspector at all times in weighing the packages of salt.

12. All ground salt manufactured and put up for the market shall be legibly marked on each keg, box, sack, bag, or other pack age containing the same, with the words "ground solar," "ground steam," as the fact may be, such marking to be done in letters.

13. The average grain of salt boiled in kettles shall be the standard of "fine salt," and shall be branded as such. All salt coarser than the average grain of kettle salt manufactured by Chapin, steam, pan, or other process, shall be branded "packers," and the coarsest salt made by same processes shall be branded "C packers C." Solar salt shall be branded "solar," and if screened the two qualities shall be designated "C solar C" for coarse, and "F solar F" for finer. No salt shall have these brands unless of first quality, of its respective grain in all respects. Salt discolored in the manufacture or from any cause not of first quality shall be branded "second quality" in letters two inches in length, and have no other inspection-mark. But the manufacturer may work all such salt over again if preferred. Lower grades of salt may be put in old barrels, and shall be branded "refuse" without other marks.

14. Every manufacturer shall keep his premises used for the storage of salt in packages in a neat and clean condition, so that salt, while awaiting inspection or shipment, shall not be liable to be rendered wet or dirty, and shall keep the same protected from the weather; and all salt not kept in a state of preservation, and neatly and carefully packed in tiers not more than three barrels high, so as to remain in sound, merchantable condition, after the same has been inspected and branded, shall be repacked or otherwise disposed of according to its quality.

18. For any neglect or refusal to comply with either or any of the foregoing rules or regulations, or for any evasion or violation of the same, on the part of the manufacturers of fine or steam salt, or any person or persons in their employ, a penalty of ten dollars is hereby imposed, to be paid to the inspector or his deputies, on demand or record in a court of justice, with costs as provided by law. All the regulations shall be held to apply to the manufacturer of salt by other processes than boiling in kettles.

19. All salt finer than the average grain of fine salt may be branded "Dairy Salt," if found of sufficient purity, after having been submitted to a chemical analysis, otherwise no salt shall be branded "Dairy Salt."

The salt-producing territory of Michigan has been divided by the State Inspector of Salt into ten inspection districts, as follows:

District No. 1, East Saginaw.
" " 2, Saginaw City.
" " 3, Carrollton.
" " 4, Zilwaukie and Melbourne.
" " 5, Portsmouth and Bay.
" " 6, Bay and Essexville.
" " 7, Salzburg, Wenona, and Banks.
" " 8, Caseville, Port Austin, New River, and Port Hope, Huron Co.
" " 9, Sand Beach and White Rock, Huron Co.
" " 10, Oscoda and East Tawas, Iosco Co.

The salt-producing capacity of the State is 1,800,000 barrels, or 9,000,000 bushels.

Statement of salt made and inspected in the State since the establishment of the State inspection law in 1869:

Comparative statement to 1876.

	1869.	1870.	1871.
Fine salt, barrels.....	513,989	568,326	655,923
Packers' salt, "	12,918	17,869	14,677
Solar salt, "	15,264	15,507	37,645
Second quality, "	19,117	19,659	19,930
Refuse salt, "	8,870	7,618	4,262
	569,688	628,979	732,437

		1872.	1873.
Fine salt,	barrels	672,034	746,702
Packers' salt,	"	11,110	23,671
Solar salt,	"	21,461	32,267
Second-quality salt,	"	19,876	20,706
		724,481	823,346

		1874.	1875.
Fine salt,	barrels	960,757	1,027,886
Packers' salt,	"	20,090	10,233
Solar salt,	"	29,391	24,336
Second-quality salt,	"	16,741	19,410
		1,026,979	1,081,865

PRICES—MARKET PROSPECTS.

Statement of prices of salt received by the East Salt Manufacturing Company of East Saginaw:

Price per barrel, 1866	$1 80
" " " 1867	1 77
" " " 1868	1 85
" " " 1869	1 58
" " " 1870	1 32
" " " 1871	1 46
" " " 1872	1 46
" " " 1873	1 37
" " " 1874	1 19
" " " 1875	1 10

The markets for Michigan salt are the States of Ohio, New York, and Indiana, and through the entry ports of Buffalo, Erie, Ashtabula, Cleveland, Sandusky, and Toledo; throughout the West and Northwest, through the ports of Chicago, Milwaukee, and Duluth.

The prospects for an increased demand for Michigan salt are improving every year; and as long as a system of inspection is maintained, and a proper care is exercised by the manufacturer in the making of salt, this condition of the markets must continue.

COLLATERAL PRODUCTS OF MICHIGAN BRINES.

As shown by the chemical analyses, Michigan brines contain, besides salt, percentages of chloride of calcium, chloride of magnesium, and bromide of magnesium.

Chloride of calcium, which forms the largest proportion of the waste mother liquors, after the salt has been extracted from the brine, is now having a value for various purposes. Its concentrated solution is used as a bath in the putting up of canned fruit. It is also employed in the manufacture of chloride of barium and artificial sulphate of baryta.

In some localities, it has also found very extensive use in the manufacture of artificial stones by the Ransom patent. The process consists in mixing sand and silicate of soda by a pug mill into a mass of putty-like consistency. In this condition, it is pressed into moulds of any form and shape. After removing the pattern or mould, a strong solution of chloride of calcium is poured over the moulded form, which so hardens the surface that it can be removed to a tank containing a solution of chloride of calcium, in which it is allowed to remain a certain length of time until the entire form becomes perfectly hard. The decomposition which takes place in the stone between the silicate of soda and the chloride of calcium forming silicate of lime, which is the cementing material. The salt produced is afterward washed out by repeated soakings and washings in fresh water.

Artificial stone made in this way has a fine texture, great durability, and when properly and carefully made equals in most respects the best varieties of the native sandstone.

Chloride of magnesium also contained in the mother liquors of the salt works is a source for the manufacture of magnesia. A caustic solution of lime precipitates the magnesia as a hydrate, from which the calcined magnesia can be made by calcination. Magnesia finds considerable use in the manufacture of rubber goods and in pharmacy.

Bromine contained in the brines, as a bromide of magnesium, is now being extensively produced from the refuse bitter waters of the salt manufacture. Bromine is largely used in the arts and pharmacy. The annual American product of bromine is now over 130,000 pounds.

The refuse salt obtained from the waste brines has a value as a manure, and should find more general use.

INDEX.

PART I. AND APPENDIX A.

APPENDIX B.

PART II.

PALÆONTOLOGY.

FOSSIL CORALS.

BY

C. ROMINGER.

PALÆONTOLOGY.

THE stratified rocks forming the surface crust of our globe are very frequently found to contain petrified corals, shells of mollusks, bones of vertebrates, vegetable remains, or impressions thereof.

The ancients were already well acquainted with this fact, but up to the eighteenth century naturalists and philosophers were greatly troubled in seeking for a satisfactory explanation of the origin of these peculiar forms, so similar to living organisms, yet made of stone.

One of the first theories on the subject was, that fossils were a *lusus naturæ*, or play of nature—that is, an effort of nature to produce organic forms, a moulding of life shape from inanimate material, without fully accomplishing the task to the final act of the inspiration of life. The Mosaic account of creation is in full accord with such views, and it is not at all improbable that Moses, or whoever was the writer of the biblical accounts of creation, derived his first thoughts upon the process of creation from the observation of fossils and meditation concerning their origin. It no doubt appeared to him more reasonable to accept them rather as half-finished work than as the remains of once living bodies, whose position within the rock was inexplicable to him; and in analogy with this conception, he imagines man created by the double process, first, of moulding his form from earth, and then of the divine inspiration of life.

During the fourteenth century the hypothesis of the origin of fossils by *lusus naturæ* began to lose credit, and it became generally recognized that they were the veritable remains of once living organisms. This being acknowledged, the thought of ascribing the origin of fossils to the scriptural deluge recommended itself as plausible, and they were at once, without critical examination of the correctness of this view, universally believed to be the remains of the animals which perished during this catastrophe, which belief was obstinately held up to the end of the eighteenth century. At that time, with the progress made in natural history, so many facts contradicting this theory had accumulated, that it could no longer be held. It was clearly recognized that the deluge could not account for fossils generally; that there existed an immense difference in the age of fossils, and that a large number of animal and vegetable creations came and disappeared again, in long-continued succession, involving the lapse of spaces of time far exceeding former conceptions of the age of the globe.

The study of the fossils and of the conditions under which they were found threw an entirely new light on the earth's history. Formerly the fossils were mere objects of curiosity; now they became important witnesses to a long series of progressive changes which the earth must have undergone ages and ages before man was created, and before the scriptural deluge could have occurred; of changes which were rarely sudden reversals of the existing conditions, but which were from the beginning and are now in constant quiet action—an endless, shifting motion, destroying here and building up there, with a slowness almost imperceptible, but, in the long lapse of time, astounding in its effects. The attentive study of fossils led to the discovery that, in the series of rock beds composing the earth's crust, certain animal forms were confined to a certain definite group of strata, which, in ascending to higher beds, disappeared gradually or abruptly, and were replaced by new forms; the same changes were noticed to occur frequently in ascending higher and higher. It was further ascertained, on examination of far remote localities, but built up by an equivalent succession of rock beds, that, in the distribution of fossils throughout the strata, the same order is found to exist—that is to say, the equivalent strata contain in different places the same, or at least very similar fossils. By deduction from this rule, we may infer that strata containing the same fossils have the same relative age; we have in the fossils a standard criterion for the determination of a certain geological horizon, irrespective of the character of the rock, which may be widely different in remote equivalent beds, and independent of direct observation of the succession of the beds, which may be hidden from view, or be complicated by irregularities, either through the absence of certain layers, or through the intercalation of new ones not observed in other localities under comparison. In the fossils we have always an infallible guide, in cases where lithological and stratigraphical characters would leave us in an inextricable perplexity, regarding the position of certain strata.

The value of palæontology, as fundamental to all our geological knowledge, is at present generally understood. Such of the States as have instituted a geological survey of their territory have shown their appreciation of its importance by making liberal provisions by law for a careful collection of fossils, and for the subsequent description and delineation in their report of all new and interesting forms.

During the progress of the geological survey of Michigan, a rich harvest of fossils has been made, the class of corals in particular being well represented in the collections. Our law provides that due attention shall be paid to the description and figuring of new or imperfectly known specimens. The number falling within this category is so great that the limited compass allowed for the present report will not admit of their being all described.

Being compelled, therefore, to make a selection out of the mass of material, I proposed to the Geological Board to give a more elaborate treatise on the indigenous fossil corals, omitting all description of mollusks and other fossil remains treated of and so amply illustrated in the reports of other States, while the corals have received comparatively little attention, notwithstanding that they belong to the forms most significant of the age of strata. The Board consented to this plan, and I hope the general reader as well as the scientist will not be displeased at being offered a carefully elaborated monograph of this class, instead of a superficial description of a great variety of species from all classes. These were the alternatives, as the fixed limits of the volume, as already stated, would not permit my entering upon a critical examination of the whole field of palæontology.

The species descriptions are illustrated by photographic figures, printed by the new Albertotype process. The figures are necessarily somewhat imperfect, because their convexity would not allow their entire surface to be within the proper focus of the instrument. Their absolute correctness in other respects, however, compensates fully for these unavoidable imperfections.

The figures of the plates could not be numbered without great inconvenience to the printer, on which account I have adopted a rule applying to all, which I think will serve the purpose.

In all the text references the upper right-hand figure is 1; the upper left-hand figure is 2; the lower left-hand figure is 3, and the lower right-hand, 4. Some plates have several figures on each of their two or four principal divisions. In these cases, to save the reader from mistakes and confusion, I have been very explicit in my descriptions, in indicating the particular figure referred to.

CORALS.

CORALS are sea animals of low organization. The general structure of their body, in the simpler forms, is that of a membranaceous bag, frequently plicated into radially arranged folds. This bag has only one central opening, which serves both as mouth and anus, and is surrounded by a variable number of retractile hollow tentacles. In the compound forms the individuals are frequently so intimately united, that the exact demarkation of one body from the other is lost.

Circulation imperfect, not propelled by a heart. Nervous system very rudimentary; no special organs of senses. Propagation partly by eggs, forming in the plications within the bag, and ejected at maturity through the central opening, partly by buds sprouting from the surface, or by division and individualization of single parts of the body. Some corals are entirely soft and fleshy; others secrete a horny or stony basal skeleton or domicil, into which the fleshy parts can be partially retracted. All the fossil corals belong to this latter tribe, and this stony Polyparium is the only portion of them preserved. Soft corals, not capable of preservation, have left no traces within the rocks, although, from analogy of present conditions with former, we have a right to assume that they were not missing in the ancient fauna.

The systematic arrangements under which corals have been described by various naturalists are very different.

Milne-Edwards is one of the writers who has paid special attention to the fossil forms of corals. I consider it, therefore, for the present purpose, most appropriate to adopt his system as a basis. It requires, however, important rectifications, which I will make as I proceed with my descriptions.

CLASSIFICATION OF POLYPES.

BY MILNE-EDWARDS.

I. *Corallia.*

II. *Hydroida:* soft, not represented in fossil condition.

The Corallia are divided into three orders:

1. *Zoantharia.*
2. *Alcyonaria.*
3. *Podactinaria.*

Of these, the first order includes the principal part of all the fossil corals; the second is only represented by Graptolites, and the third has no palæozoic representative.

The Zoantharia are divided into seven sub-orders:

1. *Malacoderma:* soft, not fossil.
2. *Apora:* recent coralline forms.

Milne-Edwards placed the genus *Palæocyclus* with this sub-order, but its affinities are decidedly nearer to forms placed in another sub-order, the Z. rugosa.

3. *Perforata.*—Abundantly represented in the mesozoic and recent coralline fauna, but not in the palæozoic. The genus Protaræa, placed here by Milne-Edwards, belongs to the next following order, the *tabulata,* and the genus *Pleurodictium,* likewise enumerated among the Zoanth. perforata, is created by simply mistaking the casts of a Michelinia for a particular type of organization, very appropriately connected with the specific by-name of "*problematicum.*"

4. *Tabulata.*

5. *Rugosa.*

These last two orders comprise nearly all palæozoic corals, and will form the special object of consideration in subsequent pages.

6. *Tubulosa.*—An order formed to include the genus *Aulopora* and *Pyrgia,* both of which genera are in intimate relationship with certain types placed under the Zoanth. tabulata, with which I am going to describe them.

7. *Zoanth. caulicula.*—These have no representatives of palæozoic date.

Zoantharia tabulata.—The corals comprehended under this sub-order are composed of tubular polyp cells, septate by transverse diaphragms, and radiated by vertical crests, which in some forms are very well developed, in others remain in rudimentary condition, or are entirely obsolete in individuals. Two principal groups of tabulata are distinguished:

I. *Milleporidæ.*—Compound polyparia built up by two structural elements; of larger radiated tubes, forming the visceral cavities for the animal, and of a cœnenchymatose tissue surrounding the tubes, likewise either of tubular structure, or of a cellulose vesiculose nature.

II. *Favositidæ.*—Compound polyparia formed of aggregated tubules of equal structure, without intervention of any other tissue element between the tube walls. The radiation of the tubes by vertical crests is often more rudimentary in its development than in the former order of Milleporidæ.

The palæozoic forms of the *Milleporidæ* are represented by the genera: Heliolites, Lyellia, and Plasmopora, to which Milne-Edwards adds Propora, Battersbyia, and Fistulipora. The latter genus has only an external resemblance to the Milleporidæ. It belongs to the Bryozoa, as I have already demonstrated in an essay published in 1866, in the proceedings of the Academy of Natural Sciences, of Philadelphia.

The genera Propora and Battersbyia I was not able to recognize among the American fossils, unless a form which I have provisionally named *Houghtonia* should be identical with the Propora.

The second order of Zoanth. tab., the *Favositidæ*, is grouped by Milne-Edwards into six sub-orders:

1. Favositinæ. 2. Chætetinæ. 3. Halysitinæ. 4. Pocilloporinæ. 5. Seriatoporinæ. 6. Thecideæ. From these the Chætetinæ have to be eliminated as a type belonging to the Bryozoa.

The genera arranged under the Pocilloporinæ, Seriatoporinæ, and Thecideæ are in perfect conformity of structure with the Favositinæ, and I see no reason for their separation from them—with one exception, that of the genus *Columnaria*, which is a form of peculiar type, exhibiting no great affinity with the genus Thecia, which has been placed by Milne-Edwards in the same sub-order with it.

The sub-order Halysitinæ includes the genera Halysites, Syringopora, Fletcheria, Thecostegites, and Chonostegites. The latter two genera I place under the Favositinæ as a form intimately related in structure to Michelinia. The genus Thecostegites is only created through mistaking compact, short-jointed specimens of Syringopora tabulata for the type for a new genus, which assertion I shall prove farther on by giving a detailed description of the species. I have, in view of the above statements, reduced the six sub-orders of Favositidæ to three, namely, *Favositinæ*, *Halysitinæ*, and *Columnariæ*, under which headings I will describe the genera and species found in the State of Michigan, taking the liberty sometimes of drawing into the descriptions specimens found in the foreign territory of the neighboring States, when I find it necessary for a full illustration of a certain group of organisms, of which the material found in the State is too imperfect. In the production of photographic figures specially, I had frequently to resort to specimens not found in Michigan localities—not that I am without indigenous ones of the same order, but because these are in a less perfect condition.

MILLEPORIDÆ.

HELIOLITES, Guettard.

Large visceral tubes, circular, scarcely or not at all projecting above the general surface, radiated by twelve longitudinal crests, not reaching the centre, and often being only low, spinulose carinæ. Numerous transverse diaphragms intersect their channels. Cœnenchym abundant, formed of much smaller, not radiated, polygonal tubules, which, divided by regularly disposed, transverse diaphragms, represent vertical rows of subquadratic cell spaces filling the interstitial space between the larger circular tubes. No lateral anastomosis between tubes or cell spaces.

Several species of Heliolites occur in the Niagara group of Michigan. The specimens are all found in silicified condition, and the more delicate surface characters have suffered partial obliteration by the process of petrification.

HELIOLITES MEGASTOMA, McCoy.

Visceral tubes about two millimeters wide. Orifices crenulated by a cycle of twelve low vertical crests. Diaphragms flat, closely set. Cœnenchym tubules about half a millimeter wide. Interstitial spaces filled by them, subject to many variations in different specimens; in some the distance between the larger circular tubes is smaller than their own diameter, in others it is larger. External mode of growth convex, or in subplane expansions, covered by a concentrically wrinkled epitheca on the impressed lower concave side. It is a common species in the Niagara group of Drummond's Island, Point Detour, and many other localities; in the drift deposits of the Lower Peninsula it also frequently occurs. The Niagara group of Indiana, Iowa, Kentucky, etc., and the Silurian strata of Bohemia inclose forms perfectly identical with those of Michigan.

Plate I.—Fig. 3 represents a silicified specimen from Point Detour, natural size, the structural details of which will all be seen more distinctly by using a weak magnifier, when looking at the figure.

HELIOLITES PYRIFORMIS, Hall.

Tubes about one millimeter wide, radiated by a cycle of twelve spinulose, vertical crests. Diaphragms flat, simple, or anchylosed with the spinulose, vertical crests into an irregularly cellulose mass, filling the tube cavities. Cœnenchym of minutely tubular structure, divided by transverse septa. Interstitial spaces between the larger tubes equal to or larger than one tube diameter. External growth, subglobular.

The mode by which the specimens are preserved alters their appearance considerably. Some of the specimens, with simple transverse diaphragms exposed to weathering, are apt to have the diaphragms of the larger tubes destroyed, and the channels of the larger tubes are seen all open, surrounded by the well-preserved mass of the smaller cœnenchym tubules. In other specimens where the vertical crests, intermingling with the diaphragms, give the larger tubes more strength, the cœnenchym is found destroyed and the larger tubes are preserved, and present themselves as free cylindrical, longitudinally carinated columns. Still other specimens are found, in which, by incrustation of the wall substance, the tube channels are narrowed, and the contrast between the larger and smaller tubes is diminished; these have a spongious aspect, and appear at first glance to be a fossil of totally different structure from the more regularly formed specimens. It is sometimes difficult to distinguish this species from the next described species, *Heliolites interstinctus.* This species is found in association with the former kind at Drummond's Island, and in the other mentioned localities in Michigan; it is likewise common in the drift. The Niagara group of Iowa and Wisconsin incloses the same form.

Plate I.—Fig. 2 represents two specimens from Drummond's Island, in natural size.

HELIOLITES INTERSTINCTUS, Linn.

Visceral tubes from one to one and a half millimeter in width. Vertical crests quite prominent, almost reaching the centre, and composed of rows of spinules pointing obliquely upward with their apices. Cœnenchym composed of minute, polygonal, transversely septate tubules. Interstitial spaces between the larger tubes usually much exceeding one tube diameter. Diaphragms rarely flat, and simple, generally complicated into a cellulose network with the spinulose, vertical crests, with a nodular projection in the centre, formed by the converging apices of the spinules. No central columella. In vertical sections the channels of the larger tubes are scarcely distinguishable from the surrounding septate cœnenchym, because the intersection of the spinules with the diaphragms divides the interior of the larger tubes into small cell spaces similar to the surrounding cœnenchym tissue. The visceral tubes always resist decay better than the cœnenchym, and are preserved as slender, longitudinally carinated columns, held together by a portion of undestroyed cœnenchym. The mode of growth is in discoid, subplane expansions, with a concentrically wrinkled epithecal crust on the lower side.

It is of rare occurrence in Michigan; occasionally specimens are found in the drift of the Lower Peninsula, but it is a very common species in the Niagara group of Indiana, Kentucky, Tennessee, etc.

Plate I.—Fig. 1 is a specimen from Louisville, Ky., in calcified condition. Specimens from the Silurian strata of Bohemia perfectly correspond with the American form.

HELIOLITES SUBTUBULATUS (?) McCoy.

Visceral tubes only half a millimeter wide, with twelve delicate marginal crenulations around the orifices. Cœnenchym tubular, very minute. Interstitial spaces between the larger tubes broad. Transverse diaphragms simple, regular, disposed at close distances.

External growth in convex, rounded masses. I have identified this form with McCoy's species on account of a general resemblance to his figures, but had no opportunity to compare specimens. It occurs in the Niagara group of Point Detour, Drummond's Island, etc.; also in Iowa, at Masonville.

Plate I.—Fig. 4, lower specimen found at Marblehead, of Drummond's Island, natural size; upper specimen from Masonville, Iowa.

PLASMOPORA.

Milne-Edwards.

Visceral tubes circular, not projecting above the general surface, radiated by twelve well-developed vertical rows of spinulose projections. Cœnenchym formed of stout vertical laminæ, which partly appear as the extraneous continuation of the radial crests of the tubes. They intersect each other in irregular manner, inclosing tubular spaces between, which are transversely septate, like the tubules of the cœnenchym of Heliolites; but while in the latter they are actually closed tube channels, in the cœnenchym of Plasmopora no closed tube walls seem to exist, but only lacunæ between the vertical plates intersecting each other. Diaphragms of visceral tubes numerous, flat, but usually complicated by intersection with the vertical rows of spinules almost reaching to the centre.

The cœnenchym usually resists weathering better than the tubes—large, open channels being found to occupy the places of the latter in such specimens.

Plasmopora and Heliolites are in structure so similar that it often becomes difficult to make a distinction between the two forms.

PLASMOPORA FOLLIS, Milne-Edwards.

Tubes from one to one and a half millimeter in diameter, separated at their circular crenulated orifices by interstitial spaces equal to a tube diameter or smaller. Vertical laminæ of the cœnenchym often holding a position toward the tubes as of external radii, and inclosing, by mutual junction and intersection by transverse dissepiments, vertical rows of cell spaces very similar to the cœnenchym of Heliolites; but the vertical walls of these septate pseudo tubules are much stouter than the tubular walls in Heliolites, and comparatively much stouter than the transverse septal laminæ dividing them. Grows in pyriform or subcylindrical, club-shaped masses of moderate size, not often exceeding that of a man's fist; the conical base is attached and exhibits a rudimentary epithecal crust; in the subcylindrical specimens, the cœnenchym cells and orifices on the side faces of the stems are usually closed, and only those of the convex terminal disk apert. Rarely found in the Niagara group of Point Detour, and sometimes in the drift of Michigan. It is a very common species, however, in the Niagara group of Indiana, Kentucky, and Tennessee.

Plate III.—Fig. 2 represents two species of Plasmopora, arranged in a group to economize space. The two upper figures are small silicified specimens of Plasmopora follis; the elongated one was found at Paul's Station, Indiana; the other, of rounded form, is from Charleston Landing, Indiana.

PLASMOPORA ELEGANS, Hall.

Synon., Heliolites elegans, Hall.

Heliol. spinipora, Hall.

Plasmopora scita (?) Milne-Edwards.

Tubes a little over half a millimeter wide, radiated by twelve prominent longitudinal rows of spinules obliquely directed upward, and nearly reaching the centre. Diaphragms complicated and anchylosed with the spinulose projections. Cœnenchym composed of very stout vertical lamels, with delicate transverse leaflets intersecting them. Intervals between the tubes about as large or larger than a tube diameter. Growth pyriform or globular. Found in the drift deposits of Michigan. Common in the Niagara group of New York, Indiana, and Kentucky.

Plate III., Fig. 2.—The two lower specimens, both silicified, are from Paul's Station, Indiana.

LYELLIA.

Milne-Edwards.

Visceral tubes circular, with orifices projecting above the general surface, radiated by twelve conspicuous vertical rows of spinules, and transversely septate by subplane diaphragms.

Cœnenchym abundant, formed of convex, vesiculose, horizontal plates of unequal size, extending in interlacing layers across the intertubular interstices, and inclosing blister-like cavities much resembling the vesiculose tissue of a Cystiphyllum.

LYELLIA AMERICANA, Milne-Edwards.

Synon., Heliolites macrostylus, Hall.

Tubes $1\frac{1}{2}$ to 2 millimeters wide, radial crests almost extending to the centre, and decurrent on the outer projecting part of the orifices, but not prolongated across the interstices, which are divided into a network of irregular angular cell spaces, or are, in weathered specimens, of blistered aspect. Transverse diaphragms subplane, often warped, closely set. Interstices between the tubes larger than one tube diameter. Vesiculose plates of cœnenchym of irregular, coarser, or smaller size, frequently found partially destroyed by decay, in which cases the tubes present themselves as free, longitudinally carinated columns, held together by such of the cœnenchym as escaped destruction. Some of the specimens of Sarcinula represented by Goldfuss are doubtless weathered specimens of Lyellia. (*Vide* Sarcinula costata, Goldf. Tb. 24 f. 11.) Growth in large convex expansions, with an epithecal crust on the lower, often concave side, or of lenticular or pyriform shape, with conical basal side. Found abundantly on Drummond's Island, Point Detour, and in other localities of Niagara exposures in Michigan; of frequent occurrence also in the drift of the Lower Peninsula, and common in the Niagara group of Iowa.

Plate II.—Fig. 1. Surface view of a silicified specimen from Point Detour, Lake Huron. Fig. 2. Side view of a weathered specimen presenting the tubes as partially free columns connected by the remains of the cœnenchym vesicles.

LYELLIA PAPILLATA, Nov. Spec.

Tubes circular, not projecting above the general surface, crenulated at the margins by twelve spinulose vertical crests. Diameter of tubes about 1½ millimeter. Interstitial spaces as wide as a tube diameter, or narrower, obscurely radiated on the surface by arrangement of the cœnenchym vesicles in conformity with the radial crests of the inside. Diaphragms convex, with deeply depressed margin, projecting within the orifices as rounded monticules, decorated with granules. In weathered specimens the tubes stand out as free, longitudinally carinated columns, as in the former species. Mode of growth convex hemispherical above, flat or concave at the lower side, which is covered by a concentrically wrinkled epitheca, or sometimes incrusting other bodies. Found abundantly in the Niagara group of Point Detour and at Drummond's Island.

Plate II.—Fig. 3 is a silicified specimen from Point Detour, Lake Huron.

LYELLIA DECIPIENS, N. SP.

Flat, undose expansions of laminated structure. Tubes one millimeter wide, orifices not projecting, crenulated by twelve marginal crests. Diaphragms slightly convex. Interstitial spaces usually larger than one tube diameter, their surface delicately reticulated by circumscribed cell spaces, as in Heliolites, but in vertical sections exhibiting a distinctly interlacing vesiculose structure, and not a tubular cœnenchym. Found in the Niagara group of Point Detour and Drummond's Island. Exteriorly it fully resembles Heliolites interstinctus.

Plate III.—Fig. 1 represents a silicified specimen from Point Detour, Lake Huron.

LYELLIA PARVITUBA, N. SP.

Tubes one millimeter wide, with projecting orificial rims, radiated within by prominent spinulose crests, and on the surface of the interstices by the converging arrangement of the cœnenchym vesicles. Interstitial spaces about equal to a tube diameter, vesicles rather coarse. Diaphragms subplane, granulose. Growth explanate, discoid, with a concentrically wrinkled epitheca on the lower side. Rarely found in the Niagara group of Drummond's Island. In the Niagara group of Indiana and Kentucky this species is very common, and is partly found silicified, partly in calcified specimens with finely preserved structure.

Plate II.—Fig. 4 is a calcified specimen from Louisville, Ky.

Various other forms described by Billings under the name of Heliolites are by structure true Lyellias, as *Heliolites affinis*, Billings; *Heliolites speciosus*, Billings; *Heliolites exiguus*, Billings: all found at Anticosti Island.

HOUGHTONIA.

N. Gen.

Tubes circular, with projecting rims; cavity lined by twenty or more longitudinal crests, and transversely septate by subplane diaphragms. Cœnenchym formed of irregularly lacunose cell spaces anastomosing amongst themselves, and frequently by pores with the tube channels. Intertubular interstices narrow—the tubes are often in immediate contiguity, so that the intertubular cœnenchym becomes restricted to the corners left between the joining tubes. No pore communication between the contiguous tube walls.

HOUGHTONIA HURONICA, N. Sp.

Globular masses, from the size of a man's fist to that of a foot in diameter, with a basal scar of attachment. Tubes from two to three millimeters in diameter. Interstitial spaces narrow, or tubes in partial immediate contiguity without intervention of cœnenchym cells. Vertical crests spinulose. Diaphragms numerous, slightly concave, and usually coincident with linear constrictions of the tubes. By intersection of the vertical crests with these constricted annular rims, the inner surface of the tubes becomes cancellated by regular, square-shaped conical pits, the bottom of which is often, but not always, perforated, and communicates with the cell spaces of the surrounding cœnenchym.

Occurs in the Hudson River group of Drummond's Island, associated with Columnaria stellata. It is likewise found abundantly in the upper part of the Cincinnati group at Madison, Indiana; more rarely in the lower strata of the same locality.

Plate III.—Fig. 3 is a lateral view of a specimen from Drummond's Island, split open. Fig. 4 is a surface view of the same.

Note.—Since the above was written, I have noticed in the second palæontological report of Ohio the description of *Columnopora cribriformis*, which is generically identical with *Houghtonia*, but Mr. Nicholson erroneously asserts the absence of intertubular cœnenchym cells, and thinks the tubes directly anastomosing by large lateral pores. This is not the case in tubes contiguous to each other, where the walls are imperforate; but in case of development of intermediate cœnenchym cells the tubes connect by pores with the cœnenchym, and in this way indirectly with each other.

FAVOSITIDÆ.

SUB-ORDER, FAVOSITINÆ.

COMPOUND polyparia, formed of intimately connected elongato-conical tubes, diverging from an imaginary axis, and frequently originating from a single mother-tube by prolific lateral gemmation, constantly repeating.

In some forms the tubes are in close connection in their whole length; in others the tubes become free at their ends. In contiguity the tube channels are anastomosing by lateral pores. Transverse diaphragms generally intersect the tube channels, but are sometimes absent, either from being destroyed, or from non-development, which latter is usually found to be the case in forms with very stout thickened tube walls. The inner tube cavity is, in the majority of Favositinæ, radiated by a cycle of longitudinal crests, or rows of spinules or squamiform horizontal leaflets projecting from the walls, which are separated by deep intervening furrows. In other forms the crests are obsolete, the radial structure being indicated only by shallow longitudinal furrows, and in others still the tube cavity is entirely destitute of crests or longitudinal furrows.

The following genera are representing this sub-order: 1. Favosites; 2. Alveolites; 3. Limaria; 4. Cladopora; 5. Striatopora; 6. Dendropora; 7. Thecia; 8. Vermipora; 9. Quenstedtia; 10. Michelinia.

FAVOSITES.

Massive or dendroid polyparia, with polygonal or circular orifices, not or rarely projecting above the general surface, and opening almost rectangularly to it. Tubes intersected by transverse diaphragms, either simple, or compound through the anchylosis of several plates meeting at angles, or rendered imperfect by partial plates not anchylosed. Tube cavity exhibiting twelve longitudinal furrows, and having the band-like intermediate spaces frequently decorated with one or several vertical rows of spinules, or with a row of horizontal, squamiform leaflets. These characters of radiation are, however, not in all species equally distinct, becoming in some specimens nearly obsolete, while in others of the same kind they may be exhibited in obvious development. The rows of squamose projections, peculiar to certain Devonian forms, by coming in contact and adhering together at their joined edges, form compound, perfect, or incomplete diaphragms, interposed between the regularly formed simple diaphragms, and in some specimens these prevail to such an extent as to altogether exclude the regular diaphragms.

Milne-Edwards proposed for Favosites of the above indicated structure the name *Emmonsia*, but the character of the diaphragms in the forms in question is so variable and inconstant, that one and the same specimen, or even the same identical tube channels, may at a certain period of growth be intersected by compound complicated diaphragms, exhibiting at another only simple, straight diaphragms like other forms of Favosites, while in the prolongation of the tubes they may be divided again by compound or imperfect septa. A character so changeable and peculiar to almost every one of the Devonian species of Favosites can not be used as a generic distinction for those which have it in a more marked degree than the others. Milne-Edwards has also confused with his Emmonsia a species which stands in no special relationship to the other forms; his Emmonsia cylindrica is a true typical form of a *Michelinia*.

The genus Favosites and the whole family of Favositoids had comparatively a very brief period of existence. The first forms appear in the upper Silurian deposits (Clinton group). During the Niagara period and the Devonian era, Favositoids abounded, and were the prevailing representatives of coralline life. The carboniferous strata inclose only a few of these forms, and in later deposits no representative of the genus is known. The Silurian forms differ from the Devonian Favosites by invariably having simple diaphragms, and by the spinulose character of their radial crests. The majority of the Devonian forms, instead of longitudinal rows of teretiform spinules, have rows of horizontal squamulæ, which, as already mentioned, sometimes coalesce into transverse compound laminæ, taking the place of the regular diaphragms, which case never occurs in a Niagara species.

FAVOSITES FAVOSUS, GOLDFUSS.

Synon., CALAMOPORA FAVOSA, Goldfuss.

FAVOSITES NIAGARENSIS, Hall, in part.

Tubes polygonal, of uniform size in the same specimens, but in different specimens variable, from a diameter of six millimeters to that of two. Internal circumference of tubes longitudinally striate by twelve furrows, with intermediate, broader, band-like spaces, which are crowded with slender spinulose projections, either in irregularly dispersed position, or arranged in longitudinal or transverse undulating rows, in accordance with the undose, transverse wrinkles of growth visible on the outside of the well-preserved tube walls. Diaphragms convex or flat, or even deeply concave, closely approximated or wide apart. All these variations of structure are sometimes observable in one and the same specimen, but usually the different variations of form mentioned are represented by different specimens. The diaphragms are marked with concentric wrinkles of growth parallel with the polygonal outlines of the tubes, and their entire surface is ornamented by delicate granules or spinules similar to those projecting from the side walls of the tubes. The margins of the diaphragms at their junction with the side walls are deflected into siphon-like depressions, frequently twelve in number, and coinciding with the twelve longitudinal furrows. In many specimens only five or six such siphonal depressions are developed, while in the circumference of some of the very large tubes I counted twenty. These latter are exceptions. In certain specimens the diaphragms connect with the side walls without any perceptible depression.

Lateral pores connecting the tubes, of moderate size, surrounded by a raised rim, forming on each side of the polygonal tubes, according to its width, a single, or double, or triple row. The pores are never much crowded, and hold no definite position in relation to each other in the adjoining rows, sometimes found alternating, sometimes opposite, or irregularly disseminated.

External form of polyparia hemispherical, or discoid, lenticular, with a concentrically wrinkled epithecal crust on the lower centrally attached side.

Occurs abundantly in the Niagara group of Drummond's Island, Point Detour, and all along the south shore of the Upper Peninsula of Michigan; also common in the drift deposits, and in the Niagara group of Wisconsin, Iowa, etc. The above species description comprises specimens so much differing in aspect that it seems strange to present them as belonging to one species. A Favosites with tubes six millimeters wide and one with tubes measuring only two are in great contrast. It may be said also that specimens with convex diaphragms and rough spinulose tube walls bear little resemblance to others having perfectly even diaphragms and almost smooth tube cavities; yet on careful examination of large collections of these forms, we find them all so much linked together by intermediate gradations that no line can be drawn between one and another.

Plate IV. represents four specimens which I consider as varieties of Favos. favosus. Fig. 1 is the fragment of a large silicified specimen with tubes about four or five millimeters in width, flat diaphragms with numerous marginal depressions, and with delicately spinulose tube walls. Found at Drummond's Island. Fig. 2 is a specimen from Point Detour, with still larger tubes of similar structure. The edges of the cells are noticed in the figure to be faintly crenulated by the twelve longitudinal furrows. Figs. 3 and 4 are specimens with convex diaphragms, of different tube size, with well-developed marginal depressions; surface of diaphragms and inner face of tube walls spinulose. Found associated with the former.

Plate V.—Fig. 2 is a specimen fully agreeing with Fig. 1, Plate IV., but of smaller tube size. Favosites Gothlandica, of Goldfuss, corresponds with this specimen; Favosites Niagarensis, Hall, includes forms of this kind also, but the name Gothlandica is applied to so many entirely different forms of Favosites, that I totally abstain from using it. The name Niagarensis, Hall, I have restricted to a form with smaller tubes.

FAVOSITES NIAGARENSIS, HALL.

Tubes about one and a half millimeter wide, of equal size in the same specimens, polygonal. Diaphragms flat, placed at various distances, sometimes very close, sometimes more than one tube diameter apart. Inner surface of tubes delicately spinulose. Spinules in irregularly dispersed position. Pores situated in close proximity to the angles of the tubes, not very numerous.

External growth in convex masses, with an epithecal crust on the lower side. Occurs associated with Fav. favosus in the Niagara group of Michigan, Iowa, Kentucky, etc. It differs from that species principally in the position of the pores near the angles, and in the small tube size; is not connecting with the specimens, Fig. 2, on the same plate, by gradation, an obvious break existing between them.

Plate V.—Fig. 1 is a silicified specimen from Point Detour.

FAVOSITES HISPIDUS, N. SP.

Tubes a little over one millimeter and a half wide, equal, polygonal, radiated by long projecting spinules almost reaching to the centre. Spinules disposed in irregular longitudinal rows, unequal in size, and more than twelve in number in the circumference of a tube. Diaphragms flat, closely set. Pores very numerous, generally forming two rows on each side. Of convex, discoidal growth, with an epitheca below, as in the other forms. Occurs associated with the preceding species in the Niagara group of Drummond's Island and Point Detour.

Plate V.—Fig. 4 is a silicified fragment found at Point Detour.

FAVOSITES VENUSTUS, HALL.

Synon., ASTROCERIUM VENUSTUM, Hall.
FAVOSITES HISINGERI, Milne-Edwards.

Tubules small, not over one millimeter wide, rounded-polygonal, of equal size. Tubes radiated by long spinules, as in the former species. Spinules in twelve distinct longitudinal rows. Diaphragms flat, or gently convex, closely approximated. Pores in one, rarely in two rows on each side.

Grows in large, massive expansions, with an epitheca on the lower side.

Found abundantly in the Niagara group of Michigan, and loose in the drift; it likewise occurs in the Niagara strata of Iowa, Indiana, Kentucky, and New York.

Plate V.—Fig. 3 is a silicified specimen from Drummond's Island.

FAVOSITES OBLIQUUS, N. SP.

Tubes polygonal, compressed, like an Alveolites, and opening obliquely to the surface. Large diameter of tubes, three millimeters; small diameter variable according to the degree of compression. In rare instances the tubes are not compressed, or only slightly so, and open rectangularly to the surface. The inner circumference of the tube walls is striate, by twelve longitudinal furrows with intermediate band-like spaces, each of which bears several longitudinal rows of spinules. Diaphragms subplane, with from eight to twelve marginal depressions, which, together with the longitudinal furrows and spinulose interstices, give the orifices a very decorative, stelliform aspect. The surface of the diaphragms is covered with delicate spinules, like the rest of the inner surface of the tubes. Lateral pores form a single row on each side, wherein it differs from Alveolites, which has larger pores, confined to the two lateral edges, or to their vicinity.

Large, undose expansions, with an epithecal crust on the lower side. Common in the Niagara group of Drummond's Island and Point Detour; also found in the drift of the Lower Peninsula; occurs likewise near Masonville, Iowa.

Plate XXVIII.—Fig. 2, silicified specimen from Point Detour. The Niagara group of New York and Indiana contains a few other species of Favosites, which are not found in the formation of Michigan; these are:

FAVOSITES PYRIFORMIS, Hall.

(Astrocerium, Hall.)

It grows in globular or pyriform masses, with a narrow, conical basal end, surrounded by an epithecal crust. Tubes rounded-polygonal, unequal in the same specimens, and in different specimens varying from one and a half to three millimeters in diameter. Diaphragms flat, moderately close. Tube channels radiated by longitudinal rows of spinules. Pores not very numerous, in a single or double row on each side. Not figured.

Another species, which I name *Favosites spongilla*, is common in the Niagara group at Paul's Station, Indiana. It is likewise of pyriform, conical growth, with subramose excrescences from the discoid upper surface, like some forms of bathing sponges. Tubes small, not over one millimeter wide, with slightly dilating, subrotund orifices. Diaphragms convex. Tube cavity surrounded by rows of spinules. Pores not clearly visible in the small silicified specimens, not larger than a walnut. I have not figured the latter two species, as they are not found in Michigan, but have thought it well to mention them as well-marked characteristic forms of the Niagara group.

FAVOSITES HEMISPHERICUS, Yandell and Shumard.

Synon., Favosites turbinatus, Billings.
Not Fav. hemisph., Milne-Edwards.

Through misapprehension, Milne-Edwards described, under the name Emmonsia hemispherica, as synonymous with Yandell and Shumard's species, a Favosites entirely different from the specimens originally designated by that name. All the original specimens of Fav. hemisph. kept in Dr. L. P. Yandell's collection are identical with *Favosites turbinatus* of Billings. We have to restore, therefore, the name hemisphericus to this species, for which it originally was intended, and give to Milne-Edwards' species the name Favosites Emmonsii, in place of Emmonsia hemispherica, which genus, for reasons mentioned above, can not be accepted.

Favosites hemisphericus is one of the best marked species of Favosites; it has a wide range of variations, but its peculiar mode of growth makes it easily distinguishable from any other form.

The tubes of this form are about two millimeters in diameter, of unequal size, rounded-polygonal; tube cavity generally smooth, intersected by simple flat diaphragms. It occurs rarely that the diaphragms are compound and angular on the surface, formed by anchylosis of lateral, squamiform projections. Lateral pores large, usually in a single row on each side, and moderately distant. Sometimes, however, two rows of pores may be observed on a side. The mode of growth mentioned as the most characteristic feature of this species is nevertheless quite variable. We find polyparia of subspherical or of biconvex lenticular form, or in cylindrical, irregularly flexuose, root-like masses, over a foot in length, or in elongated horn-shape, all of which forms proceed from a single proliferous mother-tube. At first the polyparium is attached by its narrow and usually excentrical apex, but soon it becomes free, and the apex is folded over by the spreading margins of the rapidly enlarging corallum. The tubes diverge in graceful curves from an imaginary central axis toward the periphery. Those ends, terminating on the lateral faces of the corallum, have their walls thickened in their peripheral portion, and their orifices are all closed by opercula of concentric annular structure, with a central opening while growing, which is finally closed by a solid nodular piece. The margins of the opercula are frequently decorated by twelve carinæ converging from the margins toward the centre, but not reaching it. In specimens with excessively thickened wall substance, these radial carinæ are very obscure, or entirely obliterated. The orifices terminating on the convex disk of the corallum are all open, more thin-walled than the others, and of more pronounced polygonal form. It often happens that these centrally situated, thinner-walled tubes have been destroyed by weathering, while the exterior lateral tube ends, of massive structure, have resisted and been preserved. The upper end of such specimens is deeply excavated, and the lenticular forms are transmuted into concave, patelliform dishes. The elongated, horn-shaped specimens terminate in this case with a funnel-shaped excavation resembling the calyx of a Cyathophyllum, which resemblance is augmented by the exposure of the side faces of the septate tubes, arching from the centre to the periphery, which bear a deceptive likeness to the radial lamellæ, with intermediate vesicular cell spaces of the calyx of a Cyathophyllum.

This species is equally common in the upper part of the Helderberg group and in the Hamilton strata in Michigan, and in the equivalent rock beds of other States east and west of it.

Plate VI.—Figs. 1 and 2 represent two silicified specimens of cylindrical growth. A part of the orifices in Fig. 1 is closed by opercula plainly exhibiting the twelve marginal radial carinations. Fig. 2 shows near the left margin opened tube channels with dimly visible lateral pores. The central part of the specimen is formed by the casts of the tube channels, with deep incisions in the place of the diaphragms, and papillose prominences represent the lateral pores. Fig. 3 is a weathered specimen of lenticular form, having a dish shape presenting opened silicified tube channels, intersected by diaphragms, and perforated by lateral pores. On the centre of the specimen I fastened artificially a small horn-shaped specimen, resembling the calyx of a Cyathophyllum. Fig. 4 is a calcified specimen, in the shape of a Dutchman's nightcap, found in the Hamilton group of Thunder Bay.

On Plate X., Fig. 2, a calcified specimen of similar growth to that on Plate VI., Fig. 3, presents the angular tubes of a specimen split open, with diaphragms and pores faintly indicated. The latter belongs to the upper Helderberg limestone, and was found in the drift of Ann Arbor. Fig. 1, Plate VI., is a specimen from the corniferous limestone of Port Colborne. Fig. 2, Plate VI., is found in the drift. Fig. 3, Plate VI., is from the Falls of the Ohio. The small horn-shaped specimen in the centre is from the drift of Ann Arbor.

FAVOSITES EMMONSII, N. SP.

Synon., EMMONSIA HEMISPHERICA, Milne-Edwards.

FAVOSITES ALVEOLARIS, New York Reports.

Tubes unequal, rounded-polygonal, from one to one and a half millimeter in diameter. Tube channels longitudinally striate by a cycle of twelve furrows; of the intermediate band-like spaces, each one bears a vertical row of horizontal squamæ, which are in alternating position in the adjoining rows. Diaphragms rarely simple, straight, generally compound, of anchylosed, lateral squamæ, presenting an angular, substellate surface; or the interlacing squamæ remain free, and constitute imperfect septa, instead of complete transverse diaphragms. Pores large, forming in single or double, or even triple rows on each side, according to its width, and in places they are much more numerous than in others. It is often noticeable that tubes, for a certain part of their length, are intersected by simple, straight diaphragms, without complication by lateral squamæ, and again, both above and below, are found divided by very irregularly interlacing compound septa. This form grows in large convex masses, or in discoid expansions, with a concentrically wrinkled epitheca on the lower side. Found in the upper Helderberg limestones of Mackinac, and in Monroe County, in calcified condition. Silicified specimens, partly in the shape of casts, are frequently found in the drift. The corniferous limestone of Sandusky, Ohio; of Port Colborne, Canada; of the Falls of Ohio; of Charleston Landing, Indiana, and of a great number of other localities, can be mentioned as abounding in specimens of this coral.

Plate VII.—Fig. 1 is the side-view of a calcified specimen, being a fragment of a larger mass, found at Charleston Landing, Indiana; lateral pores distinctly visible in the figure. Fig. 2 is a silicified specimen from the drift of Ann Arbor. It shows the inequality in the size of tubes (in some specimens in still greater contrast), by which I was induced to consider these forms as a distinct species (*vide* "American Journal of Science and Arts," November, 1862, Favos. heliolitiformis), an opinion which I have since changed. Other specimens are found in which the tubes have nearly all an equal size.

FAVOSITES HAMILTONENSIS, N. SP.

Synon., FAVOSITES ALPENENSIS, Winchell.

FAVOSITES DUMOSUS, Winchell.

Tubes rounded-polygonal, unequal in the same specimens and in different specimens, variable from one and a half to two and a half millimeters. Walls stout. Diaphragms regular, simple, but frequently with lateral squamæ interposed, which occasionally become anchylosed with them and disturb their regularity, but never to the same degree as in the former species. Connecting pores large, forming a single row on each side. Rows of lateral squamæ, in some specimens very well developed. Other specimens or portions of specimens have smooth tube channels. Mode of growth globular, or tuberose, or in coarse ramifications, often incrusting other bodies with the basal portion. Abundantly found in the Hamilton group of Thunder Bay and Little Traverse Bay, and in the drift deposits.

Plate VII.—Fig. 3 is a specimen from Stony Point, Thunder Bay. Fig. 4 is found in the limestone bluffs of Petosky, presenting a vertical section through a specimen identical with Winchell's *Favosites dumosus*, which is often found in more slender ramifications, but also in rounded, tuberose form, in no way differing from the typical specimens of Hamiltonensis. *Favosites Billingsii* I have named a form nearly related to F. Hamiltonensis, which is the prevailing species in the Hamilton strata of Widder, C. W., and in the Hamilton group of New York. It grows in large lenticular disks, sometimes three feet in diameter; the lower side has a central point of attachment and is covered by an epithecal crust. Tubes rounded-polygonal, unequal, from two to three millimeters wide. Diaphragms flat, with marginal, punctiform depressions, similar to Favos. alveolaris, Goldfuss. Pores forming a single row on each side. Lateral squamæ rudimentary or absent. Not figured.

FAVOSITES EPIDERMATUS, ROMINGER.

Vide "Silliman's Journal," November, 1862.

Tubes from two to three millimeters wide, subequal in the same specimens, of obtusely polygonal outlines. Tube channels longitudinally striate by a cycle of twelve well-marked furrows, each of the intermediate band-like spaces bearing a row of horizontal squamæ, sometimes very prominent, and at others in rudimentary condition and partially obsolete. Diaphragms simple, flat, or warped by marginal depressions, more rarely of broken, angular surface through complication with the lateral squamæ, as in Favosites hemisphericus. Pores comparatively small, surrounded by an elevated rim, in a single or double row on each side, never very much crowded. Grows in discoid, subundose expansions, with a delicately wrinkled epithecal crust on the lower side, having a narrow conical centre serving as point of attachment. Found in the upper limestones of Mackinac Island, and of frequent occurrence in the drift; likewise common in the corniferous limestone of Canada, New York, Indiana, and Kentucky. From the forms with deeply furrowed, crenulated orifices, and with irregular, compound diaphragms, insensible transitions exist to specimens with almost smooth, faintly furrowed tubes and with simple, straight diaphragms. In the size of the tubes also a considerable variation exists in different specimens.

Plate VIII.—Fig. 1 is a silicified specimen from Caledonia, N. Y., with beautifully crenulated orifices, exhibiting the longitudinal furrows and intermediate squamose projections. Fig. 2 is a silicified specimen found in the drift of Ann Arbor, seen from the lower side. Fig. 3 is a specimen from Port Colborne, showing the diaphragms with marginal depressions, and the general surface aspect.

FAVOSITES CANADENSIS.

(*Vide* "Silliman's Journal," November, 1862.)

FISTULIPORA CANADENSIS, Billings.

Undose expansions, with an epithecal crust on the lower side, sometimes of digitato-ramose or reticulated growth, with orifices on all sides of the stems. Tubes of two strikingly different sizes. The larger ones, about one millimeter wide, are circular, dispersed at subregular intervals between a mass of smaller subangular tubes about one third the size of the circular tubes. The specimens have a great resemblance to Heliolites porosus, or, as Mr. Billings thinks, to Fistulipora. The radiated structure of the tubes and the development of lateral pores are sufficient to prove the Favosites type of the species. The larger tubes are always lined with a cycle of twelve rows of horizontal squamæ; the smaller tubes are usually smooth, or exhibit only rudimentary squamæ. The diaphragms of the larger tubes are compound, by complication with the squamæ; in the smaller tubes the diaphragms are simple; all the tubes are connected by abundant lateral pores disposed in longitudinal rows. The orifices in certain spots of the surface are often found closed by opercula.

Found in the upper Helderberg strata of Mackinac and in the drift deposits of the Lower Peninsula; also abundantly occurring in the corniferous limestone of Canada, New York, Indiana, and Kentucky.

Plate VIII.—Fig. 4 is a silicified specimen from the drift of Ann Arbor.

Plate XV.—Fig. 3 is a reticulated branching variety found at the Falls of the Ohio, kindly lent to me by Dr. James Knapp, of Louisville.

I have from the same locality some subramose specimens of similar structure, but with larger tubes in contiguity and fewer interstitial smaller ones. These form a transition link to another species to be described hereafter (Favosites radiciformis).

FAVOSITES TUBEROSUS, N. SP.

Compare FAVOSITES TROOSTII, Milne-Edwards, and FAVOSITES BASALTIFORMIS PARS, Goldfuss.

Tubes rounded-polygonal, unequal in size, variable, between two and three millimeters in diameter, with larger tubes up to five millimeters occasionally intermingled. A cycle of twelve longitudinal rows of stout, horizontal squamæ lines the inner circumference of the tubes. The squamæ of the joining rows alternate in position, are not separated by intermediate furrows, but often slightly interlock with each other. Pores large and very numerous, two or three rows on each side, surrounded by a small pit instead of a projecting rim, and one of them is generally situated directly beneath each of the squamæ.

Diaphragms regular, complete, but often compound, angular on the surface through intersection with the lateral squamæ.

On the lateral surface of the subcylindrical polyparia, many orifices are found closed by concave opercula of concentrically wrinkled structure. Some of them have a small opening in the centre, which is finally closed up when the operculum is finished.

Found frequently in the drift of Michigan in silicified condition, partly in hemispherical masses, with a flat under side covered by an epitheca, or in elongated, cylindrical or tuberose form. Similar specimens occur in the corniferous limestone of Canada, New York, and at the Falls of the Ohio. At the latter locality, large convex masses are found, which are often erroneously identified with Favosites maximus, Troost. They are absolutely identical in structure with the described smaller forms.

Plate IX.—Fig. 1 is a representation of two small silicified specimens from the corniferous limestone of Port Colborne. The upper specimen seems to me identical with the American specimen of Favosites basaltica figured by Goldfuss. Its base and the lower specimen exhibit orifices closed by concave opercula. Fig. 2 is a silicified specimen from the Falls of the Ohio, presenting open tube channels intersected by diaphragms, and with the walls perforated by very numerous pores. It shows at the same time the divergence of the tubes from a basal centre. The rows of lateral squamæ are not as conspicuous in that specimen as in many others.

FAVOSITES WINCHELLI, Rominger.

Vide "Silliman's Journal," November, 1862.

Massive convex polyparia, composed of rounded-polygonal tubes from three to four millimeters in diameter. Diaphragms complete, simple, warped and depressed at the margins into several siphon-like pits, or the whole diaphragm is depressed into one deep excentrical funnel. Tube walls striate by twelve well-marked longitudinal furrows, destitute of lateral squamæ. Pores small, surrounded by a projecting rim, in one or two rows on each side, and somewhat remote in position.

Found frequently in the drift deposits of Michigan. Some specimens are inclosed in a white sand rock, associated with Oriskany sandstone fossils ; others originate from the corniferous limestone, and various specimens were collected by me from the Hamilton group of Thunder Bay. It is not uncommon in the corniferous limestone of Canada, New York, and at the Falls of the Ohio.

Plate IX.—Fig. 3 is a silicified specimen from the Hamilton group of Alpena. Fig. 4 is from the corniferous limestone at Port Colborne, C. W.

FAVOSITES RADIATUS, N. SP.

Tubes unequal, rounded-polygonal, one and a half to two and a half millimeters in width, radiated by twelve prominent rows of lateral squamæ with intervening deep linear furrows. Diaphragms simple, straight, or warped by marginal, siphon-like depressions; the pores are numerous, forming from one to three rows on a side. A small pit surrounds each of them, as in Favosites tuberosus. The tubes of some specimens exhibit the lateral rows of squamæ only in rudimentary development, and are nearly smooth on the inside, with flat, moderately distant diaphragms. In other specimens the squamæ project with their elongated linguiform apices nearly to the centre of the tubes.

Grows in large convex masses. Found in the Hamilton group of Thunder Bay, also at Eighteen-mile Creek, near Hamburg, N. Y.

Plate X.—Fig 1 represents a surface view of a partly silicified fragment of a larger convex mass, found in the Hamilton group of Alpena.

FAVOSITES NITELLA, WINCHELL.

Tubes rounded-polygonal, subequal, stout-walled, not fully one millimeter in width. Tube channels smooth or beset with distant lateral squamæ. Diaphragms partially simple, regular, partially of complicated, irregular form, through intersection with the lateral squamæ. Pores large, distant, in a single row on each side. Mode of growth globular or pyriform or digitato-ramose. Resembles in structure Favosites Hamiltonensis, differing from it only by much smaller tube size.

Plate XI.—Fig. 4 represents specimens from the blue shales of the Hamilton group of Little Traverse Bay. Similar specimens are found in the Hamilton strata of Thunder Bay.

FAVOSITES PLACENTA, N. Sp.

Tubes less than one millimeter wide, rounded-polygonal, subequal or unequal, larger tubes and smaller tubes clustered together in separate spots, or single circular tubes dispersed between smaller subangular tubes, as in Favos. Canadensis. Diaphragms partially straight, simple, partially complicated, with lateral horizontal squamæ. Pores large, distant, in a single row on each side. Grows in discoid, undose expansions, with a concentrically wrinkled epitheca covering the lower side. Transition forms, of digitato-ramose form, connect this species most intimately with the former species, Fav. nitella. The specimens with single circular tubes dispersed through the mass of smaller subangular ones show a close affinity to Favosites Canadensis. Although specimens from different localities exhibit numerous minor variations, I consider this a well-marked species characteristic of the Hamilton group, from its base to the highest beds. It occurs in the upper strata of Partridge Point, in Thunder Bay, in the next lower strata of Stony Point, in the massive limestones forming the nucleus of the hillocks at Phelps' quarries, and at Broadwell's and Trowbridge's mills on Thunder Bay River. In the outcrops of Little Traverse Bay it is a frequently seen form ; the drift deposits of the Lower Peninsula likewise contain many specimens. The Hamilton strata of Bosanquet township in Canada contain it in particularly regular, discoid specimens, which caused me to name it *Placenta*. Similar forms are common in the Hamilton group of New York.

Plate XI.—Fig. 1 represents small specimens from Widder, C. W., one presenting the upper surface with subequal tubes, the other the under side covered by an epithecal crust. Fig. 2 gives specimens from the same locality, with unequal tubes, approaching in structure Fav. Canadensis. Fig. 3 is part of a large expansion from the Hamilton strata at Broadwell's mill, on Thunder Bay River.

FAVOSITES RADICIFORMIS, N. Sp.

Cylindrical and apparently procumbent creeping stems of variable thickness, from the diameter of a finger to that of a man's wrist, and often several feet in length, with anastomosing or straddling branches. Tubes of two sizes—the larger ones circular, from one to one and a half millimeter wide, the smaller ones angular, filling the interstitial spaces between the larger tubes. Walls stout. Diaphragms rarely regular, straight, usually complicated with the rows of lateral squamæ, as is the case in Favosites Emmonsii. Pores large and moderately numerous. The terminal parts of the stems are always formed of comparatively thin-walled, regularly formed tube orifices. On the lateral faces of the stems the orifices are often considerably narrowed and disfigured by incrassation of the tube walls, while the lateral pore channels retain their usual diameter, and become transformed into long vermicular ducts of nearly equal size with the principal tube channels. Such specimens are very unlike, in external appearance, those with normally formed tube orifices.

I have united within this species two forms, which differ from each other in the size of the tubes and of the stems, but otherwise correspond in structure. The form with larger stems and coarser tubes is found in the upper Helderberg limestones of Michigan, but particularly well preserved in the limestones of the Falls of the Ohio, and at Charleston Landing, in Indiana. The smaller form of more delicate structure is peculiar to the Hamilton group, and is found at Thunder Bay, often also in the drift associated with other Hamilton fossils.

Plate XII.—Fig. 1 represents a silicified specimen from the Falls of the Ohio, with unusually well-preserved surface characters; the central figure in the second tier of the plate is a similar specimen of smaller size, and the two stems to the left of it are silicified specimens of the smaller variety, found in the Hamilton strata of Alpena. To the right of the central figure the upper fragment represents a horizontal section through a specimen formed of tube casts, narrowed by incrassation of the walls, and connected by radial branches, which are the casts of the lateral pore channels. The lower figure is a vertical section through a similar specimen, in the peripheral parts likewise presenting the tube casts in a lateral view; the centre of the specimen presents not casts, but the actual tube channels, intersected by transverse diaphragms, and in unaltered, not incrassate condition. The outer lower stem is a specimen with abnormally incrassate tube walls, to show the contrast in external appearance of various modifications of the species.

FAVOSITES LIMITARIS, N. Sp.

Ramified and reticulated stems, from five to fifteen millimeters in thickness, forming horizontally explanate expansions or erect fruticose ramifications. Tubes very thick-walled, opening nearly rectangularly to the surface, with circular orifices, the walls forming either a solid, undefined interstitial mass, or, in another state of preservation, the polygonal outlines of each tube are visible on the surface of the interstices as delicate engraved lines. Several varieties are observed, in regard to the mode of growth and the size of tubes. The tube orifices rarely exceed the diameter of one millimeter; often they are smaller, and in some forms they are all equal in a specimen; others have smaller and larger orifices intermingled. A part of the orifices on the side faces of the stems are often found closed by opercula, situated below the outer edge of the channels; in the interior parts of the tube channels diaphragms are not regularly developed, and are of rare occurrence. Pores large, distant, and irregularly dispersed. In older stems the tube channels not unfrequently become considerably narrowed by excessive incrassation of the tube walls, while the pore channels gain in length and width, and appear on the surface as vermicular, transverse channels connecting the tube channels, which latter are, in their narrowed condition, hardly larger than the connecting pore channels. In certain specimens the orifices are at a slightly oblique angle to the surface, and surrounded at the lower external rim by a raised margin, which approximates this species to the forms of Favositoids comprehended under the name Cladopora, in indication of which similarity of structure I selected for it the name *limitaris*, a "*joining, transitory form.*"

The different well-marked varieties, which I have considered as constituting one species, are found in the corniferous limestone of Michigan, Canada, New York, Indiana, and Kentucky, usually in silicified condition; finely preserved specimens are also found in the drift deposits of Michigan.

Plate XIII. represents four varieties of the species. Fig. 1 is the usual form found in the drift; it is likewise the most common variety in the corniferous strata of Canada West (Port Colborne) and at Caledonia, N. Y. The faintly developed lips at the lower margins of the orifices are perceptible in the figures, and in one specimen the sharply defined polygonal outlines of each tube are also plainly seen. Fig. 2 is found in the drift of Ann Arbor; stems erect, with fruticose ramification; tubes smaller than in the former variety. Fig. 3 grows in much stouter branches than the others; the stems are usually compressed, elliptical in circumference; orifices very unequal in size. The portrayed specimen is from the Falls of the Ohio, but the same form is also found in the upper limestones of Mackinac Island. Fig. 4 resembles closely form No. 3, and occurs in association with it at the Falls of the Ohio; its tubes and stems are in all their proportions smaller. On Plate X. casts of this species are represented (Fig. 3) as they occur in the drift. The conical, subangular form of the tube channels, the almost total absence of diaphragms, the dispersed position of the pores, and the mode of gemmation of one tube from the other, are plainly conspicuous in the figures.

FAVOSITES CLAUSUS, N. SP.

Clustered, rapidly branching and anastomosing flexuose stems, varying from one half to one centimeter in thickness. Tubes unequal, the larger ones circular, measuring in different specimens from one half to one and a half millimeter in diameter; the smaller tubes filling the interstices between the larger ones are subangular. Orifices at the ends of the branches all open; on the sides of the stems most of them are found closed by opercula. Opercula flat or convex, some of them decorated with twelve marginal carinæ radiating toward the centre. Diaphragms partly simple and regular, but largely intermingled with irregular partial septa, formed by the development of lateral squamæ analogous to the vertical rows of leaflets in other species of Favosites. Pores numerous. Under this species I comprehend several varieties which closely resemble each other in general structure and mode of growth, but which may possibly be distinct forms. They occur in the Hamilton group and in the corniferous limestone.

Plate XIV.—Upper left-hand figure represents a silicified specimen from the Hamilton group of Thunder Bay River, near Broadwell's mills. Similar ramifications are found in the Hamilton strata of Widder and Arcona, in Canada. The tubes of this form are smaller than in the forms of the Helderberg group. The right-hand specimen in the upper row of the plate is from the corniferous limestone found in the drift of Ann Arbor; its tubes are nearly all of equal size and closed by opercula.

In the left-hand figure in the lower tier, from the Falls of the Ohio, the large circular tubes are in great contrast with the smaller subangular ones. The right-hand lower figures are single branches from the usual variety occurring in the corniferous limestone of Michigan, Canada, New York, and in the Western States. The specimens selected are also from the Falls of the Ohio.

FAVOSITES INTERTEXTUS, N. SP.

Irregularly reticulated masses of cylindrical or compressed elliptical stems, from one to two centimeters in thickness. Tubes quite unequal, stout-walled, the larger ones circular, the smaller subangular, filling the interstitial space between the larger tubes. Size of the larger tubes not much over half a millimeter. In the centre of the stems the tube channels are regularly formed, with moderately thick walls, and intersected by complete or incomplete squamiform diaphragms, and connected by distant pores. In the peripheral portions of the stems, the tube channels, by habitual thickening of the walls, have shrunk to filiform thinness, while the lateral pores have become more profusely developed and equal in width to the shrunken tube channels. Hereby a network of anastomosing ducts is formed, which can not be properly observed in fully-preserved specimens; in the drift, however, weathered specimens frequently occur in which the casts only of these reticulated ducts are preserved in silicified condition, the wall substance having all decayed. No one would likely recognize in these networks the casts of a Favosites if parts of the fully-preserved coral were not found in immediate contiguity to such networks. The contracted tube channels usually expand again to their normal diameter in close proximity to the surface. Found in the upper limestones of Mackinac and in the drift of the Lower Peninsula.

Plate XV.—Fig. 1 represents reticulated tube casts with the central portions of the stems formed by normally shaped tube channels. The object is too minute in the specimen. On Plate X., Fig. 4, similar casts of somewhat coarser stems are represented. On Plate

XV. the upper left-hand figure is a palmate branch found in the drift of Ann Arbor; some specimens have much stouter stems, while others are only of the thickness of a lead-pencil, forming reticulated clusters.

FAVOSITES DIGITATUS, N. SP.

Cespitose masses of subparallel anastomosing stems of the thickness of a finger, or single stems with more straddling branches. Tube walls stout, joining under polygonal outlines, lined by a cycle of vertical rows of horizontal squamæ, usually fewer in number than the normal twelve. Diaphragms sometimes regular, frequently incomplete, replaced by the lateral squamæ. Pores large. Tubes in different specimens variable, from one to one and a half millimeter in diameter. The polygonal form of the orifices and the generally well-developed squamæ within the tube channels render this form at once recognizable from other branching forms of Favosites, which have their orifices always more rounded, nearly circular.

It occurs in large clustered masses in the black, shaly limestones of the Hamilton group, on the shore of Lake Huron, from Thunder Bay Island, northward; similar masses are inclosed within the limestones of Little Traverse Bay, in beds of various horizons, and preserved in calcified condition. On Thunder Bay River it is found in silicified condition in the lower beds near Trowbridge's mills; in the drift of the Lower Peninsula, also, silicified specimens associated with other characteristic Hamilton fossils can often be picked up.

On Plate XV., the six right-hand figures of the lower tier are silicified specimens, of various tube size. The two outer figures and the lower central branch are from the drift of Ann Arbor; the other three branches are from the north fork of Thunder Bay River; the lower small branch has considerably thickened tube walls, forming within the polygonal, truncate, disciform tube ends a central proboscis-like prolongation. The cespitose specimens from the dark limestones, from the shore of Lake Huron and from Little Traverse Bay, can not be successfully represented by photography on account of their sombre color.

ALVEOLITES, Lamark.

Massive convex or expanded laminar, rarely ramose, polyparia composed of intimately united, compressed tubules, intersected by transverse diaphragms, connected by lateral pores, and longitudinally crested on the inside. The tubes in the massive or laminar forms are prostrate, diverging from a central point, and open obliquely to the surface; in the ramose forms the tubes are ascending and arching outward from an imaginary central axis, as in branching forms of Favosites. Tube walls moderately stout and not expanded at the orifices, the inner margin of which is appressed to the body of the polyparium and lost in a common interstitial surface; the outer margin projects as a sharp lip. Cavities of tubes lined with longitudinal crests or rows of spinulose projections, which normally should be twelve in number, but it is rarely the case that all of them are found developed. Usually two or three of the crests, or crested rows of spinules, grow large and conspicuous; the others have a more rudimentary development, or have sometimes become obsolete. Diaphragms comparatively more distant and irregular than in Favosites. Pores very large, situated on the two lateral edges of the compressed tubes, or at least in close proximity to them. The genus Alveolites appears contemporaneously with Favosites, for the first time, in the upper Silurian strata.

ALVEOLITES NIAGARENSIS, N. Sp.

Convex hemispherical masses of concentrically laminated structure, covered by an epithecal crust on the lower concave side, or undose, discoid expansions composed of superimposed layers of prostrate tubes, diverging with a slight spiral twist from a central vertex, several of which are sometimes observed on an expansion. The compressed tubes are always more convex on the upper sides, with a corresponding concavity of the lower sides, which rest on the convexities of the subjacent tubes. The compression is sometimes only moderate, and the outside of the oblique orifices is formed by a projecting arched lip; in other specimens the compression is stronger, the orifices become narrow, lanceolate, or fissure-like, with an appressed subplane lip on the outer side. The orifices of the majority of specimens are surrounded by a cycle of denticules, corresponding to longitudinal rows of spinules along the inner surface of the tube walls. The rows are rarely fully twelve in number, and some of them are always more strongly developed than others. In some specimens no denticulation of the orifices can be observed, and the tube channels are found to be almost smooth; this is not in all cases owing to a want of development of the crests or spinules; these seem often to have been obliterated by imperfect preservation in the process of petrification.

Diaphragms somewhat distant and oblique. Pores large, marginal, causing a pouch-like dilatation of the tube wall at the spot where situated. Diameter of tubes in the wider transverse direction varies in different specimens, from a half to one millimeter, which difference in size greatly alters their aspect. The degree of compression of the tubes, their more erect or more prostrate position in various specimens also cause numerous variations in their appearance, but no tangible line between one and another of the forms exists. I have, for this reason, considered all of them as representing the modifications of one and the same species. It occurs in great abundance in the Niagara group of Drummond's Island, at Point Detour, and in other localities. It is often found also in the drift of the Lower Peninsula. The specimens are all silicified and in but few of them are the more delicate structural characters well preserved. Certain specimens found in the drift exhibit principally the silicified casts of the tube channels, which have the form of flattened bands with rounded mamiform protrusions and inter mediate indentations of the lateral margins; on the summit of each protrusion a pore channel or its cast is situated.

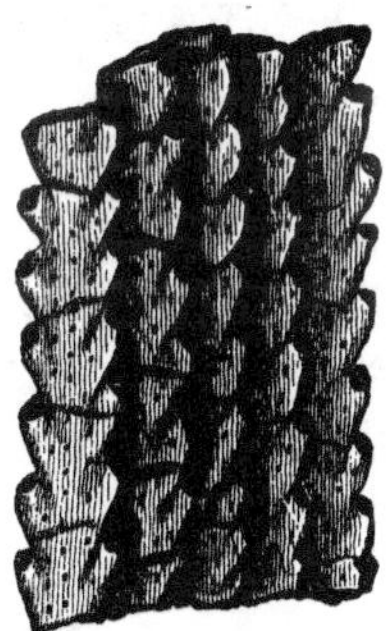

Plate XVI.—Fig. 1 represents a silicified specimen from the drift of Ann Arbor. Fig. 2 is found at Drummond's Island. The latter specimen exhibits the longitudinal rows of spinules very distinctly, but the object is too small to be properly seen in the not magnified figure.

ALVEOLITES SQUAMOSUS, Billings.

Convex masses of irregular growth, covered by an epithecal crust on the partially free, centrally attached under side, or sometimes incrusting other marine bodies. Tubes in the broader, transverse direction from one half to one millimeter in diameter, and in the other direction quite variable, in accordance with the degree of depression of the tubes, which are convex on the upper side and concave on the lower. Orifices very oblique, with a sharp lip on the outer margin. Tube channels longitudinally crested by twelve well-developed rows of spinules, of which generally some are larger than the others. Diaphragms not very close, and irregularly oblique. Pores large, marginal, but not causing a pouch-like dilatation of the tubes as in the Niagara species.

Found in the upper Helderberg limestones of Michigan, and in the drift; common also in the Helderberg limestones of Canada, New York, Ohio, Louisville, etc.

On Plate XVI., Fig. 3 is a silicified specimen found in the drift, giving a surface view; Fig. 4, likewise found in the drift, is composed of casts of the tubes. They are delicately punctured by impressions of the longitudinal rows of spinules. They exhibit the laterally situated pores and the distant, irregular diaphragms. The figures are of natural size.

ALVEOLITES VALLORUM, Meek.

(Palæontology of Mackenzie River.)

Specimens resembling the forms described by Mr. Meek, from Mackenzie River, are frequently found among the drift pebbles of Lake Superior. In some of them the tube walls are preserved; in others only the casts of the tube channels, which have the form of narrow, flat bands, connected with each other by short marginal bridges, representing the pore channels. The bands are longitudinally striate by fine, punctiform impressions, and transversely intersected by numerous closely approximated diaphragms. The width of the tube casts is about one millimeter, and their thickness one fourth of a millimeter.

Plate XVII.—Fig. 3 is a silicified specimen split in two, formed of tube casts. Found on the shore of Lake Superior, at Whitefish Point. Among the pebbles of the same locality other specimens of Alveolites are found, which agree with Alveolites squamosus, Billings.

ALVEOLITES SUBRAMOSUS, N. SP.

Incrusting expansions of irregular form, dependent from the incrusted object in the first stages of growth, subsequently of mamillate or digitato-ramose form. Orifices not over half a millimeter wide, margined on the outer side with a convex projecting or a flattened appressed lip; denticulated by crests, one of which in the median line of the inner body side of the tubes is much more prominent than the others. Pores large, rather remote. Diaphragms distant. Found in the Hamilton group of Thunder Bay, at Stony Point, and other localities. In mode of growth it perfectly resembles the branchlets from the Devonian strata of the Eifel, described by Milne-Edwards under the name of Alveolites subequalis, but its tubes are more minute and more strongly compressed than in that form.

Plate XVIII.—Fig. 4 represents calcified specimens from Stony Point, Thunder Bay, etc.

ALVEOLITES GOLDFUSSII, BILLINGS.

Undose, discoid expansions, with an imperfectly developed epitheca on the lower side, exhibiting the prostrate tube walls diverging from a central point of attachment. Orifices oblique to the surface, rarely denticulated at the margins, but interiorly, spinulose longitudinal crests are found well developed in polished sections. The tubes are seen in various degrees of compression in the same specimens; usually their transverse diameter is twice larger than their height, but sometimes tubes nearly as wide in one direction as in the other, and almost erect, as in an ordinary Favosites, can be observed. The size of the tubes is larger than in Alveolites squamosus, measuring in the larger diameter from one and a half to two miliimeters.

Pores large, situated on the lateral edges of the tubes. Diaphragms well developed, irregularly oblique or straight transverse. Found in the Hamilton strata, of Thunder Bay region, near Sunken Lake; more common in the Hamilton group of Widder, C. W., and in the Hamilton strata of Iowa.

Plate XVII.—Fig. 2 gives a surface view of part of a specimen from Widder, C. W.

LIMARIA STEININGER.

Synon., CŒNITES EICHWALD.

Small branching stems or laminar expansions, composed of thick-walled, conico-cylindrical tubules, with transversely compressed orifices, opening obliquely to the surface, surrounded on the outer side by an exsinuated lip, bearing two teeth projecting into the cavity. From the median line of the inner side of the walls, another tooth-like crest projects between the two outer ones. The tubes are connected by lateral pores, and intersected by transverse diaphragms. The diaphragms are regularly found in the thin-walled tube portions, but are rarely developed in tubes with thickened walls.

From Alveolites, Limaria differs only by more conical, stout-walled tubes, of less compressed and more rounded form in the central or basal parts of the polyparia. The number of longitudinal crests is in Limaria more restricted than in Alveolites, and rarely exceeds three. The three dentiform projections at the orifices of Limaria are the only structural difference separating it from the genus Cladopora, which has smooth, not crested tube channels; there are also, however, in species of Cladopora indications of crests, and the generic arrangement of many of the species in question is more a matter of individual arbitration than based upon any obvious typical difference.

LIMARIA RAMULOSA, HALL.

Found in the Niagara group of Lockport, etc. I have not been able to find it in Michigan. Another form of ramulets, which, according to the denticulated structure of their tube orifices belong to the genus Limaria, is *Cladopora verticillata* of Winchell and Marcy. It is of common occurrence in the Niagara group of Indiana, Wisconsin, and Kentucky, but has not been met with in Michigan.

LIMARIA LAMINATA, HALL.

Thin, undose, laminar expansions covered by an epithecal crust on the lower side. Tubes stout-walled, forming a massive interstitial surface between the orifices, which is sometimes larger than a tube diameter, other times less. Orifices, if well formed, crescent-shaped and less than half a millimeter in diameter. The convex side of the crescent forms a more or less projecting lip, with two rather obscure, dentiform crests; on the concave side of the crescent another more conspicuous crest occupies the median line. The specimens exhibit on their surface at various intervals certain centres, around which the orifices are disposed in spirally twisted rows; the concave sides of the orifices are always directed toward these imaginary central points. Of common occurrence in the Niagara group of Drummond's Island, and at Point Detour, but many of the specimens have by silicification lost the finer details of structure.

Plate XVIII.—Fig. 2 represents a specimen from Point Detour, of natural size.

LIMARIA CRASSA, N. SP.

Grows in thick, laminar expansions, of undose surface, covered on the lower side by an epitheca. Often several such laminæ are superimposed, and sometimes two leaves stick together at the epithecal side, and a lamina with orifices on both sides is the result. Orifices variable in the same specimens. If normally formed they are kidney-shaped, separated by massive interstitial spaces formed by the thick tube walls. They open obliquely to the surface, with a lip on the outer margin. In other tubes the lip scarcely projects, and the orifices appear as an unsymmetrically oval opening surrounded by a massive interstitial surface. Often, also, the tubes are joined, with nearly erect, subangular, less thick-walled orifices. On the inner side of the walls a conspicuous crest projects from the median line, and on the outer walls two others of smaller size fork over the opposite one; by a great thickening of the walls, the crests become obsolete. Pores are large and numerous. Diaphragms developed in the thinner-walled tubes. Found in the Niagara limestone of Point Detour, Drummond's Island, and in the exposures of the Niagara group along the shore of Lake Michigan, in the west part of the Upper Peninsula.

Plate XVIII.—Fig. 1 represents fragments from Point of Barques on Lake Michigan (southwest of the mouth of Manistic River).

CLADOPORA, Hall.

Ramose and anastomosing stems or laminar expansions, with orifices on one or both sides, composed of thick-walled, elongate, conical tubules, opening obliquely to the surface, with dilated orifices. Tubules laterally connected by pores. Diaphragms have originally been denied by the author in his genus Cladopora, but their occasional development is proved by many actual observations, although usually the tube channels, in specimens, are found open throughout all their length.

The tube cavity of Cladopora is said to be destitute of longitudinal furrows or crests, in distinction from Limaria and Striatopora, but this is merely through habitual obsolescence of a character which properly belongs to the entire Favositoid family, and which in some of the most characteristic species of Cladopora has been recognized in rudimentary development.

CLADOPORA LAQUEATA, N. Sp.

Large, reticulated, horizontal expansions, formed of round or compressed elliptical stems, from two to four millimeters in diameter, with narrow, intervening loops of elongate, lanceolate form. Tubes very thick-walled. Orifices separated by broad interstitial spaces, transversely oval, somewhat dilated, nearly one millimeter wide in transverse direction, with a stout lip on the exterior margin; the interior margin impressed and confluent with the massive interstitial surface. Pores plainly discernible. Diaphragms sometimes noticeable, closing off the peripheral tube ends. By silicification the finer surface details of the specimens are generally much impaired.

Occurs in the Niagara group of Point Detour, and all along the exposures of the south shore of the Upper Peninsula.

Plate XVIII.—Fig. 3 represents a fragment of a large expansion in silicified condition. Found near Seul Choix, on shore of Lake Michigan. In mode of growth this species bears much resemblance to Cladopora reticulata, Hall; but the latter is a more delicately built species, with smaller, nearly circular tube orifices.

In the drift deposits of Michigan, specimens of *Cladopora multipora*, Hall, are often met with.

CLADOPORA LICHENOIDES, N. SP.

Irregularly undose, laminar expansions, covered by an epithecal crust on the lower side, which is formed by prostrate, flattened tubes, coalesced intimately and diverging horizontally from a central apex. Toward their peripheral ends the tubes bend into a suberect position and lose their flattened form, becoming rounded and dilated near the orifices. These are sometimes nearly upright, and join with acute margins, resembling an ordinary Favosites; at other times the obliquity of the orifices is more pronounced, and the outer tube margins form an arched projecting lip, while the inner margin merges into a narrow, common, interstitial surface. The flattened tubes, forming the base of the expansions, connect by numerous lateral pores situated on both edges; the erect, more rounded portions of the tubes have the pores irregularly dispersed over their circumference.

Diaphragms sparingly developed at irregular, remote intervals, often closing the peripheral tube ends, under the form of opercula. The tube cavity is generally smooth, without crests or longitudinal furrows, which induced me to place this species with Cladopora, and not with Alveolites, under which it might otherwise be classed with propriety. Found frequently in the drift of Michigan. It occurs in place in the corniferous limestone of the Falls of the Ohio, in Canada and New York, etc.

Plate XVII.—Fig. 1 gives a surface view of silicified specimens from the Falls of the Ohio. Fig. 4 is a specimen found in the drift of Ann Arbor, exhibiting the casts of tubes seen from the basal side of an expansion. The flattened form of the prostrate channels, with numerous short marginal pore connections, the gemmation of young tubes from older ones, the disposition of distant diaphragms, the more rounded and dilating peripheral tube ends, bent into sub-erect position—all can be studied in such casts to much better advantage than in the most perfectly preserved specimens.

CLADOPORA FISHERI, BILLINGS.

Synon., ALVEOLITES FISHERI, Billings.

Palmate, laminar expansions, attached by a clumsy, massive root portion to other bodies. Orifices on both sides of the leaves, opening obliquely to the surface, with a sharp lip on the exterior side; the inner tube margin merges into a common interstitial surface, of variably broader or narrower extent. The thickness of the tube walls and the obliquity of the orifices vary much in different parts of the specimens, and accordingly the surface characters are quite changeable. On the terminal edges of the fronds the tubes are thin-walled and the orifices join with sharp, crested outlines. In the central and basal portions of the expansions, the walls are thickened, and the oblique orifices separated by intervening solid interstitial spaces, margined on the exterior side by a lip, which surrounds a transversely oval, or often a nearly circular mouth. Sometimes the orifices are not lipped, and form shallow, undefined depressions in the massive wall substance, at the bottom of which the narrower part of the tube channels begins. Again, these superficial pits are circumscribed by polygonal, carinated outlines. A difference also exists in the upper and lower surfaces of the fronds, which seem to have grown in horizontally spreading direction. The upper side is always marked by sharper, more projecting contour lines, while on the lower surface all the contours are dull and rounded.

The orifices are about one half a millimeter wide, or somewhat larger, oval or kidney-shaped on the external margin; the inner tube portions are round or subangular. Pore channels are large and numerous. Diaphragms frequently developed under the form of superficial opercula, frequently noticed also in the inner portions of the tube channels, but in specimens with very stout-walled tubes rarely observed. The original specimens described by Billings were found in the Hamilton group of Widder, C. W., in calcified condition; identical, but silicified specimens occur in the Hamilton group of Thunder Bay, and in boulders of the drift which inclose other characteristic Hamilton fossils. Entirely similar specimens are found in the corniferous limestone of the Falls of the Ohio, and at Charleston Landing, Indiana.

Plate XIX.—Fig. 1 represents a silicified specimen from the drift of Ann Arbor. Fig. 4 is a specimen from the Hamilton group of Widder, C. W., the typical locality for Mr. Billings' specimens.

CLADOPORA CANADENSIS, N. SP.

Palmate, laminar expansions, like the former species, with which it is found associated and agreeing in general structure. Tubes much smaller. Orifices at the ends of the fronds subrotund or triangular, with a convex, centrally indented lip on the outer side. On the stouter central and basal parts of the expansions, the lips are appressed, opening, transversal, fissure-like, or the lips have, besides the central indentation, two lateral ones, giving the orifices an arched, semi-lunar form. On the under side of the fronds the orifices are impressed into the massive interstitial wall substance, with a shallow depressed space surrounding them, which is defined by very obtuse rounded, subpolygonal outlines. On the upper surface, all is raised into stronger relief. Found in the Hamilton group of Widder, C. W.

Plate XIX.—Fig. 3 is a representation of one of these specimens.

CLADOPORA TURGIDA, N. SP.

Stout laminar expansions, with orifices on both sides. Tubes thick-walled, with a narrow cylindrical channel, which dilates near the surface into transversely oval or kidney-shaped oblique orifices, spreading, with the inner part of the margins, into a common interstitial surface, on which, by slightly raised carinæ, the polygonal outlines of each tube are defined. The outer margin projects as a short lip sinuated on both sides, or simply straight. In well-preserved specimens, on the expanded part of the orifices, longitudinal furrows are faintly developed, as in the genus Striatopora. A difference is noticeable between the upper and under side of the fronds.

Pores well developed. Diaphragms rarely observed excepting as opercula. Diameter of orifice a little over one millimeter; internal tube portions half a millimeter. Found in the Helderberg group of Mackinac Island, at Port Colborne, C. W., and likewise in the drift of Ann Arbor.

Plate XIX.—Fig. 2 is a silicified fragment found in the drift of Ann Arbor.

CLADOPORA CRYPTODENS, Billings.

Alveolites cryptodens, Billings.

Cylindrical polyp stems, from five to ten millimeters in diameter, with distant, dichotomous, straddling ramification. Tubes opening with oblique dilated orifices, which either join with acute edges, each of them being a circumscribed pit, or have the inner part of the walls spread into an indefined, common interstitial surface, from which the convex lips forming the front margin of the orifices project like the teeth of a rasp. Tube size variable in different specimens; in the variety with larger tubes the transverse diameter of the dilated orifices is about one and a half millimeter, the interior cavity of the channels measuring about a half of one millimeter. In the variety with smaller tubes the orifices measure about one millimeter externally, and the internal channels one third of a millimeter. The tube cavities usually appear to be smooth, but in well-preserved silicified specimens, cleared by acids of the surrounding limestone, the tube channels exhibit three crests, two projecting from the exterior side of the wall, and one intermediate between the two, from the opposite inner wall side. These crests are not noticeable on the dilated orificial part of the tubes, but are distinctly seen in the neck of the channel, where the narrower part begins. Transverse diaphragms are rarely found developed. Pores are large and irregularly dispersed. The crested condition of the tube channels would bring this species under the genus Limaria, or perhaps under Alveolites, where Billings placed it, but, considering the general habitus of the specimens, I have placed them under Cladopora, as being nearest related to the forms composing this genus, which is only deprived of crests through the incomplete development of a character typical for the whole family to which it belongs.

Found in the upper Helderberg limestones of Michigan, New York, Canada, and in the Western States; also common in the drift deposits of Michigan.

Plate XX.—Fig. 1 represents several fragments of branches with the larger tubes. Orifices somewhat variable in different branches. Fig. 2 is the variety with smaller tubes, corresponding in all particulars with the larger tubed form. All the specimens figured are selected from the Falls of the Ohio, as being better preserved than those from any other locality.

CLADOPORA ROEMERI, Billings.

Alveolites Roemeri, Billings.

Cylindrical or compressed branching stems of about five millimeters diameter. Orifices comparatively large, oblique to the surface, and joining with their expanded margins in an indefined interstitial surface, or under subangular, obtusely crested outlines, inclosing shallow, obliquely funnel-shaped pits, the outer margins of which project as arched lips; the inner walls of the pits spread insensibly, merging into the lips of the adjoining pits. External diameter of orifices about one millimeter; interior tube channel one third of a millimeter. The orifices are frequently closed by opercula situated below the external margins. Diaphragms in most of the specimens sparingly developed. Pores large and irregularly disposed.

Occurs in the Hamilton strata of Widder, Canada West, in calcified condition. Silicified specimens are found in the corniferous limestone and in boulders of that formation, mingled with the drift of the Southern Peninsula.

Plate XX.—Fig. 3 represents specimens from the typical locality of Widder, Canada West.

CLADOPORA ALPENENSIS, N. Sp.

Branching cylindrical stems, from five to ten millimeters in diameter. Orifices slightly oblique, dilated, joining under linear polygonal outlines on an even, narrow, interstitial surface; external margins not projecting as a lip, excepting a small nodular projection in the centre of the outer margin, which gives the transversely widened, elliptical mouths a faint kidney shape. The inner expanded margin of the orifices is very delicately striate in radial direction. Diameter of orifices externally about one millimeter; internal tube cavity about half a millimeter wide. Diaphragms rarely noticed. Pores large and irregularly dispersed.

Found in silicified condition in the upper strata of the Hamilton group of Thunder Bay.

Plate XX.—Fig. 4 represents a few of the branchlets. The linear polygonal outlines of the tubes are recognizable in the figures; the striation of the margins is too delicate to be seen on them.

CLADOPORA LABIOSA, Billings.

Alveolites labiosa, Billings.

Small, branching, reticulated stems, from two to five millimeters in diameter, growing from an attached, massive root portion in horizontally spreading direction. Orifices oblique to the surface, subcircular, surrounded on the exterior side by a prominent convex lip; the interior part of the orificial tube walls spreads into an undefined, flat, interstitial surface. By wearing of the surface the lips often become deeply sinuated in the centre, and then the orifices are acutely triangular. In certain specimens considered to be a variety of this species, the closely crowded small orifices are surrounded by small pits impressed in the thick wall substance, and open on the surface with less obliquity than in other specimens, and with only a small lip developed on the exterior margin. The size of the tubes differs somewhat in the specimens, but a more obvious difference in appearance is caused by the variations in the width of the interstitial spaces. In some specimens the orifices are separated by interstices less than the diameter of a tube, while in others the interstitial space is two or three times as large. In adult parts of stems the intervals between the orifices are always greater than they are near the terminal branchlets. The diameter of tubules at the orifices is about half of one millimeter; internally the channels are narrower. Within the cavity of some tubes, on the outer side of the walls, two crests can be noticed by looking into the orifices, but in others of equally well-preserved specimens no crests are recognizable. Lateral pores well developed. Transverse diaphragms have not been observed. The casts of tubes often found in drift specimens are always uninterrupted, thread-like, laterally connected by short transverse bars representing the pores, and exhibiting the intercalation of new young tubules, connecting by a perforation at the apex with their mother-tubes.

Found abundantly in the drift of Michigan, in a porous cherty rock containing many other corniferous limestone fossils. In Canada and New York it is common in the corniferous limestone; occurs also at the Falls of the Ohio.

Plate XXI.—Fig. 2 represents a number of branchlets of variable form. The two lower figures on the left side are excepted; they are described under the name of *Cladopora rimosa;* but in the lower tier of this plate the smaller central specimen is considered as a variety of *Cladopora labiosa.*

CLADOPORA RIMOSA, N. SP.

Reticulated expansions of small teretiform or elliptically compressed stems, much resembling the former species. Orifice openings very oblique to the surface, transversely compressed, fissure-like, margined by a sharp closely-appressed lip on the outer side. Diameter of orifices in transverse direction from one half to two thirds of a millimeter; interior tube channels cylindrical and much narrower. Interstitial spaces large and flat. This form is the usual associate of Cladopora labiosa, and may perhaps be only a variety of that species; but the two forms are so constant, not merging into one another through transition forms, that I believe them to be distinct. Found in the drift of the Lower Peninsula.

Plate XXI.—Fig. 2. The two lower left-hand stems; the larger forked specimen is broken off from a disciform basal expansion incrusting the stem of a Cyathophyllum Hallii.

CLADOPORA PINGUIS, N. SP.

Horizontally expanded, branching and anastomosing stems of usually compressed elliptical form, but sometimes cylindrical. Diameter of stems from five to ten millimeters. Orifices in the older stems subreniform shallow pits, impressed into a massive common wall substance, composing broad interstitial spaces. The actual tube opening, commencing at the bottom of these pits, is narrow, fissure-like, and margined by a small lip which does not project above the pit. In the ends of the branches the tube walls are less thickened, and the orifices not surrounded by pits, subcircular, margined by a moderately projecting convex lip. These terminal parts of the ramifications resemble the specimens figured as Clad. labiosa. The three right-hand branchlets and future collections may demonstrate the three last-described species to be only modifications of one; but for the present this direct affinity between them is not proved, wherefore I point them out as specifically distinct. Found associated with the other forms in the drift of the Lower Peninsula.

Plate XXI., Lower tier.—The two larger specimens were found in the drift of Ann Arbor, in a porous cherty rock, originating from decomposition of a siliceous limestone, of which sometimes an unaltered nucleus forms the centre of the boulders. The specimen in the centre below the two figures represents a variety of Cladopora labiosa.

CLADOPORA PULCHRA, N. SP.

Small cylindrical stems, from three to five millimeters in thickness, growing in reticulated ramifications, composed of thick-walled conical tubules, diverging in a curve from an imaginary longitudinal axis, opening almost at a rectangle to the surface, with circular orifices separated by interstitial walls wider than a tube diameter. The end of each tube either projects as a small monticulose protuberance above the general surface, and is defined from the adjoining tubes by delicate linear furrows circumscribing polygons, or the lower half only of each tube wall projects under the form of a low semicircular lip. In other specimens the single ends of the tubes do not project, and are not defined in their circumference, their orifices opening on the massive surface as simple circular perforations, surrounded at the outside by a shallow depressed area. Tube diameter at the orifices one third to one half millimeter, near the centre of the stems much narrower. Lateral pores numerous, in unequally dispersed position. Diaphragms sparingly developed. On the casts of the tubes which frequently occur in weathered drift specimens, a cycle of longitudinal carinations is faintly visible. In its structure this elegant small species approaches Favosites limitaris, which could likewise be not inappropriately arranged under the genus Cladopora. The thick-walled conical tubes, the greater obliquity of the orifices to the surface, with a sometimes well-developed prominent lip, bring this form nearer to the Cladopora type than to Favosites. Very common in the drift boulders of the corniferous formation in Michigan ; it occurs in place in the Helderberg limestones of Canada, and at the Falls of the Ohio, near Louisville.

Plate XXI.—Fig. 1 represents a number of variations, amongst which are found stems with smaller tubes and with larger tubes, with projecting monticulose orifices and with lipped mouths, or with massive surface of the stems, with the orifices impressed as shallow pits. Some of the stems represented exhibit also sharp, linear, polygonal furrows circumscribing the tubes.

CLADOPORA ROBUSTA, N. SP.

Palmato-ramose, occasionally reticulated stems, of round or compressed elliptical form, growing in horizontal expansions, spreading sometimes over the space of several square feet. Stems attaining a thickness of from one to two centimeters. Tube openings oblique to the surface, with gently dilating orifices, joining under subacute margins, by which the surface is divided into a network of rhomboidal spaces with rounded corners. The lower angle of the rhomboids is formed by the projecting semicircular lips of the orifices, which, by wearing off, become emarginated and acutely triangular in shape. Transverse diameter of orifices about one millimeter, in other varieties smaller. Diameter of tube channels below the peripheral surface one quarter to one half of a millimeter. Tube walls stout, thickening near the periphery. Lateral pores distant. Diaphragms sometimes observed, but not developed in the majority of the specimens. Several varieties, in manner of growth and size of tubes, can be distinguished.

Found in the corniferous limestone and in the Hamilton group. The Hamilton specimens occur in the vicinity of Alpena, on Thunder Bay ; the specimens of the corniferous strata are frequently found in the drift of Michigan, but the Falls of the Ohio is the locality where this species can be found in greatest perfection and in greatest abundance. The represented specimens are from that locality.

Plate XXII.—Fig. 1 represents two silicified branches with larger tubes. Fig. 2 is a branch of smaller tube size.

CLADOPORA IMBRICATA, N. Sp.

Cylindrical ramified stems, attaining a diameter of two centimeters, attached by a massive basal expansion. Tubes opening very obliquely to the surface, with narrow, transversely compressed orifices, joining under rhomboidal outlines. The sharp subarcuate lips forming the exterior margin of the orifices are closely appressed to the body of the stems, and arranged in an imbricating order like the scales of a fish.

Transverse diameter of orifices two millimeters, by a width of only half a millimeter across the centre of the lanceolate mouths. Internally the tube cavity becomes nearly circular and much narrower, not over half a millimeter in diameter. Pores distant. Diaphragms have not been observed. Some specimens found in the drift of Michigan seem to belong to this species, which is not uncommon in the Helderberg limestones at the Falls of the Ohio.

On Plate XXII., lower tier, the two outer stems on the right-hand side are figures of silicified specimens found at the Falls of the Ohio.

The next two species described, found in the Helderberg limestones at the Falls of the Ohio, have not been recognized in the strata of Michigan, but in order to give the description of this tribe of corals more completeness, I have allowed myself, in behalf of science, to transgress a step beyond the prescribed limits. It is very probable, however, that future collectors will find these forms in Michigan.

CLADOPORA ASPERA, N. Sp.

Cylindrical stems, from one to two centimeters in thickness, growing in horizontally spreading, reticulated ramifications, which are attached by a massive basal expansion. The tubes composing the basal part are prostrate, diverging toward the circumference of the disk; the orifices are compressed, fissure-like, covered by a scaly, flat lip, while the inner part of the walls forms an undefined, common interstitial surface. The orifices of the stems are of quite different shape; their tubes diverge from an imaginary axal line in an ascending curve toward the periphery of the stems, opening there in various degrees of obliquity, under crested polygonal outlines, which inclose shallow conical pits, at the bottom of which the tube channels open as narrow, transverse, more or less curved fissures, about one millimeter wide in the longer direction, and one quarter of a millimeter in the shorter. The body side of these pits is formed of spreading walls, which help to form the front part of the orifices next above. The outer half of the pits is formed by the obliquely truncated ends of the extremely massive tube walls, and projects under the form of a clumsy lip, giving the stems a very rough appearance. The outer transverse diameter of the orificial pits is nearly two millimeters; the compressed, band-like tube channels become circular at a short distance in from the peripheral ends, and are about one third of a millimeter in width. Pore channels distant. Diaphragms have not been noticed.

Plate XXII., Lower tier.—Upper third figure from the right side represents a silicified fragment of a reticulated expansion, from the Falls of the Ohio.

CLADOPORA EXPATIATA, N. SP.

Reticulated expansions of cylindrical or compressed palmate stems, of a diameter of from one to two centimeters, attached by a massive basal expansion. Tubes of the basal part diverging outward, prostrate, and more compressed than those of the stems, with a sharp scaly lip at the outer margin. Tube walls generally very stout. Orifices of the stems variable in the same specimens. Usually they open with no great obliquity to the surface, and join under irregular, polygonal crested outlines inclosing deep conical cell pits, narrowing into cylindrical tube channels. The dilated margins are not converted on the outer side into a lip, but form a uniform network, as in a Favosites. Often also, by incrassation of the tube walls, the cell pits become partly filled, and shallower in the expanded marginal portion, while the crests of their circumference are rounded off. In other specimens the tubes open with greater obliquity to the surface, and do not join with crested margins encircling orificial pits, but the body portion of the orificial walls spreads into a common interstitial surface, and the front walls project as sharp semicircular lips. Transitions from one of the surface characters described into the other can be followed out in nearly every larger specimen. The end branches generally differ somewhat from the older stems, and the orifices of the upper surface of the prostrate expansions are not quite alike to those of the under side. The dilated orificial pits are nearly always wider in the transverse direction of the stems than in the vertical; their diameter is about one and a half millimeter; that of the inner tube channels about one third to one half millimeter. Pores distant. Diaphragms sparingly developed. From the former species, this one differs in having smaller tubes, and less compressed, nearly circular orificial openings; but great similarity exists between them, and by reason of the great variability in the surface structure of both, it is sometimes hard to tell to which class certain specimens belong.

Plate XXII., Lower tier.—The three left-hand figures are silicified fragments from the Falls of the Ohio, representing a few of the modifications in which the species occurs.

STRIATOPORA, HALL.

Ramose stems, composed of thick-walled conical tubes, opening on the surface with oblique dilated orifices, in all particulars corresponding with the structure of Cladopora, from which they mainly differ by a cycle of longitudinal furrows radiating across the expanded tube margins, a difference which, as previously remarked, is not at all peculiar to Striatopora, but belongs to the essential family characters of all Favositoids, and happens to be more obviously developed in the forms called Striatopora than in the next related Cladopora. In addition to the longitudinal furrows, the intermediate band-like spaces also sometimes bear rows of spinules; and as another peculiarity in Striatopora, the abundant development of lateral pores may be mentioned.

STRIATOPORA HURONENSIS, N. SP.

A single fragment of a stem eight millimeters in diameter is the only specimen I have seen; but as being one of the first representatives of the genus, and positively differing from Striatopora flexuosa, Hall, found in the same geological horizon, I thought it proper to describe even a fragment when well characterized.

Orifices obliquely funnel-shaped, joining with edged margins. The body side of the orificial walls is spreading and forms part of the exterior walls of the orifices above; the outer side of the oblique orificial funnels is margined by an erect semicircular lip. Diameter of orifices in transverse direction two millimeters; in longitudinal three millimeters. Twelve deep longitudinal furrows, with intermediate obtuse crests, give the cells a star form. The tubes are distinctly intersected by diaphragms with marginal depressions. Pores are somewhat obscured by the rough silicified surface of the specimen, but are recognizable. Found in the Niagara group of Point Detour, Lake Huron.

Plate XXIV.—Fig. 2, upper fragment, natural size. *Striatopora flexuosa*, Hall, has not been observed among the fossils of the Niagara group in Michigan.

STRIATOPORA RUGOSA, HALL.

Synon., CYATHOPHORA IOWENSIS, Owen.

Stems with dichotomous branches, from five to ten millimeters in diameter, composed of very thick-walled tubes opening obliquely to the surface, with dilated mouths, bounded on the exterior side by a prominent semicircular lip. The inner body side of the walls of the orifices is flattened,spreading into a common, broad, interstitial mass. Diameter of orifices two millimeters; of interior channels one millimeter. Pores large, distant. Diaphragms not observed. The radial striæ are, in all the numerous specimens which I have examined, totally obsolete, for which reason this form would have a more appropriate place under the genus Cladopora.

Occurs frequently in the Hamilton strata of Thunder Bay, and is found in the drift.

Plate XXIV., Fig. 2.—The left-hand figure represents a stem from Thunder Bay.

STRIATOPORA CAVERNOSA, N. Sp.

Stunted ramifications of cylindrical or compressed stems, from one to two centimeters in diameter. Tubes large, in comparison with the size of the stems, and very unequal through the frequent intercalation of young tubes. Orifices oblique to the surface, rounded, or of irregular shape, joining with obtusely edged stout walls. They form gradually dilating, spacious, deep funnels, which are longitudinally grooved by a cycle of twelve well-marked striæ. A remarkable abundance of large irregularly dispersed pores perforates the tube walls within the orificial funnels, and even close to their external edges. Diaphragms flat, well developed. Diameter of full-grown tubes at the orificial ends from two to three millimeters; internal tube cavities one millimeter wide. Occurs in the drift of Michigan, associated with corniferous limestone fossils, and is found in place in the corniferous limestones of Port Colborne, Canada West; rarely also at the Falls of the Ohio.

On Plate XXIII., Fig. 3, are small silicified fragments found in the drift of Ann Arbor.

STRIATOPORA LINNÆANA, Billings.

Dichotomously branching stems, from a few millimeters to one centimeter in diameter. Orifices moderately oblique to the surface, joining under acute polygonal margins, which inclose funnel-shaped orifices, and project on their outer margin as prominent lips. Tubes very unequal in size, through the frequent intercalation of young tubes. Orificial margins grooved by a cycle of twelve deep furrows, and the interstitial, band-like spaces are decorated with longitudinal rows of spinules, which in the narrower neck portion of the tube channels project as stelliform radii. Pores large and very abundant, perforating also the expanded parts of the orificial walls. Diaphragms well developed in some of the specimens. Diameter of the peripheral tube margins about two millimeters; of interior parts one millimeter or less.

Occurs in the Hamilton group of Thunder Bay in silicified condition, and at Widder, in Canada West, in calcified form.

Plate XXIII., Fig. 5.—The three upper specimens were found at Thunder Bay, near Alpena; the three lower specimens are from Widder, Canada West. Fig. 6 of the same plate represents a larger form, found in the corniferous limestone of the Falls of the Ohio, which does not seem to differ much from the Hamilton form, except by a more robust growth, and by less definitely circumscribed orifices.

DENDROPORA, Michelin.

The corals, one of which is described by Michelin under the name of Dendropora, have been placed by Milne-Edwards with the sub-order Seriatoporinæ, through misapprehension of their structure, attributing to them a central columella which does not exist. Their structure is in all essential points identical with the Favositinæ. Milne-Edwards divides these forms into three genera: Dendropora, Rhabdopora, and Trachypora, according to certain surface characters which I have not considered important enough to justify the separation. In the following pages, therefore, I use the name Dendropora for all of them, and give the subjoined definition of the term *Dendropora:*

Branching and frequently reticulated stems, variable in diameter from one millimeter to more than one inch. The stems are attached to other bodies by an incrusting basal expansion; they are composed of very thick-walled, intimately united conical tubules, diverging from an imaginary axal centre in ascending curves. The tube channels are laterally connected by pore channels and transversely septate by diaphragms. The interior tube ends are only moderately thick-walled, but in approaching the periphery the walls thicken very much by the addition of concentric layers within the expanding channels, and constitute by their intimate union a broad interstitial surface separating the orifices. In some forms this interstitial surface is covered by spinulose ridges and granulations; in others by flexuose longitudinal rugæ, or by a combination of both granules and rugæ, with intermediate punctiform or short fissure-like porosities, which are not cell spaces of an independent tissue element, but are merely superficial punctations and engravings of the substance of the tube walls. The orifices usually project with their margins above the general surface, but sometimes they appear as impressed pits, or have at least no projecting rim. Their form is either circular or elongate elliptical. Sometimes they are disposed in regular longitudinal rows on the stems, but are also often irregularly dispersed. The obliquity of the tube mouths to the surface is variable, and in some species they open almost rectangularly to it. In a part of the species the tube channels are longitudinally striate, as in Striatopora, but usually this striation is obscure.

DENDROPORA ORNATA, N. SP.

Circular stems, from one to two centimeters in diameter, with dichotomous ramification. Orifices circular or oval, rising above the surface by a monticulose circumvallation, or nearly even with it, of unequal size and irregularly dispersed over the massive interstitial surface of the stems, which is usually wider than a tube diameter, with exception of the ends of the stems, where the orifices are separated by comparatively narrow intermediate walls. The interstitial surface is decorated by granules and short ridges disposed in loose radial order around the circumference of the orifices. Peripheral diameter of orifices about one and a half millimeter; within they gradually contract to a diameter of not more than half a millimeter. The terminal ends of the branches have somewhat larger orifices with thinner walls, greater obliquity to the surface, and are surrounded by a more or less projecting lip on the exterior side, as in the case of specimens of Cladopora or Striatopora, from which these parts differ only by the granulated edges of the interstitial walls. In polished vertical sections through calcified stems, the tubes are found to be decorated with a cycle of longitudinal rows of spinules, and the development of distant transverse diaphragms and of large connecting pores can likewise be ascertained. Found rarely in the Hamilton group of Thunder Bay, but very common in the Hamilton strata of New York, at Darien, Eighteen-Mile Creek, Seneca Lake, etc.; at Widder, in Canada, it also sparingly occurs.

Plate XXIII.—Fig. 1 represents specimens from Darien, in calcified condition.

Plate XXIV., Fig. 2.—Lower figure to the right is a young silicified branchlet found at Alpena, Mich. It exhibits a scar of attachment at the lower end. The ends of the branches are formed of thin-walled tubes with nearly contiguous orifices. The granulose decorations of the interstitial surface are obscure in this specimen.

DENDROPORA NEGLECTA, N. SP.

(Compare *Favosites polymorpha*, Billings, *Canad. Journ.*, 1859, p. 111, Fig. 12, with exclusion of the other figures.)

Stems from five millimeters to two centimeters in diameter, with irregularly straddling branches. Orifices very unequal, circular or oval, narrow, funnel-shaped, oblique, or almost rectangular to the surface, surrounded by a prominent rim, or nearly even with the interstitial surface, which is quite spacious and decorated with ridges and granulations as in the former species. Many of the stems, however, are nearly smooth on the surface, either through the wearing off of the decorations or through original want of their development. Older stems are sometimes found with nearly solid surface, the orifices having become narrowed to minute punctiform openings by excessive incrassation of the tube walls. The central portions of the stems are always formed by thinner-walled tubes or tube ends, with subangular outlines and of regu lar Favosites structure, having connecting pores, transverse diaphragms, and being longitudinally striate by faint spinulose ridges.

Found in the drift of Michigan, associated with other fossils of the corniferous limestone formation. It is found in place at Port Colborne, Canada, at Caledonia, N. Y., and at the Falls of the Ohio. At the latter place some large stems, over one inch in diameter, are found, which are usually much altered by silicification ; but most of these specimens have, on small circumscribed spots of the stems, the surface characters finely preserved, and exhibit longitudinally oval, funnel-shaped orifices of equal size, two millimeters in length and one and a half in transverse direction. The broad interstitial surface is either smooth or decorated with obtuse papilli. Lateral pores and transverse diaphragms distinctly observable. These may constitute a different species from the former.

Plate XXIII.—Fig. 4 represents silicified stems of the usual form found in the drift in Michigan, and in the corniferous limestone of Port Colborne ; the outer stem on the right side is altered by thickening of the tube walls, but in other specimens the alteration reaches a still higher degree.

DENDROPORA ELEGANTULA, Billings.

Synon., Trachypora Elegantula, Billings.

Small ramified stems, from two to five millimeters in diameter. Orifices longitudinally oval, oblique, effuse above, the remainder of the circumference being edged by a projecting rim; they are arranged in four longitudinal rows on the stems, but often the regularity of the rows is disturbed by interposition of single orifices in the intervals between. Interstitial spaces broad, decorated with flexuose and interlacing rugæ, covered by delicate granules, and rendered minutely porous by a superficial punctiform and fissure-like perforation of the wall substance. On the surface the walls of the single tubes are quite undefined, while in the centre of the stems the walls are much thinner, and are well defined from one another, exhibiting lateral connecting pores and transverse diaphragms. The bottom of the conically dilating orifices is generally formed of a stout obliquely situated diaphragm. Diameter of orifices in transverse direction one millimeter; in longitudinal one and a half millimeter; internal tube cavity much narrower.

Occurs rarely in the Hamilton group of Thunder Bay, near Broadwell's mills, where it is associated with several other species of Dendropora. The specimens represented on Plate XXIII., Fig. 2, are from the Hamilton group of Widder, C. W., the locality from which Billings described his original specimens.

DENDROPORA ALTERNANS.

Stems of about four millimeters in diameter, with remote oval orifices in quincuncial position, forming about five loose, alternating, longitudinal rows in the circumference of a stem. Diameter of orifices lengthwise from one and a half to two millimeters, and one millimeter in transverse direction. Margins raised into an obtuse circumvallation. Surface minutely punctate by acutely pointed granules, but not ornamented with longitudinal rugæ. Occurs associated with the former species in the Hamilton group of Thunder Bay River, near Broadwell's mills.

Plate XXIV., Fig. 1.—The two larger stems on the upper rock-piece are representations of this form in natural size.

In the upper right-hand corner of the same piece a small, flat, basal expansion and a stem of another smaller species of Dendropora are represented. The tubes of these are arranged in distant, irregularly quincuncial order; the interstitial surface exhibits the same ornamentations by rugæ as Dendropora elegantula, but the species is, on the whole, smaller, and the arrangement of the tubes is different.

The material at my command is not sufficient to enable me to give full characteristics of the latter kind, but I think it is specifically a distinct form.

DENDROPORA PROBOSCIDALIS, N. SP.

Small reticulated branchlets, not much over one millimeter in diameter. Orifices forming proboscidal, spoon-like projections, disposed in five or six longitudinal alternating rows on the circumference of the stems, or of more irregularly dispersed position. Interstitial surface longitudinally rugose, and dotted by punctiform and fissure-like porosities. Diameter of orifices about one third of a millimeter. Occurs with the former at Broadwell's mills; rarely also at Partridge Point, Thunder Bay, in the highest beds of the formation.

Plate XXIV., Fig. 4.—The lower group of stems gives a magnified view of the branchlets. Enlargement two diameters.

DENDROPORA (?) RETICULATA, N. SP.

With doubt I arranged, under the genus Dendropora, the coral of which a description follows: Reticulated horizontal expansions of small cylindrical stems about two millimeters in diameter, composed of moderately thick-walled conical tubules, the outlines of which in their longitudinal extension can be distinctly seen. Orifices erect, circular, with free margins. Stems similar to Aulopora spicata of

Goldfuss, in external structure, but more minute, the diameter of the tubes being only one third to one half millimeter. Interstitial surface smooth, neither rugose nor granulose. Found in the upper strata of the Hamilton group at Partridge Point, and in the lower beds on Thunder Bay River, at Broadwell's mills.

Plate XXIV.,—Fig. 1. The lower piece represents a reticulated expansion from Partridge Point, Thunder Bay. On the same plate, Fig. 4, the upper row of stems are magnified fragments (two diameters) of the same kind, found at Broadwell's mills, on Thunder Bay River.

THECIA, Milne-Edwards.

Massive or rarely dendroid polyparia with the general structure of Favosites. Tube walls very thick, forming, by their junction under defined polygonal outlines, solid interstitial spaces as wide or even wider than a tube diameter; sometimes, however, the walls do not exceed in thickness those of an ordinary Favosites, and the dilated tube margins join with edged polygonal margins. Tubes radiated by twelve spinulose, longitudinal crests almost extending to the centre, with intermediate, narrow, linear furrows. The internal crests of the orifices are sometimes prolongated externally, and extend as low radial rugæ across the surface of the interstitial spaces from one tube into the other; or the interstices, if large, are irregularly granulose on the surface. Transverse diaphragms well developed, flat or convex, projecting within the orifices as a central boss and covered with spinules or granules like the other surface of the tube cavity. Lateral pores large and abundant. Tubes frequently subject to incrassation at the expense of the lumen of the tube cavities, while the pore channels retain their original diameter and become longer. The external appearance of such specimens becomes thereby considerably altered, and in silicified specimens, in which the silex is deposited in the peculiar concentric, annular dots so often noticed, the structure becomes so much obscured that it would be impossible to recognize their true nature if it were not that other, better preserved specimens, only partially altered in this way, can be found amongst them. The genus Protaræa of Milne-Edwards, placed by him with the Zoantharia perforata, is intimately related to Thecia. It is composed of short conical tubules, communicating by lateral pores, radiated by twelve granuloso-spinulose crests, and intersected by convex diaphragms of spinulose surface. The tubules are incrusting and never attain any great length.

THECIA MAJOR, N. SP.

(Compare Favosites Forbesii. Roemer, Silur. Fauna of Tennessee.)

Discoid, lenticular expansions, covered on the lower side by a concentrically wrinkled epitheca, with diverging striæ, indicating the outlines of procumbent tubes, which bend into an erect position before they open on the upper surface of the disks. Diameter of tubes two millimeters, joining under well-marked, obtusely crested, polygonal margins, which inclose dilated orificial pits. Walls stout, but variable in thickness in different portions of the same specimens. Twelve radial crests extend half way to the centre; their edges are decorated with two rows of granulose spinules. Diaphragms numerous, partially flat, partially convex, forming a monticulose projection with spinulose or granulose surface. Pores large and abundant. Occurs in the Niagara group of Drummond's Island, Point Detour, and in many other localities on the south shore of the Upper Peninsula. Found also in abundance at Charleston Landing, Indiana; at Louisville, Ky., and in many Niagara outcrops of the West.

Plate XXV.—Fig. 1. Specimens in calcified condition seen from the upper and lower side, both from Charleston Landing, Indiana. Fig. 2 represents a silicified specimen found at Point of Barquès, on Lake Michigan. The upper end of the specimen exhibits well-preserved tube orifices with radial crests, convex diaphragms, spinulose surface decorations, etc.; the lower portion is formed of tube casts with flat diaphragms, crenulated at the circumference by the indentations made by the radial crests of the walls; the perfect correspondence of the structure of Thecia with Favosites is most beautifully to be seen in the represented specimen.

THECIA MINOR, N. SP.

(*Vide* Roemer, Silur. Fauna of Tennessee, Tb. 2, Fig. 4.)

THECIA SWINDERIANA.

General structure perfectly conformable with the former species. Discoid expansions covered on the lower side by an epitheca, concentrically wrinkled, and exhibiting the prostrate tube channels diverging from the centre. The main difference between the two forms lies only in the size of their tubes, which in this latter form is only one millimeter instead of two, as in the former. The specimens vary considerably in their surface characters. Some have only moderately stout tube walls, and join with gently dilating mouths under edged polygonal margins. With the increase of the thickness of the walls the orifices lose their circumscribed form, and the thickened walls combine into a common, broad, interstitial surface impressed with small, circular, radiated cell pits. The radial crests often extend across the interstitial spaces from one orifice into the other as superficial rugæ, mingling with additional irregular rugæ and granulations by which the interstitial surface is decorated. By a still greater degree of incrassation of the tube walls the orifices become almost closed, punctiform, while the lateral pore channels remain as large as ever, and prolongate in proportion to the thickening of the wall substance. Such specimens appear as massive expansions, perforated by horizontal vermicular channels, of stelliform arrangement around the narrow, punctiform, central tube channels in vertical position, and their identity with the other well-formed specimens would scarcely be supposed, if all possible gradations from normally formed ones to the disfigured altered specimens were not plentifully found associated with them. Found at Point Detour, Drummond's Island, and in other Niagara outcrops, in association with the former species; occurs also in the drift of the Lower Peninsula, and in the Niagara group of Indiana and Kentucky.

Plate XXV.—Fig. 3 represents a calcified specimen found at Louisville, Ky.; the Michigan specimens are all silicified, with not nearly so well-preserved surface characters.

THECIA RAMOSA, N. SP.

Stout, branching, and sometimes reticulated, anastomosing stems, from half an inch to two inches in diameter, composed of thick-walled, conico-cylindrical tubes ascending and diverging from a central imaginary axis. Orifices unequal, of polygonal form, from one to two millimeters wide at the edges of the dilating margins, radiated by twelve prominent spinulose crests, extending through the whole length of the channels. Transverse diaphragms partly simple and complete, partly incomplete, represented by lateral squamiform, horizontal leaflets. Pores large and very numerous. Older stems are often much altered in appearance by excessive thickening of their tube walls, and contraction of the tube channels, with obliteration of the radial crests. It is sometimes difficult to distinguish them from similarly altered stems of Favosites radiciformis, with which they are found associated. Occurs in the upper Helderberg strata of Mackinac Island, and is not uncommon in drift boulders on the Southern Peninsula of Michigan. It is found in great perfection and frequency in the Helderberg limestone's of the Falls of the Ohio. The silicified specimens represented on Plate XXV., Fig. 4, are from the latter mentioned locality.

VERMIPORA, HALL.

(Twenty-sixth Annual Report of the State Cabinet.)

Ramified twigs, composed of contiguous, subparallel cylindrical tubules, multiplying by lateral gemmation, slowly diverging in their parallel ascending course from a central imaginary axis, and becoming disjunct near their peripheral ends, which project on the surface as single proboscidal siphuncules. Tubes intersected by remote transverse diaphragms, and connected by lateral pores. Vertical radiating crests not observed.

Mr. Hall places these forms with the Bryozoa, and gives of their structure a description different from mine. He has overlooked the principal Favositoid characters of the tubes, *diaphragms*, and *lateral pores*, but I think these organs can be found in his specimens as well as in those I have under consideration.

VERMIPORA NIAGARENSIS, N. SP.

Short club-shaped branchlets about one centimeter in thickness. Tubules half a millimeter wide, slowly diverging from an imaginary central axis in a curve. The outer free end of the tubes is more abruptly bent, and opens rectangularly to the surface of the stems. In the interior of the stems the tubes are polygonal by mutual pressure; the free ends are perfectly circular, annulated by delicate wrinkles of growth, and in some a faint longitudinal striation is observable. Transverse diaphragms flat and distant. Pores large, irregularly dispersed. Found in the Niagara group of Point Detour, Lake Huron, and in Iowa, near Masonville.

Plate XXIV., Fig. 3.—Lower figures are specimens from the Niagara group of Masonville, Iowa, magnified about two diameters.

VERMIPORA FASCICULATA, N. SP.

Small branching stems, from two to five millimeters in diameter; tubules one half millimeter wide, ascending in almost parallel fascicles in the stems, until their ends, with an abrupt bend outward, become free. Diaphragms, intersecting the tubes and connecting pores, are plainly observable, as well as the intercalation of new tubes by lateral gemmation.

Found in the Hamilton group of Thunder Bay, and frequently in boulders of the drift, which, according to the rock character and associated fossils, belong to the corniferous limestone formation.

Plate XXIV., Fig. 3.—The upper specimens artificially crowded together. A part of them represent specimens of the corniferous limestone found in the drift; the outer specimen on the right-hand side and the slender central stem are from the Hamilton group of Alpena. Magnified two diameters.

QUENSTEDTIA, N. GEN.

Single cylindrical tubules, multiplying by lateral gemmation of either single tubes, or many at once, surrounding the mother-tube in a verticil, and remaining for a while in close contact with it, and amongst themselves. After some distance the young tubes bend outward with their ends, which separate and become free diverging branches, which, in their turn, again become mother-tubes by renewed gemmation. The tubes are intersected by remote transverse diaphragms. In places of contiguity they connect by lateral pore channels, and in well-preserved specimens longitudinal rows of spinulose crests project from the inner side of the tube walls.

QUENSTEDTIA UMBELLIFERA.

Synon., AULOPORA UMBELLIFERA, Billings.
AULOPORA CORNUTA, Billings.

Tubules about two millimeters in diameter, delicately annulated by wrinkles of growth. At variable intervals, single tubes, or from six to twelve in a verticil, sprout from their sides and remain closely attached to them and to one another for the length of about five millimeters, when they bend outward and separate, radially diverging as free branches, which themselves soon throw out new verticils. The central tube always grows straight on, at intervals continuing to gemmate. Loose stems with a verticil of branches at the end have remote resemblance to a small Crinoid head on its stem. Within the circle of branch tubes the central tube is generally dilated by a bulbiform inflation. The basal apices of the young tubes do not communicate with the older tube by simply opening into it, but by a narrow circular pore, narrower than the entire width of the channels. Besides these connections with the basis, the young tubes connect by lateral pore channels with the old tube, and laterally also among themselves. Diaphragms are quite distant, and not always observable; the longitudinal rows of spinules also are only noticed in very favorably preserved specimens, but are sometimes very well developed. By examination of larger clusters it can be ascertained that the same stems which usually send forth verticillate branches often also give off single or only two or three branches. Mr. Billings considers these as a different species, and names them Aulopora cornuta, but frequently both forms are often seen as parts of one and the same colony of stems.

Found in the drift of Michigan, associated with fossils of the corniferous limestone. It is common in the corniferous limestone of Port Colborne, C. W. I also discovered several specimens fully identical with the form of the corniferous limestone, in the Hamilton group of Thunder Bay.

Plate XXXIII., Fig. 3.—The upper figures grouped together are specimens from the drift, natural size.

QUENSTEDTIA NIAGARENSIS.

Tubes fully two millimeters in diameter, branching from a mother-tube in irregular clusters, and diverging after a short space of contiguity with production of new lateral tubes. Lateral pores are large and surrounded by a projecting rim. Longitudinal crests, or rather rows of spinules, distinctly seen. Diaphragms are not preserved in the specimens from Michigan ; others found in Iowa exhibit them. Found in the Niagara group of Point Detour, Lake Huron, and at Masonville, Iowa.

Plate XXXIII., Fig. 3.—Lower solitary specimen, found at Point Detour.

MICHELINIA, De Koninck.

Including Chonostegites, Milne-Edwards.

Compound polyparia formed of elongate, conical tubes, intimately connected in their whole length, or in rare instances with the contiguity interrupted at intervals by constrictions. The tube channels are in places of contiguity connected by lateral pores ; their cavity is intersected by a succession of diaphragms of compound, irregularly vesiculose structure, and the sides of the tubes are longitudinally striate by numerous linear furrows, with intermediate rows of spinulose prominences. This structure is in general conformity with the structure of Favosites, from which it differs in the vesiculose nature of the diaphragms, and in having a much greater number of longitudinal furrows. In Favosites these never exceed the number 12, but in Michelinia they are more than double that number. The tubes of Michelinia are usually also of much larger size than in Favosites. The genus Michelinia appears nearly contemporaneous with Favosites in the upper Silurian strata. A small nummiform species, which to my knowledge has not yet been described, occurs in the Niagara group of Tennessee. Another somewhat larger but very similar form is found in the lower Helderberg strata of Schoharie County, N. Y., which is described by Mr. Hall under the name of Michelinia lenticularis. None of these have been found in Michigan. The Devonian formation contains a variety of forms, nearly all of which are represented in Michigan. Formerly the casts of small specimens of Michelinia were through misapprehension classed under the name of Pleurodictyum problematicum, as being a fossil of peculiar organization. I have exposed this error in an article published in 1862 in *Silliman's Journal.*

MICHELINIA CONVEXA, D'ORBIGNY.

Hemispherical masses, with a depressed, turbinate, discoid under side, covered by a concentrically wrinkled epitheca, formed of diverging, large, conical tubes of unequal size and of rounded-polygonal outlines, the larger ones attaining a diameter of one centimeter; walls stout. Transverse diaphragms globoso-convex, composed of larger and smaller irregularly interlacing vesiculose plates. Vertical furrows in the circumference of a tube about forty, with intermediate rows of short, spinulose projections. The surface of the diaphragms is generally smooth; in rare instances they are covered with granular prominences. Pore openings small, surrounded by a projecting rim, irregularly dispersed, and in some parts much more crowded than in others. Found in the drift, associated with corniferous limestone fossils in silicified condition. Very common in the corniferous limestone of Port Colborne, C. W.

Plate XXVI.—Fig. 1, view from above; Fig. 2, view of the lower side of silicified specimens from Port Colborne.

MICHELINIA CYLINDRICA, Milne-Edwards.

Synon., Emmonsia cylindrica, Milne-Edwards.

Michelinia intermittens, Billings in parte.

Synon., Favosites Maximus, Troost.

Large, convex masses, formed of slowly diverging, subparallel, obtusely polygonal, sometimes circular tubes of unequal size, from five to seven millimeters in diameter. The tubes have either straight walls, or are at regular, short intervals constricted by ring-like carinæ projecting into the tube cavity. The carinæ, caused by constriction of the walls, correspond with each other in the adjacent tubes, but the contiguity of the tubes is usually not interrupted by them. The tubes with straight walls are polygonal in outline; those with constrictions are circular; transitions from one form into the other are noticeable, sometimes in the same specimens. Inner surface of tubes longitudinally striate and densely covered with irregularly dispersed, spinulose projections, which also spread over the surface of the diaphragms. Diaphragms compound, of interlaced, vesiculose plates, not near so convex as in the former species, and in close approximation. Lateral pores very irregular, and of different sizes; in the specimens with constricted tubes they are confined to the dilated parts, interstitial between the annular, projecting carinæ. Occurs with the other species in the drift deposits of Michigan; it is the most common species of the genus at the Falls of the Ohio, and is found in many localities of Ohio and Indiana.

Plate XXVI.—Fig. 3 gives a side view of a silicified specimen from the Falls of the Ohio. Fig. 4 is a surface view of a large, convex mass from the same locality.

MICHELINIA FAVOSITOIDEA, Billings.

Convex masses of diverging, intimately united, polygonal tubes, of unequal size, from three to five millimeters in diameter. Basal part broadly attached with the centre; marginal parts free and covered by an epitheca. Diaphragms nearly flat, often simple, and scarcely vesiculose, closely approximated; other times the vesiculose character is more pronounced. Pores small, irregularly distributed. Longitudinal striæ and spinulose rows much more delicate and minute than in the other species.

Found in the drift of Michigan, and in the corniferous limestone of Canada and New York.

Plate XXVII.—Fig. 4 represents a silicified specimen found in the drift of Ann Arbor.

MICHELINIA INSIGNIS, N. SP.

Lenticular convex disks of large size, formed of diverging tubes, prostrate on the lower side, and composing by their united walls an epithecal crust with diverging, radial rugæ, and with annular, concentric wrinkles of growth. Diameter of tubes from two to three millimeters. Tubes sometimes moderately stout-walled and joining with acute margins of polygonal outlines; at other times the walls are thickened, somewhat dilated at the orifices, with obtuse rounded interstitial margins. In the same specimens elsewhere, the orifices of the tubes may be projecting, with raised circular margins, and the sides of the tubes may be found only in loose lateral contiguity with teretiform walls, and annulated by fine wrinkles of growth, with faintly indicated longitudinal striation. The tube cavity is lined by from thirty to forty longitudinal rows of spinules or spinulose ridges, which project nearly to the centre of the tubes as radiations. Diaphragms closely set, concave, simple or compound, of vesiculose plates. Pores numerous, small, irregularly dispersed. Found silicified in the Hamilton group near Alpena, also in the Hamilton group of Darien, N. Y., in calcified condition; likewise in the Helderberg group of the Falls of the Ohio, and in several other localities of Kentucky, Crab Orchard, etc.

Plate XXVII.—Fig. 1 is a fragment of a large mass in calcified condition, found at the Falls of the Ohio, presenting a vertical section. Fig. 2 is a silicified specimen from Alpena, Thunder Bay, seen from the under side. Fig. 3 is the same, seen from above.

MICHELINIA TROCHISCUS, N. SP.

Synon., ASTRÆA STYLOPHORA, Eaton.

Small hemispherical masses, not often exceeding the diameter of two inches, usually smaller. The depressed conical or flat basal side is covered by a concentrically wrinkled epitheca, and is attached by a broad central scar to other marine bodies, to Gasteropod shells, Crinoid stems, and very frequently to the surface of Fistulipora. (See Worth. Geol. of Illin., Vol. III., Pl. 9, Fig. 1*b*.) Tubes very unequal, rounded-polygonal, from four to seven millimeters wide. Cavity longitudinally striate by numerous spinulose crests. Diaphragms irregular and not much crowded. Pores dispersed without order.

Occurs in the Hamilton group of Thunder Bay, and is very common in the Hamilton group of New York. The small specimens found in the upper Helderberg limestones of Michigan, Ohio, and Indiana, which are the forms to which Pleurodictyum problematicum has principally to be referred, are almost the same, if not an identical form with Michelinia trochiscus. I have not figured this species.

MICHELINIA CLAPPII.

Synon., CHONOSTEGITES CLAPPII, Milne-Edwards.

HAIMEOPHYLLUM ORDINATUM, Billings.

MICHELINIA INTERMITTENS, PARS, Billings.

Convex or discoid masses, formed of tubular, closely aggregated, subparallel or diverging polyp stems, from five to eight millimeters diameter, multiplying by marginal buds. Tubes annulated by alternate constrictions and dilatations into an urn shape of the intermediate segments, having horizontally spreading margins, which unite with those of the adjoining tubes, forming continuous laminar floors, whereby the otherwise free tubes are held together and communicate with each other by transverse channels crossing the laminæ.

In some specimens the constrictions are not so deep as in others, and the tubes then come in more intimate contact with their sides, which in such case communicate by lateral pores, and fully resemble the tubes of an ordinary form of Michelinia. The tubes are transversely intersected by interlacing vesiculose diaphragms of compound structure; the channel walls longitudinally striate by furrows and rows of spinules, conformable with the structure of Michelinia.

Occurs frequently in the drift of Michigan, and is common in the corniferous limestone of Canada and New York; it is rarely seen at the Falls of the Ohio, where Michelinia cylindrica, a closely related form, is abundant.

Plate XXVIII.—Figs. 3 and 4 represent a side view and a surface view of silicified specimens.

HALYSITINÆ.

Colonies of tubular polyp cells, multiplying by lateral gemmation, radiated by a cycle of twelve longitudinal crests or rows of spinules, and transversely septate by diaphragms of variable form, straight or funnel-shaped. The tubes are either free, loosely attached to each other, or laterally connected into laminar rows, or again distant and connected by short transverse branches, sometimes indiscriminately anchylosed into irregular conglomerated masses. The subordinate genera are Halysites, Syringopora, Cannapora, and Aulopora.

HALYSITES, Fischer.

CATENIPORA, Lamark.

Elliptical tubes, intimately connected at their lateral edges into chain-like single rows, which form erect laminar expansions, bent into tortuous curves, and composing, by the mutual junction and intersection of the laminæ, a network of irregular loops. Tubes radiated by twelve longitudinal crests, and transversely septate by closely set flat diaphragms. No lateral connection between the tubes by pores.

HALYSITES CATENULATA, Linn.

Synon., Halysites esharoides.

Catenipora labyrinthica, Goldfuss, etc.

A great variety of forms of the chain coral are found which in general structure are perfectly alike, but differ widely in the size of the tubes, in the shape of the orifices, and in the mode of reticulated connection between the catenate laminæ. Some specimens have elongate, lanceolate orifices, in others the form is oval, and in others still nearly circular. In those with large elliptical orifices the longer diameter is often five millimeters, and the shorter in the transverse direction three millimeters; in others the proportions of the diameters of the orifices are two and a half millimeters by two millimeters. In the smallest built specimens they measure one millimeter only in the long direction, and one half in the shorter. The loops of the laminæ are in some forms narrow, in one direction nearly as wide as in the other; in other specimens the loops are large, or the flexuose laminæ may for long distances run in close proximity, parallel with each other, before they make occasional connection by short transverse branches. The contrast between these various forms is very great, and it is evident that various specific forms exist; but while attempting to define them, I found so endless a series of transitory connecting forms that I desist from making a distinction, and use here the collective name of H. catenulata for all. Found in the Niagara group of Michigan, as one of the most widely distributed characteristic fossils; likewise common in the Niagara group of other States east and west. The first specimens of the chain coral are found in the upper beds of the Hudson River group, in the west portion of the Upper Peninsula of Michigan, but their preservation is so imperfect that it is impossible to determine whether these oldest specimens represent another species or not.

Plate XXIX.—Figs. 1, 2 and 4 represent three of the many varieties in which the coral is found associated in the strata of Drummond's Island and of Point Detour, all in silicified condition. Fig. 3 of the same plate I considered sufficiently characteristic to be described as a distinct species.

HALYSITES COMPACTUS, N. SP.

Tubes oval, in chain-like, lateral conjunction; but these laminæ are so closely approximated, that no retiform loops are formed by them. They come in contiguity with each other from all sides, and leave only small, angular, lacunose interstices in the corners of their intersection, which are not larger than the tube orifices themselves. By this close approximation of the tubes on all sides many of them become pressed into a polygonal form and resemble a Favosites, from which they differ, however, in the absence of lateral pores. The diaphragms of the tubes are closely approximated, flat, concave or convex in the same specimens. Their diameter is about one and a half millimeter. Found in the Niagara group along the outcrops of the Upper Peninsula, at the shore of Lake Michigan.

Plate XXIX.—Fig. 3 represents a lateral section and a surface view of a specimen found at Epoufette Point. In a stratum of an outcrop at the mouth of Manistique River this species is quite common.

SYRINGOPORA, GOLDFUSS.

Synon., THECOSTEGITES, Milne-Edwards.

Aggregated, sub-parallel, tubular polyp stems, multiplying by lateral budding, and at irregular intervals connected with each other by short, transverse, tubular branchlets. The tubes are intersected by numerous irregularly funnel-shaped diaphragms, and radiated by twelve longitudinal rows of spinules, which are sometimes obsolete. The colonies of erect stems are at the base formed of horizontally prostrate and attached ends, very much resembling the creeping expansions of Aulopora, from which the young colonies are often hard to be distinguished.

SYRINGOPORA VERTICILLATA, GOLDFUSS.

Large aggregations of parallel or diverging tubular stems, from two to three millimeters in diameter, keeping a distance of from two to five millimeters apart, across which they connect at various not very close intervals by narrow, transverse, branch tubules, of which two or three are always sent off at nearly the same height, but not in true verticillate position. The tubes are filled by invaginated, irregularly funnel-shaped diaphragms, attenuated at the lower ends into long siphons. The longitudinal rows of spinules are rarely well preserved in the tubes of the specimens which are all found in silicified condition. The colonies of stems are often large, several feet in diameter; their basal portions, composed of prostrate, irregularly reticulated expansions of stems, differ considerably from the erect parts, and among the specimens of colonies a great many variations occur as regards the size of the tubes or their mode of growth. In some the stems are distant, in others near; in some perfectly straight, in others flexuose or geniculated, with regular, verticillate side connections, or with dispersed side arms branching off at remote intervals or in closer proximity. These associated forms, sufficiently contrasting in the extreme, I have not attempted to divide into several species, but consider as variations of Syringopora verticillata, whose enumerated specific characters can not of course retain the limited form, applying only to a single variety which accidentally fell into the hands of Goldfuss, the first describer of this species. Found abundantly in the Niagara limestone of Drummond's Island, Point Detour, and in nearly all other fossiliferous outcrops of the formation in the western part of the Upper Peninsula.

Plate XXX.—Fig. 1 represents a silicified specimen from Drummond's Island, closely similar to the specimen figured by Goldfuss. Fig. 2 has somewhat smaller tubes, with less regularly disposed, transverse branch channels and more flexuose stems than the other. With the above-described specimens others are found, which seem to agree with *Syringopora cancellata* of Milne-Edwards. They are composed of flexuose tubes about one and a half millimeter wide, in loose, irregularly reticulated colonies, with the curved stems alternately contiguous and diverging. Transverse connecting channels remote, short, and clumsy. Longitudinal rows of spinules and funnel-shaped diaphragms, quite plainly exhibited in some of the specimens. I have not figured this form for want of space.

SYRINGOPORA ANNULATA, N. Sp.

Small colonies of closely approximated, tubular stems of jointed aspect, with sharply projecting rings of growth, and with numerous verticillate, transverse tubules connecting the stems at short intervals. Diameter of tubes about one and a half millimeter. Diaphragms of the elongated, funnel-shaped form peculiar to the genus. Found at Point Detour in the Niagara limestone, and in the drift deposits of the Lower Peninsula.

Plate XXXII., Lower tier.—The two left figures represent silicified specimens found in the drift of Ann Arbor.

SYRINGOPORA TENELLA, N. Sp.

Irregularly reticulated colonies of tubules, one millimeter in width, or less. The tubules branch in the same manner as Aulopora, and directly connect with each other by approximation, without the intervention of narrower, transverse channels, as in other species of Syringopora. The tubules exhibit a faint longitudinal striation on the outside wall, and the cavity is lined by a cycle of twelve spinulose crests. Diaphragms funnel-shaped, but not always developed; the channels are often found open throughout.

Found in the Niagara group of Point Detour, Drummond's Island, and in the drift. Occurs also in Indiana and Kentucky.

Plate XXX.—Fig. 4 represents a small specimen found in the drift, seen from the basal side, with creeping, prostrate tubules. On the upper side of the specimen the tubules are bent into an erect position.

SYRINGOPORA FIBRATA, N. SP.

Large convex colonies, with closely approximated subparallel or diverging tubules half a millimeter in diameter, laterally connected by numerous short transverse channels, branching off at close intervals from the circumference of the thread-like stems. The distance separating the stems is variable—sometimes less, sometimes more than one tube diameter. Radial crests long, very distinct, twelve in number. Diaphragms direct transverse, not funnel-shaped. This species very frequently grows up in intimate connection with expansions of Stromatopora. The tissue of the Stromatopora fills out all the interstices left between the tubules, which in such specimens are usually further apart than in those growing solitary. Both hold in their growth an equal passus, and the addition of new layers to the Stromatopora coincides with the growth of the tubules. It resembles Syringopora compacta, Billings, found in the strata of Anticosti; but in that species the tubules are in almost perfect contiguity, and their diaphragms are distinctly funnel-shaped.

Common in the Niagara group of Point Detour, Drummond's Island, and frequently found in the drift. It occurs also in the Niagara group of Indiana, Kentucky, and Iowa.

Plate XXX.—Fig. 3 gives a surface view of a silicified specimen from Drummond's Island.

SYRINGOPORA PERELEGANS, BILLINGS.

Colonies of tubular stems, from one and a half to two millimeters in diameter, formed at the base of prostrate tubes, multiplying by bi- or tri-partite ramification, in the same manner as Aulopora, by production of one or two young tubes sprouting from the basal portion of their flanks, which creep on for some distance, while the mother-tube bends its orifice into an erect position, after having given off the branches. The spreading, prostrate, basal tubes, flattened on the lower side, come in multiple contact with their sides and grow together into an open, reticulated expansion, or are so densely crowded as to form an uninterrupted basal leaf, from which the tubes singly ascend into a vertical, subparallel position, and then grow up with remarkably straight stems, if not disturbed by accidental impediments.

The stems in the erect growing parts of the colonies are remote from each other about the width of a tube diameter, or more, and are connected by slender, transverse tubules at intervals of from one half to one centimeter. The tubes are annulated by delicate wrinkles of growth, with periodical, sharper offsets, causing an articulated appearance. Internal structure longitudinally striate by spinulose crests, and intersected by funnel-shaped, irregular diaphragms prolongated with the lower apex into long siphons.

Occurs in the upper Helderberg limestones of Mackinac; frequently also in the drift, associated with corniferous limestone fossils, and in the corniferous limestones of Canada, New York, and of the Falls of the Ohio.

Plate XXXI.—Fig. 2. The small specimen attached to the lower left-hand corner of the other specimen represents a fragment of a laminar, basal expansion with erect, circular orifices, found in the drift. Figs. 3 and 4 are silicified specimens from the Falls of the Ohio—the one with larger sub-flexuose tubes, the other with more slender and straighter tubes.

SYRINGOPORA MACLUREI, Billings.

Tubes about three millimeters wide, flexuose, occasionally touching each other, and then diverging again, or at other times of more regular, subparallel growth, with interstitial intervals usually larger than a tube diameter, and with remote, slender, transverse tubules of connection. This coral resembles the former species, differing from it only in having a larger tube size, and a more irregular mode of growth, but in many instances it becomes difficult to decide whether a specimen belongs to one or the other form.

Plate XXXI.—Fig. 1 represents a fragment found in the drift of Ann Arbor, exhibiting the terminal portion of a colony. In Fig. 2 the large specimen, also, from the drift, is seen from the basal side, with the prostrate, creeping, reticulated tube portions. The basal expansions of the former species, represented in the same figure, do not always grow in uninterrupted leaves, as in the fragment represented, but often in an open network like that in the larger figure. In some specimens the tubules are more nearly approximated than they are seen to be in Fig. 1.

SYRINGOPORA TABULATA, MILNE-EDWARDS.

Synon., THECOSTEGITES BOUCHARDI, Milne-Edwards.

Large, convex colonies of diverging, subparallel, straight tubules, forming incrustations of other marine bodies with their creeping, Aulopora-like, basal ends, which subsequently continue to grow in an erect position. Tubules about one millimeter wide, closely approximated, with intervals narrower than a tube diameter; the transverse connecting tubules branch off in subregular, verticillate position, and correspond in all tubes in certain levels, by the lateral anchylosis of which almost uninterrupted laminar floors are formed; this is, however, not an invariable structure. The same specimens often exhibit portions in which the transverse branchlets are not verticillate, but in irregularly dispersed position, and in which no laminar floors intersecting the colonies are perceptible. The tubules are distinctly radiated by twelve spinulose crests, and on the surface of the tubules a dull, longitudinal striation is usually noticed. Diaphragms funnel-shaped, with tubular invaginated ends. The floors of connecting processes are in some specimens moderately distant, as in that represented on Plate XXXII., upper specimen to the right. These are the typical form of Milne-Edwards' Syr. tabulata. In other specimens, particularly those of smaller size, forming incrustations of shells, etc., these floors are in close approximation, and form a series of superimposed laminæ, separated by small vesiculose interstices. Milne-Edwards, misapprehending their structure, described them as the type form of a new genus, Thecostegites; but a little more careful examination would necessarily have shown him the specific identity of his Syringopora tabulata with his Thecostegites Bouchardi, both described as occurring at the Falls of the Ohio, from which locality the specimens represented on Plate XXXII. come. The upper convex specimen on the left side of the plate is the form corresponding with Milne-Edwards' Thecostegites. He has described similar other forms under the names of *Syringopora Verneuilli*, *Syr. Cleviana*, and Mr. Billings describes a form under the name of *Syringopora Hisingeri*, all of which are distinguished from one another by trifling modifications in their manner of growth. I consider them as mere varieties of one and the same species for which I retain Billings' name.

SYRINGOPORA HISINGERI.

It differs from Syringopora tabulata by its more distant, somewhat flexuose tubules, with side connections in dispersed position, and not in verticils. The tubules vary in size from half a millimeter to one millimeter. The three lower specimens in the upper tier of Plate XXXII. represent various fragments of this form, found in the drift. Other specimens are found in which the tubules are still further apart. The last-mentioned forms are all found associated in the corniferous limestone of Michigan, Canada, Ohio, New York, Indiana, Kentucky, etc.

SYRINGOPORA NOBILIS, BILLINGS.

Colonies of large tubes, from five to eight millimeters in diameter. In some the tubes are quite remote from each other, and connected by distant, transverse branch channels; others have the tubes more closely clustered and of smaller size. I am not positive of the specific identity of these forms, but provisionally arranged them under Billings' name, intended for the form with large, remote stems. Found in the corniferous limestone, and in the Hamilton group of Michigan and Canada; similar forms occur in the Hamilton group of Iowa.

On Plate XXXII., lower tier, right-side figure, is represented a specimen found in the drift of Ann Arbor, associated with corniferous limestone fossils; the adjoining central specimen is a young specimen with closely clustered tubes, found in the Hamilton group of Alpena.

CANNAPORA, Hall.

(*Compare* Fletcheria, *Milne-Edwards.*)

Colonies of closely approximated, erect tubules with stout walls, sprouting from an incrusting basal expansion formed of prostrate tubules growing and multiplying in the same manner as an Aulopora. The erect ends of the tubules are annulated by wrinkles of growth and by sharp-edged, periodical offsets marking an interruption and renewed growth from the inner circumference of the old orifices. The sides of the tubes are partly connected by horizontal expansions of the walls, partly in direct contiguity, in which latter case the otherwise circular tubes are pressed into a polygonal shape, and connect in the contiguous parts by lateral pores. The orifices are slightly dilated at the margins, radiated by twelve spinulose projections, rows of which extend through the whole length of the tubes. Diaphragms are not often developed, direct transverse, and not funnel-shaped as in Syringopora. Considerable affinity exists between Cannapora and Aulopora.

CANNAPORA JUNCIFORMIS, Hall.

Tubules from one to one and a half millimeter in diameter, forming large colonies of convex growth, with regular, subparallel stems in the larger masses; but in smaller specimens, representing incrusting basal portions, the tubes are sometimes agglomerated in irregular manner. Structure in conformity with the above given general generic description. Found in the Niagara group of Drummond's Island, and sometimes in the drift. In New York State it is found in somewhat lower position in calcareous layers of the Clinton group. The tubes of the New York specimens are somewhat smaller than those of the specimens from Drummond's Island.

Plate XXXIII., Fig. 4.—Lower specimen on left-hand side is a silicified young colony from Drummond's Island; the lower figure on the right-hand side is a fragment of a specimen from the Clinton group of Brockport, N. Y.

AULOPORA, Goldfuss.

Colonies of prostrate, stout-walled tubes, attached with their lower flattened side, multiplying by latero-basal gemmation. One or two young tubes sprout from the lateral edges of the base of the creeping tubes near the orifices, which then rise from the prostrate into an erect position, while the new branches creep on, until they again send off branches in the same manner, which latter, by coming in contact in their spreading growth, adhere together and form reticulated loops, or, if closely crowded, continuous laminar expansions. Other species grow, by union of their tubes, into compact, thicker masses. It is rarely the case that they compose ramified branches. The tubes nearly always exhibit a faint, longitudinal striation and longitudinal rows of spinules encircling the inner cavity in more or less rudimentary development. Remote, isolated diaphragms are sometimes observed, but usually the tube cavities are open throughout their entire length. Lateral pores connecting the contiguous tubes channels do not seem to exist. The orifices project with free circular margins ; occasionally, through being closely crowded, the orifices of a limited spot may become polygonal from mutual pressure. Certain minute Bryozoa, in manner of growth resembling an Aulopora, have been confounded with this genus ; one of them is *Aulopora arachnoidea*, Hall ; these have no affinity with Aulopora, their structure being the same as in the jurassic and cretaceous genera Proboscina, Berenicea, or Stomatopora, whose utriculous walls are perforated by numerous microscopical pores, comparable to the minute punctations of the shell of a Terebratula. These punctations can be distinctly seen in well-preserved specimens of Aulopora arachnoidea, collected at Richmond, Indiana.

AULOPORA SERPENS (?) Goldfuss.

Prostrate expansions of conical tubules, one sprouting in a linear row from the basal part of the orificial end of the other ; or at times two of them fork off, and meeting others in the course of their growth, unite laterally with them and inclose irregular loops. All the tube ends, after the departure of a branch tube, bend into an erect position and usually grow no further. The width of the tubes of different specimens varies from one to two millimeters. The identification of this species with the European form, described by Goldfuss, is made with some hesitation, and is intended rather to express their great resemblance than a full identity. Found in the Hamilton group of Thunder Bay and Little Traverse Bay, incrusting other corals.

Plate XXXIII.—Fig. 2 represents a specimen from Little Traverse Bay incrusting a Stromatopora.

AULOPORA CONFERTA, WINCHELL.

Incrusting, reticulated, or continuous laminar expansions formed of laterally anchylosed conical tubules, arranged in fan-like, spreading order by emanation from the prolific gemmation of a single mother-tube according to the bilateral, forking mode of growth exhibited in the generic description. The club-shaped tubules are about one millimeter wide across the thickest part; the channels of the erect, circular orifices measure about half of a millimeter. Found abundantly as incrustation of other corals in the blue fossiliferous shales of Little Traverse Bay.

Plate XXXIII.—Fig. 1 represents a solid incrustation of the surface of a Stromatopora by this species of Aulopora.

AULOPORA ERECTA, N. SP.

Massive, incrusting expansions formed of very stout-walled tubes, about two or two and a half millimeters in diameter. On the basal side of the expansions, broke loose from the incrusted body, the prostrate, flattened tubes are noticeable, grown into a dense agglomeration by repeated rapid gemmation. From this basal sheet the tubules bend into a vertical position, and continue to grow in this direction for some length parallel with each other, and producing no more side branches at the rapid rate of the prostrate portions.

These erect tubes are circular, closely approximated, or sometimes in intimate, mutual contiguity, pressing each other into a sub-polygonal shape. The orifices exhibit a cycle of longitudinal furrows and intermediate rows of spinulose projections in rudimentary development. Diaphragms are generally not developed. Occurs in the Hamilton group at Stony Point, Thunder Bay.

Plate XXXIII.—Fig. 4, upper specimen.

COLUMNARIÆ.

CONSISTING OF THE SINGLE GENUS COLUMNARIA.

COLUMNARIA, GOLDFUSS.

Goldfuss at first included within this genus several corals which have a different structure; he acknowledges, in the appendix to his work, however, that the coral called by him Columnaria sulcata is only a weathered specimen of Cyathophyllum quadrigeminum. Columnaria lævis is also, in all probability, generically different from his Columnaria alveolaris, which alone is at present considered the typical representative of the genus. In Goldfuss's characteristics is expressly stated the absence of transverse diaphragms in the tubes, although in his figures the diaphragms of the tubes are so distinctly delineated that I can not conceive how they escaped his observation. I define the genus as follows:

Convex colonies of contiguous, polygonal, or rarely of free circular tubes, growing from a few attached mother-tubes by rapidly multiplying lateral gemmation. Tubes radiated by vertical lamellæ of alternately larger and smaller size, the larger ones in some species reaching to the centre, or not. Number of lamellæ from twenty to forty.

Transverse diaphragms simple, flat, moderately close in position. Walls not perforated by pores, thin, and inseparably united in the forms with polygonal tubes, appearing to be formed of simple laminæ dividing the adjoining cavities, but in favorably preserved specimens the duplicity of the walls is positively observed.

COLUMNARIA ALVEOLATA, GOLDFUSS.

Convex, large colonies, sometimes attaining a diameter of several feet, composed of intimately connected tubes diverging from a basal centre. Lower side covered by a concentrically wrinkled epitheca; central part attached. Tubes quite unequal in the same specimens and in different specimens. In some they vary from two to five millimeters; in others, tubes one centimeter in width, and smaller ones of only two and three millimeters, are intermingled. Radial lamellæ from twenty to forty, according to the size of the tubes, not reaching to the centre. Transverse diaphragms flat, closely set, usually smooth in the centre, and only at the outer circumference intersected by the radial crests. It is rarely the case that the lamellæ extend as low carinations over the surface of the diaphragms to the centre. The figures of Goldfuss exhibit the radii as alternately reaching the centre; this is, as already stated, very unusual with specimens from the Trenton group, while it is regularly seen in the specimens from the Hudson River group and Niagara group. Milne-Edwards considers both forms as one species, but I think they differ sufficiently to be set down as two species. To the Trenton form Goldfuss's name, Alveolata, is applied by most of the palæontologists; for the Hudson River group species, Hall's name, Columnaria (Favistella) stellata, is adopted, although it is not perfectly certain whether Goldfuss had not also a Hudson River group specimen under consideration.

The Trenton strata of the Escanaba River and of St. Joseph Island, in Lake Huron, contain an abundance of this coral, but the specimens are not very well preserved, being transformed into dolomite spar, which is a very unfavorable material for the preservation of the finer structural details. This coral is also frequently found in the Trenton group of Illinois, at Dixon, and in the lead-bearing strata of Wisconsin and Iowa, where it is often found in silicified condition, and finely preserved.

Plate XXXIV.—Fig. 1 is the surface view of a specimen from the Trenton group of St. Joseph Island. Fig. 2 is a fractured surface exhibiting a vertical section of a specimen from Escanaba River. Fig. 4 is a specimen with very large and unequal tubes. found in the Trenton group, at Dixon, Illinois.

COLUMNARIA STELLATA, Hall.

Synon., Favistella stellata, Hall.

Convex masses of similar structure with the former species; the tubes are somewhat less unequal in the same specimens, varying in size between three and six millimeters. Radial lamellæ from twenty to thirty, alternately larger and smaller, the larger ones extending to the centre. Diaphragms flat, closely set, intersected by the radial lamellæ, which only in the peripheral circumference form continuous vertical leaves. The crests continued to the centre of the diaphragms are merely superficial. Found abundantly on the north side of Drummond's Island, in the shales of the Hudson River group. The equivalent exposures in Bay de Noquets, opposite Escanaba, do not contain any. It is likewise found in the upper part of the Hudson River, or Cincinnati group, near Madison, Indiana, and in other localities along the Ohio River.

During the progress of the survey, I found specimens which I consider as identical with this species in the Niagara group of Point Detour, in which formation it was not known to occur.

Plate XXXIV.—Fig. 3 gives a surface view of a specimen from Drummond's Island (Hudson River group).

Plate XXVIII.—Fig. 1 is a silicified specimen from the Niagara group of Point Detour.

COLUMNARIA HERZERI, N. Sp.

Colonies of tubes, partially in close contiguity, of polygonal form, and intimately united with their walls; partially free, circular, laterally joining into chain-like rows, not unlike Halysites, or opening singly on the surface. Diameter of tubes three millimeters. Structure otherwise entirely corresponding with the associated form, Columnaria stellata. Is described by Nicholson under the name Favistella calycina.

The specimens were found by Rev. H. Herzer, of Louisville, in the Cincinnati group of Kentucky. It may only be a modification in the growth of the usual form C. stellata. Not figured. The specimens are too imperfect for photographic delineation.

ZOANTHARIA RUGOSA, MILNE-EDWARDS.

So called in allusion to the radial rugæ or plications of the stony, calcareous polyp cells, which are the only parts of these animals that have been preserved. The Zoantharia apora of a similar structure are distinguished from these by a difference in the arrangement of the radial plications. Milne-Edwards assumes four primary plications in the cycle of radii in the Zoantharia rugosa, and six primary plications in the Zoantharia apora, and deduces therefrom, in an elaborate essay, a law of symmetry, according to which the multiplication of the radii in the cycles takes place, and by which he endeavors to demonstrate that in case a new plication or lamella is formed in the interstice between two older plications of a certain value in the cyclical order, in all interstices, limited by plications of the same value, the intercalation of a new lamella takes place simultaneously, and this law he supposed to be governing the growth of Zoantharia rugosa, as well as of the Zoantharia apora. In the latter order this rule seems to be in force, but it does not apply to the growth of the Zoantharia rugosa.

The radial plications of the Zoantharia rugosa are arranged in four primary fascicles, separated from each other by more or less conspicuous gaps. These fascicles, apparently segments of a cycle of rays, are in reality bilaterally situated in symmetrical position on an axal line, dividing the apparent cycle in two halves. The two fascicles on one side are equivalent to those of the opposite side, but differ from one another. For better illustration, we may compare the circumference of a polyp cell to a horseshoe with narrow, almost closed aperture. Opposite this aperture, in the centre of the curve, two fascicles meet with their equivalent sides, leaving an obscure, narrow gap between them, the centre of which often exhibits a solitary, independent plication. This gap may, in distinction from the other gaps, be designated by the name of *central gap*. At the ends of these fascicles, remote from the central gap, and directed toward the aperture of the horseshoe, the plications become gradually shorter, and, seen from the peripheral surface of the polyp cells, do not extend to the apex of the conical polyparium, but terminate above, nearer the calycinal margins. Another gap separates these shorter plications on each side from the joining fascicles of plications, which extend to the ends of the arms of the horseshoe. This pair of gaps are the *lateral gaps.* The further ends of this second pair of fascicles approach each other again, in the aperture of the horseshoe, leaving another larger gap between themselves than the other fascicles, which may be termed *apertural gap;* its centre is, like the opposite obscure gap, occupied by a solitary plication. The plications of this second pair of fascicles are longest and extend to the apex of the polyparium on their end joining the lateral gaps, and shortest at the apertural gap. This is the order in the structure of all the polyp cells of the Zoantharia rugosa. If, during the progress of growth, new plications are added to the cycle of existing ones, the new ones are only inserted at those ends of the four fascicles which are directed toward the apertural gap, while the already existing plications are never disturbed by interposition of new ones, excepting, as indicated at the four ends of the fascicles, directed to the apertural gap; furthermore, the addition of new plications at the four ends of the fascicles is not always contemporaneous in all, or in the opposite corresponding ones, for otherwise the lamellæ in each equivalent bundle should be equal in number, which is not always the case. This bilateral structure of the polyp cells of the Zoantharia rugosa has been observed by several palæontologists, and been mentioned by them as a peculiarity of certain species; but the late Dr. Kunth, of Berlin, was the first to demonstrate this bilaterality to be an essential character of all the Zoantharia rugosa, and to exhibit with clearness the peculiar mode of multiplication of the lamellæ in this order. If we examine a Streptelasma or a Zaphrentis, we find the outer surface of the polyp cells longitudinally striate, by broad, convex bands or ribs, and by intermediate, narrow, linear furrows. The furrows correspond to the crest-like plications on the inside of the calyces, the ribs to the interstitial spaces between them. Three of such longitudinal furrows are, on each of the polyp cells, more conspicuous than the others; they correspond to the gaps between the bundles of lamellæ. In the furrow corresponding to the apertural gap, the other furrows from both sides converge at acute angles, like the barbs of a plume, to its keel, gradually becoming shorter as they approach the margins of the calyx. The two other obvious furrows, corresponding with the lateral gaps, are, on the side nearest to the apertural gap, joined by similar parallel furrows extending into the apex; on the other side the furrows abut against it at an acute angle, and decrease in length as they ascend. The central gap is not indicated on the outside, because the furrows on both its sides are parallel with it, as new plications are never intercalated in this place.

The annexed sketches will cause the descriptions to be understood at a glance. We perceive, by looking at the figures, that

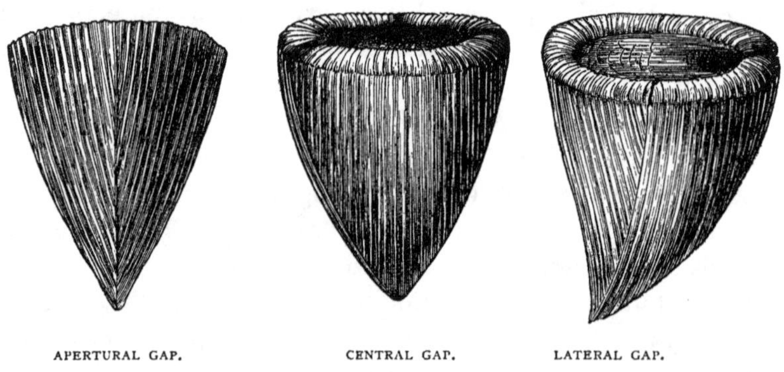

APERTURAL GAP. CENTRAL GAP. LATERAL GAP.

in the apertural gap the striæ must have a pinnate position, because on both of its sides new plications are constantly added to the ends of the fascicles; for the same reason we see them on the lateral gap on one side pinnate and on the other parallel, because no new plications are ever inserted there, and in the central they are all parallel because no implantation occurs on any of its sides.

All Zoantharia rugosa have this structure, but the four principal septal divisions do not present themselves in all with equal conspicuousness. In some the cycle of plications in the calyces is almost uninterrupted, and they appear as if of truly radial structure; in others the division lines between the fascicles are well marked by gaps, which on the bottom of the end-cells dilate into depressions called *septal foveæ*. The apertural fovea is always the largest, and an indication of it is noticeable in all forms of this order, while the two lateral gaps rarely become so distinct as to dilate into septal foveæ. The central gap is almost in every instance obscure, scarcely noticeable. Mr. Kunth, in speaking of the position and the development of these foveæ, justly remarks that if only one of the four foveæ is well developed, it is always the apertural fovea which he calls *principal fovea;* but he is in error when he adds, "only in rare instances the opposite fovea is best developed." This case never happens; in symmetrically curved, horn-shaped polyp cells the apertural fovea is either in the median line of the convexity of the curve or on the concave side. Not unfrequently the largest fovea is found in a lateral position with respect to the curvature of the polyp cells. But even if we find the largest fovea in such lateral position, it does not follow that one of the lateral foveæ has been developed in preference to the others; on close examination, it will always be found that the septal striæ on the surface converge from both sides toward the median line of that fovea, which unmistakably proves it to be the apertural fovea; if it were the lateral fovea the striæ would converge toward it only from one side, or if the central, they would be all parallel, which is never observed.

Milne-Edwards divides the Zoantharia rugosa into four families: the Stauridæ, Cyathaxonidæ, Cyathophyllidæ, and Cystiphyllidæ. These sub-divisions, however, are artificial, not being based on important differences in the plan of structure.

Stauridæ are described as polyp cells with well-developed, radial lamellæ, which intersect the whole length of the corallum as uninterrupted, vertical leaves, which are at intervals connected by short, interstitial, transverse leaflets. The lamellæ are grouped in four fascicles, which have their limits marked by very obvious septal gaps visible within the cells under the form of a four-armed cross. The enumerated genera of Stauridæ are: Stauria, a Silurian coral; Metriophyllum, a Devonian form; Polycœlia, of Permian age. No coral which could be identified as belonging to one of these genera has been found in Michigan.

Cyathaxonidæ are described as single polyp cells, with well-developed radial lamellæ, extending as uninterrupted leaves through the whole length of the corallum, and uniting in the centre into a cristiform columella. The interstices between the lamellæ are said to be open throughout without diaphragms or transverse, interstitial leaflets. This family characteristic is based on imperfect observation. The lamellæ do not unite in the centre into a cristiform columella, and their interstices are not open all their length, but have transverse leaves intersecting them, the conically protruding centres of which leaves, one invaginated into the other, form the cristiform columella, and not the united central ends of the vertical lamellæ, which do not perfectly reach the centre under the form of uninterrupted vertical leaves; their inner termination is only a superficial carination on the conical centres of the diaphragms. This structure does not materially differ from the structure of many genera of the Cyathophylloids, particularly of some forms of Zaphrentis and Trochophyllum. The latter genus may be said to differ from Cyathaxonia only in the inverted direction of their invaginated diaphragms. In Trochophyllum the diaphragms form deep, funnel-shaped depressions in the centre of the cells, which, in their invaginated condition, likewise compose a solid central axis, turned inward instead of projecting. Cyathaxonia is not found in the strata of Michigan. The specimens described from the upper coal measures as Lophophyllum proliferum, McChesney, is a genuine form of Cyathaxonia, entirely corresponding in structure with the forms of Cyathaxonia, described by Milne-Edwards, from the sub-carboniferous strata of Kentucky. Palæontologists examining these well-preserved specimens observed at once the existence of transverse leaves across the radiated interstices of the calyces, and hesitated on that account to identify them with Cyathaxonia; had Milne-Edwards examined his type specimens somewhat more carefully, he would have noticed in them the same transversal leaves.

CYATHOPHYLLIDÆ.

Simple or compound polyparia formed of cell cups margined by a cycle of plications of an apparently radial position toward the centre of the cells, but actually disposed according to the bilateral plan peculiar to the whole order of the Zoantharia rugosa.

The polyparia are built up by a successive series of such cups, one invaginated into the other, with gradually increased size. In some forms the cups are clearly defined in their superposition by a more or less distinct lamination in the structure of the polyparia; in others the union of the cups is more intimate. The plications of the incased cups corresponding, and clasped over one another, grow together and form continuous vertical laminæ, while the side walls of the cups unite into a common external wall of more massive structure; only the bottoms of the cups escape the general agglutination of the parts and remain free laminæ separated by an interstice from the adjacent cup bottoms. These laminar cup bottoms are, in the description of Cyathophylloid corals, considered under the name of diaphragms. In a portion of the Cyathophylloid family the interstices between the crest-like plications of the end cups are free and open; in other generic groups the interstices are up to the margins of the calyces traversed and filled with vesiculose plates, which divide them into small cell spaces.

The family of Cyathophylloids is represented by numerous modifications of its type, which will be specially considered in the generic descriptions. Milne-Edwards has adopted thirty-five genera of Cyathophylloids, and a large number of additional generic names, partly synonymous with the above, are used in the works of palæontologists. A careful study of the various forms has convinced me that a large proportion of the promulgated genera have been negligently established upon an examination of insufficient material and with incorrect appreciation of structural characters, individual peculiarities being often mistaken for important generic differences. In passing the genera in review, I will have frequent occasion for rectifications and changes in the arrangement, by which the number of the genera will be greatly reduced.

Cystiphyllidæ are pointed out as the fourth family of the Zoantharia rugosa, composed of the single genus Cystiphyllum. These corals differ from the true Cyathophyllum merely in having but a rudimentary development of the plications, which never compose continuous vertical leaves. The plications of Cystiphyllum are low crests much obscured by the blistered surface of the calycinal walls, which are entirely composed of vesiculose plates. In vertical sections the polyparia appear to be built up by a superimposed succession of layers of vesicles, disposed in accordance with the shape of the end cups.

An uninterrupted chain of transition forms between Cystiphyllum and the corals of the Cyathophylloid family exists, and the relations of Cyathophyllum proper and Cystiphyllum are so close that I think it unnatural to separate this genus from it as representing a different family type.

The formations of Michigan inclose a great many corals of the

Cyathophylloid family. The frequent fragmentary condition of the specimens and the altering effects of petrification prevent, in many instances, an exact identification of all the collected specimens, for which reason I have restricted myself to the description of those forms only of which I had satisfactory material for examination.

The genus Cyathophyllum, which gave the name to the entire large family, is not the primitive type form in which its first representatives appeared; the oldest forms of the Cyathophyllides were of the less complicated structure of Streptelasma and of Zaphrentis, which existed already in the lowest strata of the Trenton period. Cyathophyllum and many other diversifications of the type commence to appear in the upper Silurian beds. The Devonian period was the time of their greatest development, and after the carboniferous period we find the whole family exterminated, leaving no representative in the periods subsequent to the Permian strata.

CYATHOPHYLLUM, GOLDFUSS.

Simple or compound polyparia, each polyp cell surrounded by its own perfect wall. Vertical lamellæ well developed, forming continuous leaves through the whole length of the corallum, and extending to the centre, or near to it. The interstices between the lamellæ in the peripheral area (formed by the ascending walls of the calyces) are divided into small vesiculose cell spaces by short, transverse leaflets extending from one lamella to the other, and filling the calycinal interstices up to the outer margins. The central area (formed by the bottoms of the cell cups) is transversely septate by continuous simple diaphragms, or by compound plates formed of several convex, anchylosed pieces; these diaphragms are also intersected by the radial lamellæ reaching to the centre, or gradually vanishing in the middle. Surface of vertical lamellæ either smooth or granulose, with entire or with denticulated edges. Many species of Cyathophyllum have the side faces of their lamellæ decorated by low, equidistant carinæ, ascending in a curve from below and outward to the upper and inner edges, where they terminate as acute denticulations, or have the form of transverse trabeculæ, the carinæ of both sides of the leaves being coincident.

This carination is very obvious in a certain species first described in the geological reports of New York under the name of Strombodes helianthoides, which subsequently has been selected as the type form of the genus *Heliophyllum* (Heliophyllum Hallii), whose only distinguishing character from Cyathophyllum rests in the carinated surface of its lamellæ. If this distinction had been carried out strictly, and had all the forms agreeing in structure with Cyathophyllum, and at the same time having the surface of the lamellæ decorated by carinæ, been placed under the genus Heliophyllum, little objection could be urged against the arrangement, but no attempt has been made to do so. Milne-Edwards, the founder of the genus, while he describes one form as Heliophyllum Hallii, comes out with another equally characteristic Heliophyllum under the designation Zaphrentis cornicula, simply because that species has a somewhat large septal fovea, its only structural similarity to Zaphrentis. Other forms with the Heliophyllum character well developed he continues to consider as Cyathophylla, as, for instance, Cyathophyllum helianthoides, Cyath hexagonum, Cyath. rugosum, etc.

Carinated lamellæ are also regularly observed in the genera Diphyphyllum, Acervularia, Phillipsastræa, and in others. Another consideration depreciating the value of the carinations of the lamellæ as a generic mark is their frequent total obsolescence in specimens which by all other characters belong to a certain carinated species. Having the alternative before me then, either to adopt Heliophyllum and to substitute that name for a great many others well established, or to restore a few species now named so to their nearest relatives, the Cyathophylla, many of which participate in the same character of carination, I felt inclined to take the latter course as the simplest and most satisfactory.

CYATHOPHYLLUM HALLII, MILNE-EDWARDS.

Synon., HELIOPHYLLUM HALLII, Milne-Edwards.

Simple turbinate polyp cells, attached by the small basal apex, and frequently by additional root-like prolongations from a part of the side-walls. The conical shape of the cells varies considerably in different specimens, and changes during the progress of growth. A specimen may begin with a narrow cylindrical base, and then suddenly spread its end cell into an expanded dish form, or another may very regularly and gradually dilate into curved, horn-shaped cells, or the conical calyces of the base, after attaining a certain diameter, may stop to dilate and continue to grow on, maintaining the same size, into long, cylindrical stems, straight, or curved, or geniculated by interruptions in the growth, with constrictions and deflexions. In regularly formed specimens the calyces are shallow, bell-shaped, with broadly spread margins; other specimens have deeper calyces, with nearly erect margins. The radial lamellæ are alternately shorter and longer, but equal in size near the calyx margins, forming a uniform, uninterrupted cycle, with exception always of a faintly indicated apertural gap and septal fovea. The longer lamellæ extend as somewhat flexuose crests to the centre. Often a lamella continues across the calyx from the centre of the apertural gap to the opposite side, and the other lamellæ abut against it from both sides in symmetrical order. The bottoms of the end cells are usually raised into obtusely rounded, monticulose protrusions, on which the lamellæ unite with interlaced, twisted ends; or sometimes the lamellar crests fade away before reaching the centre, which then is formed by a smooth, naked spot of narrow extent. The most obvious character of this species are the arched carinæ extending across the lateral faces of the lamellæ from the outer peripheral side and below, to the upper and inner edges of the lamellæ; the carinations correspond on both faces and project on the edges of the lamellæ as obtuse, transverse bars or as acute dentations. The carinæ of different specimens vary considerably in degree of approximation; in some about eight carinæ are in the space of one centimeter, while others may have as many as fifteen within the same space. The radial lamellæ are acute, linear, and the interstices between them are completely filled by vesiculose, transverse plates arranged in imbricated superposition, in arched rows, ascending from within and below, upward and outward, diagonally to the direction of the carinæ. In the central area the polyparia are intersected by diaphragmatic, transverse plates, usually compound, of several pieces, inclosing larger vesiculose, interstitial cavities, which, by intersection with the vertical lamellæ, are divided into cellulose spaces of a much coarser kind than the interstitial cell spaces of the peripheral area. Associated with the specimens exhibiting plainly the carinated character of the lamellæ, others entirely similar to them are found with very obscure carinations. The calyces of the largest specimens attain a diameter of about six centimeters. The average number of lamellæ, in the circumference of calyces four centimeters wide, is from seventy-five to eighty-five. The external mode of growth is subject to a great many variations, from the short, broadly turbinate cell to long, cylindrical stems, with all sorts of irregularities by constrictions, flexions, etc. Occurs in the upper Helderberg group, and in the Hamilton group of Michigan, Canada, New York, Ohio, and in the Western States. The specimens of different localities and of different strata show some differences, but not in a degree to justify their separation into several species.

Plate XXXV., Upper tier.—The three left-hand figures are medium-sized specimens, found in the Hamilton group of Widder, C. W.; the two outer calyces are short, turbinate; the adjoining specimen exhibits an irregularly distorted cylindrical growth. The third upper figure from the left is found in the Hamilton group of Thunder Bay; the lamellæ on one side of the calyx are plainly carinated, while on the other side scarcely any traces of carination can be observed.

CYATHOPHYLLUM JUVENIS, N. SP.

A very constant form found in association with the preceding species, resembling it in all particulars, but in all proportions smaller. The arched carinæ are closely approximated, twenty-four on the space of a centimeter. Number of lamellæ from sixty to seventy in the circumference of calyces two and one quarter centimeters wide, which is about the largest size observed. Found in the Hamilton group of Thunder Bay, Little Traverse Bay, at Widder, C. W.; also in the upper Helderberg strata of New York, Ohio, Kentucky, etc.

Plate XXXV., Upper tier.—The three smaller specimens on the right side of the plate; the longer cylindrical specimen is of larger size than usual.

CYATHOPHYLLUM CORNICULA.

ZAPHRENTIS CORNICULA, Milne-Edwards.

Single, conical, symmetrically curved polyparia, annulated by fine wrinkles of growth, and by distant, shallow, rounded constrictions; delicately striate in longitudinal direction by septal furrows; apex pointed; calyx deep, with suberect margins gently spreading near the edges. Bottom of calyces variable; there are specimens in which the calyx gradually narrows into an obtuse pit; in others the bottom is reflected into a moderately convex protrusion, on which the lamellar crests unite; or this protrusion of the reflected bottom is of annular form, with a depression in the centre, which is confluent with a well-developed septal fovea situated on the convex side of the curvature of the horn-shaped polyp cells. The lamellæ are alternately large and small, denticulated on the edges and carinated on the side faces; from sixteen to eighteen carinæ on the space of one centimeter's length. Number of lamellæ in calyces of two centimeters diameter, from seventy to eighty. Lamellar interstices of the peripheral area filled with vesiculose, transverse plates up to the margins of the end cups, but the edges of the lamellæ remain free to some extent, more so than in the former species. The central area is intersected by well-developed transverse diaphragms, of somewhat irregular compound structure, joining the outer vesiculose area with depressed margins. The largest sized specimens are about six centimeters long, by a diameter of four centimeters at the calycinal margins; but the majority of specimens are much smaller. It occurs in the upper Helderberg strata of Michigan, Ohio, Canada, New York, and in the Western States, as one of the most abundant and characteristic fossils of that horizon.

Plate XXXV., Lower tier.—The left-hand group of specimens represents different variations of the kind found in the drift of Ann Arbor, all in silicified condition, with exception of the upper largest specimen, which is calcified; the other specimens are from the Falls of the Ohio, and from Columbus, Ohio.

CYATHOPHYLLUM SCYPHUS, N. SP.

Conical polyp cells, symmetrically curved, or irregularly constricted and geniculated, pointed, or with a broad scar of attachment. Calyx deep, spacious, with erect margins; bottom narrowing into an obtuse point, or somewhat flattened. Lamellæ linear, equal near the margins, but unequal in length, the larger ones uniting in the centre. The two lateral and the apertural gaps always plainly indicated; particularly distinct is the apertural gap, which has no determined position with regard to the curvature of the polyp cells. The surface of the lamellæ is smooth; their interstices filled with vesiculose plates. The central area is transversely septate, by compound vesiculose diaphragms. Number of lamellæ in calyces three and a half centimeters wide, 125 to 130. Polyp cells of larger size, measuring about two inches across the calyx and about three inches in length. Surface longitudinally ribbed by septal furrows, and intermediate rounded carinæ. Found in great numbers in silicified condition in the lower beds of the Hamilton group, at Long Lake, north of Alpena.

Plate XXXV., Lower tier.—The two right-hand specimens. One exhibits a view of the calyx, with distinctly visible indication of the apertural and the two lateral gaps; the other gives a side view of a polyp cell.

CYATHOPHYLLUM GENICULATUM, N. SP.

Large conical polyp cells of much interrupted growth by smaller constrictions and by deeper abrupt truncations of the old calyces, and renewed growth from their centre of a new calyx in considerably deflected direction, often making a perfect right angle with the old cell, which interruptions, frequently repeated, result in the production of distorted, geniculated, conico-cylindrical polyp stems. The basal portion of these stems exhibits sometimes a small scar of attachment at the pointed end; at other times broad scars, extending some distance upward along the sides, are noticed on the lowest cell with truncate base. The latter more permanently attached stems are usually of a more regular, straight, conico-cylindrical form ; the others, feebly attached stems, by breaking loose and falling into any accidental position, were obliged to alter the direction of their calyces, and if by subsequent currents or other causes their position was changed, they had to accommodate themselves again to the new position, and this, I suppose, is the true reason of their distorted growth. The calyces of the polyp cells are deep, gradually tapering, with inclined suberect margins. Lamellæ delicate, linear, subequal near the margin, crenulated at the edges, and obtusely carinated on the side faces. Apertural gap well marked. Interlamellar interstices of the peripheral area filled with vesiculose plates. Central area traversed by compound vesiculose diaphragms, which are much intersected by the vertical lamellæ. Diameter of large calyces from five to six centimeters. Number of lamellæ in calyces four centimeters wide, 112. Found in the upper shaly strata of the Hamilton group, at Partridge Point, Thunder Bay.

Plate XXXVI.—Lower figure represents the peculiar mode of growth of the polyp cells. Some specimens found at Widder, C. W., in the Hamilton group, are of entirely similar growth, but these evidently are only a modified form of Cyathophyllum Hallii, with obscure lateral carinæ.

CYATHOPHYLLUM HOUGHTONI, N. SP.

Erect, conico-cylindrical polyp cells, with a strong latero-basal attachment. Surface obtusely wrinkled, rarely interrupted by acute annulations. Calyx deep, with steep side walls, and erect, slightly dilating edges. Bottom of cells about one third as wide as their outer margin, subplane or gently convex, with depressed circumference, crossed by the lamellæ, of which three or four are always much stouter than the others and coalesce in the centre. Sometimes the centre of the cell bottoms is depressed, with a ring-like elevation surrounding the depression, of smooth surface. Lamellæ alternately larger and smaller, linear near the bottom of the calyces, roof-shaped on the ascending walls, and frequently explanate into a blistered plicated membrane near the margins. The surface and the edges of the lamellæ within the calyces are covered with granulations and by short, interrupted, transverse carinations or rugosities. The transformation of the linear radial crests into roof-shaped plications on the ascending side walls of the calyces alters the structure of the peripheral area considerably. There are no small, vesiculose, interstitial plates developed in the interstices between the radial crests, as in the outer area of other Cyathophylla; the lamellæ themselves open in two diverging leaves, which join in the interstices into a continuous calycinal membrane of a blistered structure. The calycinal surface represents a complete laminar bag folded into plications, with the acute edges of the folds directed inward, and the rounded curve turned outward. The coral is formed by invagination of a series of such bags, which have elongated, blister-like intervals between them, but are in intimate connection by the edges of their crested plications, which correspond to each other and combine into vertical laminar dissepiments extending through the whole length of the corallum. In the marginal portions of the calyces, however, the crests are often interrupted in their vertical continuity by the extension of the blister-like interstices between the calycinal bags across several of the plications which have lost their edged crest form through spreading into a tent-shape. This structure frequently causes an exfoliation of the surface of the specimens, with exposure of the outer blistered surface of the bags, by which even small fragments can be identified as belonging to this species. The central area is septate by transverse diaphragmatic plates of much regularity. The vertical lamellæ intersect them as continuous leaves nearly to the centre. Occurs as the prevailing species in the Hamilton group of Thunder Bay and of Little Traverse Bay. A coral described by Hall under the name of Chonophyllum ellipticum, from the Hamilton group of Iowa, agrees in structure with the described form, but not with Chonophyllum. A similarly built species is found in the upper Helderberg strata of Kentucky, but both of these, according to their mode of growth, seem to differ specifically from our form.

Plate XXXVI.—In the upper tier of figures are views of different specimens found at Little Traverse Bay. The central larger specimen presents a polished section.

CYATHOPHYLLUM RUGOSUM, Milne-Edwards.

Synon., Astræa rugosa, Hall.

Astræiform colonies of polygonal, intimately united stems of a diameter from one to one and a half centimeter, which in some specimens of a certain state of preservation are separable, and present longitudinally ribbed polygonal stems, annulated by transverse wrinkles of growth. Calyces joining, with gradually ascending side walls, inclosing conical cell pits; or the end cells are formed by an abrupt, narrow, central pit, with horizontally expanded, discoid margins. The bottom of the cells is sometimes formed by diaphragms with a smooth central spot; usually the lamellæ reach to the centre and intermingle there, forming a twisted knot. Number of lamellæ in the circumference of the calyces from 35 to 45; their edges are crenulated, the side faces traversed by arched carinæ, which in some specimens are almost obsolete, in others very distinct. Interlamellar interstices traversed by small vesicles filling them to the margins of the calyces. The centre of the stems is transversely septate by diaphragms, intersected in their outer circumference by continuous vertical lamellæ; centrally their continuity is interrupted, and the ends are merely carinations on the upper face of the diaphragms.

Milne-Edwards describes paliform lobes and the development of a rudimentary columella in this species, but neither one nor the other structure can be recognized. The centre of the calyces in some weathered specimens protrudes with a degree of convexity exhibiting the twisted ends of the radial lamellæ, but no paliform lobes, much less a columella. Found in the Helderberg limestones of Mackinac Island, and in the drift of the Lower Peninsula. It is also common at the Falls of the Ohio, at Sandusky, and in many other localities.

Plate XXXVII.—The upper row represents a polished, horizontal section, and a lateral view of another specimen with stems separable from each other.

CYATHOPHYLLUM DAVIDSONI.

Synon., ACERVULARIA DAVIDSONI, Milne-Edwards.

ACERVULARIA PROFUNDA, Hall.

The corals described under the name Acervularia Davidsoni and Acerv. profunda, which latter I consider merely as a variety of the former, are in structure identical with Cyathoph. rugosum. The genus Acervularia is represented as having its central portion of the polyp cells surrounded by an internal wall, but neither the above-mentioned corals nor the typical forms of the genus Acervularia (Cyath. pentagonum and Cyath. ananas of Goldfuss) exhibit an internal wall. In the circumference of the abrupt inner cell-pits of all these forms a sort of annular demarkation is conspicuous in transverse sections, because the shorter ones of the alternately larger and smaller radial lamellæ terminate there with somewhat thickened edges, but they never combine into a closed, ring-like wall.

The specimens described by Milne-Edwards are from the Helderberg limestones of the Falls of the Ohio; the Michigan forms identified with it in the subsequent description are found in the Hamilton group.

Growth in large, convex masses, or in lenticular, discoid expansions, covered on the lower depressed, conical, and centrally attached side with a concentrically wrinkled epithecal crust. Stems multiplying by marginal and central gemmation from the calyces; sometimes single stems are free and circular; usually the growth is astræiform, with intimately connected polygonal calyces, surrounded by acute linear crested edges. The margins of the calyces are usually broadly explanate, discoid, rarely gradually descending into the more abrupt, bell-shaped, central excavation proper to all forms, on the rounded bottom of which the lamellæ unite, or which, in rarer instances, exhibits a narrow diaphragm sparsely intersected by lamellar crests. Diameter of calyces about one centimeter, but quite variable. Lamellæ long and short, in alternation, but equal in size near the calyx margins, crenulated at the edges, and decorated by arched carinæ crossing their flanks; from thirty-six to forty lamellæ in the circumference of a calyx. Interlamellar interstices filled with delicate, transverse, vesiculose plates. The central area is distinctly septate by diaphragms, which are not much intersected by vertical crests; on the circumference of the central area, in polished transverse sections, a more compact ring is visible, formed by a thickening of the longer lamellæ, and by the abrupt termination of the alternating shorter ones within this circle, but not a trace of an actual inner wall is developed. By comparing specimens from different strata and different localities, a number of minor variations may be observed, but I do not consider them important enough to make specific distinctions. This form approaches also so near to Cyathophyllum rugosum of the upper Helderberg group, that a strict distinction between them is almost impossible.

Occurs abundantly in the Hamilton strata of Thunder Bay, and of Little Traverse Bay; is also a common form in the Hamilton strata of Iowa.

Plate XXXVII., Fig. 4.

CYATHOPHYLLUM CRISTATUM, N. SP.

Astræiform calyces, bell-shaped, joining with polygonal, suberect margins; diameter of cells about two centimeters; about thirty-six alternately large and small stout lamellæ in the circumference, with crenulated edges and lateral carinations; the larger lamellæ extend over the bottom of the cells to the centre; interlamellar interstices large, filled with coarse, transverse, vesiculose plates. Central area irregularly septate by vesiculose compound diaphragms. Occurs rarely in the Hamilton strata of Little Traverse Bay; its structure is much coarser than in Cyathophyllum Davidsoni, with which it is associated.

The specimens were not sufficiently perfect for photographic delineation.

CYATHOPHYLLUM COALITUM, N. SP.

Astræiform masses of very large, polygonal polyp cells measuring about four centimeters in diameter, each one surrounded by its own complete wall. Surface of calyces expanded, discoid, with an abrupt but shallow central pit, the reversed bottom of which conically projects, covered by the central ends of the radial crests. Lamellæ linear, subequal, from sixty to seventy in the circumference of a calyx, crenulated by transverse trabeculæ (bars), which are the ends of lateral, arched carinæ decorating the side faces; about fourteen carinæ on the length of one centimeter. Interstitial spaces filled with vesicles arranged in arched rows running diagonally across the carinations. Central area traversed by transverse, larger plates, which are much intersected by the vertical lamellæ. The structure of this coral is identical with Cyathophyllum Hallii, from which it differs principally in its cespitose, compound growth. Found frequently in silicified condition in the drift, connected with fossils of the corniferous limestone.

Plate XXXVIII.—Fig. 4 represents a fragmentary specimen from the drift of Ann Arbor.

CYATHOPHYLLUM RADICULA, N. SP.

Small single polyp stems, about one centimeter in diameter, conical at the base, cylindrical in their prolongation, annulated by numerous sharp constrictions caused by periodical interruptions in the growth of the cells, which commences again with contracted base from the centre of the old cells. The bases of the stems are strongly attached to other bodies, and the attachment is often strengthened by excrescences from the sides of the stems. Calyces not as deep as wide, with erect, ascending sides, slightly expanded near the margins, and surrounded by about sixty alternately larger and smaller crenulated lamellæ. Bottom of cells flat, formed of a smooth or faintly carinated or granulose transverse diaphragm; in some other specimens the lamellæ extend to the centre, and the bottoms of the cells are more rounded, concave. A septal fovea is rarely indicated. Found in the Niagara group of Drummond's Island, at Point Detour, and in the Niagara group of Iowa.

Plate XXXIX., Fig. 3.—The left-hand, outer vertical row of specimens is from Point Detour; the central row represents specimens from Masonville, Iowa; the right-hand row may be a different species. It occurs in the Niagara group of Louisville, and of Charleston, Indiana; the stems are of longer cylindrical growth, often curved and geniculated; their calyces rarely exhibit a naked diaphragm in the bottom, and the crenulated lamellæ generally reach to the centre. The surface of the stems is in both kinds longitudinally ribbed by septal striæ.

CLISIOPHYLLUM, Dana.

Simple conical polyp cells with the general structure of Cyathophyllum, differing from it in the shape of the calycinal bottom. Radial lamellæ linear, with prominent free edges within the end cells; the interstices between the lamellæ are traversed by transverse, vesiculose plates, but these do not fill the interstices up to the margins of the lamellæ, as is usual in Cyathophyllum, and the inclosed vesiculose spaces are somewhat larger. The broad central area of the polyp cells is formed of high, projecting, conical diaphragms, one incasing the other, and crested on the surface by the central ends of the radial lamellæ. The apertural septal fovea well developed.

CLISIOPHYLLUM ONEIDAENSE, Billings.

Conico-cylindrical, sometimes elliptically compressed polyparia, annulated by numerous transverse wrinkles and intermediate linear constrictions. The stems are frequently flexuose; their width is from three to five centimeters, by a length of sometimes over one foot in cylindrical specimens; the conical cells are shorter, with a diameter equal to that of the former. The basal ends of the larger stems often, for some length, grow in the form of narrow cylindrical pedicles, the surface of which is ornamented with numerous stout spinulose projections, which also extend, but rarely, for some distance higher over the upper, more dilating portions of the stems. The calyces are spacious, with steep side walls, terminating with erect or only slightly expatiated margins. Lamellæ near the calycinal margins of alternately larger and smaller size; further down the sides the lamellæ are all of one size; the smaller intercalated ones remain confined to the outer margin. A conspicuous septal fovea interrupts the cycle of the lamellar crests, causing a deep, siphonal depression in the peripheral circumference of the cell bottoms, which are broad, rising into a strong cone carinated by the radial lamellæ uniting on its apex in somewhat twisted manner. Number of lamellæ in specimens of four centimeters calyx diameter, from 85 to 90, and at the margins of the calyces an equal number of small rudimentary folds are intercalated.

Found in the upper Helderberg strata of Mackinac, at the Falls of the Ohio, at Port Colborne, in Canada, and frequently in the drift deposits.

Plate XL.—The upper tier represents various silicified specimens found in the drift, left-hand and lower central specimen ; the other two are from the Falls of the Ohio. The right-hand specimen exhibits the invaginated, conical diaphragms almost extending across the whole width of the stems, surrounded only by a narrow peripheral area.

LITHOSTROTION, FLEMMING.

Compound polyparia, formed of cylindrical stems, enveloped by a perfect epithecal wall, and either loosely approximated, with circular orifices, or intimately united, and joining under polygonal outlines by mutual pressure. Structure very similar to Clisiophyllum. The outer area is divided into small cellulose spaces by the interposition of vesiculose, transverse plates between the vertical lamellæ ; the inner area, which is not defined from the outer area by an intervening wall, is formed by diaphragms reflected into large protruding cones, carinated by the radial crests uniting on them and invaginating into one another. The laterally compressed, crest-like apices of the invaginated cones grow together and form a continuous, thin axal lamina pervading the whole length of the corallum.

LITHOSTROTION MAMILLARE, EDWARDS & HAIME.

LITHOSTROTION PROLIFERUM, Hall.

Large colonies of remote, cylindrical stems, from one to two and a half centimeters in diameter, multiplying by gemmation from the margins of the calycinal disks, or astræiform masses of intimately united, polygonal stems of similarly variable sizes, and unequal in the same specimens through the intermixture of frequent young cells. Calyces moderately deep, obliquely spreading in the margins, and more abruptly excavated in the inner circumference. Bottom of cups reflected into a large, conical protuberance, carinated on the sides by the converging ends of the radial lamellæ, and terminating with a laterally compressed cristiform edge. From thirty to forty lamellæ in the circumference of a calyx; and sometimes indications of rudimentary, intermediate plications are noticeable. The clusters of singly growing stems cover sometimes spaces of large extent, and not a specimen with astræiform, polygonal calyces is found among them; in other localities the astræiform colonies are the prevailing form; this seems to indicate a difference between the two forms, but specimens are found, and that not rarely, in which one part of the stems is free, circular, and another intimately united, pressing each other into the polygonal form. As no difference in the structure can be observed in the two forms, I am inclined to consider them modifications of one species, whose difference in mode of growth is perhaps only dependent upon local conditions existing at one and another place. Occurs in the carboniferous limestone of Wildfowl Bay, and at Bellevue and Grand Rapids, Michigan.

Plate LV.—The upper tier represents two specimens from the carboniferous limestone of Wildfowl Bay—one with astræiform, polygonal calyces, the other with partial free circular stems.

The specimen lying across the bottom of the lower tier in the same plate is a singly grown stem of the same species.

BLOTHROPHYLLUM, Billings.

Conico-cylindrical polyparia, single, or in cespitose clusters, produced by prolific calycinal gemmation of a few parent cells. The structure of the stems, as being built of a series of invaginated cups, is particularly obvious. The bottom of these cups has the shape of transverse diaphragms, smooth in the centre, or superficially carinated by the central ends of the radial, crest-like folds, into which the side walls of the cups are plicated. These crests of the superimposed cups unite into continuous vertical laminæ within a narrow circle intermediate between the central and the peripheral areas, but are interrupted in their continuity outside or inside of it. Inside, on the diaphragms, the plications fade away as superficial, low carinations; in the outer peripheral area their continuity is interrupted for other reasons; the margins of the incased plicated cell cups dissolve connection and begin to diverge; gradually widening gaps open between the laminar cup margins, which at first continue to repose on each other's crests, but finally also these become disjunct, and they remain so until at the peripheral surface the edges of the cup membranes join again into a common epithecal wall, which closes off from the outside the cavernous gaps between them. Some of the forms have a well-developed septal fovea; in others it is not very distinct.

BLOTHROPHYLLUM DECORTICATUM, Billings.

Large polyp stems, conical at the base, cylindrical and flexuose above, attaining a diameter of over two inches and a length exceeding one foot. Surface, if perfect, covered by a continuous epithecal crust, longitudinally striate by septal furrows and annulated by deep wrinkles and constrictions. The conical basal part is decorated with strong nodular spinulosities, as the polyp cells of the associated Clisiophyllum, with which it stands in structural relationship. Calyces moderately deep, with steep sides, explanate margins, and broad bottoms, in the form of irregularly concave diaphragms, smooth in the centre, and on one side depressed into a deep septal fovea. The lamellæ are acute, very prominent linear crests on the ascending side walls of the calyces, but become lower and almost obsolete near the expanded peripheral margins; in the broad marginal interstices between them smaller plications are regularly intercalated.

The peripheral part of the polyparia formed by the expanded laminar cup margins, with large gaps between them, and supported only by their ends, united in an epithecal cuticle, is very fragile and rarely found in good preservation. The plurality of specimens have lost their epitheca, and the laminar margins stand out free, surrounding the stems like broad collars; or they have been destroyed, and only the central cores are found, presenting an exfoliated surface, and consisting of a cycle of stout vertical lamellæ, which incloses the central series of diaphragms. Occurs in the drift of Michigan, and is found in place at the Falls of the Ohio, and in the corniferous strata of Canada.

Plate XLI.—Silicified specimens from the Falls of the Ohio. The right-hand weathered specimen exhibits the centre of a polyp stem intersected by diaphragms. The left-hand specimen has at the conical base preserved its continuous epithecal wall; above it the surface is exfoliated and shows the coarse, blister-like cavities intermediate between the invaginated series of renewed cell cups.

BLOTHROPHYLLUM CÆSPITOSUM, N. SP.

Aggregated, conico-cylindrical polyp cells of a much interrupted, articulated growth, by constantly repeating constrictions and dilatations of the cell cups. The constrictions of the stems are acute angular, without interruption of the continuity of the surface walls; in other instances the continuity is interrupted, and a more or less broad, expanded rim of the older cell cup projects with free edge at the places of constriction. The polyparia multiply by gemmation of many young cells at once from the end cups of the older stems. The clustered stems become attached to each other by their acute, annular edges; the joints of the obliquely diverging stems are generally oblique to each other in proportion to the inclination of the stems—one joint, so to say, being pushed sideways over the other in this direction. The calyces are shallow, with obliquely spreading side walls. Radial crests not very high, linear, and projecting most on the more vertical portions of the cup walls, dilating into tent form on the marginal, expanded portions of the calyces. Edges of the plications denticulate and surface granulose. At the margins of the calyces smaller, rudimentary plications are alternately interposed between the larger ones. Diaphragms forming the bottom of the cups flat, with several siphonal depressions in their circumference, but with no distinct septal fovea; their centre usually smooth, sometimes carinated by the ends of the lamellæ. By the united linear, crest-like portion of the plications a cycle of vertical lamellæ is formed around the central diaphragms; the area exterior to this cycle is formed by superimposed, plicate, sometimes blistered, laminar cup-walls, partially connected by the edges of the lamellæ, otherwise separated by irregular, blister-like cavities, but uniting again in the peripheral wall. Diameter of stems from two to three centimeters. Found in the Niagara group of Drummond's Island, at Point Detour, etc., in silicified, generally much decayed and altered condition.

Plate XLII.—Surface view and lateral view of specimens from Point Detour.

CHONOPHYLLUM, MILNE-EDWARDS.

Single turbinate polyparia, composed of invaginated, radially plicated cell cups, which are intimately united within the central area, and form with their linear plications continuous vertical crests, extending through the whole length of the corallum, and uniting in the centre into a somewhat twisted fascicle, but without composing a solid central axis. The interlamellar interstices of this central fascicle or core are traversed by transverse vesiculose plates, but no larger transverse diaphragmatic septa are observable. In the peripheral area the structure is entirely different. The connection between the invaginated cups becomes more loose, the linear plications open themselves and spread horizontally, forming gradually widening and moderately convex, band-like folds of the expanded laminar cup walls, which are superimposed in well-defined, membraniform layers, one reposing on the granulose prominences of the surface of another, and more intimately connecting in the linear furrows between the plications, which correspond to the interlamellar spaces of other Zoantharia rugosa, but were confused by Billings with the lamellæ. In his description of Chonophyllum magnificum, Mr. Billings remarks: "The grooves on the floor of the cup indicate the position of the septa, and the ridges are the equivalent of the interseptal spaces." This is an evident error. It can be directly observed in the specimens how the linear vertical crests of the central area gradually open in two diverging leaves, spreading horizontally into flattened, band-like folds, and at the same time how the spacious interlamellar interstices of the central circle become outwardly angustated in the same measure as the plications widen. In the median line of these linear interstitial spaces, confounded with the lamellæ, the rows of vesiculose transverse plates, characterizing them as true interstitial spaces, are, in all the well-preserved specimens, plainly demonstrable, anatomical facts.

CHONOPHYLLUM MAGNIFICUM, Billings.

Conical polyparia, attaining a calyx diameter of nine inches in larger specimens; some grow in short, broadly expanded polypdoms, increasing but little in length; others proportionately elongate their stems with the widening of their calyces. The pointed ends of the polyparia are attached by a small scar. The outer wall is annulated by concentric wrinkles of growth and longitudinally ribbed by septal striæ. Calyces broad, explanate, dish-shaped. Plications equal, linear, crest-like in the central parts of the calyces, but changing into tent-shape on the spreading neck part, and opening into broad bands near their peripheral circumference. The surface of the plications is densely covered with decorative granulations or papilli, visible as well on the horizontal, band-like surface as on the side faces of the linear, crest-like portions. In calyces of three inches diameter about ninety plications are counted in the circumference. In the bottom of the calyces the lamellæ become very delicately linear and twisted, or irregularly interlacing into a central fascicle. No indication of a septal fovea. Occurs in the upper strata of Mackinac Island and in the drift of the Lower Peninsula, and is common at the Falls of the Ohio, at Charleston Landing, Indiana, and in other exposures of the upper Helderberg group.

Plate XLIII., Upper tier.—The right-hand specimen is a silicified fragment of a large calyx exhibiting the band-like form of the lamellæ toward the outer margin, and their crested linear form near the central cavity; the papillose surface is likewise well seen in the figure. The other specimen gives a side view of a specimen showing the general mode of growth, and the laminated structure of the polyparia. The right-hand figure in the lower row is a calyx seen from above. All the specimens represented are from the Falls of the Ohio; the Michigan specimens were not so well adapted for delineation.

CHONOPHYLLUM PONDEROSUM, N. SP.

Patellate, depressed, conical polyparia of irregular, unsymmetrical, clumsy growth, with gemmation from the centre of the calyces, of single new cells, or, in rare instances, of from two to four confluent or imperfectly defined calyces. End cells shallow, explanate at the margins, more abruptly depressed in the centre, which is surrounded by a cycle of low linear crests uniting in it with twisted ends. Expanded marginal part radiated by flat, broad, band-like plications of papillose surface. The specimens are all formed of a heavy, compact mass of amorphous, white, ivory-like carbonate of lime, or partially silicified, and with scarcely a trace of the organic structure preserved; only in a few specimens could enough of it be seen by which to recognize the generic relations of the specimens and their correspondence with Chonophyllum. It does not seem to be the mode of petrification which obscures the structure, as we find this coral in many different localities associated with other corals exhibiting the finest details of structure, while they everywhere present the same massive, compact condition. The coral appears to have, during the progress of its growth, filled out all its cellulose cavities as soon as the fleshy parts of the animal abandoned them.

It occurs rarely in the upper Helderberg limestones, but is abundant in certain layers of the Hamilton group of Thunder Bay, and is also found in Little Traverse Bay.

Plate XLIII., Lower tier.—The left-hand figure is a specimen found in the lower limestones of Phelps' quarries, near Alpena.

OMPHYMA RAFINESQUE, PTYCHOPHYLLUM IN PARTE, MILNE-EDWARDS.

Single conical polyp cells of Cyathophylloid structure, composed of invaginated calycinal cups, the bottoms of which have the form of spacious diaphragms, either smooth or crested by the radial lamellæ uniting in the centre. The ascending side walls of the cups are encircled by linear, crest-like plications, which connect into uninterrupted vertical laminæ, within this intermediate area. At the peripheral cup margins the plications become tent-shaped, embracing one another in their superposition, but not always combining with their edges into uninterrupted vertical leaves. The interlamellar interstices are traversed by transverse plates, and divided into cellulose spaces, but the dissepiments are not independent vesiculose leaflets; they make part of the tent-shaped folds of the invaginated series of cell cups, and represent the rounded, outwardly directed flexion of the plicated cup walls, while the inwardly turned folds are sharply crested. Root-like, cylindrical excrescences from the side walls of the polyparia, by which they are attached to other bodies, are a peculiarity of the different species of Omphyma, which, however, are not exclusively so to them, but are also noticed in other forms of the Cyathophylloid family. As another distinctive character of Omphyma, the development of four septal foveæ is mentioned by Milne-Edwards, but they are generally not all equally distinct, while very frequently only one of them is obvious, the others being almost obsolete. The genus Ptychophyllum, described by Milne-Edwards as being organized like Chonophyllum, differing from it in the twisted converging ends of the radial lamellæ, forming a central false columella, is likewise in close structural relationship with Omphyma, and in the special case of Ptychophyllum Stockesii, I found its affinity with Omphyma verrucosa so great that I altered the name of the first from Ptychophyllum to Omphyma.

OMPHYMA VERRUCOSA, MILNE-EDWARDS.

Conical polyparia, attaining in larger specimens the length of one decimeter by a calyx diameter of from seven to eight centimeters. Surface of the silicified specimens generally exfoliated; if perfect, it is covered by an epithecal wall with annular wrinkles of growth, and longitudinally striate by septal furrows. From the sides of the conical walls numerous cylindrical, root-like prolongations grow out, serving for attachment of the coral to other bodies; these appendices were not distributed equally over the surface, but seemed to form only on those sides where a chance for attachment was offered by close proximity of an object. Calyces spacious, with steeply ascending sides and a gently expanded margin; bottom broad, convex, with depressed circumference, flat or somewhat concave in the centre, which may be almost smooth, or the lamellæ may extend over it as carinations, becoming twisted in the centre. On the ascending sides of the calyx the lamellæ have the form of acute linear laminæ alternating in size, a smaller and a larger one near the bottom of the calyx always united into pairs. In the marginal portions of the calyces, the two plates forming the linear crests diverge at the base, and open into a tent-shape. The four septal foveæ are scarcely ever distinct—two of them, or it may be only one, being plainly developed.

The centre of the polyparia is, in vertical sections, seen regularly intersected by large transverse plates, and the continuity of the vertical crests is interrupted. Number of lamellæ in calyces of six or seven centimeters diameter from one hundred to one hundred and ten. Associated with the elongated type form already described, which is represented on Plate XLIV., lower tier, right- and left-hand specimens, are shorter conical specimens, with broad, expanded calyx margins, and generally with a very prominent bottom, covered by twisted radial crests, seeming to be a mere variety of the former kind. The central figure between the two represents one of them. Occurs in the Niagara group of Drummond's Island, etc.

OMPHYMA STOCKESII.

Synon., PTYCHOPHYLLUM STOCKESII, Milne-Edwards.

Conical polyp cells very similar to the former species, in structure and mode of growth. Calyces spacious, rather shallow, with expanded margins; bottom of cells always raised into a monticule, on which the lamellæ unite in twisted manner. Two of the septal foveæ distinct, the other two obscure. Lamellæ united into pairs of a larger and a smaller one; of more delicate structure than in the former kind, and with narrower interstices. Their vertical continuity is complete in an inner intermediate cycle; interrupted in the central part, occupied by transverse diaphragms, and in the marginal parts, in which the horizontally expanded cup membranes are bent into zigzag lines, and superimposed in layers. Number of lamellæ somewhat larger than in the former species in specimens of the same size. External surface covered with root-like excrescences as in the other. The description given by Edwards of

Ptychophyllum Stockesii says nothing about such excrescences, but otherwise it applies exactly to the specimens now considered, which were found in the same locality as his, at Drummond's Island, associated with the other form. Other forms of Ptychophyllum, found at Louisville, in the Niagara group, and resembling *Ptychophyllum patellatum from Gothland*, have these root-like appendices also well developed. It is sometimes difficult to draw a line of distinction between specimens of these two species.

Plate XLIV., upper tier, gives various silicified specimens from the Niagara group of Drummond's Island.

A very common species in the Niagara group of Iowa, described by D. Dale Owen, under the name of *Cyathophyllum undulatum et multiplicatum*, has a structure entirely conformable with the two species of Omphyma of Drummond's Island, and must therefore be arranged with them in the same generic group.

DIPHYPHYLLUM, Lonsdale.

Synon., Eridophyllum, Milne-Edwards.

Diplophyllum, Hall.

Colonies of aggregated cylindrical polyp cells, multiplying by calycinal gemmation, but not by fissiparous mode of propagation, as Lonsdale asserts. The stems are rarely in intimate contact so as to form astræiform masses; usually some interval remains between them, and they are mutually connected by rugose or radiciform lateral prolongations of the walls, or by floors formed by periodical horizontal expansions of the calyx margins until they join at their edges. Structure of cells biareal. The outer area is formed by the external epithecal wall with a cycle of stout vertical lamellæ having crenulated edges and arched carinæ decorating their flanks. The interlamellar interstices are filled with small transverse plates, dividing them into narrow cellulose spaces. These transverse plates are disposed in arched rows, crossing the arched carinæ diagonally from within and below, upwardly and outwardly. The inner area is principally composed of flat, transverse diaphragms, which are only in their circumference intersected by the radial lamellæ; their centre is free of the crests, or the crests extend only on their upper surface to the centre. There are three different modifications in the structure. In one the demarkation of an inner and an outer area is very obscure; the vertical lamellæ reach to the centre of the diaphragms as superficial carinæ. These are exclusively Silurian forms, which might be distinguished as a peculiar generic type, but as their general mode of growth is so similar to the other biareal forms of Diphyphyllum, I prefer to leave them together. A second modification has a very broad central area, formed almost exclusively by transverse diaphragms, while the vertical lamellæ are confined to a narrow peripheral cycle; but the inner and outer cycle is not defined by an intermediate internal vertical wall. The third modification, which is generally of stouter growth than the second form, has the inner area defined from the outer by a distinct vertical wall of horseshoe shape, open on the side of the apertural fovea. The lamellæ in this latter form never transgress the inner wall, and the central part within is exclusively formed by a superimposed series of transverse diaphragmatic plates.

DIPHYPHYLLUM HURONICUM, N. SP.

Aggregated, cylindrical, flexuose stems of a diameter of from one to two centimeters, annulated by delicate striæ of growth, and by deeper wrinkles and constrictions; longitudinally ribbed by septal furrows. The stems are laterally connected by stout rugose prolongations from their walls, which in all the stems of a colony are uniformly directed to one side. Calyces moderately deep, dish-shaped, with explanate margins, radiated by about sixty linear lamellæ, which unite in a central fascicle; their margins are faintly crenulated, or not so at all. Interstices filled with vesiculose plates, which in the central part are larger and inclose somewhat coarser cell spaces, but no distinct large plates, properly deserving the name of diaphragms, are developed, and the outer and inner area are not well defined. The stems multiply by gemmation from the centre and the margins of the end cells, the marginal gemmæ remaining for a good while of a more slender, smaller size than the contemporaneous new cells sprouting from the centre. Found in the Niagara group of Drummond's Island and Point Detour.

Plate XLV.—Fig. 1 represents a side view of a cluster of stems found at Point Detour.

DIPHYPHYLLUM RUGOSUM, Milne-Edwards.

Eridophyllum rugosum, Milne-Edwards.

Of very similar sructure to the former, but its stems are smaller, less than one centimeter in thickness; the gemmation from the calyces is very prolific; from four to six gemmæ grow at once from an end cup; the stems are tortuous, geniculated, annulated by sub-regularly repeating constrictions, and by delicate linear striæ of growth; the lateral processes, for mutual attachment of the stems, are acanthiform, quite numerous. Calyces forming rounded, moderately deep excavations with slanting sides and erect margins. Lamellæ crenulated, from forty to fifty in the circumference of a calyx, and extending nearly to its centre, which is generally formed by a very narrow diaphragm, not transgressed by the lamellæ, but not separated from the outer area by an internal wall.

This species is not found in Michigan, but is a very common form in the Niagara group of Indiana and Kentucky, and because of its close affinity to the former species, I have considered it of interest to describe and represent it in this place.

Plate XLV.—Fig. 2 gives a side view of a silicified specimen from the vicinity of Louisville; the stems are of somewhat larger size than the specimens usually have.

DIPHYPHYLLUM MULTICAULE, Hall.

Syringopora multicaulis, Hall.

Flexuose cylindrical stems, from three to four millimeters in diameter, distant from each other about one tube diameter, connected by narrow, remote spurs resembling the transverse tubules of a Syringopora. Surface faintly ribbed by septal striæ, and encircled by wrinkles of growth. Calyces deep, with almost vertically erect walls, radiated by about thirty crenulated lamellæ, of which half the number are marginal; the others reach to the centre. Interstitial spaces filled with vesiculose plates. Diaphragms generally obscured by frequent intersection with the lamellæ; more rarely the central area is occupied by a flat diaphragm free of crests. I was at first inclined to consider the latter form as a separate species, but I found later that these differences constitute only individual variations of the same form.

Found in the Niagara group of Point Detour, Seul Choix, on Lake Michigan, and in the drift boulders of the Lower Peninsula.

Plate XLV.—Fig. 3 is a specimen with plainly developed transverse diaphragms; in Fig. 4 the lamellæ extend to the centre, and the diaphragms are obscure. Both specimens are found in the drift of Ann Arbor.

DIPHYPHYLLUM SIMCOENSE, Billings.

Synon., Eridophyllum Simcoense, Billings.

Diphyphyllum stramineum, Billings.

Colonies of cylindrical, subparallel, straight or flexuose stems, closely aggregated or more distant from each other, varying in different specimens, in diameter, from three to six millimeters. Surface longitudinally ribbed and annulated by wrinkles of growth. The stems laterally connect by slender transverse processes, similar to the transverse tubules of Syringopora—not, however, making communication between the visceral cavities, as in those, but merely fastening externally to the walls for mutual support, according to the necessity; in some places these are numerous and crowded, in others considerably distant. Calyces deep, with erect sides and slightly dilating margins, surrounded by about forty crenulated lamellæ of equal size near the margins, but alternately longer and shorter in the bottom part of the calyces. In some specimens these are almost totally restricted to a narrow marginal cycle, and the centre is occupied by flat, broad diaphragms with depressed circumference; in other specimens the larger lamellæ extend nearly or completely to the centre, and intersect the diaphragms as continuous vertical leaves. The same specimens often exhibit tubes with both variations of structure, plainly demonstrating how little importance can be placed in some cases on the degree in development and extension of the vertical crests. The interlamellar interstices of the peripheral area are traversed by vesiculose plates; the central area, principally formed by transverse diaphragms, is not defined from the peripheral cycle by an internal wall. Gemmation calycinal, producing single forked branches or a number of young calyces sprouting at once from the end cells. Occurs in the upper Helderberg limestone of Mackinac, and in the corniferous strata of Canada, New York, Ohio, and in the Western States; likewise found frequently in the drift of the Lower Peninsula.

Plate XLVI., Upper tier.—The left-hand figure represents a specimen found in the drift, with tubes smaller than usual; it is in all probability identical with *Diphyphyllum stramineum*, Billings. The two lower figures are different views of one specimen with larger tubes, agreeing with the type form of Eridophyllum Simcoense, described by Billings. It was found in the corniferous limestone of Caledonia, N. Y.

DIPHYPHYLLUM RECTISEPTATUM, N. SP.

Cylindrical, closely aggregated, subflexuose stems, from five to seven millimeters in diameter. Calyces with erect, vertically ascending side walls, and a broad bottom formed by flat diaphragms depressed in their circumference and smooth in the centre. Lamellæ stout, alternating in size, not crenulated, about thirty-six in the circumference of a calyx; the larger ones extend over the marginal parts of the diaphragms. Diaphragms remarkably regular, extending nearly across the entire width of the stems, meeting near the outer walls with a very narrow peripheral cycle of more minutely cellulose structure, formed by intersection of the interlamellar spaces with ascending rows of small, transverse, vesiculose plates. The species has much resemblance to Diphyphyllum latiseptatum of McCoy. Occurs in the lowest horizon of the Hamilton group, near Craford's quarry, at Middle Island, Presque Isle Lighthouse, etc. Not figured.

DIPHYPHYLLUM PANICUM.

Synon., CYATHOPHYLLUM PANICUM, Winchell.

Large colonies of diverging, partially contiguous cylindrical stems of about one centimeter in diameter, multiplying by prolific calycinal gemmation. Stems longitudinally striate and transversely wrinkled by lines of growth, and, periodically, by deeper inciding constrictions. Calyces deep, with steep side walls and slightly expanded margins. Bottom of calyces occupying about one third of the diameter of the stems, formed of vesiculose compound diaphragms, which are only in their peripheral circumference intersected by vertical lamellæ. Lamellæ crenulated at the edges and decorated on the sides with arched carinæ, from forty to fifty in the circumference of a calyx. Peripheral area filled with small interlamellar vesicles; the two areas are not defined from each other by an intervening wall. Found in the upper part of the Hamilton group, in the lime quarries near Petosky, and on Little Traverse Bay.

Plate XLVII., Fig. 3.—Two fragments, one exhibiting a vertical section through the stems, the other giving the exterior surface of the stems.

DIPHYPHYLLUM GIGAS, N. SP.

Large cylindrical stems, sometimes over one inch in diameter, growing in cespitose colonies, and multiplying by prolific calycinal gemmation of the stems. Surface covered with annular wrinkles, by which the stems attach themselves to one another. Longitudinal septal striæ very distinct. Calyces deep, with steep side walls and gently expanded margins, surrounded by about eighty subequal lamellæ crenulated at the edges by the development of arched lateral carinæ. Interlamellar interstices of the outer area filled with small, transverse, vesiculose plates. Bottom of calyces formed by flat diaphragms, smooth in the centre, and intersected in the circumference by the vertical lamellæ; no defining walls between the outer and inner area. Found in association with fossils of the corniferous limestone, in the drift deposits of Michigan.

Plate XLVI., Upper tier, right-hand figure.—Diphyphyllum (Eridophyllum) Verneuilli, a species with stems intermediate in size between this form and Diphyphyllum Simcoense, is likewise not uncommon in the drift boulders belonging to the corniferous limestone formation. Its central area, formed of smooth transverse diaphragms, is defined from the peripheral cycle by an internal wall, more or less distinctly developed. Not figured.

DIPHYPHYLLUM ARCHIACI, Billings.

Synon., Eridophyllum strictum (?) Milne-Edwards.

Cylindrical stems, multiplying by calycinal gemmation, with a diameter of from one to two centimeters, transversely wrinkled by fine striæ of growth and longitudinally ribbed by septal rugæ; in some specimens the stems are articulated by abrupt constrictions, and moderately distant; in others the growth is more uniform and the stems are in closer approximation, partly touching with their sides. Calyces generally bell-shaped, with steep sides and gently dilating margins; sometimes more shallow and of expanded form. Lamellæ crenulated by the ends of the arched carinæ decorating their sides, fifty to sixty in the circumference of a calyx, subequal near the margins, but alternately longer and shorter; the longer ones abut against a narrow inner wall formed like a horseshoe, which incloses flat transverse diaphragms; the aperture of the horseshoe is coincident with the principal septal gap. The interstices of the peripheral cycle of lamellæ are divided into small cellulose spaces by transverse vesiculose plates. Occurs in the upper Helderberg limestones of Michigan and Ohio, and in the Hamilton group of Thunder Bay; likewise in Bosanquet township, Canada. The specimens from different localities vary somewhat, but agree in general so well that a specific distinction can not be made with propriety. The Helderberg form, which I have identified with this species, is probably the same with Eridophyllum strictum, Milne-Edwards.

Plate XLVII., Upper tier.—The left-hand figure is a polished transverse section through a specimen from the upper Helderberg group, exhibiting the narrow horseshoe-shaped inner walls. The right-hand specimen, found in the same locality, exhibits a side view of the stems, interrupted by constrictions. The vertically intersected central stems have the narrow central area and the lateral carinations of the lamellæ well exposed. The right-hand figure in the lower tier of the same plate represents a cluster of stems found in the Hamilton group of Alpena, with well-preserved end cells.

DIPHYPHYLLUM COLLIGATUM.

HELIOPHYLLUM COLLIGATUM, Billings.

Colonies of subparallel stems of the structure of Diphyphyllum, with an internal narrow wall separating the outer finely cellulose from an inner transversely septate area. The growth of these colonies is entirely peculiar; the stems are regularly articulated by deep constrictions, in which constricted parts they are free. In alternation with these constrictions, the calyces become broadly expanded at certain levels, coincident in all the tubes of the colony, and join with their margins under polygonal outlines in a continuous floor of astræiform aspect. At a subsequent period the surface of the expanded calyces becomes covered up by an epithecal crust, and from the centre of each of the old calyces a new calyx grows with a contracted base, rapidly dilating above, in order to meet the others again in a common floor, which contractions and expansions follow each other in constant succession. The calyces are radiated by about fifty crenulated lamellæ, equal near the margins, but alternately longer and shorter on the sides of the calyces; the longer ones abut against the narrow inner wall. Found in the upper Helderberg limestones of Michigan, Canada, and at the Falls of the Ohio.

Plate XXXVIII.—Fig. 3 represents a side view of two silicified fragments from the drift of Ann Arbor.

PHILLIPSASTRÆA, D'ORBIGNY.

Synon., SMITHIA, Milne-Edwards.

Compound astræiform polyparia, with confluent calyces, destitute of intervening walls, but enveloped at the base of the colony by a common epithecal crust. Calyces horizontally expanded in their margins, excavated by an abrupt central pit, which is usually surrounded by an elevated monticulose rim. Radial lamellæ linear, carinated on the sides, and crenulated at the edges by the ends of the same carinations. Cycle of the lamellæ composed of alternately longer and shorter ones; the longer lamellæ unite in the centre, and form a pseudo-columellar, nodular protuberance, but do not connect into a continuous vertical axis. The shorter lamellæ terminate on the monticulose rim surrounding the central crateriform cell pit. Interlamellar interstices filled with transverse vesiculose plates, arranged in the peripheral area in arched rows crossing diagonally the direction of the lateral carinæ. The transverse septa of the centre are so much intersected by the centrally converging vertical lamellæ that the contrast in the structure of the outer area from that of the inner is very much weakened; the inclosed vesiculose interstitial cell spaces of the centre are somewhat coarser than the peripheral ones, but it is seldom that larger plates, comparable with continuous diaphragms, can be noticed. By the greater conspicuousness of these transverse plates in the centre, the genus Pachyphyllum is distinguished from Phillipsastræa; there are, however, so many gradations of transition between the two modifications of the otherwise perfectly identical types, that I consider their separation artificial and inappropriate.

PHILLIPSASTRÆA VERNEUILLI, MILNE-EDWARDS.

Size of corallites very different in various specimens. Distance from centre to centre of cell pits from one to one and a half centimeter. Diameter of the central pits varying from three to five millimeters. Number of lamellæ in the circumference of a cell from thirty-six to forty. Lamellæ linear within the inner cycle, and tent-shaped on the expanded peripheral portions of the calycinal confluent disks. Such tent-form is evidently not caused by any divergence of the two leaves composing the crests, but by the oblique lateral attachment of the interstitial vesicles to them. The crenulations of the edges of the lamellæ have the form of linear crossbars. The centre of the calyx bottom is raised into a columellar knot, and in vertical sections of calcified specimens a central string of greater density can be observed, but it is not a solid axal column ; in some specimens no indication of a columella is perceptible.

Grows in large discoid or convex masses, and is found frequently in the drift deposits of Michigan, associated with fossils of the corniferous limestone.

Plate XXXVIII.—Fig. 2 represents two silicified fragments found in the drift of Ann Arbor.

PHILLIPSASTRÆA GIGAS (?) OWEN.

PHILLIPSASTRÆA GIGAS, Billings.

Large lenticular masses covered by an epitheca on the lower side ; upper side formed by large confluent star cells perfectly resembling the smaller form, *Phillipsastræa Verneuilli.* The polyp cells are unequal, owing to the frequent intercalation of young calyces. The cells are not perfectly confluent with their horizontally explanate margins ; an obscure polygonal defining line indicates the extent of every individual calyx, but an intermediate wall is not developed. Diameter of the larger calyces over two centimeters ; diameter of inner cell pit not quite one centimeter. The circumference of the inner cell pit is raised into a rounded monticulose rim. Bottom of inner cell pit reversed into a small central boss, on which the lamellæ unite with a spiral twist. Circumference of cells radiated by from fifty to sixty crenulated lamellæ.

Found in the upper strata of the Island of Mackinac.

Plate XXXVII., Lower tier.—The left-hand figure presents a surface view of a calcified specimen from Mackinac. This form is in all particulars, except in the size of the calyces, similar to

Phillipsastræa Verneuilli, but the two forms are not found associated on Mackinac Island. It is doubtful to me whether Owen's species is identical with this form; the figures and descriptions given by him are insufficient to determine the question positively. Another large form of Phillipsastræa, for which I propose the name of *Phillipsastræa Yandelli*, is found in the Helderberg limestones of the Falls of the Ohio, and in silicified condition, often loose, in the drift of that vicinity. It differs from the described form in having much more spacious central cell pits, not surrounded by a raised rim. The bottom of the cells is formed by a large convex protuberance on which the lamellæ unite; diameter of cells from three to four centimeters; inner cell pit one and a half to two millimeters wide; exterior outlines of calyces obscurely defined. Not represented for want of space.

STROMBODES, Schweigger.

Compound polyparia, formed of radiated polyp cells united, without defining walls. The cells are either confluent, without any peripheral demarkation, or they join under obtusely crested polygonal outlines, which inclose shallow calycinal depressions with an abrupt central pit. The surface impressed with these pits forms a continuous laminar expansion, and the growth of the polyparia consists in a constantly repeated production of such laminæ; wherefore we find them formed of a superimposed series of such layers. The walls of the abrupt central depressions of the calyces, which correspond in the layers, combine by invagination into cylindrical central cores, extending, without interruption, through the whole length of the corallum; the crest-like plications in the circumference of the inner cell pits form a cycle of vertical lamellæ, which intersect this central core. The horizontally spreading marginal portions of the superimposed calyces are not in immediate contiguity; between each layer an interstice exists, which is filled with unequally interlaced, blister-like vesicles. This indicates a periodicity in the growth of the polyparia by which at one time fully finished, radially plicated, continuous laminar calyces were formed, and in time for the abandonment of the old cells and preparatory to the formation of a new layer, the old surface was covered by a coating of vesicles to serve as an under structure for the support of the new, carefully finished, calycinal floor. The radial plications of the calyces generally unite in the centre into a papillose projection ; in rare cases they die out before reaching the centre and leave a small naked spot within. The arrangement of the lamellæ into four fascicles and the development of a small septal fovea are not unfrequently noticeable in the bottom of the cells ; the steeply ascending sides of the inner pit are surrounded by crest-like plications, which grow stouter as they bend over upon the expanded marginal parts, and, in their course to the margin, repeatedly divide into narrow rounded rugæ, often five or six times more numerous than the crests of the cell pit from which they emanate. The division in this case is not conformable with the rule of intercalation of new lamellæ set forth in the introductory pages, but takes place apparently without any strict order. The plications of this expanded peripheral area are mere superficial rugæ, and do not combine into vertical lamellæ. In several species on each side of a radial ruga of the expanded calycinal surface, a row of punctiform, closely approximated pores opens, which are in alternating position on the two sides ; in perfectly intact surfaces these pores seem to be closed ; it is only in slightly worn specimens that they are open circular orifices.

STROMBODES PENTAGONUS, Goldfuss.

Strombodes striatus, D'Orbigny.

Large discoid expansions covered on the lower side with a concentrically wrinkled epitheca, and attached at the central apex. Surface of disks composed of irregularly polygonal, shallow calyces with an abrupt central depression. Diameter of the calyces very variable in different specimens, ranging from one to four centimeters. The steep walls of the inner cell pit are surrounded by about thirty stout, crest-like plications, which, reduced to a smaller number by coalescence, unite in the centre, and form there a styliform protuberance; or the bottom of the cell remains even while crossed by the carinæ. On the expanded marginal portion of the calyces the plications lose their crest form and are reduced to rounded rugæ, which, through division or through the implantation of new ones between them, multiply to three or four times their original number, and have then the form of equal, narrow, linear stripes. On both sides of each of these stripes a row of circular pores opens with closely crowded orifices alternating in position on the opposite sides. In some specimens the inner cell pits are surrounded by a monticulose raised rim; in others the surface of the calyces is roughened by blisters without a distinct radial striation; these conditions represent the different stages in the growth of the coral which it undergoes previous to the deposition of a new well-finished calycinal floor. The great difference in the size of the calyces of some specimens has induced D'Orbigny to distinguish the larger-celled form, as *Strombodes striatus*, from the smaller-celled *Strombodes pentagonus* of Goldfuss, but it is impossible to draw a dividing line between them; all gradations of sizes, from the large to the small forms, can be found associated in the same localities, and in structure not the least difference exists between them.

Occurs very abundantly in the Niagara group of Point Detour, Drummond's Island, etc., and frequently found in the drift.

Plate XLVIII.—Fig. 1 is a silicified specimen corresponding with Strombodes striatus, D'Orbigny. Fig. 2 represents the typical form of Goldfuss's species, Strombodes pentagonus.

The Niagara group of Kentucky and Indiana incloses an abundance of specimens, which appear to be in every respect identical with the above-described species, but I observe that the interstitial layers of vesicles in the specimens from Michigan are always of much coarser structure than in the specimens found at Louisville, etc.

STROMBODES PYGMÆUS, N. SP.

Calyces not defined, composing laminar surfaces dotted with abrupt cell pits, about two millimeters in width, and distant from each other six or eight millimeters. The broad interstitial surface is striate by the diverging radial rugæ of the cell cups, which meet and intermingle with those of the adjoining cells. The radial striæ are bordered on both sides by a row of circular pores as in the former species. In the centre of the pits the uniting radial crests form a small styliform projection.

Found in association with the other species in the Niagara group of Drummond's Island and of Point Detour.

Plate XLVIII.—Fig. 3, silicified specimen from Point Detour, Lake Huron.

STROMBODES MAMILLATUS, D. DALE OWEN.

Centre of calyces rising from a common interstitial surface as high, mamiform cones, excavated at the top by a crater-like, radiated pit. The radial rugæ extend over the surface of the cones and across the interstitial surface from one cell into the other, as narrow, equal-sized bands of granulose surface. In the interstices between these bands distant depressions can be noticed, but nothing similar to the rows of circular pores bordering the rugæ of the other species. The centre of the cell pits is formed by a small styliform projection. General structure as in the other species; composed of alternating layers of well-finished cup membranes, and of strata of vesicles. The size of the mamiform cones and their relative distance differ in various specimens. Width of cell pits from four to five millimeters. Distance from centre to centre from one to two centimeters. Found in the Niagara group of Drummond's Island; it is also common in the same formation in Iowa, Kentucky, Indiana, etc.

Plate XLVIII.—Fig. 4, silicified specimen form Point Detour.

STROMBODES ALPENENSIS, N. SP.

Massive horizontal expansions, covered on the lower side by an epithecal crust. Surface formed of shallow calyces, deepening in the centre into a more abrupt pit. The calyces are confluent, or imperfectly defined from each other by tent-shaped, obtuse ridges circumscribing irregularly polygonal spaces. Radial plications from thirty to forty, linear, crest-like in the circumference of the inner pits, and uniting in the centre into a twisted knot or without forming any protuberance. The crest-like plications, while diverging across the expanded peripheral cup margins, gradually widen into convex bands, separated by narrow linear furrows; their surface is ornamented with densely crowded granulations. The diameter of the calyces is very unequal in the same specimens; some of them are three centimeters wide, others only one. The internal structure of the specimens I could never distinctly observe; all the specimens are transformed into a solid white amorphous mass of carbonate of lime, resembling ivory or porcelain in a fracture, while other corals associated with them had their most delicate details of structure perfectly preserved, excepting one other heretofore described (Chonophyllum ponderosum), which is found in similarly solidified condition.

It is found in the light-colored limestones of the Hamilton group, forming the lowest beds in the quarries of Phelps' lime-kilns, near Alpena, and in a similar rock near Broadwell's mills, on Thunder Bay River.

Plate XXXVIII.—Fig. 1 is a calcified specimen from Broadwell's mills, in natural size.

In the Hamilton group of Rockford, Iowa, a coral is found which bears an almost perfect similarity to the form just described, exhibiting a well-preserved structure, consisting of membraniform layers of confluent radiated cell cups, interlaminated with strata of coarse, blister-like vesicles, entirely conformable with the structure of a Strombodes from the Niagara group. The lamellæ unite in the depressed central pits in a low obtuse boss. Mr. Hall has described this coral under the name of Smithia Johnnai, and another similarly built form as Smithia multiradiata, but they differ altogether in structure from the genus Smithia, or, what I consider as the same thing, from Phillipsastræa. The latter genus has the structure of the usual forms of the compound Cyathophylla, differing from them only by the absence of walls separating the single cell cups, while the specimens under consideration are built according to the plan of Strombodes; and, guided by perfect external similarity, I also identify the structureless specimens found in Michigan, with Strombodes.

VESICULARIA, N. GENUS.

Compound polyparia formed of a superimposed series of calycinal cups, of coarsely blistered surface, which in vertical sections appear as a uniform succession of layers of large, unequal, vesiculose plates, perfectly resembling a vertical section through a Cystiphyllum. These blistered calycinal membranous layers are radiated by plications, which are linear low crests in the circumference of an inner, broad, shallow cell pit, the bottom of which is occupied by a flat diaphragm, over which the crests converge toward the centre, gradually vanishing. The margins of the cells are broad, expanded, and confluent with each other, without demarkation. The radial plications lose, in their divergence across them, the crested form, and expand into flattened, gradually widening bands, as in Chonophyllum.

The crest-like portion of the plications in the circumference of the inner cell pit forms, by combination with the invaginated series of cups, a narrow cycle of vertical crests surrounding an inner core formed of diaphragms. In the outer area no trace of continuous vertical leaves is noticeable. Vesicularia is closely related with Strombodes; it differs from it in its broad calycinal bottoms having the shape of diaphragms, and in a prevailing disposition of all the calycinal layers to a vesiculose blistered structure, which in the other genus is only periodically so, and alternates with homogeneously formed laminar layers of more highly finished surface. From Chonophyllum it is likewise distinguished by the vesiculose structure of the superimposed cup walls; from Cystiphyllum it only differs in having a compound mode of growth with confluent cells.

VESICULARIA MAJOR, N. SP.

Discoid expansions formed of large confluent polyp cells. Calyces shallow, explanate, with a broad, dish-shaped central pit, the bottom of which is formed by a flat diaphragm. Radial plications linear, crest-shaped in the circumference of the inner pit, and extending over the surface of the diaphragms, gradually vanishing near the centre. In their divergence across the expanded marginal parts, the plications lose the crest form and dilate into low, rounded, gradually widening rugæ with intermediate linear furrows. The surface of the expanded parts of the calyces is raised into blisters, locally densely crowded, and obscuring the radial folds; in other parts singly dispersed. The central diaphragms are simple and not blistered. In vertical sections the polyparia fully resemble a Cystiphyllum, being composed of layers of coarse, unequal, interlaced vesicles. The calyces attain in some specimens a diameter of from three to four inches. Found in the Niagara group, at Point Detour, and on Drummond's Island.

Plate XLIX., right-hand figure, upper row.—In the Niagara group of Masonville, Iowa, another species of more minutely vesiculose structure occurs, which I have named *Vesicularia minor*, and represented, for sake of comparison, on the same plate with the other. The plications are very delicate, ornamented with spinulose projections; the cell pits, scarcely depressed, are only perceptible by the convergence of the plications toward certain centres. Under side of the expansions covered by a concentrically wrinkled epitheca, with radiciform excrescences for attachment to foreign bodies. Associated with these compound specimens are single polyp cells of the same vesiculose structure, which connect the compound forms so closely with Cystiphyllum, that it would have been more appropriate, perhaps, instead of establishing a new subgenus *Vesicularia*, to change Milne-Edwards' original definition of Cystiphyllum so as to include the compound forms with confluent cell cups.

VESICULARIA VARIOLOSA, N. SP.

Confluent calyces forming mamiform monticules, truncate by abrupt but shallow cell pits, the bottoms of which are formed by flat diaphragms with marginal depressions indicating the principal septal fascicles. Distance from centre to centre of the monticulose calyces about two centimeters; diameter of terminal cell pits about five millimeters. Calyces surrounded by about thirty plications, having the form of low crests in the inner circumference of the pits, but of rounded rugose form in their extension across the interstices, and on the sloping sides of the monticules. The surface of the polyparia is generally raised into irregular large blisters, which impair the distinctness and continuity of the radial plications. In vertical sections layers of interlaced coarse vesicles are found to constitute the whole polyparium.

Occurs in the Niagara group of Point Detour, and also in Iowa localities. This form is easily mistaken for Strombodes mamillatus, Owen, which occurs in its association. The well-developed flat diaphragms and entirely vesiculose structure distinguish it, however, from the latter.

Plate XLIX.—Fig. 4 represents a surface view of a silicified specimen from Point Detour.

CYSTIPHYLLUM, MILNE-EDWARDS.

Simple or loosely aggregated polyp cells, of conical or cylindrical form, enveloped by an epithecal wall, composed of an invaginated series of cell cups of compound vesiculose structure, and radiated by plications. The plications are either crest-like within the ascending part of the calyces, and dilating into flattened broader rugæ toward the peripheral margins, or are represented merely by superficial linear striæ or rows of spinules; they often become totally obsolete, and the surface of the calyces appears simply blistered, without any visible radiation; in no case do the plications combine into vertical laminæ pervading the whole length of the corallum. The arrangement of the plications into four principal fascicles is in some of the specimens very distinct. The inner area of the polyp cells is rarely intersected by transverse diaphragms; generally the central vesicles are somewhat coarser than the peripheral ones, but without demarkation between the bottom part of the calyces and the sides as in Cyathophyllum. The exterior epithecal wall is in many specimens longitudinally ribbed by well-pronounced septal striæ, while the vesiculose internal surface of the calyces may exhibit but very indistinct radial plications.

CYSTIPHYLLUM NIAGARENSE.

CONOPHYLLUM NIAGARENSE, Hall.

Conical polyp cells attached to other bodies at the base, and by additional root-like prolongations from the sides. Stems elongated, subcylindrical, or shorter turbinate, annulated by superficial constrictions with tortuous flexions, or by periodical total interruptions in the growth of a calyx, and the formation of a new cell from within. The calyces are moderately deep, uniformly spreading from an obtusely angustated bottom; margins erect; their surface is blistered, and is radially striate by spinulose crests, developed in some specimens with more distinctness than in others. The surface of the polyp stems in well-preserved condition is longitudinally ribbed by septal striæ, but it often happens that the outer walls are destroyed, and that the stems are of rough exfoliated aspect, exhibiting the concave side of the blisters composing the cell cups, and the free edges of the single invaginated cups composing the stems.

Found in the Niagara group of Drummond's Island, at Point Detour; likewise in the Niagara group of Kentucky, Iowa, and Indiana.

Plate XLIX.—Fig. 3 represents several silicified specimens of shorter turbinate and of more elongate tortuous form. The upper right-hand and the lower left-hand specimens are found at Drummond's Island; the other two at Masonville, Iowa.

CYSTIPHYLLUM AMERICANUM, MILNE-EDWARDS.

Single polyparia, surrounded by a perfect, concentrically wrinkled epithecal wall, of conical, or, in the progress of growth, of horn-shaped, curved, or straight cylindrical form. Dimensions of stems very variable, from one to two inches in diameter, and in specimens of cylindrical growth not unfrequently over one foot in length; other specimens have a much shorter turbinate form. Calyces moderately deep, with explanate margins, equally tapering toward the bottom, which is generally occupied by a few irregular blisters. The ascending calyx walls are sometimes only slightly blistered, and folded into stout radial rugæ. In other specimens the rugæ are obsolete and the blisters principally obvious. A great many variations in mode of growth, in the relative size of the vesicles, and in distinctness of plications, can be observed among the numerous specimens found in the Helderberg group and in the Hamilton strata, which, upon closer investigation, may require to be separated into different species, but for the present I have not discovered any well-established characters upon which such a division could be based.

It occurs nearly in every stratum of the upper Helderberg group and of the Hamilton group in Michigan, Canada, New York, and in the Western States.

Plate L., Upper tier.—The outer left-hand specimen is from the Hamilton group near Broadwell's mills, on Thunder Bay River; the two other specimens are from the Hamilton group of Widder, C. W. The right-hand figure (Fig. 4) in the lower tier represents silicified specimens from the corniferous limestone found in the drift.

CYSTIPHYLLUM AGGREGATUM, Billings.

Conico-cylindrical polyparia, closely aggregated, and attached to each other by the wrinkles of their surface, multiplying by calycinal gemmation. Diameter of stems from two to three centimeters. Structure conformable with Cystiphyllum; vesicles coarse; end cups moderately excavated, blistered, with faint, spinulose, radiating striæ. Epithecal walls likewise faintly ribbed by septal rugæ. Found in large clusters in the Hamilton group of Thunder Bay. Not figured.

CYSTIPHYLLUM SULCATUM, Billings.

Symmetrically curved, conical polyparia with a pointed apex. Surface gently annulated by obtuse wrinkles of growth. Calyces spacious, oblique to the axis, with erect acute margins. The surface of the calyces generally forms a continuous laminar bag without a blistered surface; the marginal part of the cups is radiated by rounded rugæ, broadest near the edges of the cups, narrowing and almost vanishing near the bottom. The arrangement of the plications into four fascicles with intermediate gaps is in this species particularly plain, and the apertural gap situated in the centre of the large curvature of the horn-shaped cells is the largest. In vertical sections the structure is found to be perfectly conformable with Cystiphyllum, composed of incased vesiculose cups. There are two varieties: in one the plications expand toward the margin of the cups into broad bands decorated with granulations; in the other form the plicæ split toward the margin into narrower fine striæ. The latter variety, which has also less obliquely erect cups, is found in the upper Helderberg limestones of the Falls of the Ohio; the other is found in the drift of Ann Arbor, on Mackinac Island, and in the corniferous limestone of Port Colborne, in Canada.

Plate L., Lower tier.—The left-hand figure (Fig. 3) represents silicified specimens from Port Colborne. Various other forms of the genus Cystiphyllum occur at the Falls of the Ohio, and at Columbus, Ohio, which I omit to describe, as not found in Michigan.

ZAPHRENTIS, Rafinesque.

Inclusive of Streptelasma, *Hall, as a sub-generic form.*

Simple conical polyparia, composed of a series of invaginated, radially plicated cell cups. The superimposed cell cups are with their side walls so intimately united, that no interstice is left between them, and all combine into one simple compact wall folded into laminar plications. The interstices between the plications are, within the terminal cups, free and open throughout. The plications of all the incased cups are connected into continuous, strong vertical leaves intersecting the whole length of the corallum. The bottom part of each cup remains free, and is separated from the subjacent one by a small interstice. It appears in vertical sections through the corallum as a transverse laminar diaphragm. These superimposed diaphragms extend from wall to wall; their peripheral margins are deflected and connect with the outer wall at an acute, downwardly directed angle. The interlamellar interstices, which are open in the end cell, become, below its bottom, intersected by the diaphragms, and are divided into coarse cellulose chambers, which must not be confused with the smaller interstitial cell spaces of the outer area in a Cyathophyllum. The latter are formed by rows of small vesiculose plates traversing the interstices in arches, ascending from the inner circumference of the diaphragms to the outer walls of the polyparium, within the end cup as well as below it. The transverse interstitial plates which make part of the diaphragms invariably approach the outer walls in a downwardly instead of an upwardly directed curve. The arrangement of the lamellæ into four fascicles is, in Zaphrentis, generally well marked, and a largely developed septal fovea in the interstice between the two apertural fascicles is considered as the leading distinctive character of the genus Zaphrentis.

The importance of the development of a septal fovea in Cyathophylloid corals has been unreasonably overestimated by Milne-Edwards. In his work on palæozoic corals, he describes twenty-nine species of Zaphrentis, simply guided by the presence of a large septal fovea, in disregard of other structural peculiarities. Fully half of these forms, named Zaphrentis, have not the structure of Zaphrentis, and belong to the true Cyathophylla, by reason of the development of transverse vesiculose plates in the interlamellar interstices of the end cups, which, as has been stated before, never occur in the interstices of the lamellæ of a Zaphrentis. As examples of Cyathophylla, so misplaced, I mention Zaphrentis cornicula, Zaphr. Guerangeri, Zaphr. excavata, Zaphr. Michelini, etc. The genus *Streptelasma*, of Hall, and his *Polydilasma*, which I consider as the same thing, differ from Zaphrentis merely in having a less conspicuous, or, sometimes, almost obsolete development of a septal fovea, and in the irregular entanglement of its radial lamellæ in the centre, constituting, in combination with the intersected diaphragms, a spongioso-cellulose pseudo-columella; or, at least, the regularity of the diaphragms in the centre is obscured by their multiple labyrinthical intersection with the vertical leaves. A strict distinction of the two genera is not possible; some forms of this group could with the same propriety be placed in one as in the other.

The Cyathophylloid corals of the lower Silurian strata generally have the structure of Streptelasma, and, considering Streptelasma as a subgenus of Zaphrentis, I begin with the description of its species first as being the oldest ones of the type, and let those of Zaphrentis follow them.

STREPTELASMA CORNICULUM, HALL.

The original specimens represented and described by Hall, from the Trenton strata of New York, are too imperfect to allow much more than recognition of the general structure. Similar and no better preserved specimens are found in the Trenton strata of Escanaba River, and on St. Joseph's Island and Sulphur Island, situated north of the other. I have represented them on Plate LI., the four left-hand figures in the upper row; the upper larger specimen is from the lower Trenton strata of Escanaba; the three lower specimens are from somewhat higher beds on Sulphur Island.

It is doubtful whether the specimens described under the same name by Milne-Edwards, from the Hudson River group, belong to the same species; they are found in much better preservation, and can therefore be more specifically described. Elongate conical, symmetrically curved, horn-shaped corals; middle-sized specimens have a diameter of about three centimeters at the calyx margin by a length of from seven to eight centimeters, but the proportion between length and width of the specimens differs; some are more elongated, others are shorter than the indicated proportions. The surface of the polyparia is covered by a perfect epithecal crust, with transverse fine wrinkles of growth, and longitudinally striate by septal rugæ and intermediate furrows. Milne-Edwards asserts the cells to be covered by an *imperfectly* developed epithecal crust, but this is an error. Calyces moderately deep, with erect acute margins, steeply inclined side walls, and a variably formed bottom, sometimes narrowed into a blunt end; at other times broader, rounded, convex in the middle. Lamellæ linear, stout, alternately larger and smaller, from 20 to 130 in the circumference of calyces, three centimeters wide. Their surface is decorated by minute granulose rugæ, crossing the side faces in an ascending direction from the inside toward the periphery. The radial crests become labyrinthically entangled in the centre of the cells, and usually form a broad convex protuberance. A small septal fovea is always noticeable, and sometimes also the lateral septal gaps are well marked. In vertical sections the centre of the polyparia is found to be intersected by well-developed transverse diaphragms; the vertical crests intersecting them divide the interstices between them into irregular cell spaces. The apices of the polyparia are pointed, and rarely exhibit a small scar of attachment. Sometimes twin cells are found, but this is abnormal.

Plate LI., Upper tier.—The largest specimen is from the Hudson River group of Drummond's Island; the other six, smaller specimens, were found at Richmond, Indiana, and at Madison. The right-hand calyces have broad convex cup bottoms with irregularly entangled lamellæ; the two upper figures to the left of the larger have a well-developed septal fovea, and a narrow, styliform, central protuberance. The lower left-hand specimen is a twin-cell.

STREPTELASMA PATULA, N. SP.

POLYDILASMA, Hall.

Short conical polyparia, about two centimeters wide at the expanded calyx margins, by a length of only one or one and a half centimeter. Calyx variable in depth in accordance with the more elongate or shortened external form of the polyp cells, surrounded by from twenty-five to thirty stout lamellar crests, with as many smaller intermediate ones, confined only to the marginal portions of the calyces. The sides of the lamellæ are transversely striate, and their edges crenulated. By the convergence of the lamellæ in the centre, a narrow columellar axis of spongiose structure is formed, which on one side is deeply exsinuated by a septal fovea; in very young specimens this axis is a horseshoe-formed erect leaf, against the circumference of which the converging lamellæ abut; the centre of the horseshoe sinus is occupied by a strong lamella.

Found in the Niagara group of Drummond's Island and Point Detour; also in the Niagara limestones of Iowa, at Masonville.

Plate XXXIX.—Fig. 1 represents a number of silicified specimens found at Drummond's Island.

STREPTELASMA CONULUS, N. SP.

Straight, conical, small-sized polyparia; the larger ones attain a diameter of one centimeter by one and a half in length; surface faintly annulated by lines of growth, not ribbed longitudinally as in the similar form Streptelasma calycula. Calyces deep, with erect margins surrounded by from twenty to twenty-five denticulated lamellar crests of larger size, and by as many intermediate rudimentary ones with likewise dentate edges; the sides of the lamellæ are ornamented with transverse rugæ. The larger lamellæ unite in the centre, as in the former species, into a horseshoe-formed cycle which incloses a narrow core of lacunose, irregularly anastomosing cell spaces; the aperture of the horseshoe corresponds with the principal septal fovea.

Found associated with the former in the Niagara group of Drummond's Island, etc.

Plate XXXIX.—Fig. 4 represents a number of silicified specimens from the above-named locality.

STREPTELASMA SPONGAXIS, N. SP.

POLYDILASMA, Hall.

Small, conical, horn-shaped polyparia, about two centimeters wide by three in length in middle-sized specimens. Calyces moderately deep, with slanting sides and slightly expanding margins, surrounded by about thirty stout crests alternating with as many intermediate smaller ones. Surface of lamellæ decorated with granules and transverse rugæ. The lamellæ unite in the centre into a spongiose axal core, resembling the tissue of a macerated porous bone. Septal fovea obscure. The apices of the cells exhibit generally a strong sublateral scar of attachment.

Found associated with the other forms in the Niagara group of Drummond's Island, and at Point Detour; also found at Masonville, Iowa.

Plate XXXIX., Fig. 2.—All the smaller specimens represent the usual form as it occurs at Point Detour. The larger specimen is from the Niagara group of Paul's Station, Indiana; it does not seem to differ much from the smaller specimens except by a central compressed cristiform projection similar to the columella of Cyathaxonia, which is broken in the represented specimen, but is distinctly developed in other specimens found there and at Louisville. I hesitate therefore to identify the larger specimen with the smaller form. The subsequently described species have all a well-developed septal fovea, and are considered to represent the genus *Zaphrentis* proper.

ZAPHRENTIS STOCKESII, MILNE-EDWARDS.

Symmetrically curved conical polyparia, sometimes elliptical in outlines by a compression in a direction transverse to the curvature. Length of cones about twice the diameter of the calyces, which in middle-sized specimens is about four centimeters. Calyces moderately deep, with erect margins and a spacious subconvex bottom, on which the lamellæ unite in an irregularly twisted, interlacing manner as low carinæ. Lamellæ linear, stout; sixty to sixty-five larger ones alternating with as many small rudimentary crests may be counted in the circumference of calyces four centimeters wide. A large septal fovea is situated in the median line of the convex side of the curved polyparia. Transverse diaphragms well developed; the crests on the upper side do not connect into continuous vertical leaves with those of the succumbent cups; the lower side of the diaphragms is generally smooth, not crested The external walls of the specimens are rarely preserved in the silicified condition, and the excoriated surface is longitudinally ribbed by the exposed vertical plications. In some specimens, however, the superficial epithecal crust is perfectly preserved. Found in the Niagara group of Drummond's Island, Point Detour, and in the same formation at Masonville, Iowa.

Plate LI., Lower tier—The two largest specimens. The upper one, on the left-hand side, is a side view of an excoriated specimen from Point Detour. The one on the right-hand side of the plate exhibits the bottom of a calyx and the position of the septal fovea; the erect marginal parts are broken off. The second figure from the left, in the lower tier, is also a young specimen of this kind.

ZAPHRENTIS UMBONATA, N. Sp.

Conical, horn-shaped polyparia resembling Zaphr. Stockesii, attaining in some larger specimens a calyx diameter of eight centimeters by twice that in length; the usual size of the specimens found is smaller. Calyces spacious, with erect acute margins and a broad bottom, which is reversed into a large, laterally compressed, prominent cone. The circumference of the larger calyces is surrounded by about eighty large lamellæ, with as many intermediate smaller ones; the larger ones unite on the central cone, ascending its sides directly or with a spiral twist. A large septal fovea is developed in the median line of the larger curved side. In vertical sections the invaginated, reversed, conical cell bottoms are observed to have grown together with their apices and to form a cellulose, pseudo-columella. Found associated with Zaphr. Stockesii in the Niagara group of Point Detour and Drummond's Island. Casts of a similar species are common in the Niagara limestones of Milwaukee. At Louisville, also, this coral occurs.

Plate LI., Lower tier.—The upper figure in the centre is one of the smaller-sized specimens found on Drummond's Island; another small specimen is represented in the lower right-hand corner of the plate. The central cone is in some specimens much more prominent than in those given here. In the lower row of the same plate the first outer specimen on the left-hand side and the third one represent other calyces of a Zaphrentis, conformable in some respects with the heretofore described associated forms, but differing in the shape of the cell bottom, which in one is formed by a large rounded protuberance, exsinuated on one side by a septal fovea, while in the other, evidently only an individual modification of the former, it is a horseshoe-formed elevated ring with a deeply depressed, smooth, central excavation. This form seems to constitute a different species from the others, but I leave the question open for further decision.

ZAPHRENTIS GIGANTEA, Lesueur.

Conico-cylindrical, horn-shaped polyparia, attaining in some specimens a size of two and a half feet in length, by a diameter of three inches. Some enlarge their diameter rapidly to a certain thickness, and then grow on in a uniformly cylindrical shape; others are in the young state, slender, flexuose, and irregularly constricted stems, and grow gradually to larger diameters. The surface of the polyparia is covered by an epitheca with shallow annular wrinkles of growth and longitudinally ribbed by septal striæ, which, however, are not in all specimens equally distinct. Calyces spacious, with erect walls, and acute, wedge-like margins; bottom broad, marginally depressed and flat in the centre. In one place of the circumference the diaphragms are more deeply depressed by a septal fovea. Radial lamellæ stout, linear, alternately long and short, but appearing nearly equal on the margins of the calyces, where the sharp crested leaves of the inside expand into low rounded rugæ. The extension of the radial crests toward the centre is subject to variations; in some the central part of the diaphragms remains smooth, and the crests are confined to their peripheral circumference; in others the crests reach as low carinæ to the centre and become irregularly entangled in their convergence, but these central portions of the crests are merely superficial, and do not intersect the diaphragms to form continuous vertical leaves. The number of lamellæ in calyces of about two and a half inches diameter is 150 to 160, half of which are of the smaller size. Found in the upper Helderberg limestones of Michigan, Canada, Ohio, and in the Western States.

Plate LII. represents specimens of smaller size, found at the Falls of the Ohio.

ZAPHRENTIS PROLIFICA, Billings.

Conical, irregularly curved polyp cells, obtusely wrinkled by annular rugæ. Middle-sized specimens about three or four centimeters wide at the calyx margin, by a length of from seven to eight centimeters. Calyces deep, spacious, with erect margins. Bottom of cells variable; most frequently its centre is reversed into a laterally compressed, more or less prominent cristiform projection, whose sides are carinated by the centrally uniting radial crests; in others the bottom is uniformly depressed convex, covered by the entangled converging ends of the lamellæ; sometimes also a flat smooth spot is left in the centre of the cell bottom, which merges into a large septal fovea. The septal fovea is, in its position, independent from the curvature of the polyp cells, but always represents the apertural fovea, whether it be in the median line of the curved cells or in lateral position. Lamellæ about 120 in the circumference of calyces three or four centimeters wide, alternately large and small. Near the calyx margin the plications have the form of low rounded rugæ with granulose surface; further inside of the calyces the rugæ transform into acute, stout, linear crests. In vertical sections the superimposed bottoms of the incased cell cups appear as large transverse diaphragms joining the outer walls with deeply deflected margins. Occurs frequently in the upper Helderberg limestones of Michigan, and in the neighboring States to the east and west; is also common in the drift boulders belonging to the corniferous limestone formation.

Plate LIII.—The upper row represents various silicified specimens, partly found in the drift of Ann Arbor, partly from the corniferous limestone of Port Colborne, C. W.

ZAPHRENTIS NODULOSA, N. SP.

Curved elongato-conical polyparia of somewhat flexuose growth, annulated by shallow constrictions and finer transverse wrinkles; vertically striate by septal furrows. The apicical portion of the polyp cells is decorated by densely crowded, stout, spinulose projections, which gradually vanish on the upper parts of the cells. Calyces deep, with erect margins; bottom formed by a narrow, almost smooth diaphragm deflected on one side into a large septal fovea. The lamellæ are sharp linear crests within the calyx; near the margins they become low rounded rugæ; about seventy in the circumference of calyces one inch in diameter, alternately of larger and smaller size. The sides of the lamellæ are decorated by irregular transverse rugæ and granulations.

Not uncommon in the drift of Michigan, in association with corniferous limestone fossils; also found in the corniferous strata of Canada.

Plate LV.—The right-hand side small specimen, in the lower tier, represents a rather small calyx found in the drift of Ann Arbor; other larger specimens dilate more rapidly, and resemble in mode of growth Zaphr. prolifica.

ZAPHRENTIS GREGARIA, N. SP.

Short turbinate, somewhat curved polyp cells, of about two inches calyx diameter by a length of from one and a half to two and a half inches. Surface annulated by sharp transverse wrinkles and distinctly ribbed by longitudinal septal furrows. Calyces spacious, with broad subplane bottoms, over which the lamellæ extend to the centres. A large septal fovea generally on the convex curved side. Side walls of calyces suberect with acute edges. Found in large numbers in the black shaly limestone strata of the lower part of the Hamilton group, on the shore of Lake Huron, north of Thunder Bay. Not represented.

Another form of Zaphrentis found in the Hamilton group of Arcona, C. W., may be mentioned here. Some of the specimens perfectly resemble Zaphrentis prolifica of the Helderberg group; other larger specimens, externally identical with them, have the bottoms of the calyces formed by broad, perfectly naked, flat, or somewhat concave diaphragms. They seem to be mere individual variations of one and the same type, first represented under the form of Zaphr. prolifica.

ZAPHRENTIS CONIGERA, N. SP.

Compare AULOPHYLLUM, Milne-Edwards.

Long, horn-shaped, conico-cylindrical polyparia, with obtusely annulated rugose surface, attaining a size of one foot in length by a diameter of one and a half inch. Calyx deep, with erect side walls and acute margins, surrounded by about 120 alternately larger and smaller lamellæ; sharp linear crests in the inside of the calyces, lowered into rounded rugæ on the margins. The bottom of the calyces is reflected and forms a large pointed cone with broad base, on which the central ends of the radial crests ascend with a spiral twist. Septal fovea comparatively small, irregular in position regarding the curvature of the horn-shaped stems. The central cones are the analogon of the transverse diaphragms, which are invaginated into one another, and become superficially attached by their crests, but do not combine into a continuous axal column. From an observation of the figures of Clisioph. prolapsum,

McCoy, called Aulophyllum by Milne-Edwards, I would suggest that a great similarity exists between them and the species under consideration; but Milne-Edwards asserts the development of an internal wall separating the inner area from the outer, of which in our specimens not the least trace can be observed. Found in the upper Helderberg limestones of Mackinac Island, and at the Falls of the Ohio.

Plate XL., Lower tier.—The central, shorter, conical specimen is from Mackinac Island. The other specimens are from the Falls of the Ohio. The latter are silicified; the first is in calcified condition.

ZAPHRENTIS EXIGUA.

Synon., HELIOPHYLLUM EXIGUUM, Billings.

Small, conical, oblique polyp cells, encircled by linear constrictions and intermediate broader rugæ. The curved conules are flattened on the longer side and quite convex on the shorter side of the curvature. Diameter of calyces one and a half centimeter in medium-sized specimens, two and a half in the largest ones; their length is about equal to their width, or a little longer. Calyces moderately deep, surrounded by about seventy alternately large and small lamellæ, denticulated at the edges and transversely carinated on the sides by granulose ridges. The lamellæ are very stout, protruding with the convexity of their edges above the margin of the outer peripheral walls of the cells. In the median line of the flattened longer side of the cells a conspicuous septal gap is developed, which extends to the centre, dilating into a small horseshoe-formed sinus around which the lamellæ are grouped. The centre of the septal gap is occupied by a single lamella, which directly connects with another coming from the opposite side. The lamellæ on both sides of the septal gap unite at their central ends in semi-pennate fascicles.

The interlamellar interstices are all free and open, whereby this form proves itself positively distinct from Cyathophyllum or Heliophyllum, under which name it has been described by Billings.

Occurs in the upper Helderberg limestones of Mackinac, and in the drift, associated with corniferous limestone fossils; it is also found in rare cases in the Hamilton group, at Broadwell's mills, on Thunder Bay River, while in the corniferous limestone of Canada, and at the Falls of the Ohio, it is quite common.

Plate LIII., Lower tier.—The six specimens in two vertical rows on the left side of the plate, and the lower one in the central row. The middle specimen in the second row is a calcified specimen from Mackinac; the next specimen below and the one in the central row are specimens from Crab Orchard, Kentucky. Of the remainder of the group, the two large specimens are found in the drift of Ann Arbor; the two smaller ones are from the Falls of the Ohio.

ZAPHRENTIS UNGULA, N. SP.

Conical, transversely compressed, and, in the direction of the compression, curved polyp cells, more flattened on the convex side of the curvature than on the opposite. Surface annulated by linear constrictions, with intermediate, broad, rounded rugæ; apex of polyparia pointed. Calyces moderately deep, gently expanded near the margins, gradually narrowing into an obtuse, transverse, central pit, which is joined by a septal fovea, situated in the median line of the flattened broader side. Lamellæ stout, subequal near the margins, but alternately long and short; the longer ones extend nearly to the centre; the bottom of the small central pit is usually free of crests. Dimensions of polyparia from two to three centimeters in transverse calyx diameter by a little more than half that measure in the opposite direction, and in length exceeding the greater width by about one fourth. Number of lamellæ in medium-sized specimens, about 90; in larger ones, 100. Found in the upper Helderberg group, at the Falls of the Ohio, and rarely in the drift of Michigan in silicified condition.

Plate LIII., Lower tier.—The two right-hand specimens; the lower one is about the largest size found.

ZAPHRENTIS COMPRESSA, N. SP.

Conical compressed polyp cells, straight, or curved in the direction of the narrow side. Large specimens have a calyx diameter of about eight centimeters in one direction, and four in the other, by a length of one decimeter. Calyces of that size are surrounded by 170 or 180 alternately small and large lamellæ, which are, within the cups, sharp linear crests, but become lower rounded rugæ on the margins of the cup walls. End cups deep, with erect, acute margins, of the shape of elongated troughs, gradually diminishing into a narrow bottom, one side of which is deeply depressed by a septal fovea situated on the median line of the longer diameter of the compressed calyces. The degree of compression is not in all specimens equally strong; some are very nearly flattened on the compressed sides, while others have a convex oval circumference. The surface of the polyparia is annulated by irregular rounded rugæ.

Found in the upper Helderberg limestones of the Falls of the Ohio. It resembles the former species, but is much larger, and is easily distinguished by the position of its septal fovea, which is on the narrow side, while that of the previous form is in the centre of the broader side.

Plate LIII., Lower tier.—The upper second figure from the right-hand side. I consider it desirable to give a figure and description of this form, not found in Michigan up to the present date, but in all probability to be discovered some day by industrious collectors.

Various other species of Zaphrentis, partly already known and described (Zaphrentis Rafinesqui, Milne-Edwards), partly new forms, are omitted from this report, as not found within the boundaries of the State of Michigan.

ZAPHRENTIS SPINULOSA (?) MILNE-EDWARDS.

Symmetrically curved, conical polyp cells, attaining a length of six centimeters by a calyx diameter of three centimeters. Calyces deep, with erect margins, surrounded by about forty-five stout lamellæ, and as many rudimentary intermediate folds near the margins of the calyces. A large septal fovea is developed on the concave side of the horn-shaped cells, and besides the two lateral septal gaps, are generally well marked in the specimens. The surface of the polyp cells is annulated by rings of growth, and the basal portion is decorated by stout spinules similar to those of Zaphr. spinulosa, Milne-Edwards. I have not seen any of the Western specimens with sufficiently well-preserved open calyces to enable me to establish their exact identification with the Michigan specimens.

Occurs in the carboniferous limestones of Saginaw Bay, on Point aux Grees, and on Charity Islands; likewise in the limestones of Bellevue, Eaton Co.

Plate LV., Lower tier.—The upper four central figures and the larger calyx to the left of them represent specimens found at Bellevue, Michigan.

AMPLEXUS, SOWERBY.

I can not find an appreciable difference between the genera Amplexus and Zaphrentis; both have the same general structure. The radial plications in Amplexus are said to be confined to the marginal parts of the polyp stems, and not to extend far across the central area, principally built up of transverse diaphragms. But it is not uncommon to see, in so-called specimens of Amplexus, the radial crests extending to the centre of the diaphragms, under the form of low superficial carinæ. On the other hand, it is equally common to notice genuine Zaphrentis forms in which the radial crests are confined to a peripheral cycle, and do not reach to the centre.

Amplexus generally grows in elongate cylindrical stems, while Zaphrentis has more of a conical mode of growth, but this is also a very vague difference; Zaphrentis frequently grows likewise in cylindrical stems, and among the associated forms of Zaphrentis gigantea, Zaphr. Rafinesqui, and Amplexus Yandelli, such a similarity in structure exists that fragments of stems of the three species are never distinguishable from each other with perfect security from mistakes. In some forms of Amplexus the septal fovea becomes obsolete, and in polyp stems where a septal fovea exists it is not as well marked in one part as in another. The genus Calophyllum, Dana, has been created to include these forms deprived of a septal fovea, but I consider such distinction superfluous.

AMPLEXUS SHUMARDI.

Synon., CYATHOPH. SHUMARDI, Milne-Edwards.

Articulated cylindrical polyp stems, composed of a succession of subconical segments, formed by periodical interruptions in the growth of the calyces, resulting in the closure of the marginal parts of the old cells by a continuation of the epithecal wall, and a renewed growth of a cell, having a narrower basis, from the inner circumference of the old one, until after a while a new contraction occurs. The surface of the stems is delicately cancellated by the intersection of the longitudinal septal rugæ with annular striæ of growth. The basal joint of the stems is of conical growth and exhibits a strong scar for attachment at the apex. The stems are composed of a cycle of vertical crests projecting from the wall into the cavity, and of a series of superimposed diaphragms intersecting the cavity of the stems and extending from wall to wall, joining it with strongly deflected margins, and only intersected by the vertical crests in the outer circumference. The end cells, which are generally only preserved in small young specimens, are of a dilated funnel shape, surrounded by from sixty to seventy alternately large and small lamellæ, with granulose surface and denticulated edges. The bottom of the calyces is generally formed by a smooth diaphragm, but sometimes the crests of the circumference extend over their surface to the centre as low superficial carinæ. The lamellæ lose their linear crested form on the edges of the calyces, where they expand into low rounded rugæ. On one side of the calyx the diaphragms are deeply depressed by a septal fovea, but the latter is not in all parts of the stems equally distinct, and becomes not unfrequently obsolete for a while. The average diameter of the stems is from two to three centimeters; the length of the joints varies from one to two centimeters.

Found in the Niagara group of Point Detour and Drummond's Island; at Masonville, Iowa; in Perry Co., Tennessee, etc.

Plate LIV., Upper tier.—The outer figure on the right-hand side of the plate is a stem from the original locality from which the species was first described (Perry Co., Tennessee); the three next fragments to the left of it are from the Niagara group of Drummond's Island; the other figures on the left are specimens from Masonville, Iowa. I find it strange that Milne-Edwards should connect this form with the genus Cyathophyllum, which has the most characteristic structure of an Amplexus.

AMPLEXUS YANDELLI, Milne-Edwards.

Conico-cylindrical flexuose stems, from two to four centimeters in diameter, annulated by fine wrinkles of growth with intermediate coarser rugæ, and frequently of a jointed structure through periodical constrictions of the calyces and continued growth of the stem without interruption of the continuity of the epithecal wall. Calyces deep, with erect margins, surrounded by about sixty alternately large and small vertical crests. The bottom of the calyces is formed by flat or warped diaphragms, depressed on one side by a deep septal fovea. The lamellæ are restricted to the outer circumference of the diaphragms, but sometimes they extend to the centre as superficial ridges.

Occurs in the corniferous limestone of Indiana, Kentucky, Canada, and is found in the drift deposits of Michigan. Some cylindrical stems, which evidently belong to the juvenile specimens of Zaphrentis gigantea, are so closely resembling Ampl. Yandelli, that I always find difficulty in distinguishing them.

Plate LIV., Lower tier.—The right-hand specimen is found in the drift of Ann Arbor; the others are from the Falls of the Ohio. The outer specimen on the left-hand side of the plate resembles considerably the basal portion of Zaphrentis gigantea. See Plate LII., base of large specimen.

INDEX.

PLATES.

Note.

The figures of the plates could not be numbered without great inconvenience to the printer, on which account I have adopted a rule applying to all, which I think will serve the purpose.

In all the text references the upper right-hand figure is 1 ; the upper left-hand figure is 2 ; the lower left-hand figure is 3, and the lower right-hand, 4. Some plates have several figures on each of their two or four principal divisions. In these cases, to save the reader from mistakes and confusion, I have been very explicit in my descriptions, in indicating the particular figure referred to.

PLATE I.

Fig. 1. HELIOLITES INTERSTINCTUS. Louisville, Niagara group.

2. ——— pyriformis. Drummond's Island, Niagara group.

3. ——— megastoma. " "

4. ——— subtubulatus. Upper specimen from Iowa; lower from Drummond's Island.

PLATE I

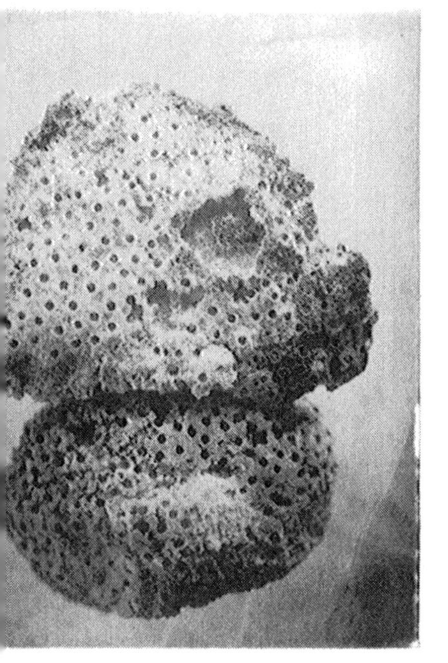

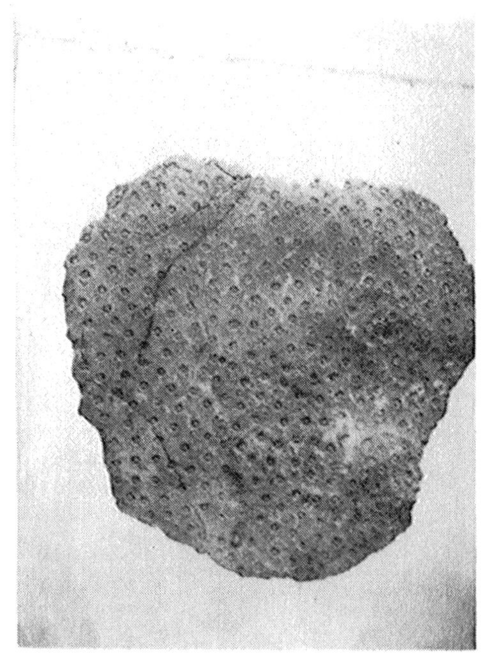

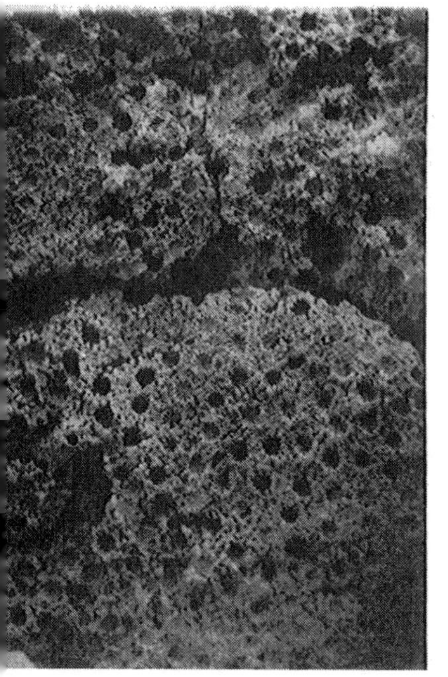

PLATE II.

Figs. 1 and 2. Lyellia Americana. Point Detour, Niagara group.

Fig. 3. ——— papillata. Point Detour, Niagara group.

4. ——— parvituba. Louisville, Ky.

PLATE III

PLATE III

Fig. 1. LYELLIA DECIPIENS. Point Detour, Niagara group.

2. PLASMOPORA FOLLIS. Upper figures, Niagara group, Indiana.

——— elegans. Lower figures, Niagara group, Indiana.

Figs. 3 and 4. HOUGHTONIA HURONICA. Hudson River group, Drummond's Island.

PLATE III

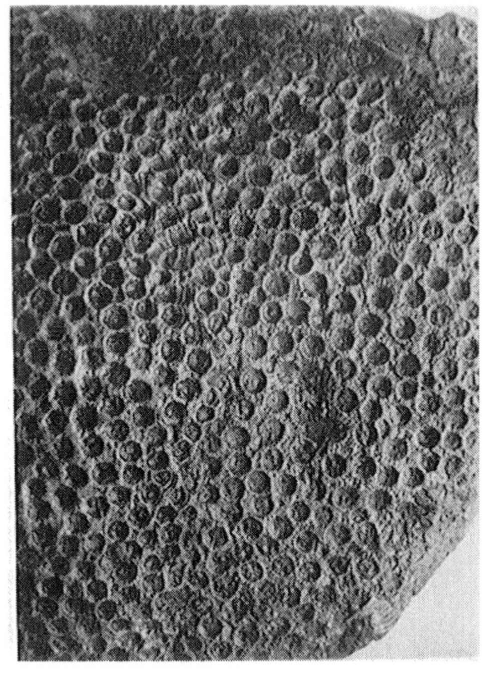

PLATE IV.

All *Favosites favosus*, from Drummond's Island, Niagara group.

PLATE IV

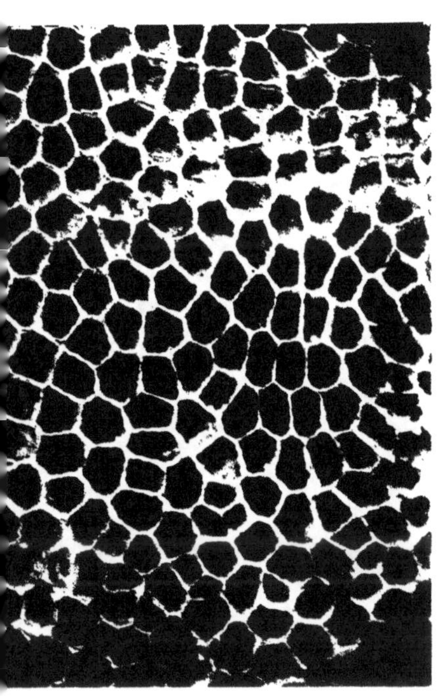

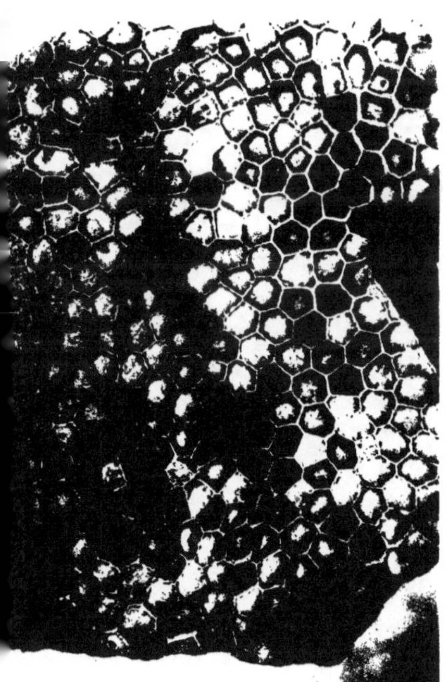

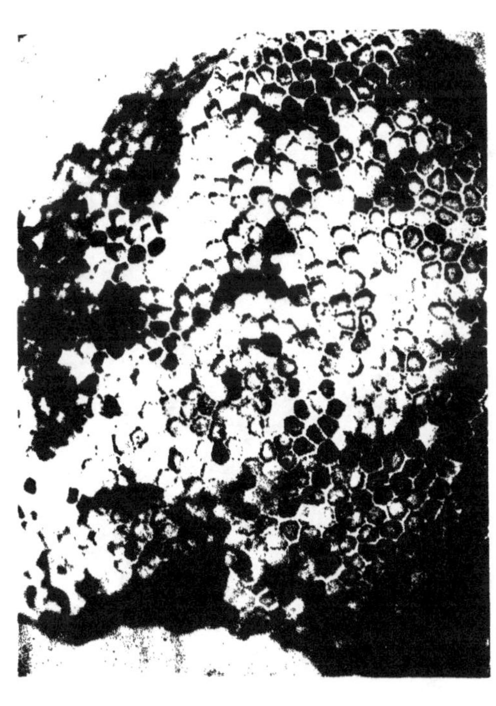

PLATE V.

Fig. 1. FAVOSITES NIAGARENSIS. Point Detour, Niagara group.

2. ——— favosus. Smallest variety. Drummond's Island.

3. ——— venustus. Drummond's Island, Niagara group.

4. ——— hispidus. " "

PLATE V

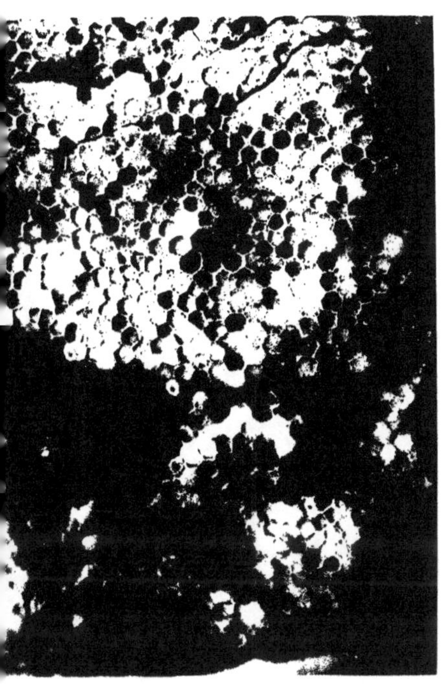

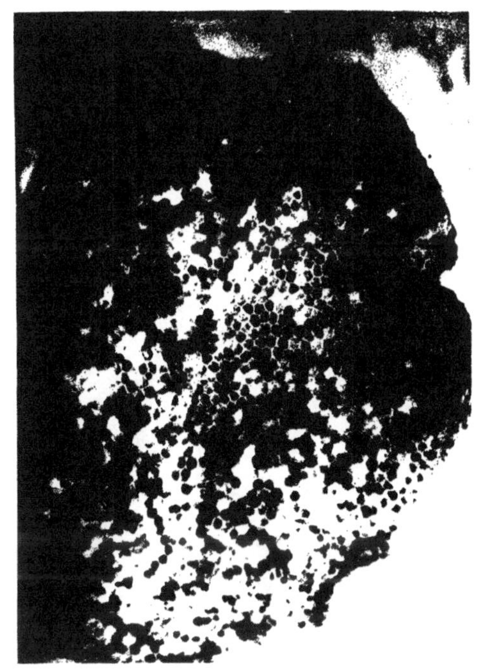

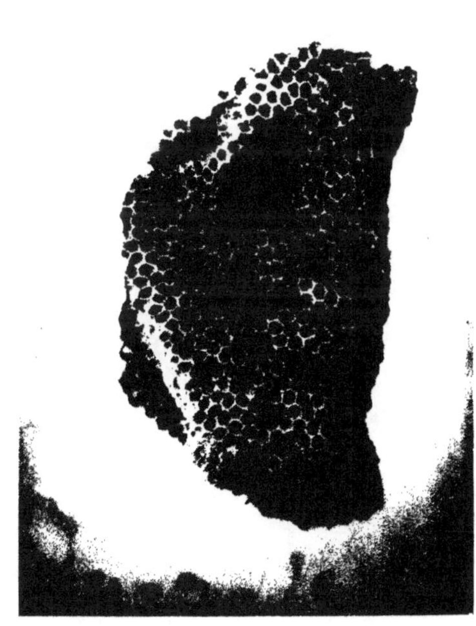

FLATE VI.

All figures FAVOSITES HEMISPHERICUS. Devonian.

PLATE VI

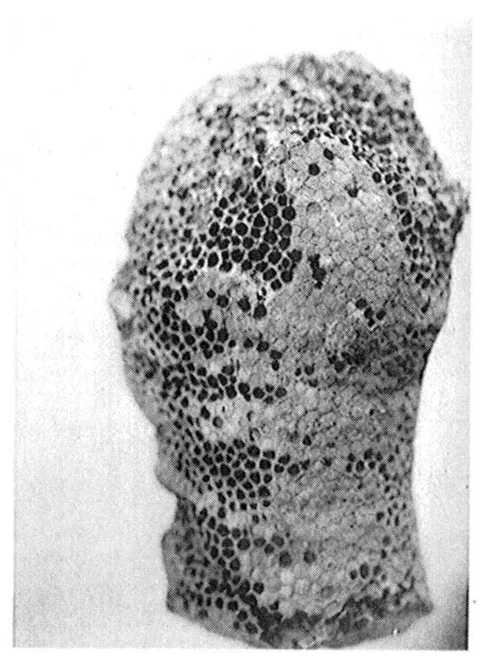

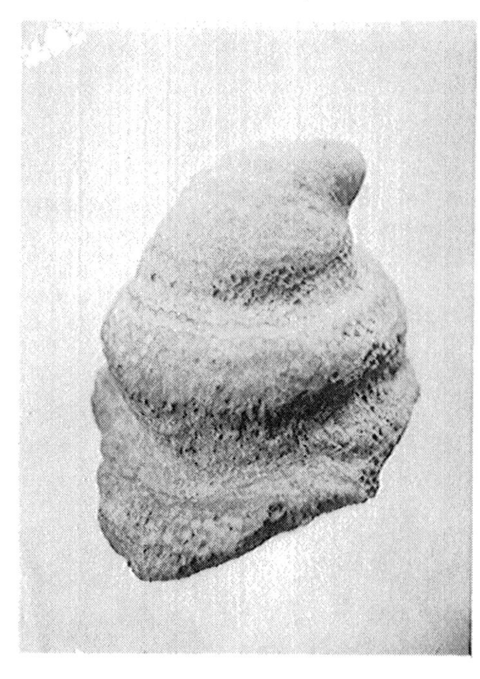

PLATE VII.

Figs. 1 and 2. FAVOSITES EMMONSII. Upper Helderberg group.

3 and 4. ——— Hamiltonensis. Hamilton group, Michigan.

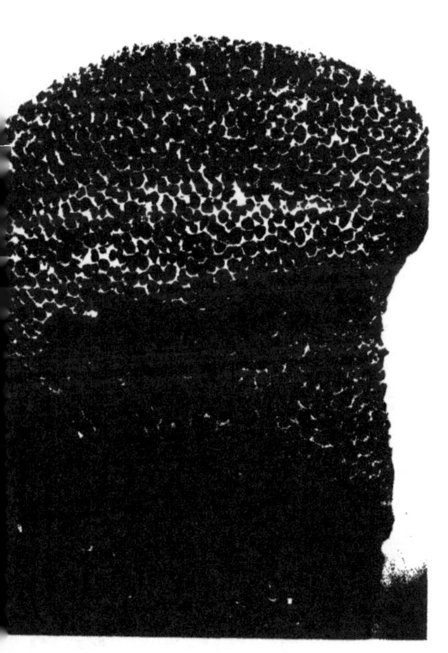

PLATE VIII.

Figs. 1, 2, and 3. FAVOSITES EPIDERMATUS. Corniferous limestone.

Fig 4. ——— Canadensis. Corniferous limestone.

PLATE VIII

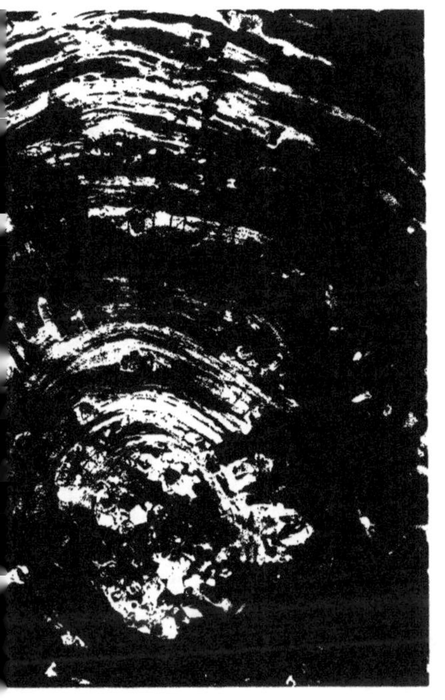

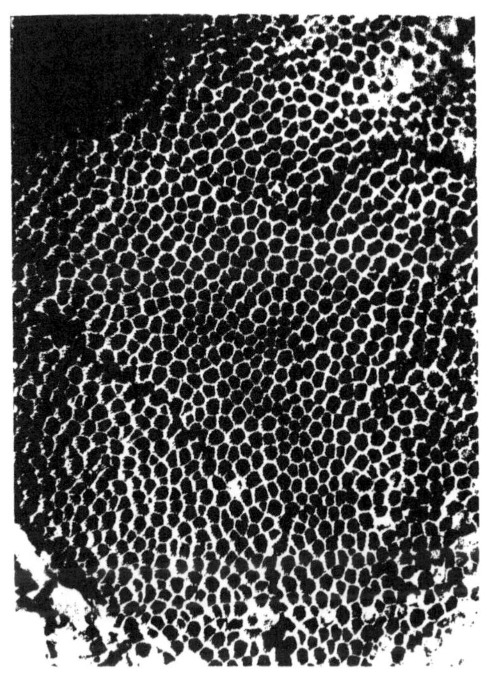

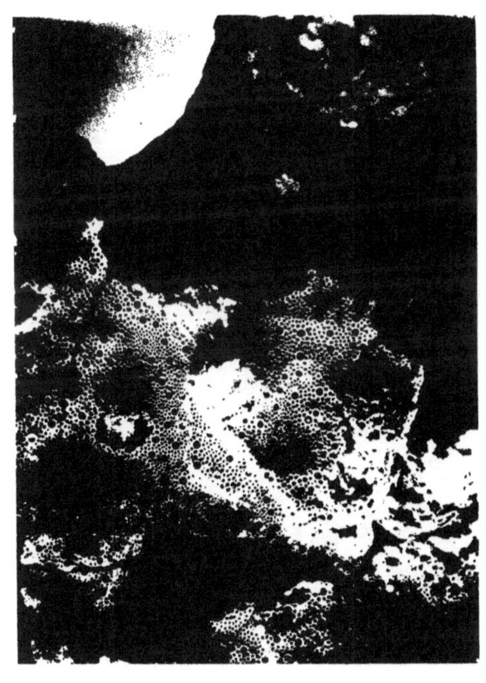

PLATE IX.

Figs. 1 and 2. FAVOSITES TUBEROSUS. Corniferous limestone.

3 and 4. ——— Winchelli. Corniferous limestone and Hamilton group.

PLATE IX

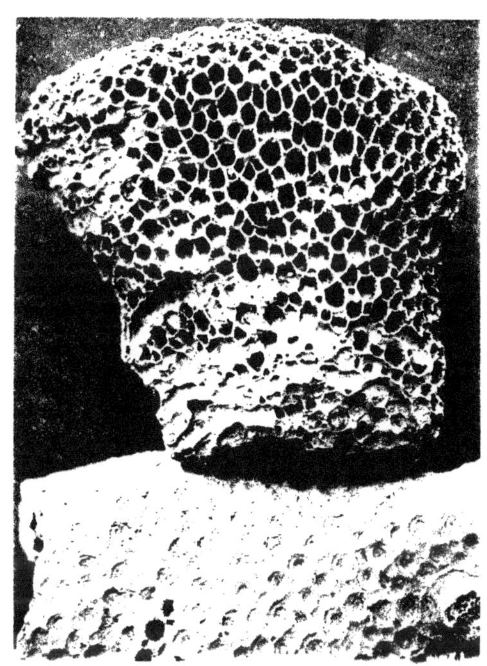

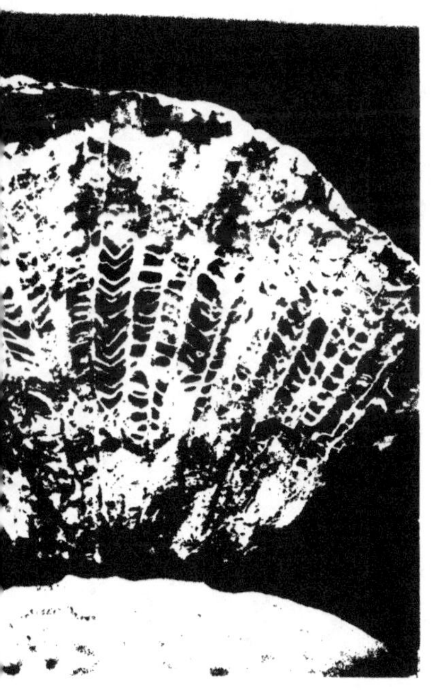

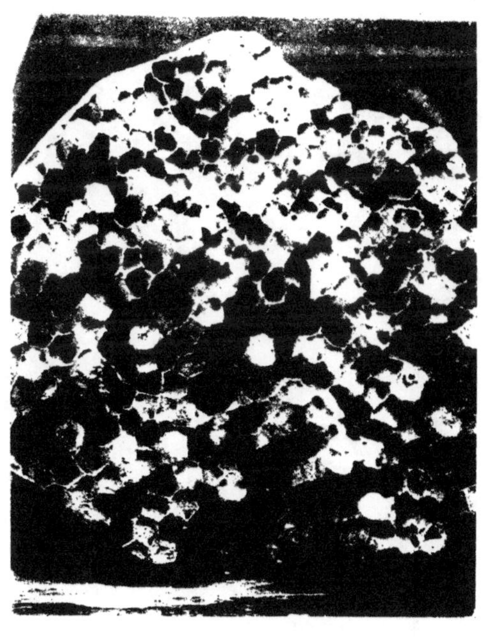

PLATE X.

Fig. 1. FAVOSITES RADIATUS. Hamilton group.

2. ——— hemisphericus. Helderberg group.

3. ——— limitaris—Casts.

4. ——— intertextus—Casts.

PLATE X

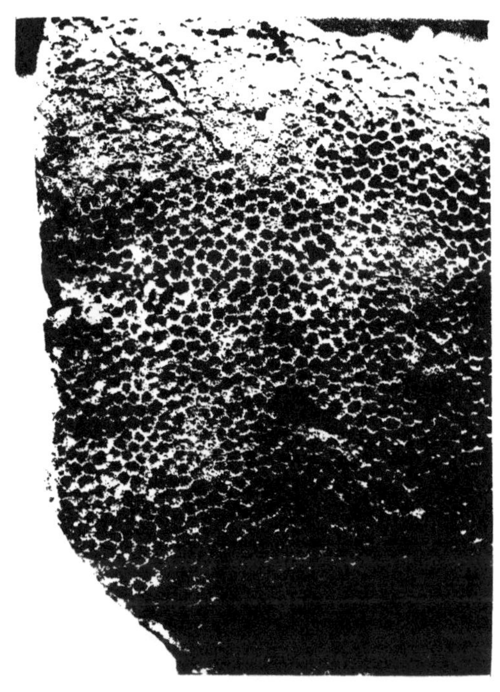

PLATE XI.

Figs. 1 and 2.	FAVOSITES PLACENTA.	Hamilton group,	Widder.
Fig. 3.	—— ——	"	Thunder Bay.
4.	—— nitella.	"	Little Traverse Bay.

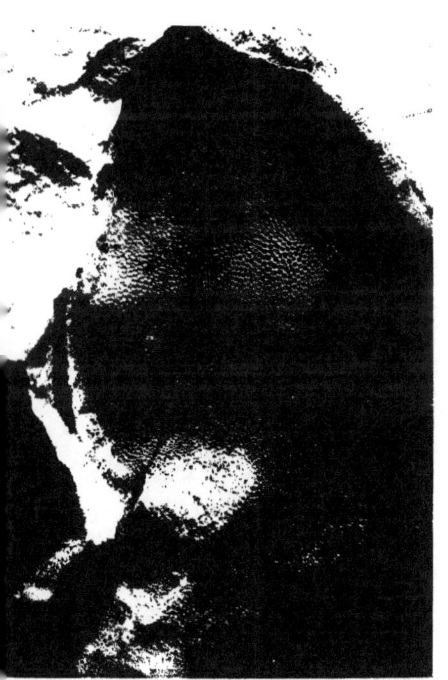

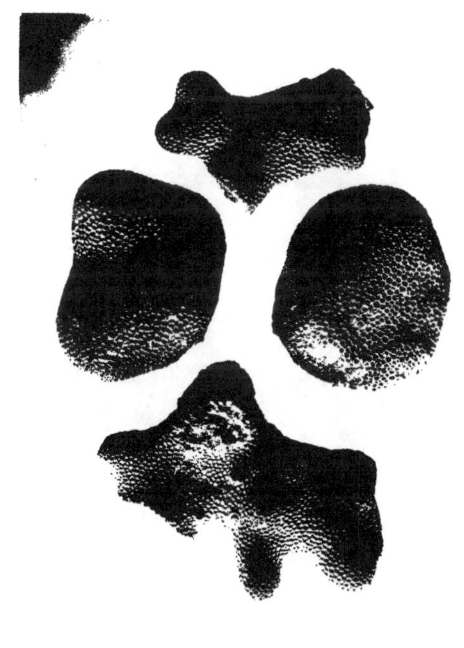

PLATE XII.

All figures FAVOSITES RADICIFORMIS. Helderberg and Hamilton groups.

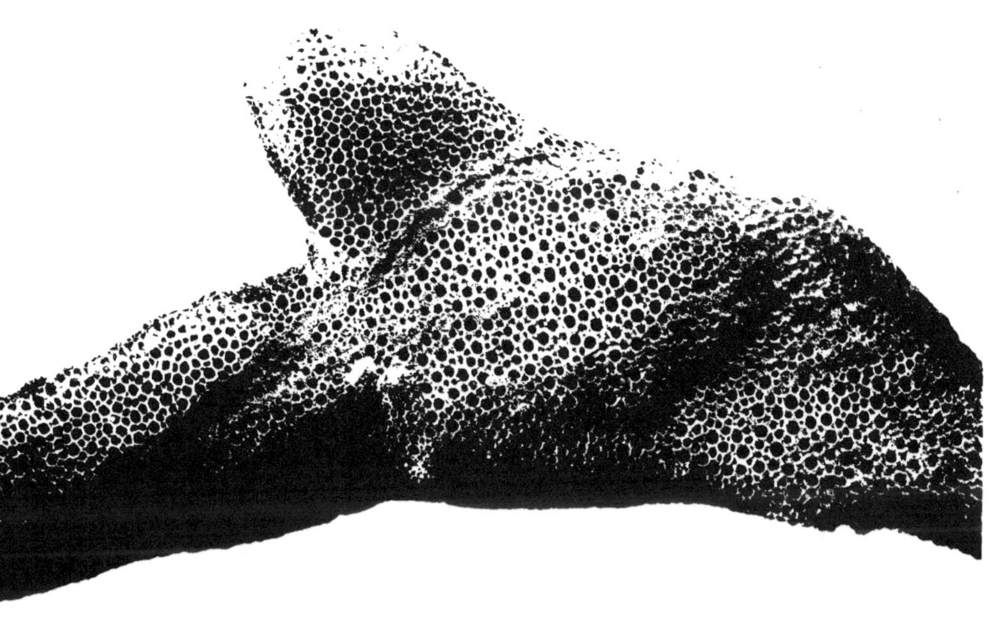

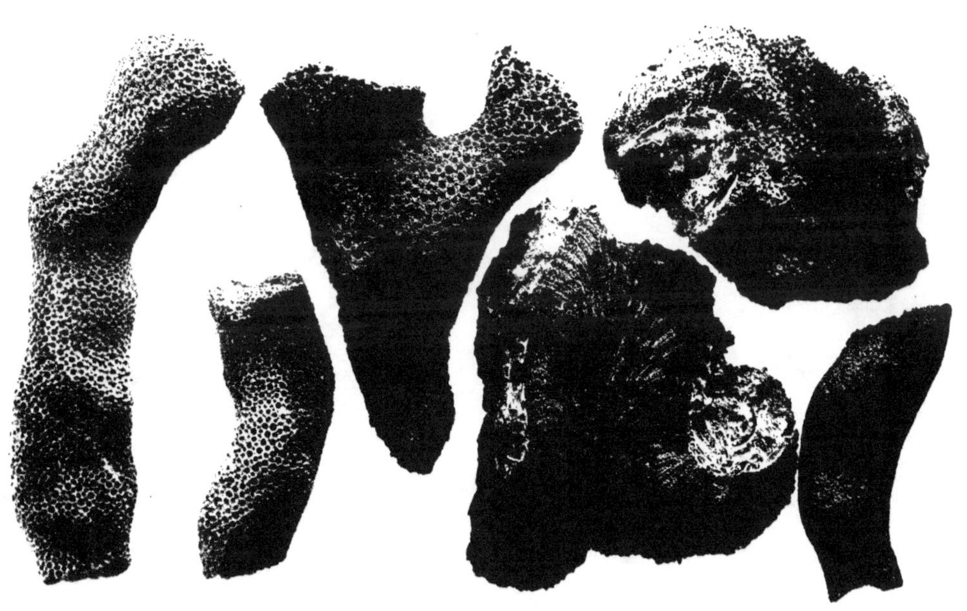

PLATE XIII.

All figures varieties of FAVOSITES LIMITARIS. Corniferous limestone.

PLATE XIII

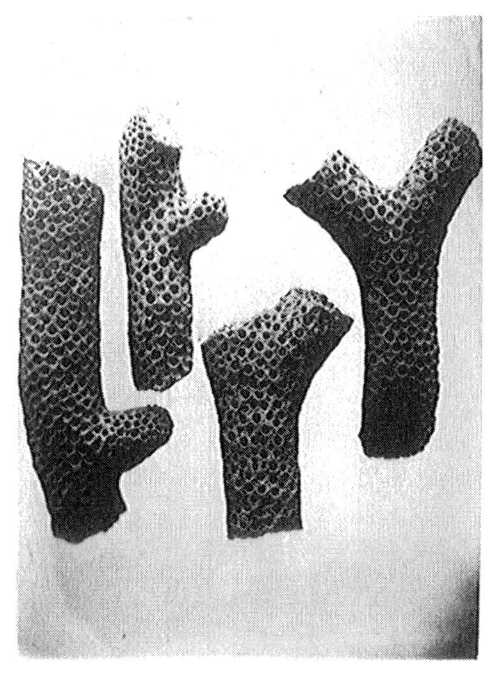

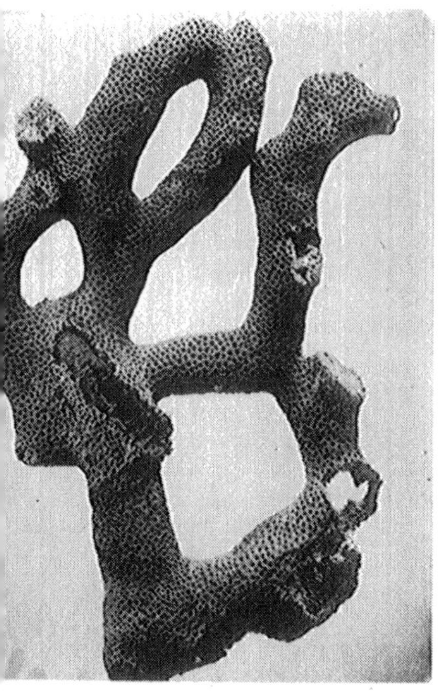

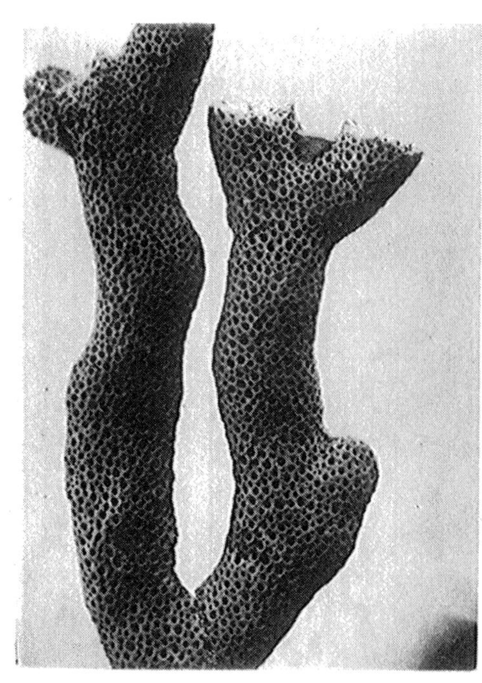

PLATE XIV.

All figures FAVOSITES CLAUSUS. Helderberg group and Hamilton group.

PLATE XIV

PLATE XV.

Figs. 1 and 2. FAVOSITES INTERTEXTUS. Corniferous limestone.

Fig. 3. ———— Canadensis.

Group 4. FAVOSITES DIGITATUS.

PLATE XV

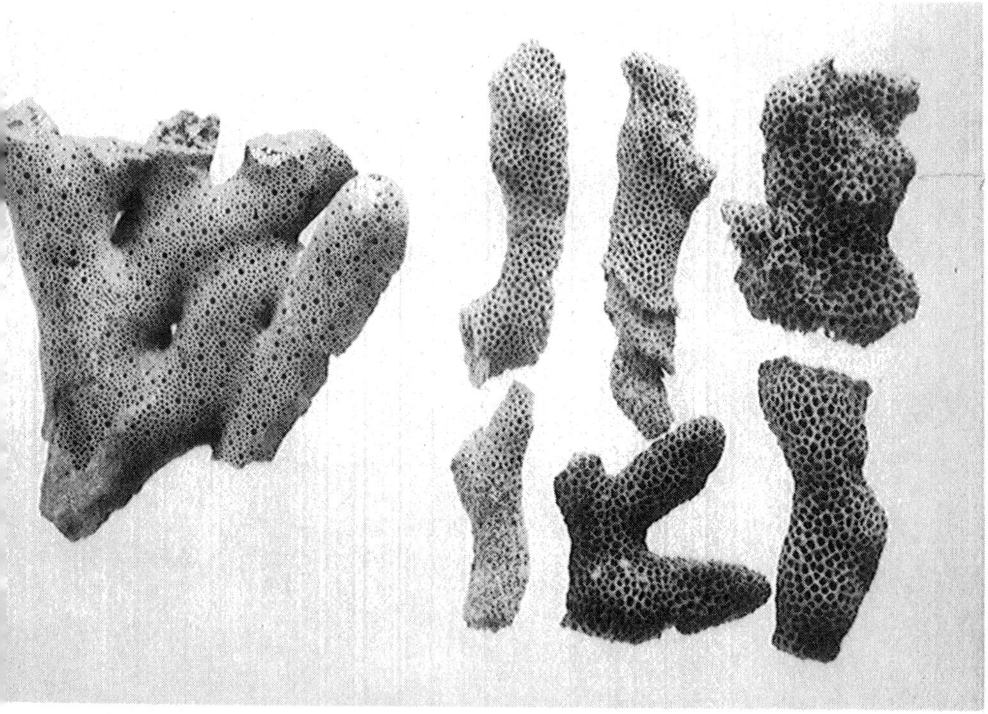

PLATE XVI.

Fig. 1. Alveolites Niagarensis. Drift. Michigan.

2. —— —— Point Detour, Niagara group.

3. —— squamosus. Found in the drift.

4. —— —— Caps of tubes. Drift.

PLATE XVI

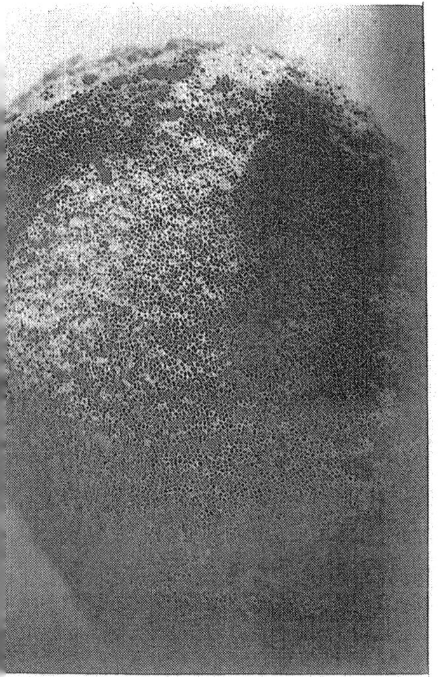

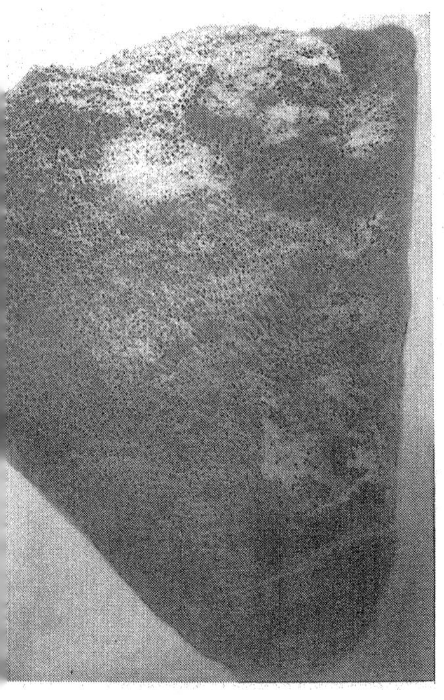

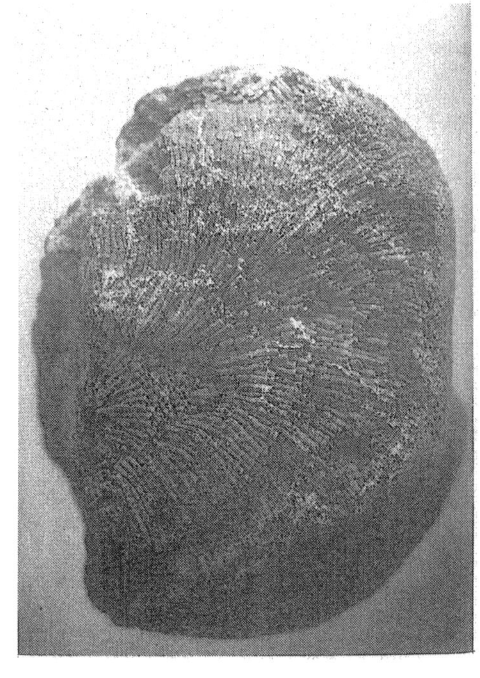

PLATE XVII.

Fig. 1. Cladopora lichenoides. Falls of Ohio.

4. ——— ——— Caps found in the drift.

2. Alveolites Goldfussii. Hamilton group, Widder.

3. ——— vallorum. Drift of Lake Superior.

PLATE XVII

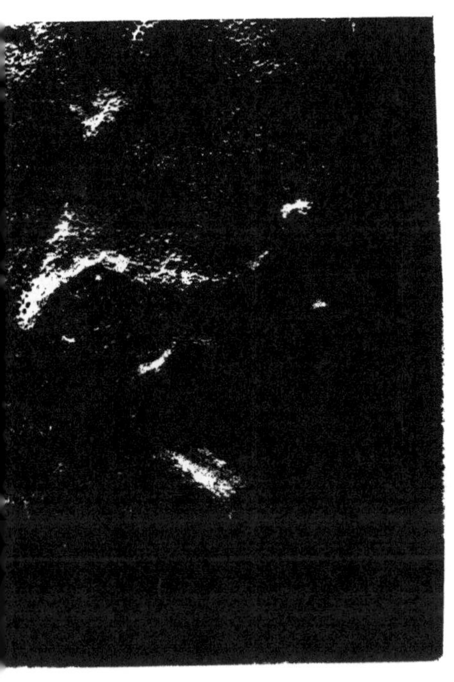

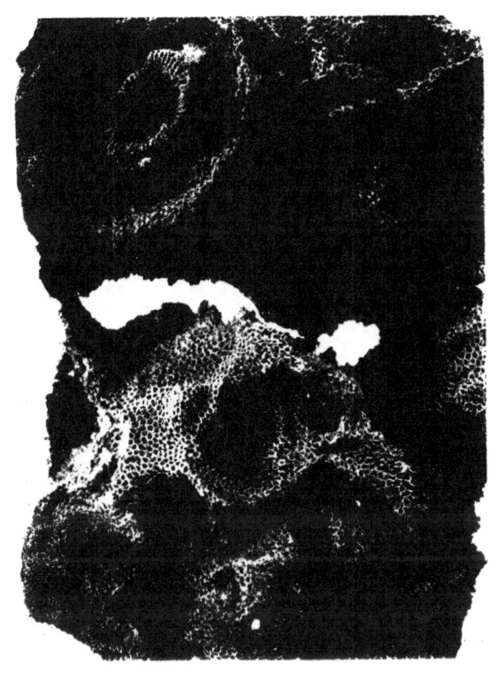

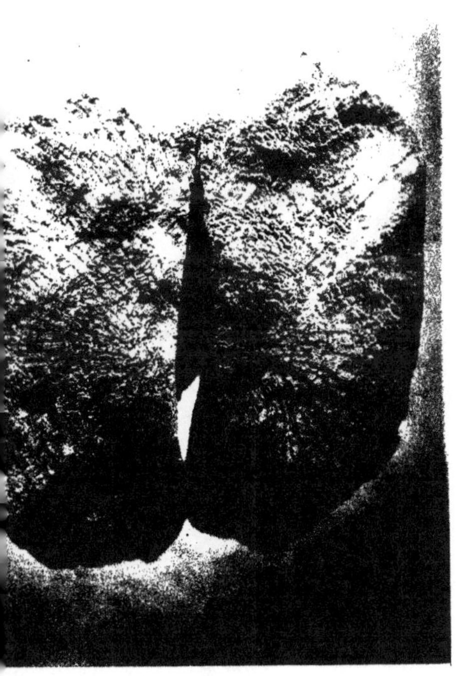

PLATE XVIII.

Fig. 1. LIMARIA CRASSA. Niagara group, Point of Barques, Lower Michigan.

2. ——— laminata. Niagara group, Point Detour.

3. CLADOPORA LAQUEATA. Niagara group, Seul Choix.

4. ALVEOLITES SUBRAMOSUS. Hamilton group Thunder Bay.

PLATE XVIII

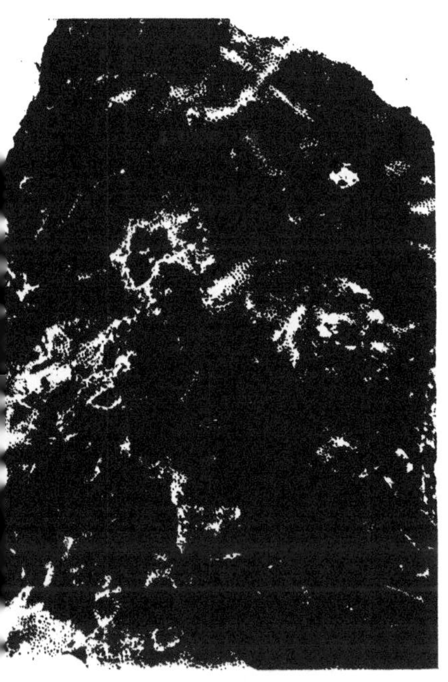

PLATE XIX.

Fig. 1. Cladopora Fisheri. Hamilton group drift.

4. ——— ——— Hamilton group, Widder.

2. ——— turgida. Corniferous limestone drift.

3. ——— Canadensis. Hamilton group, Widder.

PLATE XIX

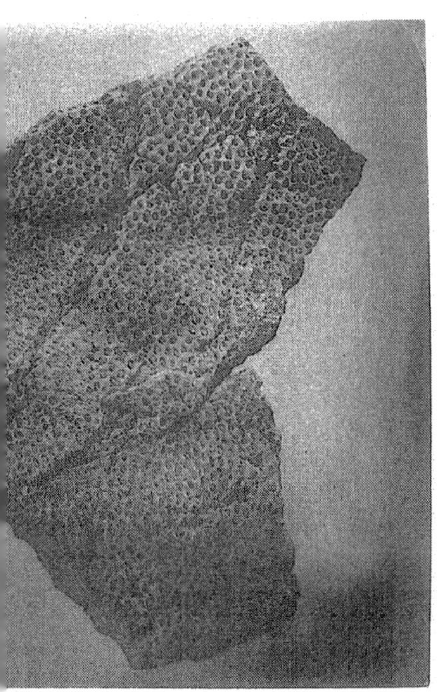

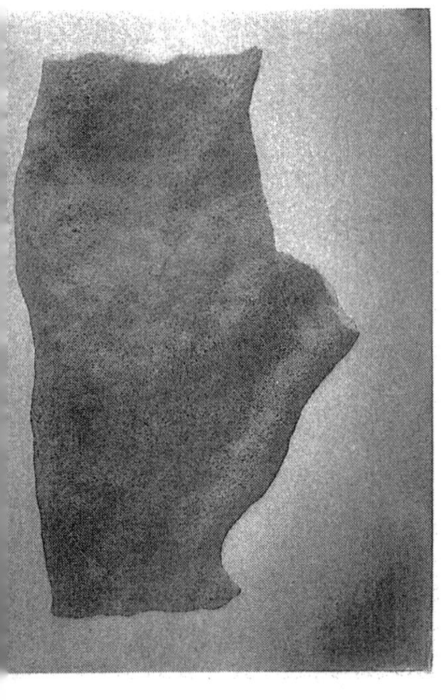

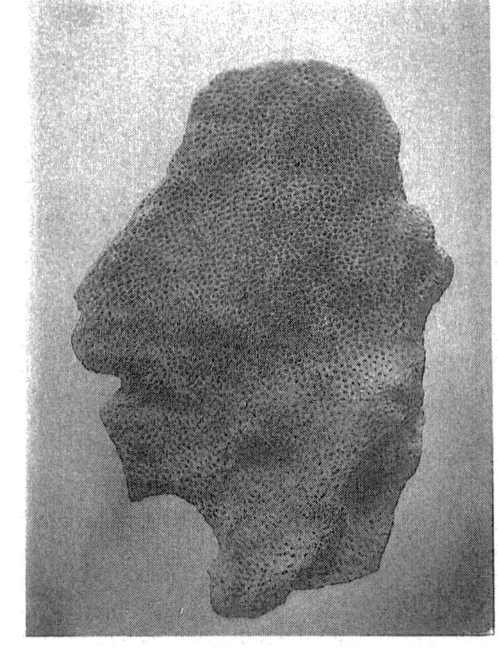

PLATE XX.

Figs. 1 and 2. CLADOPORA CRYPTODENS. Corniferous limestone, Falls of Ohio.

Fig. 3. ——— Roemeri. Hamilton group, Widder.

4. ——— Alpenensis. Hamilton group, Alpena.

PLATE XX

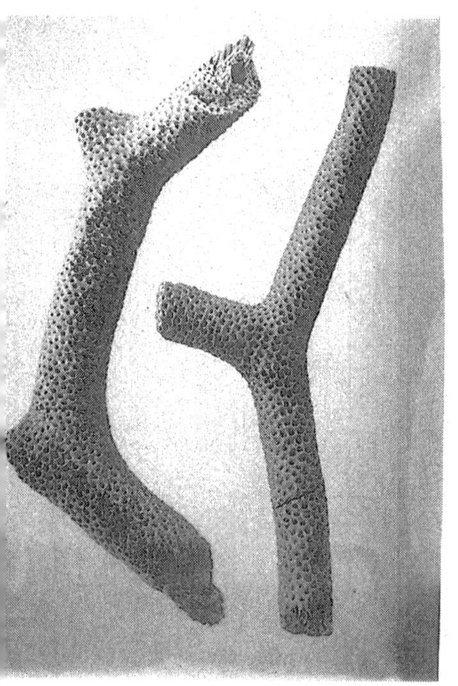

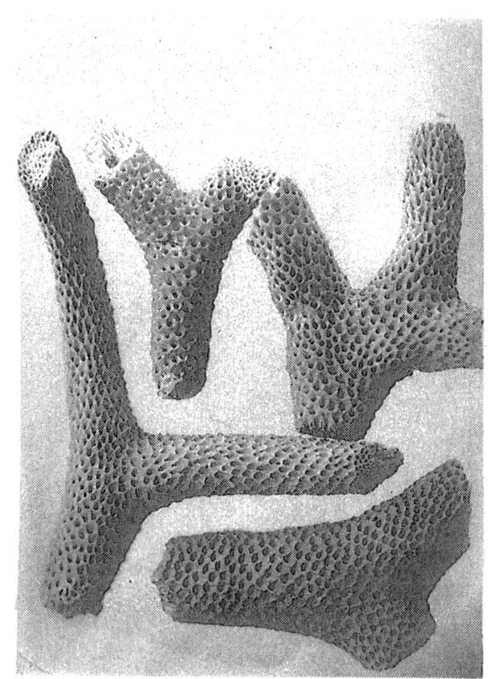

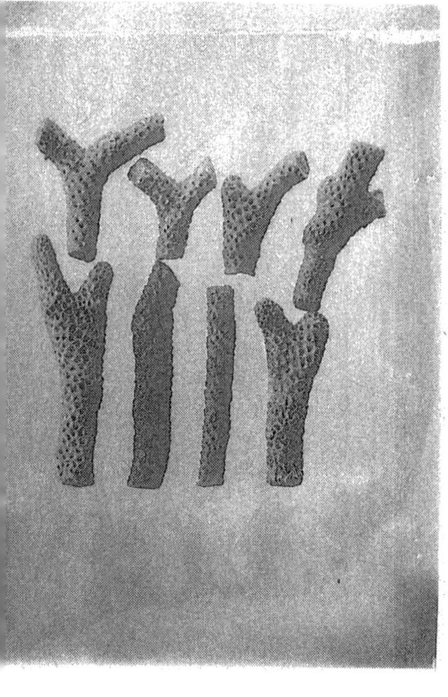

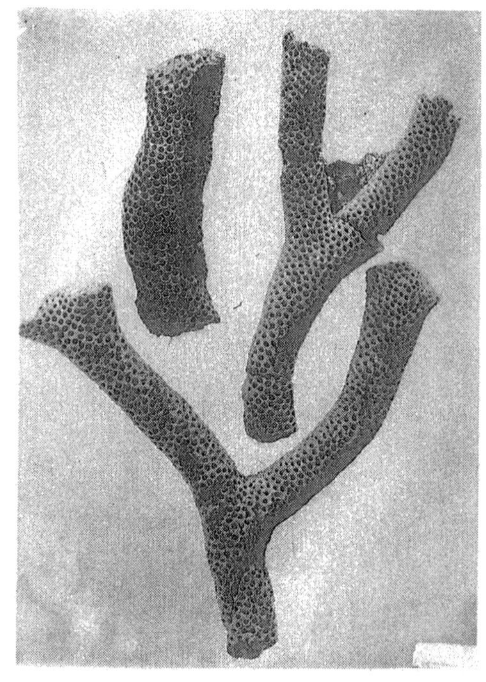

PLATE XXI.

Fig. 1. CLADOPORA PULCHRA. Corniferous limestone drift, and Port Colborne.

2. ——— labiosa. Corniferous limestone drift.

2. The two lower left-hand figures, CLADOPORA RIMOSA. Drift.

3. Lower tier, CLADOPORA PINGUIS. Drift. Central specimen at the base represents a variety of CLADOPORA LABIOSA.

PLATE XXI

PLATE XXII.

Figs. 1 and 2. CLADOPORA ROBUSTA. Corniferous limestone, Falls of the Ohio.

Lower tier, two right-hand specimens, CLADOPORA IMBRICATA. Falls of the Ohio.

Small upper specimen in the centre, CLADOPORA ASPERA. Falls of the Ohio.

Three specimens on left side, various forms of CLADOPORA EXPATIATA. Falls of the Ohio.

PLATE XXII

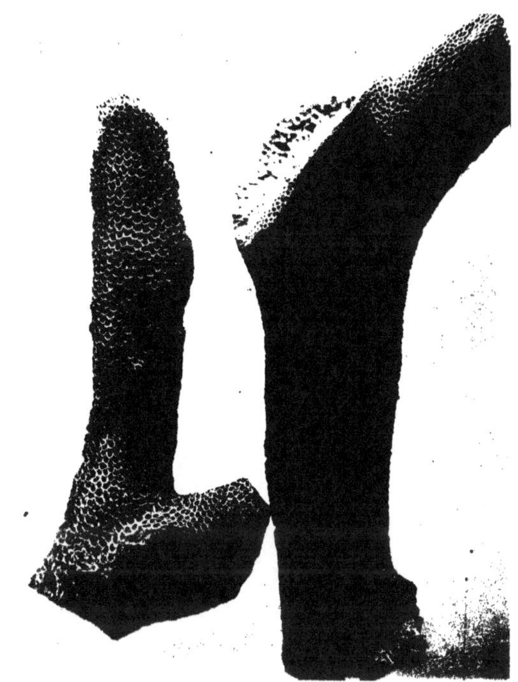

PLATE XXIII.

Fig. 1. DENDROPORA ORNATA. Hamilton group, Darien.

2. ——— elegantula. Hamilton group, Widder.

3. STRIATOPORA CAVERNOSA. Corniferous limestone drift.

4. DENDROPORA NEGLECTA. Corniferous limestone drift.

5. STRIATOPORA LINNÆANA. Hamilton group, Thunder Bay and Widder.

6. Supposed variety of the same species. Corniferous limestone, Falls of the Ohio.

PLATE XXIII

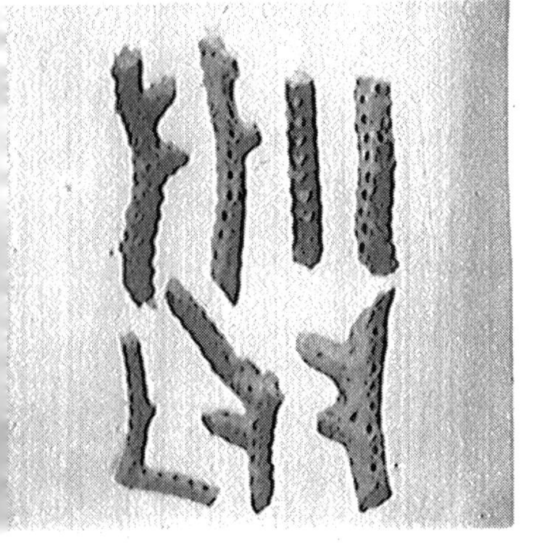

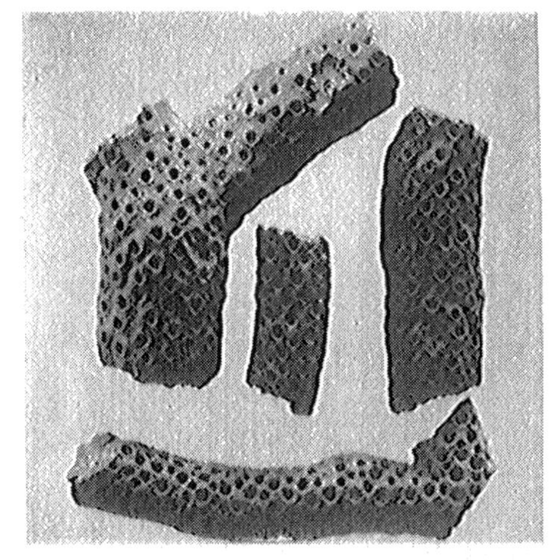

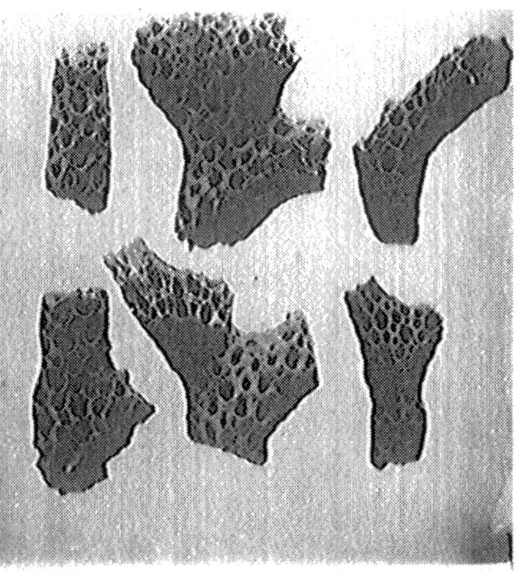

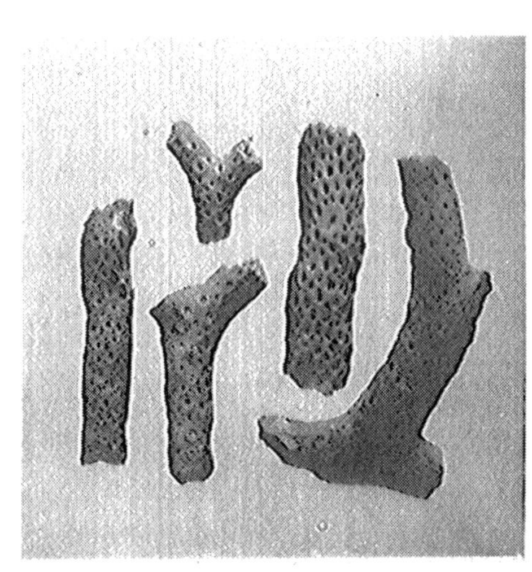

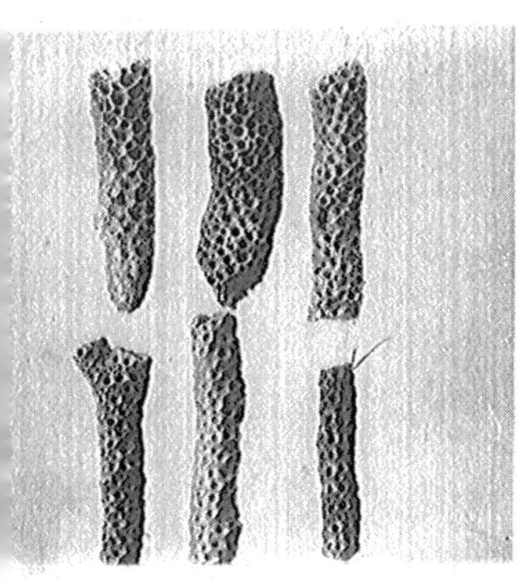

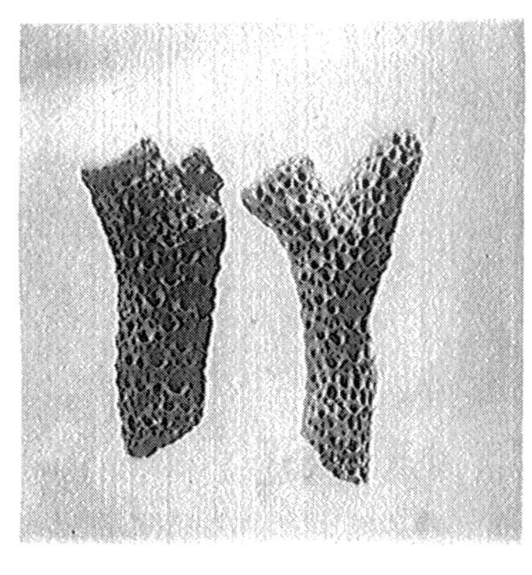

PLATE XXIV.

Fig. 1. Upper specimen, DENDROPORA ALTERNANS. Hamilton group, Thunder Bay.

Specimen at the base, DENDROPORA RETICULATA. Hamilton group, Partridge Point.

2 Upper specimen, STRIATOPORA HURONENSIS. Niagara group, Point Detour.

Lower left-hand specimen, STRIATOPORA RUGOSA. Hamilton group, Thunder Bay

Lower right-hand specimen, DENDROPORA ORNATA, juvenile specimen. Thunder Bay, Hamilton group.

3 Upper group of specimens, VERMIPORA FASCICULATA. Corniferous limestone and Hamilton group. Magnified 2 diameters.

Lower three stems, VERMIPORA NIAGARENSIS. Niagara group, Iowa. Magnified 2 diameters.

4. Upper row of stems, DENDROPORA–RETICULATA. Magnified 2 diameters. Thunder Bay.

Lower group of stems, DENDROPORA PROBOSCIDALIS. Hamilton group, Thunder Bay

PLATE XXIV

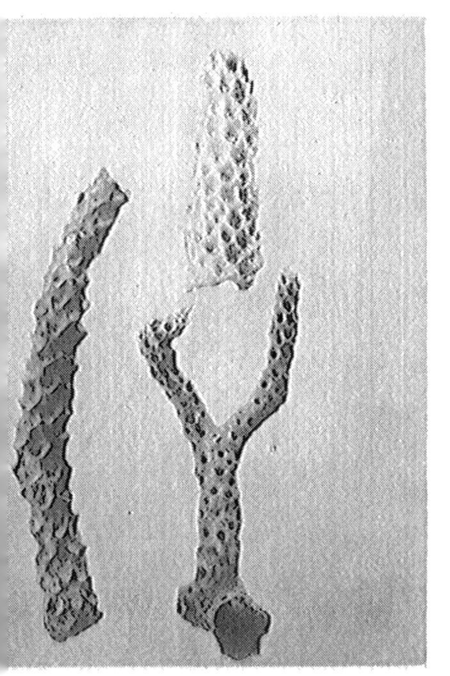

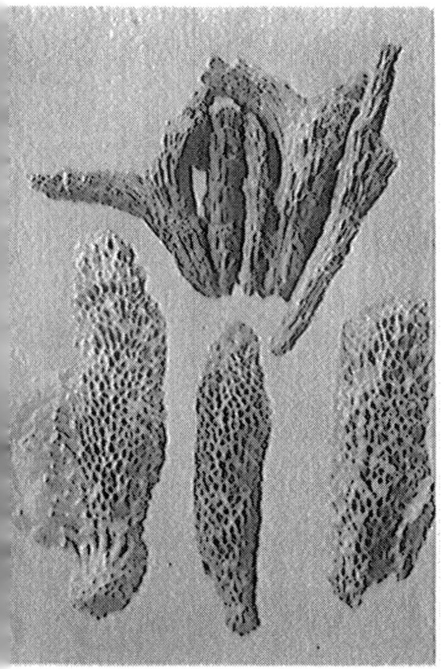

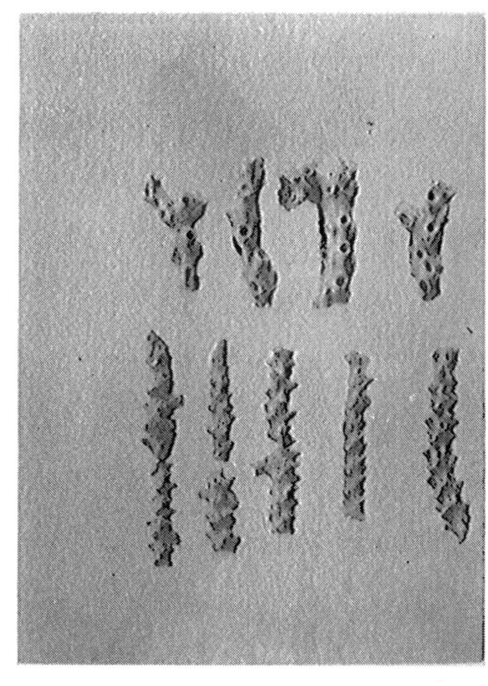

PLATE XXV.

Fig. 1. THECIA MAJOR. Niagara group, Charleston Landing.

2. ——— ——— " Point of Barques.

3. ——— minor. " Louisville.

4. ——— ramosa. Helderberg group, Falls of the Ohio.

PLATE XXV

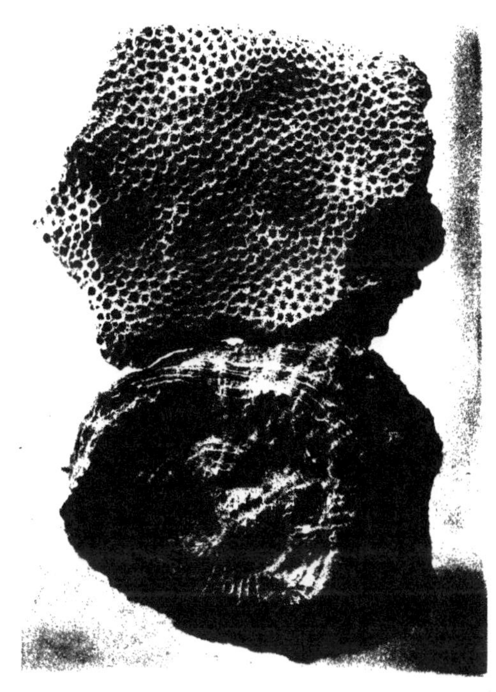

PLATE XXVI.

Figs. 1 and 2. MICHELINIA CONVEXA. Helderberg group, Port Colborne.

3 and 4. ——— cylindrica. Helderberg group, Falls of the Ohio.

PLATE XXVI

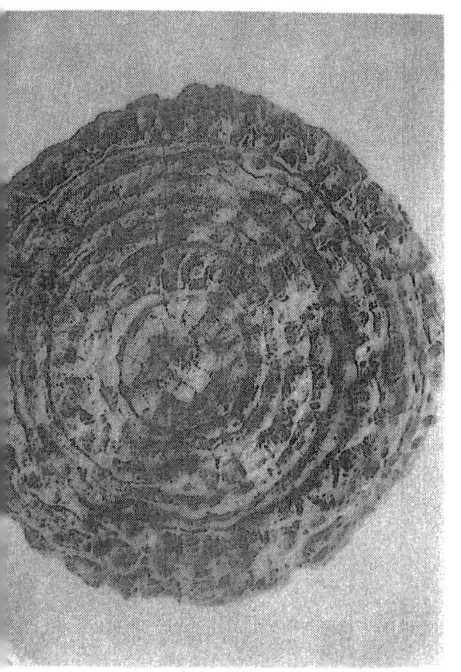

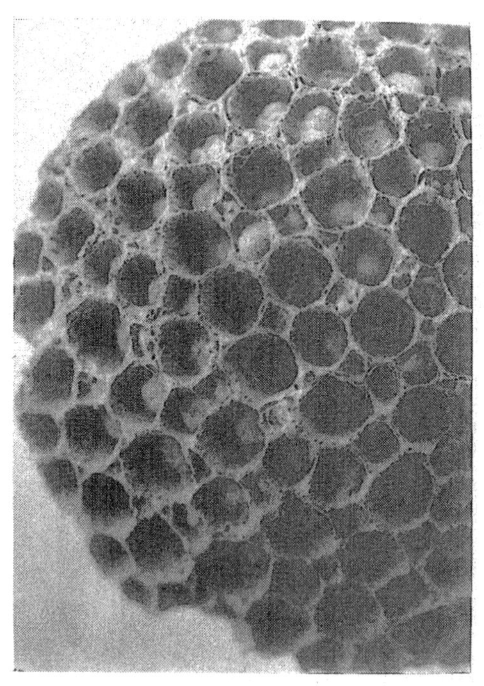

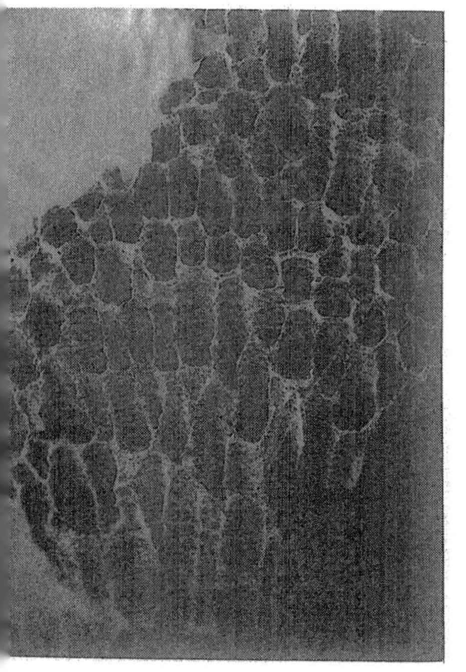

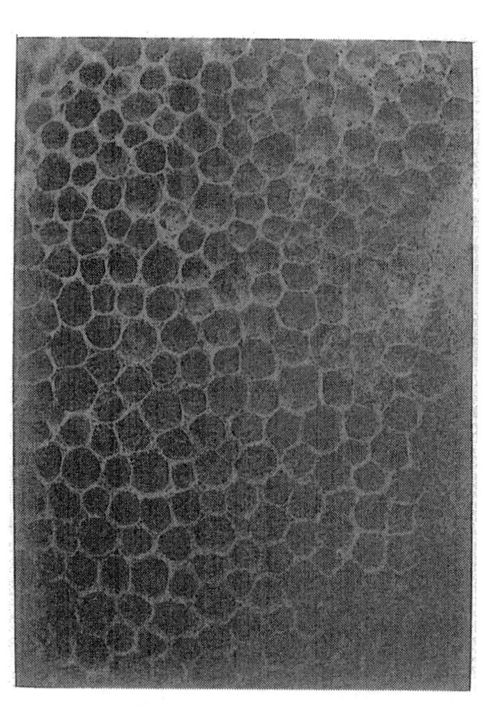

PLATE XXVII.

Figs. 1, 2, and 3. MICHELINIA INSIGNIS. Hamilton group, Thunder Bay, and Fig. 1. Helderberg group, Louisville.

Fig. 4. MICHELINIA FAVOSITOIDEA. Helderberg group, Port Colborne.

PLATE XXVII

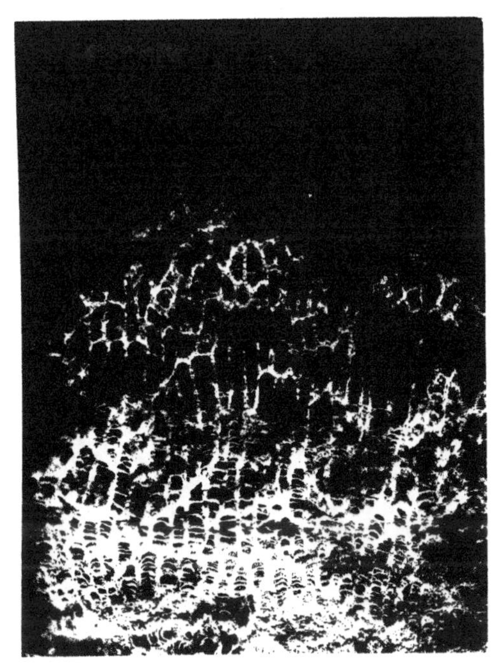

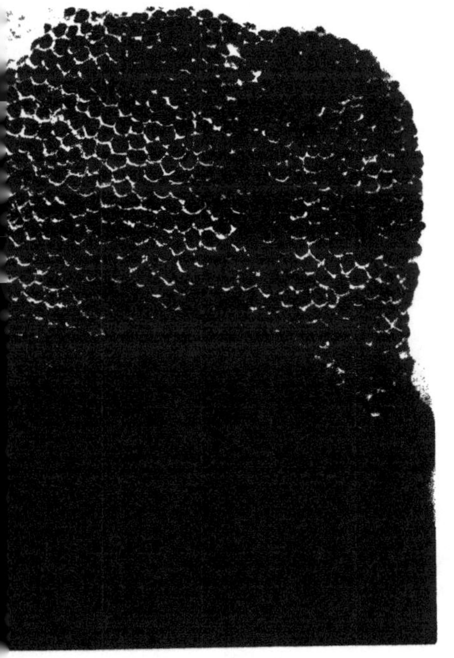

PLATE XXVIII.

Fig. 1. Columnaria stellata. Niagara group, Point Detour.

2. Favosites obliquus. Niagara group, Point Detour.

Figs. 3 and 4. Michelinia Clappii. Corniferous limestone, Port Colborne.

PLATE XXVIII

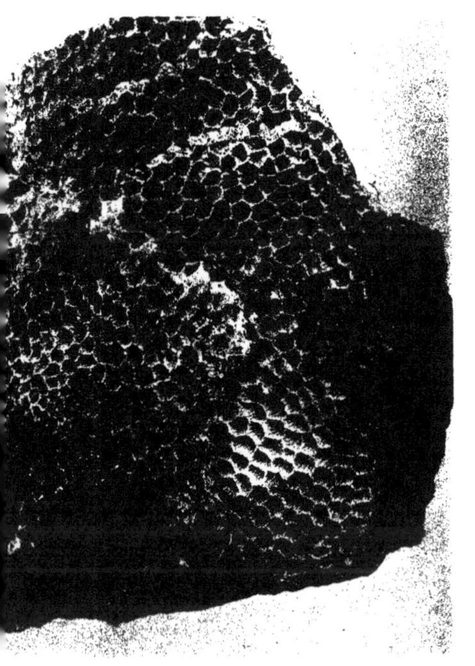

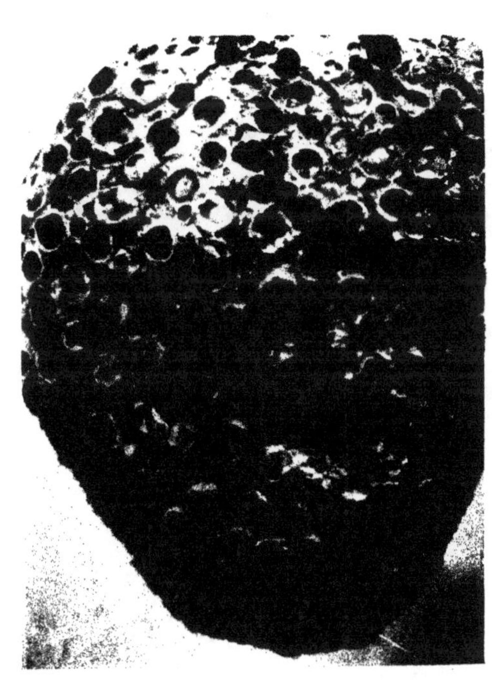

PLATE XXIX.

Figs. 1, 2, and 4. Varieties of HALYSITES CATENULATUS. Niagara group, Point Detour.

Fig. 3. HALYSITES COMPACTUS. Niagara group, Epoufette Point.

PLATE XXIX

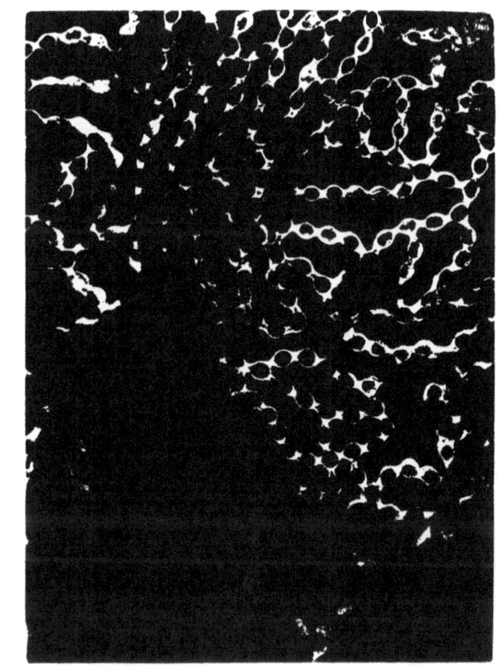

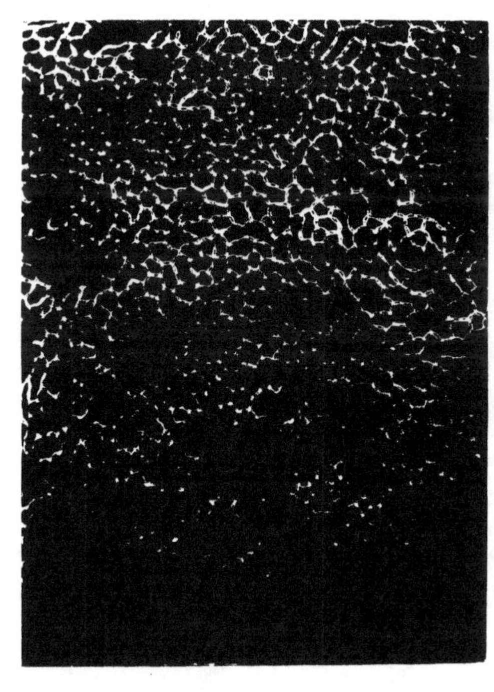

PLATE XXX.

Figs. 1 and 2. SYRINGOPORA VERTICILLATA. Niagara group, Point Detour.

Fig. 3. SYRINGOPORA FIBRATA. Niagara group, Drummond's Island.

4. —— tenella. Niagara group drift.

PLATE XXX

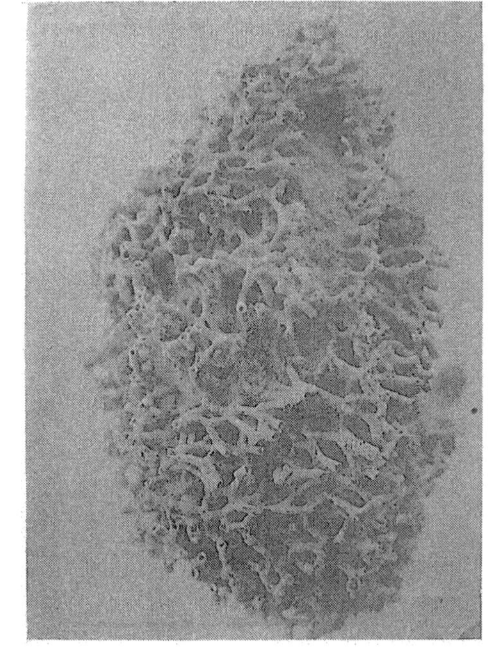

PLATE XXXI.

Figs. 1 and 2 SYRINGOPORA MACLUREI. Corniferous limestone drift. Basal expansion of Syringopora perelegans on the left lower corner of Fig. 2.

3 and 4. SYRINGOPORA PERELEGANS. Corniferous limestone, Falls of the Ohio.

PLATE XXXI

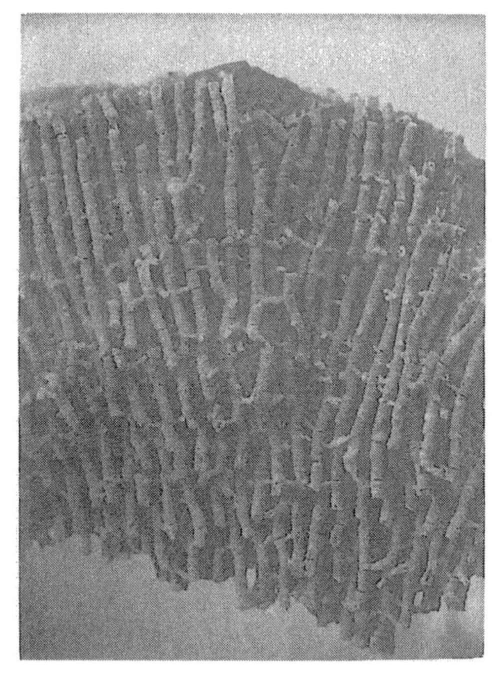

PLATE XXXII.

Upper tier, the two specimens above, SYRINGOPORA TABULATA, from the Falls of the Ohio.

Three lower specimens, SYRINGOPORA HISINGERI. Corniferous limestone drift.

Lower tier, left-hand specimens, SYRINGOPORA ANNULATA. Niagara group drift.

Central and right-hand specimens, SYRINGOPORA NOBILIS; the first from Hamilton group of Thunder Bay, the other from the corniferous limestone drift.

PLATE XXXII

PLATE XXXIII.

Fig. 1. AULOPORA CONFERTA. Hamilton group, Little Traverse Bay.

2 ——— serpens. " "

3. QUENSTEDTIA UMBELLIFERA. Corniferous limestone drift.

4. Upper specimen, AULOPORA ERECTA. Hamilton group, Thunder Bay.

Lower right hand specimen, CANNAPORA JUNCIFORMIS. Clinton group, Brockport, N. Y.

Left-hand specimen CANNAPORA JUNCIFORMIS. Niagara group, Point Detour.

PLATE XXXIII

PLATE XXXIV.

Fig. 1. COLUMNARIA ALVEOLATA. Trenton group, St. Joseph's Island.

2. ——— alveolaris. Trenton group, Escanaba River.

3. ——— stellata. Hudson River group, Drummond's Island.

4. ——— alveolata. Trenton group, Dixon, Illinois.

PLATE XXXIV

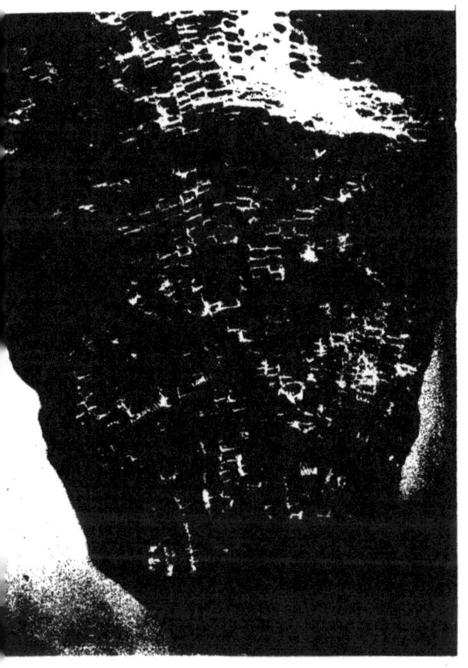

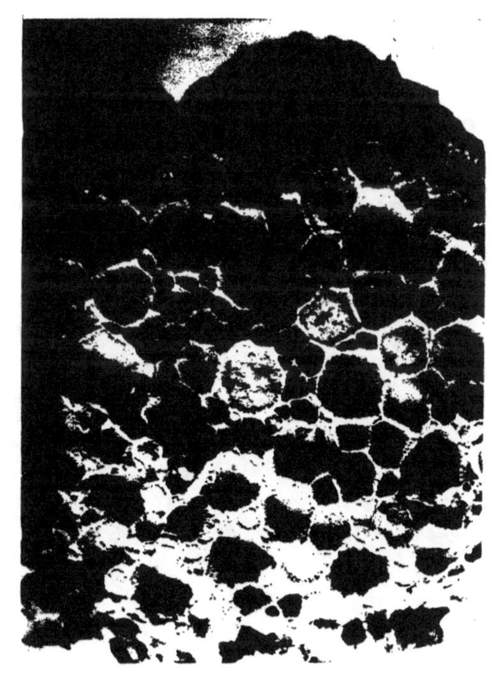

PLATE XXXV.

Upper tier, three specimens on left side, CYATHOPHYLLUM HALLII. Hamilton group, Widder.

Upper specimen in centre, same species, from Thunder Bay.

Three specimens on the right with more delicate structure, CYATHOPHYLLUM JUVENIS. Hamilton group, Widder.

Lower tier, two left-hand specimens, CYATHOPHYLLUM ZYPHUS. Hamilton group, Long Lake.

Group on the right side, CYATHOPHYLLUM CORNICULA. Corniferous limestone.

PLATE XXXV

PLATE XXXVI.

Upper tier, CYATHOPHYLLUM HOUGHTONI. Hamilton group, Little Traverse Bay.
Lower tier, ---—— geniculatum. Hamilton group, Partridge Point.

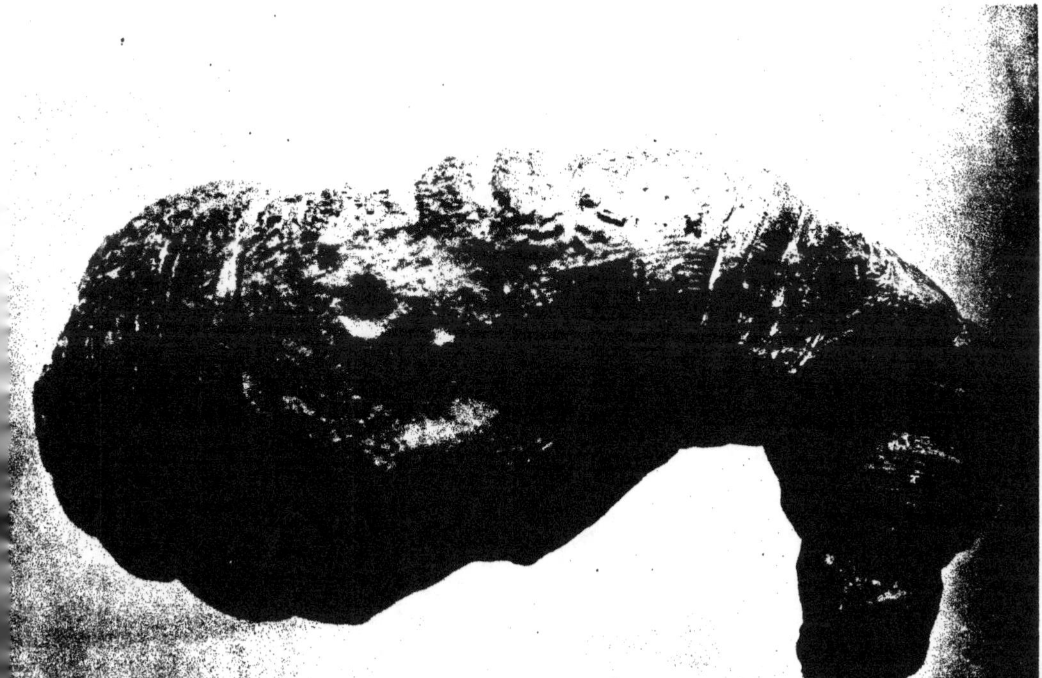

PLATE XXXVII.

Figs. 1 and 2. CYATHOPHYLLUM RUGOSUM. Helderberg group, Sandusky.

Fig. 3. PHILLIPSASTRÆA GIGAS. Helderberg group, Mackinac Island.

4. CYATHOPHYLLUM DAVIDSONI. Hamilton group, Little Traverse Bay.

PLATE XXXVII

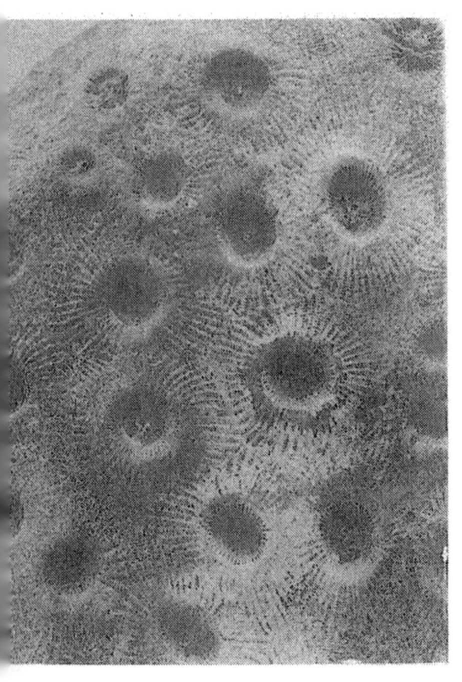

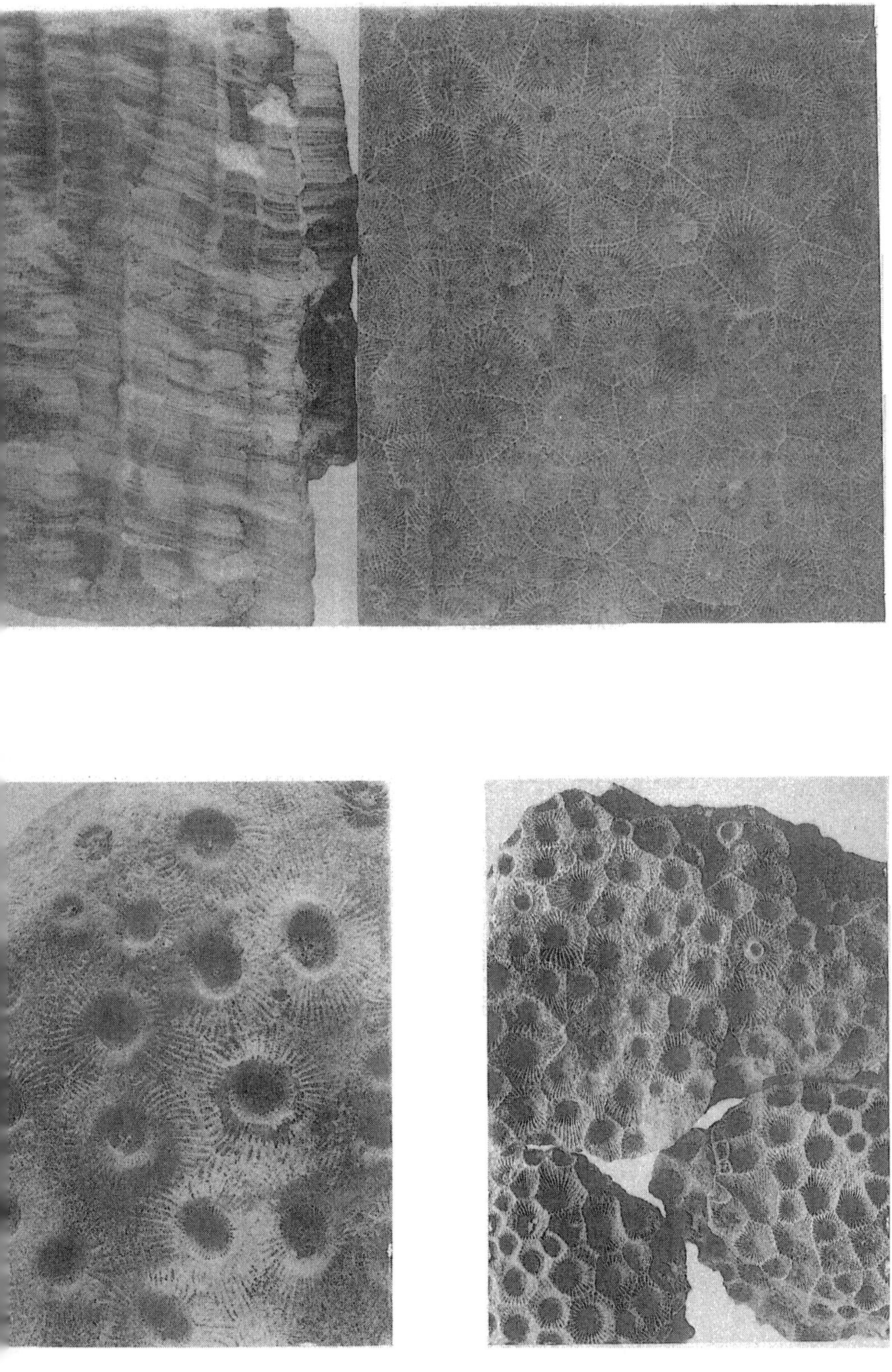

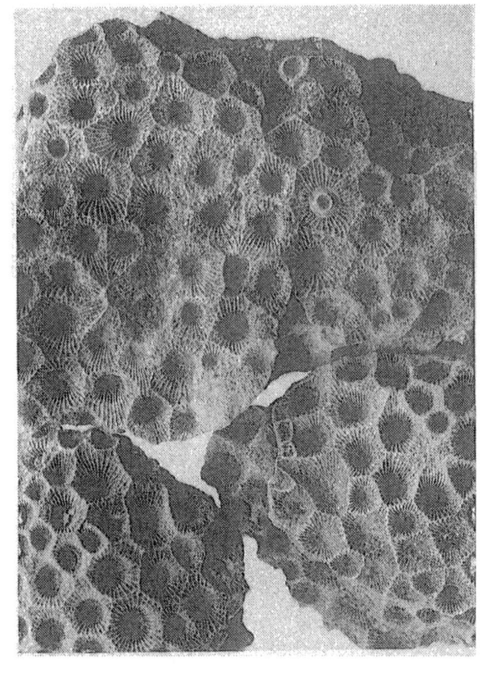

PLATE XXXVIII.

Fig. 1. Strombodes Alpenensis. Hamilton group, Thunder Bay.

2. Phillipsastræa Verneuilli. Corniferous limestone drift.

3. Diphyphyllum colligatum. " "

4. Cyathophyllum coalitum. " "

PLATE XXXVIII

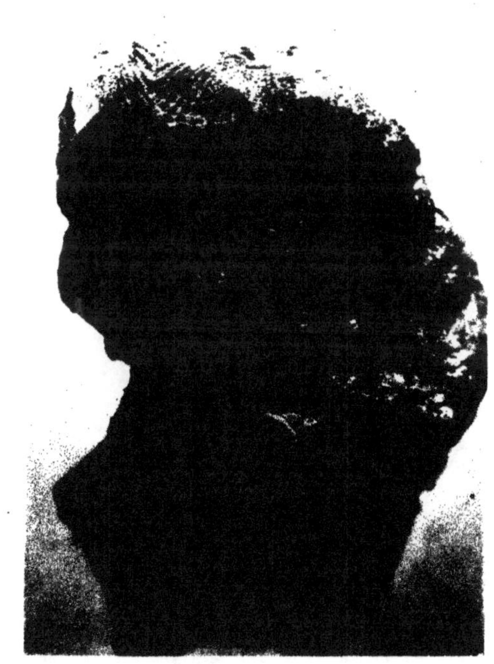

PLATE XXXIX.

Fig. 1. STREPTELASMA PATULA. Niagara group, Point Detour.

2. ——— spongaxis. " "

3. CYATHOPHYLLUM RADICULA. " Drummond's Island.

Two elongated specimens on the right a somewhat different form. Louisville.

4. STREPTELASMA CONULUS. Niagara group, Point Detour.

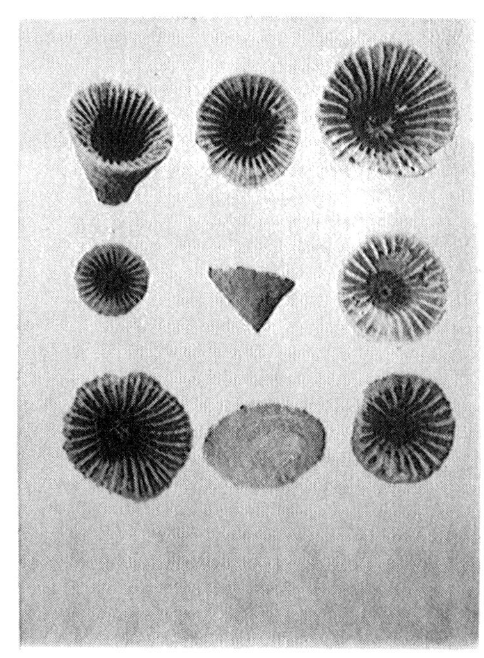

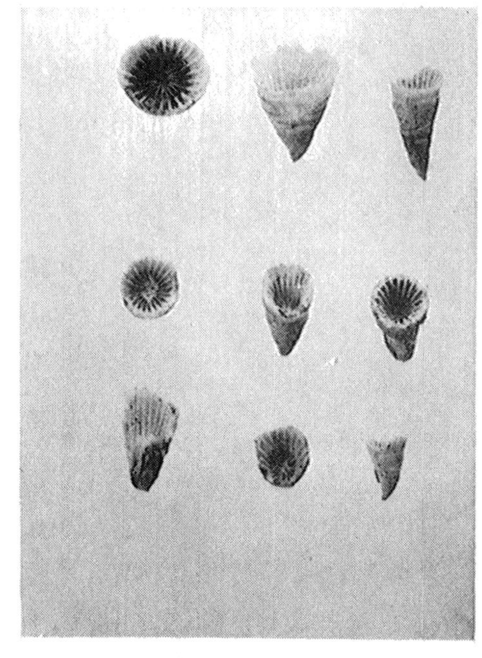

PLATE XL.

Upper tier, Clisiophyllum Oneidaense. Corniferous limestone, Falls of the Ohio.

Lower tier, Zaphrentis conigera. Corniferous limestone, Falls of the Ohio. Upper central specimen from the Island of Mackinac.

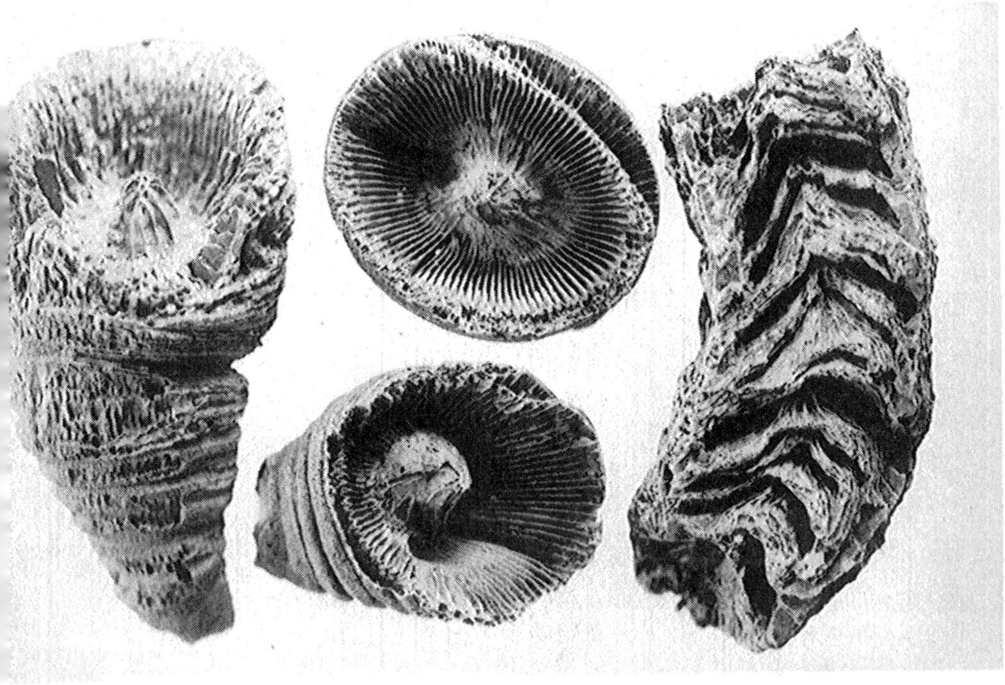

PLATE XLI.

Blothrophyllum decorticatum. Corniferous limestone, Falls of the Ohio.

PLATE XLI

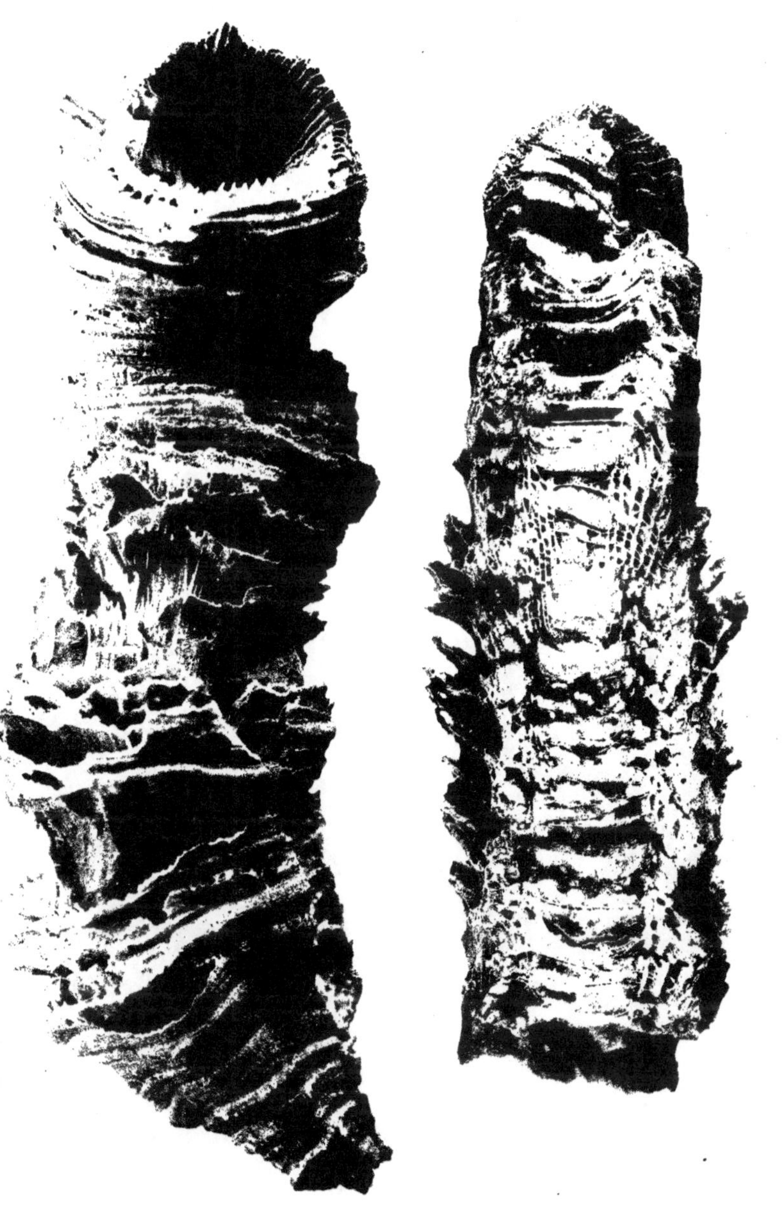

PLATE XLII.

BLOTHROPHYLLUM CÆSPITOSUM. Niagara group, Point Detour.

PLATE XLII

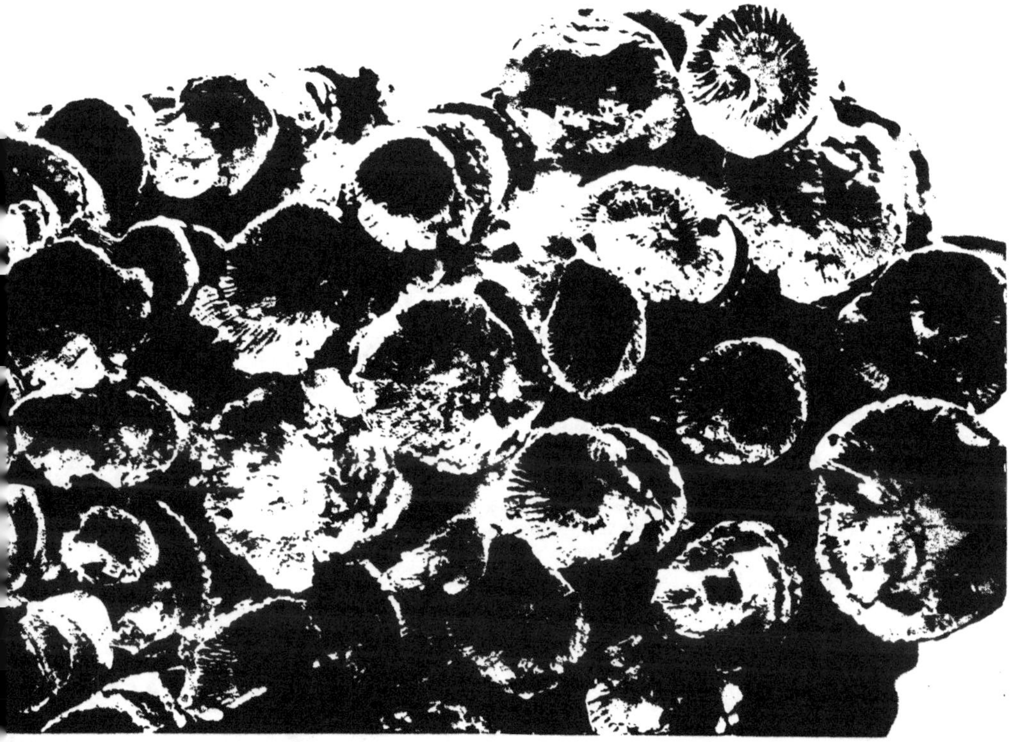

PLATE XLIII.

CHONOPHYLLUM MAGNIFICUM. Corniferous limestone, Falls of the Ohio.

Two upper and right-hand lower figures, CHONOPHYLLUM PONDEROSUM. Hamilton group, Thunder Bay.

PLATE XLIII

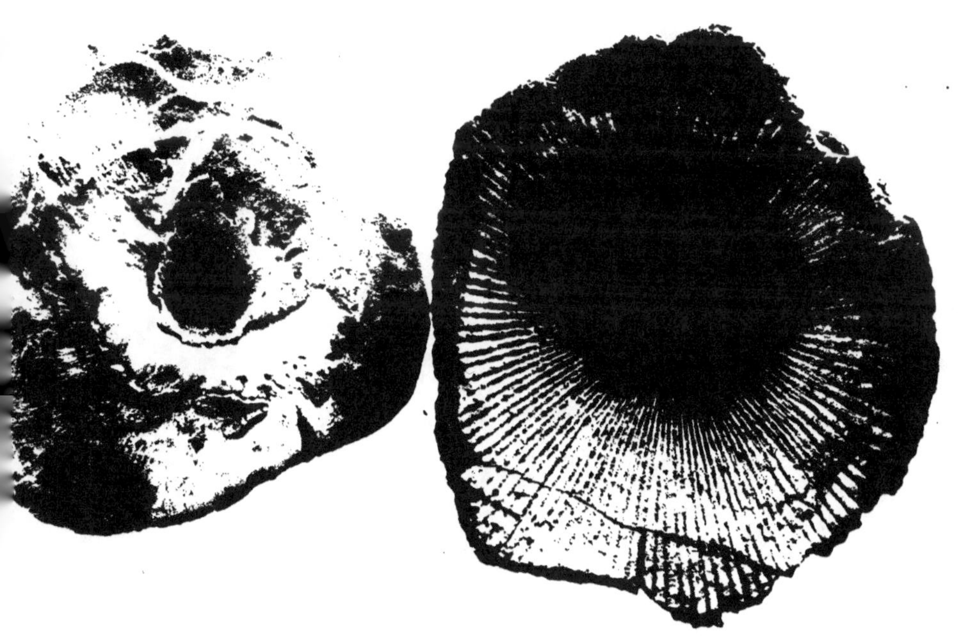

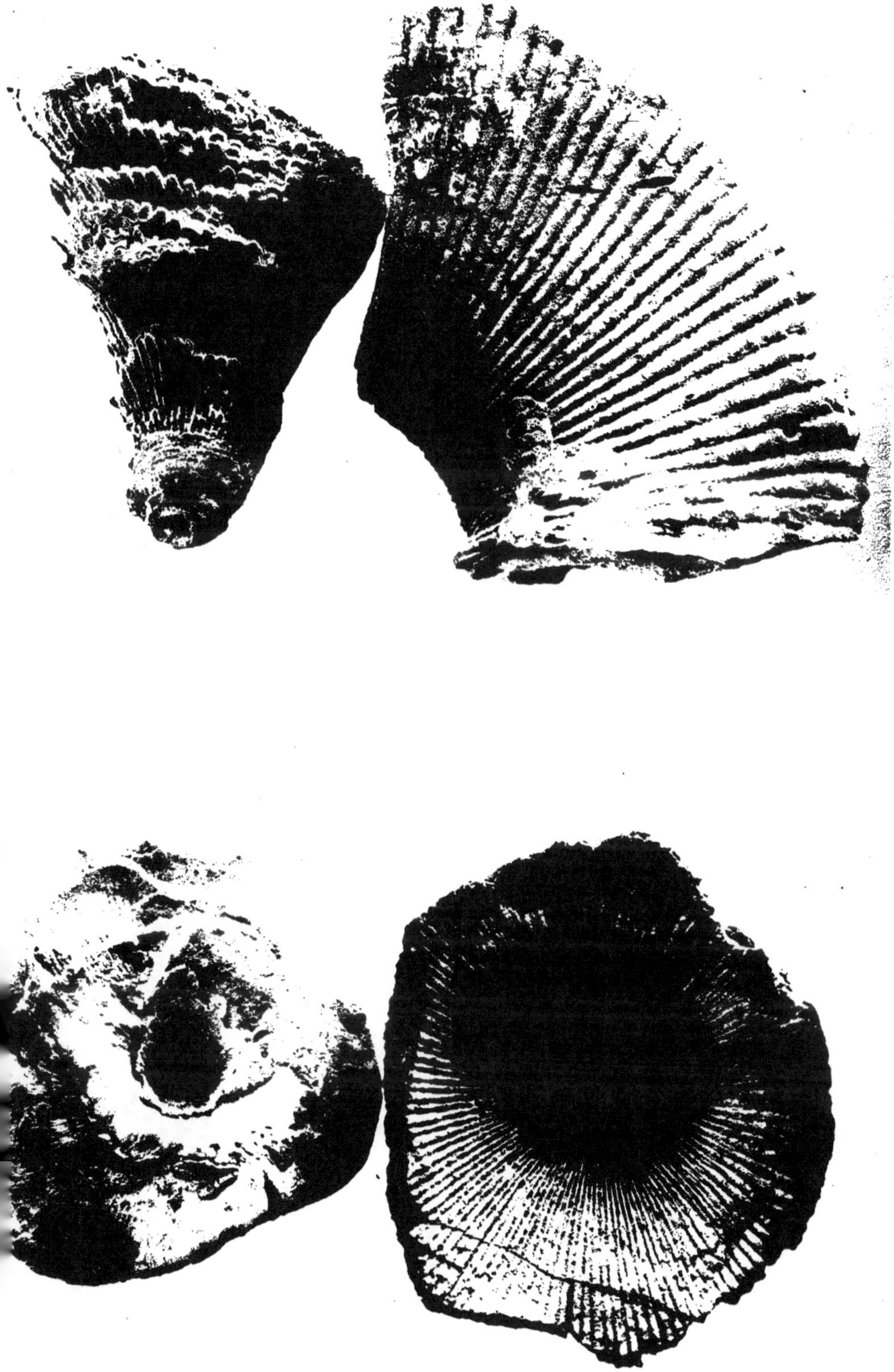

PLATE XLIV.

Figures in upper tier, Omphyma Stockesii. Niagara group, Point Detour.
Figures in lower tier, ——— verrucosa. " "

PLATE XLIV

PLATE XLV.

Fig. 1. DIPHYPHYLLUM HURONICUM. Niagara group, Point Detour.
2. ——— rugosum. " Louisville.
Figs. 3 and 4. DIPHYPHYLLUM MULTICAULE. " drift.

PLATE XLV

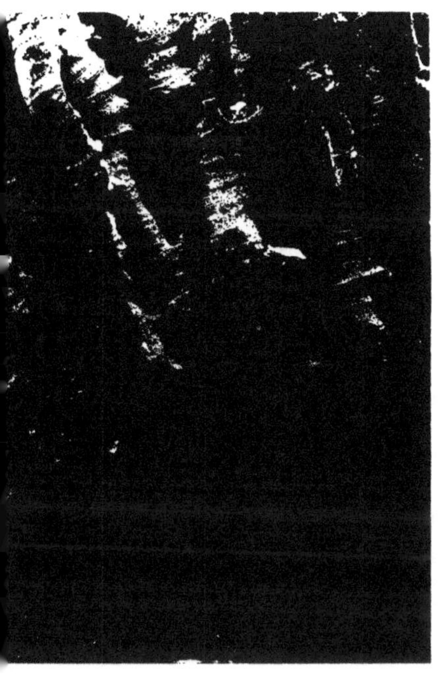

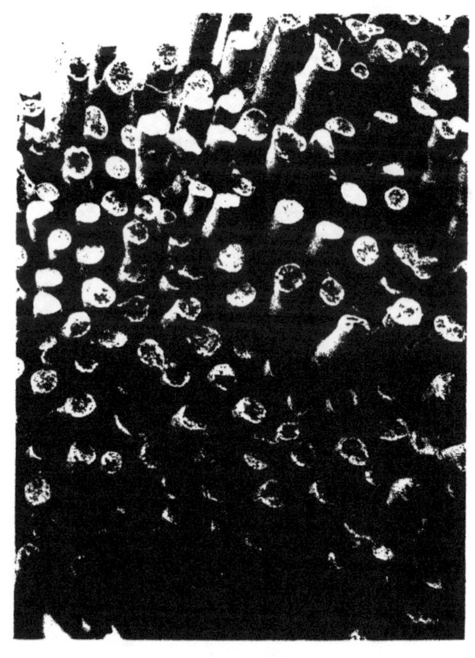

PLATE XLVI.

Fig. 1. DIPHYPHYLLUM GIGAS.

2. ——— stramineum.

Figs. 3 and 4. ——— Simcoense. All corniferous limestone forms.

PLATE XLVI

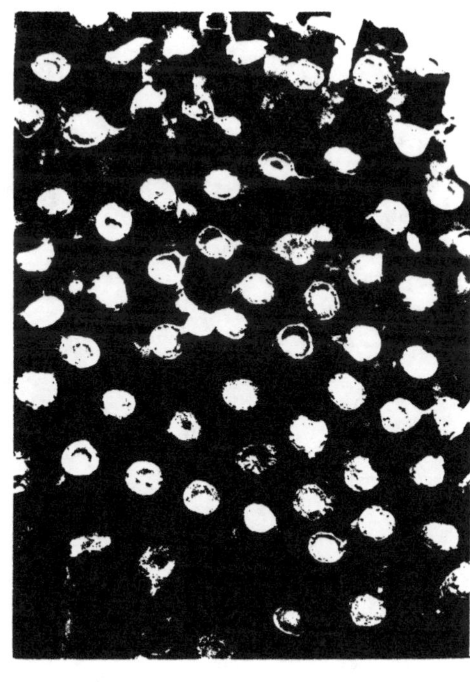

PLATE XLVII.

Upper tier, DIPHYPHYLLUM ARCHIACI. Helderberg group, Sandusky.

Fig. 4. Same species, from Hamilton group, Thunder Bay.

3. DIPHYPHYLLUM PANICUM. Hamilton group, Little Traverse Bay.

PLATE XLVII

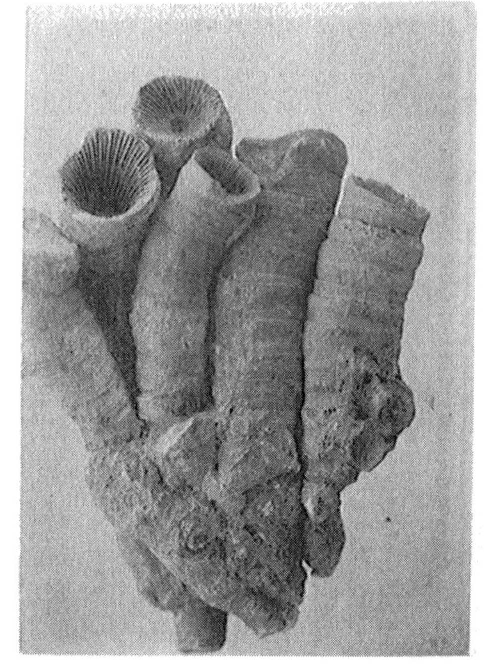

PLATE XLVIII.

Fig. 1. Strombodes striatus.

2. ——— pentagonus.

3. ——— pygmæus.

4. ——— mamillatus. All from Niagara group, Drummond's Island.

PLATE XLVIII

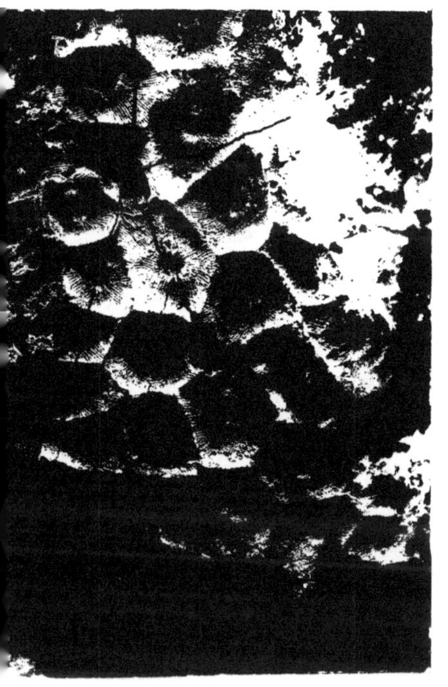

PLATE XLIX.

Upper tier, right-hand figure, VESICULARIA MAJOR. Niagara group, Drummond's Island.

Left-hand figure, VESICULARIA MINOR. Niagara group, Iowa.

Lower tier, right-hand figure, VESICULARIA VARIOLOSA. Niagara group, Point Detour.

Left-hand figures (Fig. 3), CYSTIPHYLLUM NIAGARENSE. Niagara group, Iowa and Michigan.

PLATE XLIX

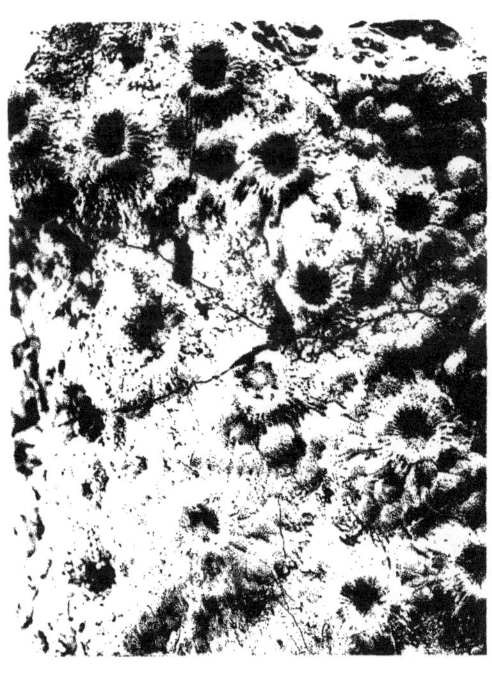

PLATE L.

Upper tier, CYSTIPHYLLUM AMERICANUM, various forms. Hamilton group, Thunder Bay and Widder.

Fig. 4. In lower tier, same species, from the corniferous limestone.

3. CYSTIPHYLLUM SULCATUM. Corniferous limestone, Port Colborne, C. W.

PLATE L

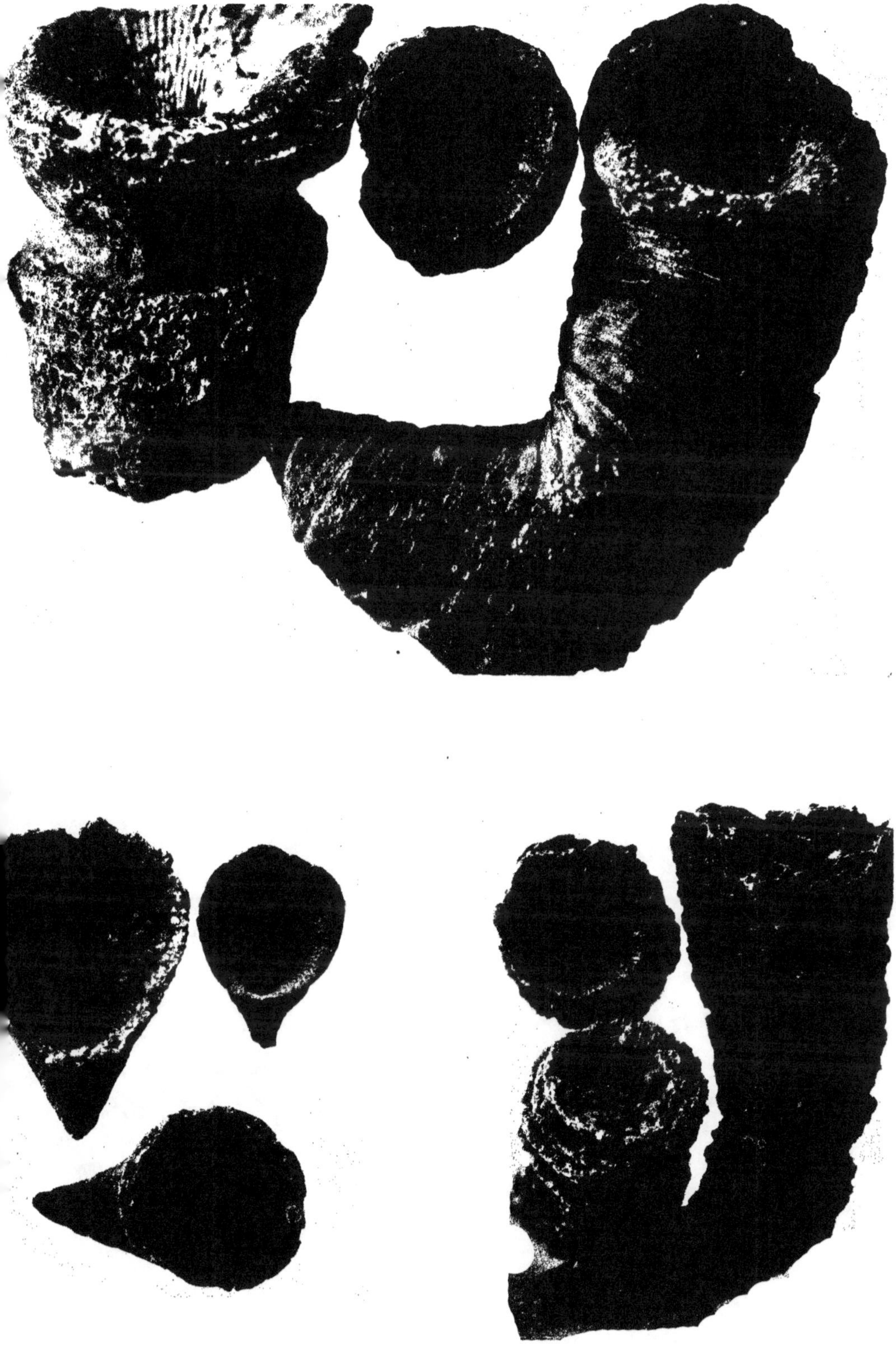

PLATE LI.

Upper tier, STREPTELASMA CORNICULUM. Four specimens on left side from the Trenton group of Michigan.

Group of seven specimens on right side found in the Hudson River group; the largest one on Drummond's Island, the others at Richmond, Indiana.

Lower tier, upper central specimen, and lowest one in the right corner, ZAPHRENTIS UMBONATA.

Other specimens, excepting the left outer and the third in the lower row, are forms of ZAPHRENTIS STOCKESII, found at Point Detour, in the Niagara group.

The two excepted lower specimens on the plate are not nearer determined.

PLATE LI

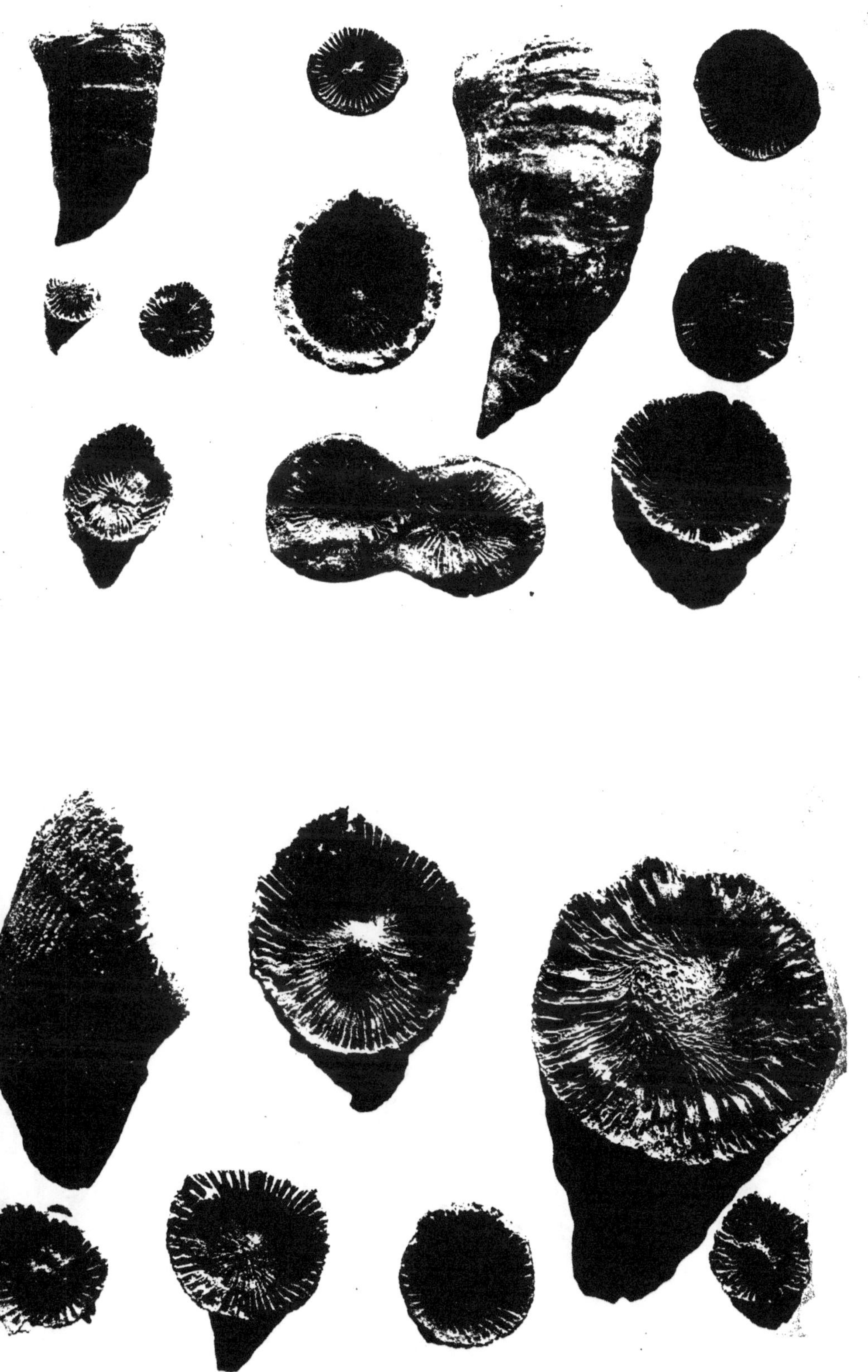

PLATE LII.

ZAPHRENTIS GIGANTEA. Corniferous limestone, Falls of the Ohio.

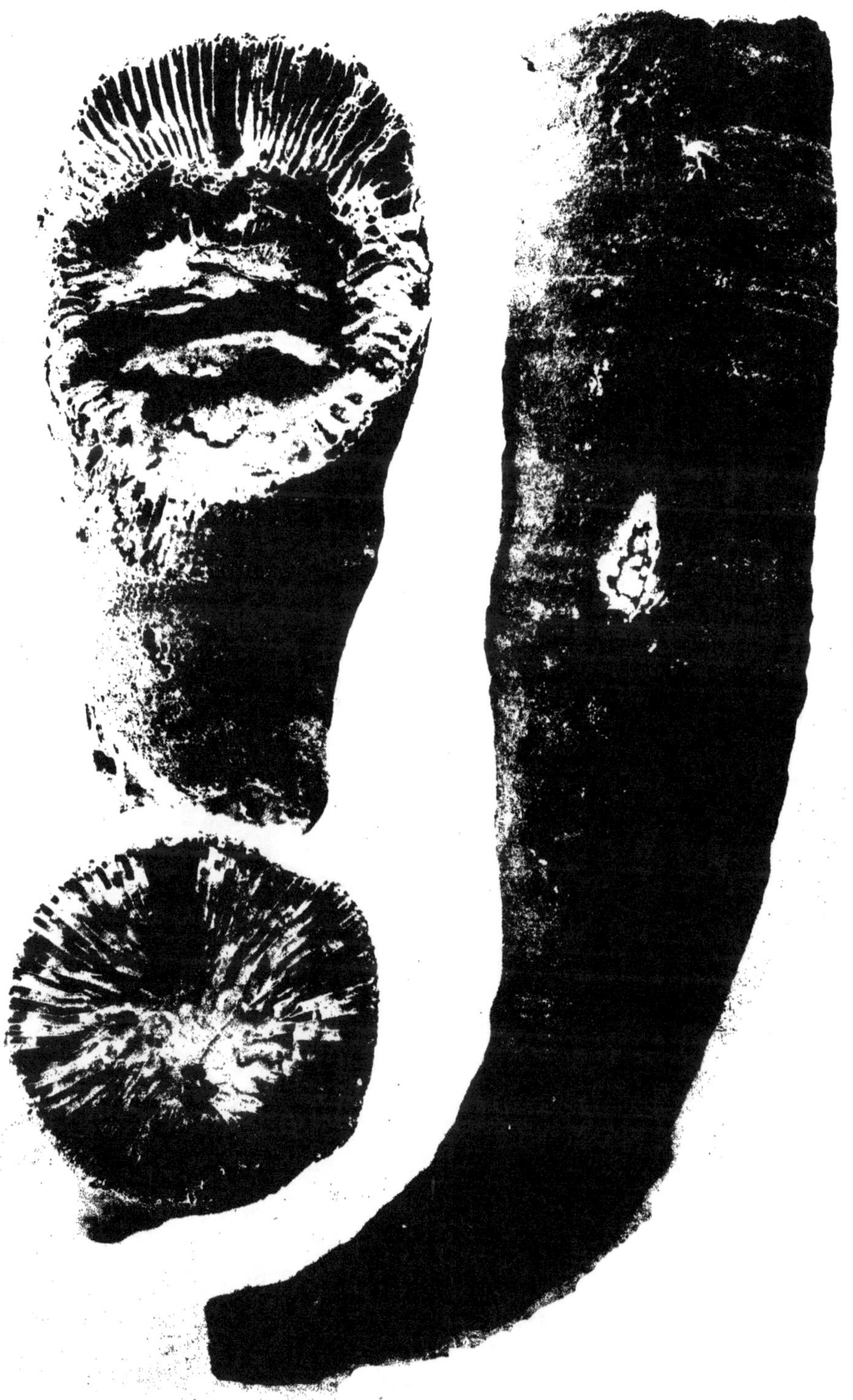

PLATE LIII.

Upper tier, ZAPHRENTIS PROLIFICA. Corniferous limestone.

Lower tier, seven specimens in the left-hand group, ZAPHRENTIS EXIGUA. Corniferous limestone from various localities.

Two right-hand specimens, ZAPHRENTIS UNGULA Corniferous limestone Falls of the Ohio.

Largest central specimen, ZAPHRENTIS COMPRESSA, from Falls of the Ohio.

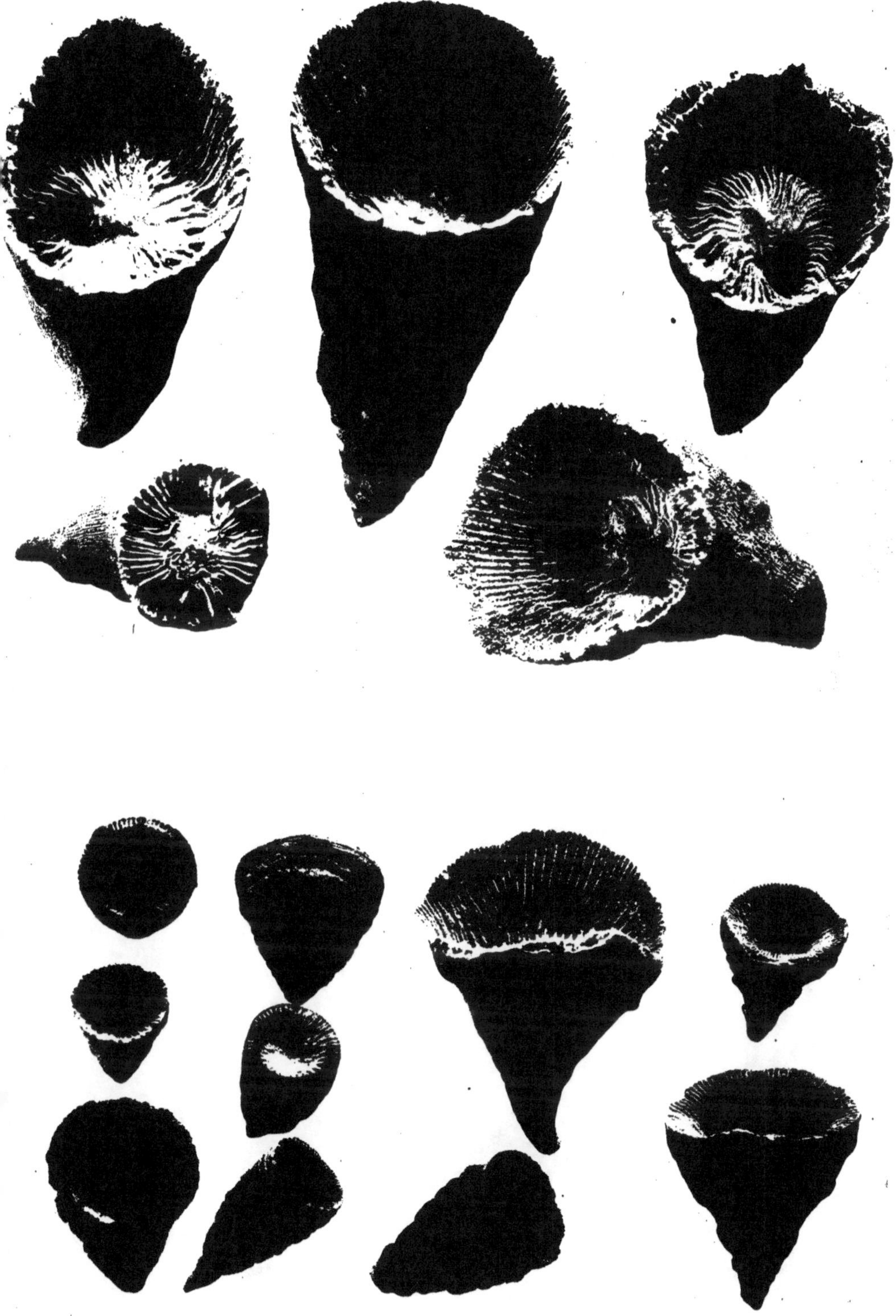

PLATE LIV.

Upper tier, AMPLEXUS SHUMARDI. Niagara group, Michigan, Iowa, and Tennessee.

Lower tier, —— Yandelli. Corniferous limestone, Michigan and Falls of the Ohio.

PLATE LIV

PLATE LV.

Upper tier, Lithostrotion mamillare. Subcarboniferous limestone, Wild Fowl Bay, Michigan.

Lithostrotion proliferum, lowest transverse stem.

Lower tier, single small specimen to the right, Zaphrentis nodulosa. Corniferous limestone drift.

Group of five specimens to the left of the former, Zaphrentis spinulosa. Subcarboniferous limestone, Bellevue, Michigan.

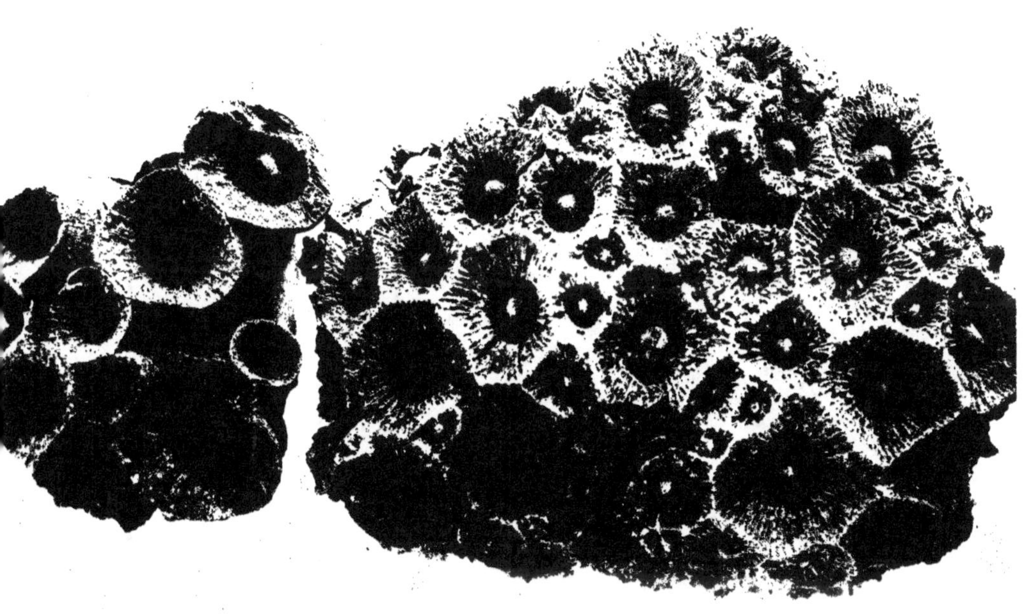

www.ingramcontent.com/pod-product-compliance
Lightning Source LLC
LaVergne TN
LVHW021100110826
845150LV00001B/131

* 9 7 8 1 4 2 5 5 6 5 9 9 2 *